Thomas Loch Garman

The Poetry of Medbh McGuckian
The Interior of Words

The Poetry of Medbh McGuckain

The Interior of Words

Edited by
SHANE ALCOBIA-MURPHY
and
RICHARD KIRKLAND

CORK UNIVERSITY PRESS

First published in 2010 by
Cork University Press
Youngline Industrial Estate
Pouladuff Road, Togher
Cork, Ireland

British Library Cataloguing in Publication Data

ISBN-13: 978-185918-465-3

Printed in the UK by J.F. Print
Typeset by Tower Books, Ballincollig, Co. Cork

www.corkuniversitypress.com

Contents

Acknowledgements

We would like to thank our contributors for their patience and willingness to engage in critical dialogue, and the editorial staff at Cork University Press for their dedication and wise counsel.

We would also like to express our heart-felt gratitude to Medbh McGuckian for permission to quote from her work and for granting us an interview – such good-natured co-operation is rare, and her contribution to this volume is inestimable. We would also like to formally acknowledge the AHRC Centre for Irish and Scottish Studies at Aberdeen for providing a venue at which many of these chapters first found an audience.

An earlier version of Michaela Schrage-Früh's essay can be found in her *Emerging Identities: Myth, Nation and Gender in the Poetry of Eavan Boland, Nuala Ní Dhomhnaill and Medbh McGuckian* (Trier: WVT, 2004).

List of Contributors

SHANE ALCOBIA-MURPHY lectures at the Department of English, University of Aberdeen, and is the author of *Sympathetic Ink: Intertextual Relations in Northern Irish Poetry* (2006).

RICHARD KIRKLAND is Professor of Irish literature and cultural theory in the English Department at King's College London. He has published widely on the subject of modern Irish writing and culture.

MICHAELA SCHRAGE-FRÜH is an assistant professor at the Department of English and Linguistics at the Johannes Gutenberg University of Mainz, Germany. She is the author of *Emerging Identities: Myth, Nation and Gender in the Poetry of Eavan Boland, Nuala Ní Dhomhnaill and Medbh McGuckian* (2004) and has published widely on Irish, Scottish and English poetry.

CATRIONA CLUTTERBUCK lectures in the school of English, Drama and Film at University College Dublin. She has published mainly on contemporary Irish poetry and its critical and cultural contexts, including work on Derek Mahon, Eavan Boland, Thomas Kinsella and Eilean Ni Chuilleanain, as well as essays on Lady Gregory, Charles J. Kickham, Brian Friel and Anne Devlin.

HELEN BLAKEMAN completed her PhD on Medbh McGuckian's poetry at Sheffield University and has lectured at Manchester University. Recent publications include an essay in 'The Body and Desire in Contemporary Irish Poetry' edited by Irene Gilsenan Nordin (2006).

ELIN HOLMSTEN is Assistant Professor of English at Dalarna University, Sweden. She completed her thesis *The Hermeneutics of Otherness in Medbh McGuckian's Poetry* at Uppsala University, Sweden, in 2006.

SCOTT BREWSTER is Director of English at the University of Salford. He is author of *Lyric* (Routledge 2009), and co-editor with Michael Parker of *Irish*

Literature since 1990: Diverse Voices (2009). He has published widely on Irish writing, the Gothic, deconstruction and psychoanalysis.

CONOR CARVILLE is Lecturer in English and American Literature at Reading University. His book on contemporary Irish cultural criticism *The Ends of Ireland* is forthcoming from Manchester University Press.

BORBÁLA FARAGÓ is currently an IRCHSS Post-Doctoral Fellow in the School of English, Drama and Film, University College Dublin. She is the author of a number of articles on contemporary Irish poetry. She is co-editor with Moynagh Sullivan of *Facing the Other: Interdisciplinary Studies on Race, Gender and Social Justice in Ireland* (2008).

LEONTIA FLYNN has written two collections of poems *These Days* (Cape, 2004) and *Drives* (Cape, 2008) and is Research Fellow at The Seamus Heaney Centre for Poetry at Queen's University, Belfast. Her study of Medbh McGuckian will be published by the Irish Academic Press in 2011.

CLAIR WILLS is Professor of Irish Literature at Queen Mary, University of London. She has published widely on Irish literature and culture. Her most recent publication is *Dublin 1916: The Siege of the GPO* (2009).

Introduction

SHANE ALCOBIA-MURPHY

Author of twelve collections of poetry, Medbh McGuckian is one of Northern Ireland's foremost poets; however, she has not won the critical acclaim accorded to her peers. While there are monographs and collections of essays devoted to the work of Seamus Heaney, Paul Muldoon, Derek Mahon and Michael Longley, McGuckian's *oeuvre* tends to be overlooked. The reason for this is, perhaps, its 'obliquity'. Indeed, it is by now a critical commonplace to describe her poetry as 'obscure', a term rarely used in approbation with regard to her work. Accurately summarising the current critical consensus, Rui Carvalho Homem writes that

> [f]ew contemporary poets with well established careers and near-canon-
> ical status will have been so hounded by one single critical *topos* as
> Northern Irish poet Medbh McGuckian. That *topos* concerns her sup-
> posed obscurity, mentioned vociferously, dismissively, apologetically, or
> with some enthusiasm, depending on the critical perspective and on the
> ensuing degree of sympathy.[1]

Reviewers of her first collection, *The Flower Master* (1982), were, in the main, perplexed by the complexity of her similes, the curious syntactical arrange-ment of her sentences, and the often unstable lyric centre of her poems. Writing for the *Sunday Tribune*, fellow poet Dennis O'Driscoll stated that McGuckian was 'a profoundly self-absorbed poet' whose work was 'merely private', the syntax of which left 'the reader confused, excluded, even bored'.[2] Although Eamon Grennan's review for *The Irish Times* was more appreciative, commenting that here was 'a talent that is surely one of the most exciting in recent Irish poetry', yet even he talks of her poems as 'unnecessarily opaque, the language straining after its own concealment'.[3] Such criticisms were not specific to male reviewers. Avril Forrest, in her piece for *The Connaught Tribune*, felt that McGuckian's 'problem in writing a poem' was not 'in finding the words and images she needs, but in gaining

1

control and imposing order on the thronging richness of her poetic imagination'.[4] However, reading her early poems after twenty-five years have
passed, one can begin to wonder what all the fuss was about. Is 'Mr
McGregor's Garden'[5] really all that 'exotic in its imagery and impenetrable in
its reference'?[6]

Mr McGregor's garden (97)	Mr McGregor's Garden
lived largely for her needle; saved the sanity of more women (55)	Some women save their sanity with needles.
'volatile [. . .] his vulgarity' (48)	I complicate my life with studies
a little ladylike sketching (33)	Of my favourite rabbit's head, his vulgar volatility,
her resident toad; in a flannel-lined box (50)	Or a little ladylike sketching
the Herbarium; 'exclusively tropical' (45)	Of my resident toad in his flannel box;
dry-rot [. . .] in the garden [. . .] grow it (44)	Or search for handsome fungi for my tropical
for the sake of a kinder climate (14)	Herbarium, growing dry-rot in the garden,
the spiky [. . .] purple head among the moss, which I took up carefully with my old cheese-knife, and turning over saw the slimy veil (43)	And wishing that the climate were kinder,
	Turning over the spiky purple heads among the moss
	With my cheese-knife to view the slimy veil.
sleepers in the goods sidings (22)	
under the animal's own control;	Unlike the cupboard-love of sleepers in the siding,
My tame hedgehog could rouse herself at half an hour's notice; on a merely wet day in August; usually after a large meal and an evening of extra liveliness; very cross if interrupted (51); wants to return; 120 respirations to the minute; weak and nervous (52)	My hedgehog's sleep is under his control
	And not the weather's; he can rouse himself
	At half-an-hour's notice in the frost, or leave at will
	On a wet day in August, by the hearth.
	He goes by breathing slowly, after a large meal,
	A lively evening, very cross if interrupted,
	And returns with a hundred respirations
	To the minute, weak and nervous when he wakens,
	Busy with his laundry.
Sleepless nights [. . .] were spent in learning the plays of Shakespeare by heart (40)	On sleepless nights while learning
Bunny came to my bedside in a white cotton nightcap and tickled me with his whiskers (61)	Shakespeare off by heart,
	I feel that Bunny's at my bedside
	In a white cotton nightcap,
	Tickling me with his whiskers.

In contrast to the reviewers' claims of 'opacity', the poem seems to have
a marked narrative clarity, established from the outset by the binary opposition between the demarcated activities of 'some women' – the domestic
'angels of the house' who while away their time with embroidery – and
those of the speaker, who locates herself outdoors and dares to improve her
mind with scientific study and art. While the speaker pointedly 'complicates'
her life, she has a heightened awareness of the strict late-nineteenth-century
conventions concerning female deportment and behaviour. However,
although she self-reflexively refers to her sketching as 'ladylike', she associates
herself with the 'vulgar volatility' of her subject; in contrast to the suffocating
confines of the domestic realm, she goes to the 'tropical / Herbarium'. That
she is alive to the pernicious effects of society's conventions can be seen in
the imagery associated with the speaker's investigations: both the 'dry-rot in
the garden' and the unkind climate connote a psychodrama wherein society's

restrictive rules can adversely affect women's 'sanity'. That she turns over 'the spiky purple heads' suggests not simply her interest in botany, but also stands as an imaginative metaphor for her combative stance with regard to patriarchy: the speaker will delve into, examine and overturn a masculinist mindset (these are phallic 'heads'), subversively using the emblem of her supposedly domesticated condition to do so ('my cheese-knife').

The second stanza continues with the same opposition between repressed, marginalised figures – 'cupboard-love'; 'sleepers in the siding' – and a more active, central self. The speaker's hedgehog is masculine, and such an allocated gender subject position garners control and power: his sleep is 'under his control'; he can 'leave at will'. Yet, in McGuckian's portrayal, this figure is depicted somewhat sympathetically: although cross and irritable, he is also, at times, aligned with the domestic realm, busy, as he is, 'with his laundry'. Following on from the speaker's unveiling and usurpation of masculinist conventions in the opening stanza, the strict demarcation of 'male' and 'female' subjectivities is broken down. Yet this reading is seemingly undermined by two factors: first, we see the speaker pacified and safely closeted away in the final stanza, taking instruction from a male precursor ('learning / Shakespeare off by heart'); second, the poem's title, 'Mr McGregor's Garden', firmly locates the world of the poem within patriarchy, one whose proprietorship is left uncontested. However, reviewers at the time ought to have been alive to the allusions within the poem ('Mr McGregor's Garden' suggests Beatrix Potter as a source), and knowing its intertext reveals a rather different conclusion.

McGuckian borrows throughout the text from Margaret Lane's biography of Beatrix Potter (1978) and, in so doing, her text becomes a dramatic monologue, with McGuckian adopting the mask of her literary exemplar. The literary self performs here a masquerade: the 'I' is both McGuckian and *not* her. Indeed, since the dramatic monologue is said to exhibit 'an overdetermined and objectified selfhood symptomatic of anxieties about claiming any kind of subject position',[7] it is thus the appropriate genre in which to explore the dislocations of self due to the material and psychic constructs imposed by patriarchy. As we have seen, this is precisely what occurs in the text. The anxieties surrounding female authorship are played out using the biographical details of someone else. Lane describes Potter's early life as follows:

> As an amateur artist, naturalist and secret chronicler she had worked absorbedly from her early childhood to her middle thirties, without discovering the true direction in which her talents lay. She had led a solitary and in many ways repressive life, a prisoner in the sterile habitat of her Victorian parents.[8]

Yet, like Peter Rabbit, she raided 'Mr McGregor's garden', and was not content to abandon the life of the mind. While on the surface the concluding stanza seems to imply resignation and the abandonment of protest against patriarchy, the details are taken from a passage in the biography which presents contentment for a very different reason: Potter had succeeded with her very first publication and had thus entered the supposedly male world of economics: having earned a cheque for £6 for her illustrations, she 'retired to bed, and lay awake chuckling till 2 in the morning, and afterwards had the impression that Bunny [the subject of her drawings] came to [her] bedside in a white cotton nightcap and tickled [her] with his whiskers'.[9] This is an image of female empowerment: just as Potter perseveres with her art, McGuckian completes her poem, one that is located in, and takes ownership of, 'Mr McGregor's Garden'.

The essays presented in this collection aim to rescue McGuckian from obscurity (in all senses). The opening chapter by Michaela Schrage-Früh re-examines the early collections and contests the rash dismissal by critics of their supposed 'apolitical' stance with regard to the Northern Irish Troubles. Building on the pioneering work of Clair Wills,[10] Schrage-Früh explores the ways in which McGuckian refers to political and overtly public concerns in her first four collections. The private and public realms are seen to overlap, with the poet exploring her own national identity by exploding stereotypical tropes and myths. The chapter has much in common with my own chapter, which focuses on McGuckian's exemplary poetics, particularly in terms of gender. Indeed, where Schrage-Früh offers an insightful reading of 'The Rising Out'[11] in terms of national politics, one could equally examine the poem in terms of its gender politics. The poem comes from McGuckian's second collection, *Venus in the Rain* (1984), one that was met with even more bafflement than *The Flower Master*. Aidan Mathews in *The Irish Times* complained about how 'strains of polemic and pillow-talk mix in a weird hybrid';[12] Peter Porter in *The Observer* was 'baffled and fed up at several almost impenetrable poems';[13] Jon Cook said that the collection confirmed her reputation as 'an obscure and esoteric writer';[14] and James Simmons felt that the collection was a bad joke, full of 'alluring nonsense'.[15] While sympathetic to the reviewers' predicament at having to present analyses when working to a tight deadline, nevertheless both Schrage-Früh and myself take issue with the dismissal of *Venus and the Rain* as simply 'spinning sumptuous Parnassian stuff out of all sorts of confused erotic and domestic perceptions'.[16] Such comments miss the politics at work in the text.

> My dream sister has gone into my blood
> To kill the poet in me before Easter. Such
> A tender visit, when I move my palaces,
> The roots of my shadow almost split in two,

Like the heartbeat of my own child, a little
Blue crocus in the middle of a book, or the hesitant
Beginning of a song I knew, a stone-song
Too small for me, awaiting a drier music.

She gentles me by passing weatherly remarks,
That hover over my skin with an expectant summer
Irony, soliloquies that rise out of sleep,
And quite enjoy saying, 'Rather a poor year.'
I continue meanwhile working on my arm-long
'Venus Tying the Wings of Love', hoping
She will recede with all my heroes, dark
Or fair, if my body can hold her bone to term.

For any that I loved, it was for their hair
That never really belonged to them, its colour
Like a line of clouds just about to crumble,
The breaking of ice in a jar. In my mind,
I try and try to separate one Alice
From the other, by their manner of moving,
The familiar closing of the unseen room,
The importunate rhythm of flowers.

If she had died suddenly I would have heard
Blood stretched on the frame, though her dream
Is the same seed that lifted me out of my clothes,
And carried me till it saw itself as fruit.

Schrage-Früh presents an engaging interpretation of 'The Rising Out', reading it in light of, and against, Yeats's 'Easter 1916', concluding that it is an inherently political poem, but one that rejects the conventional equation between female body–national territory. However, while she uncovers one intriguing intertext in the poem – an excerpt from a translation of Rainer Maria Rilke's 'Requiem for a Friend' – one could extend that part of her analysis to see a clear gender politics at work in the text. The primary intertext is not Rilke's text *per se* (nor is it Yeats's poem, though that does not invalidate her argument); rather, McGuckian takes quotations from Karen Petersen and J.J. Wilson's *Women Artists*,[17] a monograph which contextualises and historicises the lives and production of women artists from the early Middle Ages to the twentieth century. One of the early questions that Petersen and Wilson ask is: 'Is it mirroring or some deeper psychic process that causes so many double images in women's art?'[18] This accounts for the doubles that occur throughout 'The Rising Out'. McGuckian alludes to two of the examples cited by the authors when examining this question. The first is Mary Cassatt's *The Loge* (1882), a painting in which 'the fan seems *to separate one Alice from the other* Alice in the looking glass'; the second is Frida Kahlo's *The Two Fridas* (1939), which 'reflects a frequent *dream women* have of joyous embrace between *the dark sister and the fair sister*' and which presents Kahlo's feeling of being '*split in two*'.[19] What the poem explores, in part, is 'the fear that women describe of looking into the mirror one day and seeing nothing', an 'allegory of non-identity' which 'also reveals fear of desertion, of dependence upon an insufficiently integrated self'.[20] As in 'Mr McGregor's Garden', we have a clear binary opposition between the social/socialised self and the desiring, subversive, artistic self. What is being played out is a psychodrama, a fear that the subject cannot reconcile two seemingly disparate dispositions, and that it is condemned to being split in two.

McGuckian's poem, however, using the documented experiences of female artistic exemplars, attempts to resolve the conflict. The speaker declares that she will continue working on her 'Venus Tying the Wings of Love', here referring to Elisabeth Vigée-Lebrun's statement that, on the day her daughter was born, she did not quit her atelier and 'continued working at [her] *Venus Tying the Wings of Love*, in the intervals between the throes'.[21] All of the extracts cited by McGuckian centre on a key dilemma: how can one be both a mother and an artist? For example, in the concluding stanza we have a pairing together of female artists. The first is Frida Kahlo, one of whose paintings 'deals with her own miscarriage'. Petersen and Wilson relate how she 'wanted so much to have a child by Diego [her husband], but *her body could not hold it to term*'. Later, 'she took up the scene again and again, sometimes *painting the blood out over the frame* as if to warn us that life and art cannot be kept separate'.[22] The second artist referred to in the concluding stanza is the one noted by Schrage-Früh, namely Paula Modersohn-Becker, the subject of Rilke's poem in which he says: '*And finally you saw yourself as a fruit, / Lifted yourself out of your clothes and carried / that self before the mirror.*'[23] While Rilke berated Modersohn-Becker for returning to her husband and seemingly betraying her art for a life of domesticity, McGuckian's poem offers a corrective. The experiences of Kahlo and Modersohn-Becker are conjoined. When the speaker refers to 'the same seed', she is quoting Joanna Griffin's poem (cited by Petersen and Wilson) affirming the inseparability of life and art. The allusion also, significantly, establishes a connection between the contemporary female artist (McGuckian/Griffin) and those female exemplars who had to resolve their own psychodramas (Vigée-Lebrun, Kahlo, Cassatt, Modersohn-Becker): '"Her dream is my seed / Her vision my task to make the centuries see her / with such clear eyes as hers are."'[24]

The question of the self-definition of the female artist is taken up in the second chapter of this collection. Catriona Clutterbuck's analysis foregrounds 'a poetics of subjectivity' predicated through McGuckian's signature mode of semantic obscurity, by which she presents a quest for individuation 'that is truly capable of modelling the ethics of witness in the public arena'. Focused on the same collections as Schrage-Früh, Clutterbuck takes the argument concerning female poetic agency one step further; drawing on psychoanalytical theory, particularly that of Julia Kristeva, she brilliantly demonstrates that McGuckian's early poems construct self-reflexive versions of the private realm. The chapter is a perfect riposte to the readings of her work which argue that it is predicated purely on anti-logic. One such reader was Alan Jenkins: reviewing the third collection, he claimed that 'it would be a strange child (or adult) who professed to having made much of the poems in *On Bal-lycastle Beach* (1988), which for the most part exist in some vaguely inebriated, pre-rational state, monotonously accumulating vague poeticisms'.[25] In response, Clutterbuck's argument contends that McGuckian's self-reflexive texts generate a new form of logic that draws on conventional logic and anti-logic, but that privileges neither and, in the process, there emerges a 'creative renegotiation of meaning' between reader and author:

> the individual's personal filtering of experience is paramount, *and* [. . .] the version of reality so created can only be useful to that individual [. . .] if it is allowed to be open to adaptation through the questioning and input of the perspectives of others – the space for which adaptation can be generated in the work of art.

Helen Blakeman's chapter, like Clutterbuck's, draws on Kristevan theory to focus on the topic of poetic indeterminacy. The speaking subject, for Kris-teva, is a split subject, divided between conscious and unconscious motivations. The subject's signifying processes are also divided between the *symbolic* (rule-governed element of language; ordered; Oedipalised), and the *semiotic* (psychic and bodily energies which do not signify; pre-Oedipal; anar-chic). What interests Blakeman is how the irruption of the semiotic manifests itself in McGuckian's work, disrupting 'accepted notions of both signification and subjectivity'. Blakeman ably demonstrates the extent to which the 'semiotic forces of language fracture the signifying process' and, in so doing, provides a clear explanation for the so-called 'obscurity' of McGuckian's texts. Rather than constituting 'nonsense', they explore the boundary between signification and 'non-sense'. Blakeman's chapter also offers a useful comparative reading of the Symbolist texts of Stephane Mal-larmé's and McGuckian's work, convincingly demonstrating how both authors engage both in word-play and sound-play, pushing the limits of lan-guage. Blakeman's chapter is focused on *Marconi's Cottage* (1991), a collection which was well received. Like Blakeman, reviewers at the time appreciated the collection's linguistic experimentation. David Herd, writing in the *New Statesman and Society*, argued that McGuckian's 'real concern' was 'for what it might be like to cross the threshold and get outside the words into which she was "born"'.[26] Although adverting to the fact that McGuckian had 'developed a reputation for combining hyperaesthetic lyricism with baffling difficulty', Sean O'Brien does concede that she may be 'a visionary original' and that she seems to be 'interpreting experience before familiar interpretations come into play'.[27] Allison Rolls, reviewing the collection for the Galway-based journal *Krino*, perceptively noted that the poems inhabited 'that McGuckianesque twilight zone between the land and the sea'.[28] Indeed, it is precisely this notion of borders and thresholds which attracts Blakeman in her analysis.

Since the publication of *Marconi's Cottage*, the application of Kristevan theory to McGuckian's poetry has become much in vogue,[29] and rightly so since it allows critics a methodology to appreciate, and write about, a poetry that is so self-reflexive about its own production. Indeed, McGuckian herself uses one of Kristeva's texts, *Powers of Horror*,[30] to construct a late poem, 'To Such a Hermes':[31]

the nearly same (182) lower form of man (176)	I am the nearly same lower form of man, my name will be of no use to you.
we know the sound (202) uttered in one breath (198)	You know the sound, uttered in one breath.
On our land and under our skin (182) reverberates with the war (201)	On your land and under your skin I keep my life, my rhythm reverberates with the war. dying as fast as ever it can die.
a piece of waste, his wife as it were (185) with and against, further, through, beneath or beyond (188) this 'not yet a place' this no-ground (38)	My eyes were your slaves, a piece of waste, a theft. your wife as it were, with and against, further through, beneath or beyond this not-yet-a-place, this no-ground.
Céline seeks to loosen the language from itself (189) draws near to that emptiness of meaning (191); the height of bloodshed (155); Spring, which they, the birds I mean will never see again (195)	I loosen language from myself, an enemy of meaning comes near, salving my height of bloodshed with this fatherless spring the birds I mean will never see again.

The intertext for this poem centres on a state of boundary subjectivity known as 'abjection'. The 'abject', for Kristeva, is neither subject nor object; rather, it is the loss of distinction between the two, or the collapse of the boundary between self and other. With regard to the individual's psychosexual development, the abject refers to the moment when the individual begins to recognise the boundary between 'me' and 'm(other)'. Abjection occurs when this boundary is no longer secure and when the individual is drawn 'toward the place where meaning collapses'.[32] For Kristeva, literature is the privileged space in which to explore abjection:

> On close inspection, all literature is probably a version of the apocalypse that seems to me rooted, no matter what its sociohistorical conditions might be, on the fragile border (borderline cases) where identities (subject/object, etc.) do not exist or only barely so – double, fuzzy, heterogeneous, animal, metamorphosed, altered, abject.[33]

Poetry, in particular, with its willingness to play with metaphor, syntax and grammar, allows the author to reveal the arbitrary nature of language and to show that it is itself limned with the abject fear of loss: 'The one who tries to utter this *not yet a place, this no-ground*, can obviously only do so backwards, starting from an over-mastery of the linguistic and rhetorical code. But in the last analysis he refers to fear – a terrifying, abject referent' (38, emphasis added).

The speaker in 'To Such a Hermes' is 'the nearly same', 'the lower form of man'. Both quotations refer to subjected minorities on the margins of society. The poem's addressee, the 'you', can be read as the speaker divided from herself – seeing herself as other – but, more specifically, given the intertext, the persona being addressed is Louis-Ferdinand Céline, one of the authors chosen by Kristeva who best explores abjection in his work. Kristeva contends that Céline's prose avoids 'subordination', that his sentences 'do not present themselves as logico-syntactic units' and that they proceed 'by means of brief statements', by 'clauses that can be *uttered in one breath*'.[34] His work 'is a struggle, if not full of hatred at least fascinated and loving, with the mother tongue. *With and against, further, through, beneath or beyond?* Céline "*seeks to loosen the language from itself*".'[35] McGuckian, of course, struggles with her mother tongue in her writing since she feels that it marks her out as subjected: 'it's an imposed language, you see, and although it's my mother tongue and my only way of communication, I'm fighting with it all the time';[36] 'I resist and I'm angry – we're always angry, because every time we open our mouths we're slaves.'[37] More fundamentally, however, her manipulation of language allows her to explore its very limits and she, like Céline, 'draws near to that emptiness of meaning'.[38] In the poem, McGuckian 'loosens' Céline's language, thus further fragmenting it. This disruption of language allows the 'enemy / of meaning to come near', 'salving [her] height of bloodshed'. This is significant since, as Kristeva states, the 'birth-giving scene' – '*the height of bloodshed*' – is the ultimate location of abjection.[39] Her use of language allows for the irruption of the semiotic, resisting the move into the patriarchal symbolic realm. Hence, we have a 'fatherless spring' at the poem's conclusion (which itself cites an example of Céline's fragmented writing).Where the poet once felt subjected (even to a literary exemplar like Céline) – 'My eyes were your slaves, / a piece of waste' – her reconfiguration of his writing allows her to reach 'this no-ground', the realm of the semiotic.

From *Captain Lavender* (1994) to the intensely prolific period of this century, in which she has published seven collections in nine years, McGuckian's work has been marked by a deliberate linguistic experimentation which has increasingly divided the critics. On the one hand, her poetry continues to be read (negatively) as 'private and inward-turning, non-rational, built upon the inaccessible logic of dream and subconscious associations'.[40] The critical reflex here seems to stem not only from a belief that poetry must possess the virtues of prose, a mindset that resists the ambiguities that arise from a poetry built on convoluted syntax and a non-standard collocation of words, but also from a failure to discern any coherent rationale behind her poems' construction: the reader is supposedly faced with 'a language functionally indiscriminate: a poetry knot, a poetry *clot*'.[41] On the other hand, however, some critics and reviewers revel and rejoice in a language '[c]haracterized by elusive referents, by similes that compound until their ground is effaced, and sometimes by such skilful manipulations of syntax that a reader may feel shipwrecked between subject and predicate'.[42] One critic in particular, Robert Brazeau, presents a remarkable insight into her language usage when he argues that it 'offers a sense of the viability of [. . .] staging a series of linguistic and avant-garde disruptions that trouble familiar social and ideological categories'.[43] Arguing that McGuckian adopts a Wittgensteinian approach to language, whereby language as a system 'precludes understanding rather than facilitating it', he contends that she has come to the conclusion that 'if language works within stabilizing social systems to ground and delimit meaning, then language can be reworked in ways that appear illogical in order to unwrite existing designations'. Compelling evidence for this can be found in 'Pulsus Paradoxus', a poem from her 1998 collection, *Shelmalier*.[44] The poem consists of quotations taken from Ray Monk's biography of Ludwig Wittgenstein.[45]

'At first something like an image was there' (532) 'has for me a *pre*-love' (504); leaves everything as it is (533); we do not see everything as something (508); 'everything that is brown' (521) 'I take it for granted that he was incorruptible' (568); colouredness from the colour (562); 'a light shining on them from behind. That they do not themselves glow' (522) 'Is it that the word does not have an aroma of meaning' (532); 'the really faithful memory' (312)	At first there was something like an image there: he had for me a pre-love which leaves everything as it is. We do not see everything as something, everything that is brown, we take for granted the incorruptible Colouredness of colour. But a light shines on them from behind, they do not themselves glow. As a word has only an aroma of meaning, as the really faithful memory is the part of a wound that goes quiet.
'keeping magic out has itself the character of magic' (308); 'a *picture* held us captive	Keeping magic out has itself the character of magic – a picture held us captive

And we could not get outside it, for it lay in our	and we could not get outside it
language' (365); the uniform of a force that no	for it lay in our language in the uniform
longer existed (169)	of a force that no longer existed.
The target he was aiming at was the point at which	Peace was the target he was aiming at,
doubt becomes senseless (578);	the point at which doubt becomes senseless,
'peace is the last thing that will find a home' (485)	the last thing that will find a home.

The poem is a poetic manifesto which declares McGuckian's intent to move beyond the 'picture that held us captive'. The reference is to St Augustine's account in *Confessions* of how he learned to talk, one which Wittgenstein uses in his *Philosophical Investigations* to introduce the concept of the language-game:

> These words, it seems to me, give us a particular picture of the essence of human language. It is this: the individual words in language name objects – sentences are combinations of such names. – In this picture of language we find the roots of the following idea: Every word has a meaning. This meaning is correlated with the word. It is the object for which the word stands.[46]

For Wittgenstein, this 'picture' is too rigid and falsely explains the working of language and logic. '*A picture held us captive*', he says, '*and we could not get outside it, for it lay in our language* and language seemed to repeat it to us inexorably.'[47] To understand the workings of both logic and language, he focuses our attention away from words and sentences and 'on to the occasions we use them, the contexts which give them sense'.[48] The meaning of language is contextual; it does not reside, statically, in a one-to-one correspondence between name and object. Language-games, for Wittgenstein, are ways of 'inventing imaginary situations in which language is used for some tightly defined purpose'. In picturing the situation, he argues, language cannot 'be described without mentioning the *use*' to which it is put. His aim is to question the prevailing approaches to assigning meaning in language, namely the reflective and expressionist theories. The reflective theory argues that each word has meaning since it represents an object in the world, and so in a sentence meaning can be built up from its component elements. The expressionist model states that meaning is derived because language is a reflection of our thoughts (language 'translates' these thoughts). However, Wittgenstein discounts this theory since one cannot have thoughts without language. The language-game allows him to pass beyond the passive reflective and expressionist models; for Wittgenstein, the individual shapes the use of language as language shapes him/her. The rigidity of outmoded theories of language is suggested by McGuckian by the image of 'the uniform of a force that no longer existed'. The quotation refers to Wittgenstein's continued wearing of his army uniform following the conclusion of the First World War, as if it were part of his identity. The uniform was a symbol of a past age that had to be rejected. When Wittgenstein stated that philosophy '*leaves everything as it is*', he was arguing that 'in seeking to change nothing but the way we look at things' he was actually 'attempting to change *everything*'.[49] To break free from the rigidly deterministic logic of philosophy and language, one has to begin by acknowledging that meaning is culturally determined. Once this is recognised, the poet can attempt to reconfigure her relationship to language, to 'unwrite existing designations', as Brazeau argues. Hence, she can dismantle language: the word, for her, 'has only / an aroma of meaning'.

McGuckian is concerned with the limitations and possibilities of the poetic medium, as exemplified by 'Sky in Narrow Streets', from which this collection of essays takes its title:

> I drive words abreast
> Into the interior of words;
> It is murder or kindling when two meanings
> Rush together from such a distance,
> No multiplicity can distress them.[50]

Here her characteristic appropriative writing – taking phrases from pre-existent texts to form *collage poetry* – performatively enacts the thematics of the text. Quoting paratactically from C.S. Lewis's *Studies in Words*, George D. Painter's biography of Marcel Proust and Henri de Lubac's *The Faith of Teilhard de Chardin*,[51] she comments on her *ars poetica* by allowing ideas from different sources to rub up against each other. C.S. Lewis contends that the sense of a word is governed by the context in which it appears; consequently, the intrusion of an unintended or irrelevant sense is said to cause 'a semantic explosion' because 'the two meanings rush together from a great distance' (CL 12). While Lewis's series of essays intends to limit connotations and avoid unwarranted ambiguity through his technique of 'driv[ing] words of different languages abreast' (CL 2), McGuckian drives these words 'into the interior of language'. The source for this latter phrase comes from the biography of Proust in which Painter recalls the fastidious editorial practices of Louis Ganderax who would, when correcting proofs for the *Revue de France*, pursue hiatuses '"into the very interior of words"' (MP1 92). The two sources, then, assert the necessity for exactitude of meaning. Yet while Lewis and Ganderax are at pains to avoid verbicide, namely 'the murder of a word' (CL 7) through incorrect semantic usage, McGuckian's poem introduces her own caveat: 'It is murder *or kindling*' (my emphasis) when the two meanings come together. Hence, in this case, when words from the two texts are conjoined the resultant ambiguity is not necessarily destructive. That the speaker is reading the two sources against the grain is made apparent in the stanza's final line, which is taken from de Lubac's study of de Chardin: 'He to whom it is given [. . .] to see Christ *more real* than any other reality in the World,

Christ everywhere present and everywhere growing more great, Christ the final determination and plasmatic Principle of the Universe, he indeed lives in a zone where no multiplicity can distress him' (TC vii, original emphasis). McGuckian is using the phrase in a very different context from de Lubac: 'multiplicity' refers here to the multiple meanings which are generative in a poetic context. The ambiguity, for McGuckian, does not 'distress' words (however much the unwilling reader may cry 'murder').

Water-colour of trees (MP2, 3); seascapes (MP1, 281) At dawn, noon and night (MP1, 207); furniture of earth (CSL 15); promise to pay which is never going to be kept (CSL 7)	My watercolour of trees, seascapes at dawn, Noon and night, the unmade furniture of earth, Promise to pay what is never going to be kept.

This ekphrastic stanza works against Lewis's prescriptive linguistic theories. In *Studies in Words* he argues that 'verbiage' is a form of 'verbicide' when a writer uses 'a word as a promise to pay which is never going to be kept'. For McGuckian, such an emphasis on precision and exactitude is detrimental to the imagination. So, when using a phrase from Lewis like 'the furniture of earth', she does not adopt his metaphorical application ('that which is to earth as tables and chairs and so forth are to a house'); rather, she dismantles and 'unmakes' prescribed meanings. Trees are very different from a 'water-colour of trees': art transforms 'the real'. A word may have a referent, but one ought not to confuse the sign for the thing itself. To convey this idea, McGuckian, at the poem's close, cites a lesson learnt by Proust from John Ruskin's *Praeterita*. Entranced by a group of young trees in a forest, Ruskin begins to draw the branches: '"With wonder increasing every moment I saw that they 'composed' themselves, by finer laws than any known of man. At last the tree was there, and everything that I had thought about trees, nowhere"' (MP1 283). McGuckian's driving of words into 'the interior of words' is a means of capturing and conveying that sense of wonder and allows readers access to the imaginative potential of language.

In her chapter, Elin Holmsten examines this attempt by McGuckian to revitalise language. Her analysis of McGuckian's meta-representational poems contends that she is not escaping meaning; rather, her disruption of language 'allows for speaking differently, which opens encounters with otherness'. Holmsten concludes that McGuckian's 'departure from restrictive modes of writing' may well render her work 'obscure', but not in a negative sense: citing Paul Celan's response to those who had complained about the obscurity of his own verse, she writes, 'This obscurity [. . .] has been bestowed on poetry by strangeness and distance [. . .] for the sake of an encounter.' The exploration of subjectivity in this chapter differs radically from that of Clutterbuck as Holmsten's readings draw on Levinasian philosophy, which contends that 'saying is a state of openness to the other'.[52] For Emmanuel Levinas, 'to be' is 'to be for the other'; what he initiates in his work is 'an ethical relationship with alterity'.[53] The application of such theory is appropriate, and is certainly one which McGuckian has investigated. Indeed, 'A Book of Rains', a poem from a recent collection, *The Currach Requires No Harbours*,[54] cites directly from many of his essays collected in *The Levinas Reader*.[55]

the line is traced	[. . .] the line is traced
like the trajectory of the blow	in the trajectory of the blow
that is dealt (83); having nothing	that was dealt. Having nothing
at its disposal	at its disposal
that would enable it to not yield	to not yield
to the provocation (95)	to the provocation,
The time of *dying*	the time of dying
cannot give itself	cannot give itself
the other shore (140)	the other shore,
The future that death gives [. . .]	the future that death gives
is not yet time (45)	is not yet time,
when [. . .] his forsakenness	when his forsakenness
draws near (179); under the force	draws near, under the force
of the blow received (174)	of the lips of the blow received.

The above poem would fit nicely into Holmsten's section, which outlines the ways in which McGuckian's poems stage encounters with the other after death.

Scott Brewster also adopts a Levinasian theoretical model in his chapter when examining both the presence and significance of a key trope in McGuckian's *oeuvre*: the house. The house may be indicative of sheltered domesticity, but often in Northern Irish artworks the private realm is under scrutiny. Poets like McGuckian register an acute sense of vulnerability due to the all-pervasive gaze of neighbours, the police and the opposing community. Brewster demonstrates how, in McGuckian's work, the house is gradually transformed from a site figured as both refuge and trap wherein the speaker struggles to maintain privacy, to a locus in which is staged an encounter with 'the other'. The poet thus becomes more receptive to exteriority. On the one hand, we have poems like 'Sky-Writing,'[56] which is made up of fragments taken from Rilke's *Selected Letters*[57] and which features an enclosive, womb-like plenitude:

What can I do against this room (294)	What can I do against this room
which I was obliged to let grow and grow	I was obliged to let grow and grow
all through the winter (358); in the new	In the new space all through the winter?
space (372)	[. . .]
the world outside forfeits (239)	I forfeit the world outside
	For the sake of my own inwardness,
so at one with its scent (398)	I am so at one with the scent of its many wills

Here, there is not so much an acceptance of the private realm but a questioning (and ultimately a reassertion) of the speaker's powers of agency. As Susan Stanford Friedman argues, the female writer who employs the childbirth metaphor in an attempt to conjoin creativity with procreativity 'necessarily confront[s] the patriarchally imposed, essential dilemma of their artistic identity: the binary system that conceives woman and writer, motherhood and authorhood, babies and books, as mutually exclusive'.[58] McGuckian's poem, dealing with origins and originality, revisits the thematic concerns of 'The Rising Out' and yet again uses Rilke's own words against him. The occupations of mother and poet are not mutually exclusive, and the female poet can co-opt and alter the words of a male author to make them her own. On the other hand, McGuckian writes poems like 'The Over Mother'[59] (a text dismissed by David Mason as an example of 'sheer pretentiousness'),[60] which also features the house as womb,[61] but which does not bracket off the public realm:

'the sealed hotel' (M 87)	In the sealed hotel men are handled
Passion exhausts itself at the mouth (Lawrence)	as if they were furniture, and passion
'the play kisses' (M 281)	exhausts itself at the mouth. Play kisses
The circuits of the body (M 300); 'underloved	stir the circuits of the underloved body
Person' (M 259); 'the ever-resurrection' (M 228);	to an ever-resurrection, a never-had tenderness
'the never-had tenderness' (M 239); 'I'd just die	that dies inside me.
inside' (M 381); 'cleverly dead' (M 142)	
'vertical audience' (M 332); 'words can fly	My cleverly dead and vertical audience,
out' (M 184); 'climate of unexpectation' (M 144)	words fly out from your climate of unexpectation
leaky letters (M 83); 'shallowized' (M 301)	in leaky, shallowised night letters –
'What you has spoken?' (M 207)	what you has spoken?

The house is ironically depicted as a 'sealed hotel', a temporary place of residence bereft of the usual trappings of luxury and ease associated with a hotel; here, the house is clearly a contained space wherein freedom of movement is curtailed. At the time of writing, McGuckian was teaching poetry classes to the inmates of the Maze prison and so the poem exemplifies her movement away from an apolitical, sheltered locus to a more public space. The prisoners, 'handled / as if they were furniture', are at the mercy of their jailer (the poem's 'Over Mother'). Referring to the prisoners depicted in *Captain Lavender*, McGuckian states: 'I just wanted to ring the changes on their still being in a cage. They had freedom, they actually were more free – in their own world they had their own private republic, their own *Gaeltacht*.'[62] Such freedom, however, is tempered not only by the poem's overriding sense of enclosure, but by the theatricalised nature of communication which takes place therein: with 'play kisses' and 'shallowised night letters', all is covert, potentially superficial and unreal. As the poem's intertext – the biography of Anne Sexton by Diane Middlebrook – suggests, there is a distinction to be made between '"a human relationship"' and '"a letter relationship between humans"' in which "'*words can fly out* of your heart (via the fingers) and no one really need live up to them'" (M 184, my emphasis). Indeed, the speaker is left asking 'what you has spoken?'

The 'house' in a McGuckian poem is, in the words of the poet herself, 'probably the poem itself [. . .] or a symbol for the world of the poem'.[63] One could argue that the poem is 'the sealed hotel', a place in which she handles her exemplars 'as if they were furniture', where passion 'exhausts itself at the mouth'. Lawrence's *The Trespasser* here is sampled and then dropped in favour of the next exemplar. However, as in 'Sky-Writing', McGuckian uses her poem as a protest against patriarchal restrictions and as a means of asserting her words' abilities to 'fly out from your climate of unexpectation'. The latter phrase is taken from Middlebrook's biography, which cites Anne Sexton as an example of someone who benefited from 'a social experiment involving women', namely the setting up of the Radcliffe Institute, whose programme was designed to '"harness the talents of intellectually displaced women"' (M 144). The Institute's founder, May Bunting, had contended that 'many well-educated women in the Boston area were ready, after raising families, to return to full-time intellectual or artistic work but struggling for opportunity in a "climate of unexpectation"' (M 144). The 'vertical audience' sought by McGuckian is symptomatic of the poet's assertion of her own authority and of her desire to move outwards from the private realm into the public, since the phrase refers to 'the "vertical audience" of peers living and dead, measurable in the tables of contents of influential anthologies' (M 332).

Focusing on a single collection, *Had I a Thousand Lives* (2003), Conor Carville's chapter examines the rationale behind, and efficacy of, McGuckian's representation of commemorative practices, focusing particularly on the critique within many of the poems of the ideology of commemoration within Irish nationalism. The thematics of his chapter tie in well with my own, focused as it is on McGuckian's recuperative project centring on (and intending to reverse) the apparent occlusion and erasure of traumatic narratives of the past. Both chapters reflect upon McGuckian's self-reflexivity as regards language's inability to represent (or resurrect) the dead. Indeed, this is one of the key themes running throughout this collection of essays, and can be seen in 'A Religion of Writing',[64] which is the first poem that Carville looks at. (The two intertexts for this poem are Armando Petrucci's *Writing the Dead* and Theodor Adorno's *Beethoven*, cited on the left):[65]

a return to the outdoors (W 22)	Dreams as common as rain
one whom the earth has reclaimed (B 184)	returning to the outdoors
passage [. . .] from the name to the	one whom the earth has reclaimed
body (B 29); the remoteness from name to	in the passage from the name
meaning (B 172)	to the body, the remoteness
	of name to meaning.

The writing [. . .] is set low [. . .] despite	Despite the thicket, the writing
The thicket (W 58); half-empty lines, with	is set low, half-empty lines
ivy leaves and stylized fruits acting as	with ivy leaves and fruits
punctuation (W 39)	acting as punctuation.
unsteady capitals (W 28)	such unsteady capitals,
the backward *S* (W 31); the capital *L*	the backward *S*, the *L*
with foot slanting sharply downward (W 31)	with its foot slanting sharply
the *B* with detached loops (W 31)	downwards, the *B* with detached
a *G* consisting of two opposing	loops, a *G* consisting of two opposing
curves (W 38)	curves [. . .]

Despite the apparent solidity of the gravestone inscriptions, the capitals, as Carville points out, are referred to as 'unsteady', 'slanting', 'detached' and 'opposed' and the lines are 'half-empty'. Those commemorated are thus doubly erased (from life and then from language). Indeed, there is an opposition established early on between 'music' and inscription, with names (belonging to the latter). In the opening stanza, McGuckian writes that:

> the sea beauty
> Of the air was moved
> By warmed music which caused
> that question to vanish.

In contrast to this 'music', naming and names seem less effective. While 'remoteness / of name to meaning' seems, on first reading, to be an admission of failure, almost as if it were a Derridean gloss on the arbitrary nature of the sign and a disavowal of the Western belief in the 'presence' of language, the sense of the fragment's meaning alters when viewed in context. Adorno argues that '[m]usic is name in the state of absolute impotence; it is also the remoteness of name from meaning, and both are the same thing. The holiness of music is its purity from dominance over nature' (B 172). While McGuckian's poem acknowledges its limitations since it has everything to do with naming, nevertheless it attempts formally to achieve the status of 'warmed music', and it does this (in the words of Clair Wills) through 'stretched and unhooked metaphors', 'grammatical and syntactical shifts', 'endlessly migrating pronouns',[66] and, of course, through the poem's incorporation of fragmented quotations. Commenting on Adorno's unfinished, fragmentary study of Beethoven, the editor states that 'fragmentary texts may become legible as a kind of spatial configuration: a signature that can only be deciphered if the surviving fragments and drafts are arranged in a constellation determined by their *inherent meaning*' (B ix, original emphasis). The fragmentary nature of the text does not militate against the achievement of meaning; rather, as the editor claims, '[j]ust as each of the [. . .] fragments on Beethoven contains a question to answer which nothing less than the unwritten book on the composer would be needed [. . .] the constellation which the fragments form objectively together [. . .] *may cause that question* [. . .] *to "vanish"'* (B x, my emphasis). The poet's dislocating appropriative practice is perhaps her attempt to achieve the quality of music, one which can better commemorate and remember the dead.

One of the key functions of this collection of essays is to provide inter-pretative pathways into McGuckian's work, to account for its hypnotic beauty and to provide theoretical models which help explain its supposed 'obscurity'. Richard Kirkland's chapter is exemplary in each of these respects. Starting with the premise that 'the creation of human subjectivity is a neces-sarily endless process', he uses Gilles Deleuze's notion of 'becoming' to confront one of the key tensions which emerges from her work: while the poetry seems to refuse communication, at the same time each text is charac-terised by its directness of address to a 'you' (who is never identified). What emerges from Kirkland's analysis of her poems and published extracts from her diaries is a writer who continually presents incomplete narratives of self-formation: each text 'describes provisional shifting states of becoming', and it is this absence of identity which confers upon both the poet and her work their 'minority status', a Deleuzean term which denotes an unsettled and unsettling status in relation to a hegemonic standard. The texts are unnerving and 'obscure' to the reader precisely because they refuse hegemonic com-municational models; they refute fixed standards and are characterised by and fascinated with endless process.

The two remaining chapters each focus on McGuckian's 'muses'. Borbála Faragó investigates the different guises of the muse, be they men, women, angels or readers, and argues that their presence in the poetic text constitutes a manifestation of both a pre-Platonic and a post-romantic figure of the muse. In contrast, Leontia Flynn's chapter engages with specifically identified muses, namely the authors that the poet borrows from when constructing her texts. Reviewing the work that I have undertaken in the past to unearth these sources, she examines the 'strange shifting chain of authorship' which results from an appropriative practice. Her chapter rightly questions the efficacy of, and perhaps even the rationale behind, source hunting. What exactly is the reader to make of the excavated sources if we find that the poet 'appropriates language from [a biographer] who translates Mandelstam who appropriates the voice of his wife Nadezhda'? Are we then left bewildered in a hall of mirrors? How far does source hunting get us, and does the revelation of a source really provide a stable resting place for an understanding of the poems? 'What seems clear', she argues, 'is that while offering a glimpse on to bewil-dering intertextual vistas, and a commentary on its own forms, the meaning continues to elude us as far as interpretation of McGuckian's individual poems is concerned.' This is an extremely salutary conclusion as it heightens our sense of the poetry's provisional states of becoming, as noted by Kirkland.

An intertextual approach is *not* the only way to read a McGuckian poem, nor is it necessarily the best way. Leontia Flynn's essay, then, acts as a necessary corrective to the naive excesses of my own work. Nevertheless, one could argue that the unearthing of a source and the tracing of its possible relevance can aid in our understanding both of her writing process and her relationship to her exemplars. Indeed, some texts seem to invite the intertextual approach. My final example, 'Sealed Composition',[67] from her latest collection, *My Love Has Fared Inland*, is a case in point:

it is a little like returning to life (GC 112)	It is a little like returning to life,
with a new spinal cord (GC 162); 'that reddens	with a new spinal cord that reddens your throat,
your throat' (GC 182); their untended name (GC 115)	your untended name, dreaming and probing,
dreaming and probing, seeing and testing (GC 184)	seeing and testing the consolation
the consolation of new gospels (GC 192)	of new gospels.
the cloaked girl (GC 55); the all-too-human sharer of	The cloaked girl, all-too-human sharer
his flaming tomb (GC 70);	of his flaming tomb,
'flower-reading' (MC 5); the transfigured city (GC 34)	is flower-reading the transfigured
anti-city (GC 34); a lady of the mind (GC 17)	anti-city, lecturing on mercy, a lady
his mind's bride (GC 180)	of the mind, his mind's moated bride.
the seraph's second wing is reversed at the	The seraph's second wing
wrist (MC 13); the needle of happiness (GC 63)	reverses the needle of happiness
the pilot-angel (GC 81)	at the wrist, a pilot-angel,
an epiphany in black (GC 184)	an epiphany in black anxiety,
'snaps his helmet shut / on his face' (GC 172)	he snaps his helmet shut on his face.
'the slowest of heavens' (GC 73); 'going up and	The slowest of heavens, going up
Down another's stairway' (GC 143)	and down another's stairway,
angelic boat (GC 95)	smothers their angelic ivory boat
cold or intimate [. . .] tones (GC 186)	in cold and intimate tones:
'silent lips, dry' (GC 179); on the reached shore (GC 92)	their dry lips find themselves on the reached shore.

While 'sealed' connotes authoritative ratification – it bears the mark of the author to denote the text's authenticity (and originality) – the adjective also suggests that the text is a private missive for a specific audience; hence it is closed off from all other eyes. 'Composition' suggests the product, the work of art itself, but the word's definition equally calls attention to its means of production: it has been formed by combining various elements together. That these elements come from a literary exemplar is conveyed by the poem's epigraph from Goethe, a citation which at once informs the reader of her characteristic style and of its rationale: 'One learns only from those one loves.' There seems, then, to be a tension evoked by the title and epigraph: while the poet asserts the composition's originality (that it comes from her), she also intimates its derivative nature. In an interview she states:

> [t]he words are given to me [. . .] and the authors, and the translators, especially if they're dead, they are very aware of me using them and that they want it, they want me to make the same words live again in a new

way and do things with it that carries me and marks my reading of the
book and marks my learning process with them.[68]

There is clearly no anxiety of influence here, an assertion to which the
opening stanza, composed of phrases taken from Glauco Cambon's *Dante's
Craft*, a study of Dante's influence on later writers, bears testimony. In her
work, McGuckian 'tends' to the names of dead authors and in the opening line
she is in the position of Dante communing with the souls in hell. In the
Inferno, Virgil 'passes on to Dante the role of interceding for the dead with the
living' and for the dead '*it is a little like returning to life* to have the privilege of
speaking to a man of flesh and blood' (GC 112, my emphasis). For McGuckian
and the resurrected author alike the use of the intertext provides 'a new spinal
cord' and 'reddens' the throat. Of course 'reddens' initiates a tension whereby
the use of someone else's words can both be harmful ('redden' as indicative of
soreness) and life-giving ('redden' meaning 'to grow ruddy with health'). There
is no one way of reading the stanza, and indeed it intimates that nothing is
fixed or wholly determined in her work: she aligns herself with the outlook of
the Italian poet Eugenio Montale, who argues that 'dreaming and probing,
seeing and testing are one in the act of poetry' (GC 184).

The emphasis on concealment runs throughout the text: the girl is
'cloaked'; the bride is 'moated'; the male figure 'snaps his helmet shut on his
face'. McGuckian is tracing a particular use of the encoded message (or
'*trobar clus*') in literature: although it initially seems as if she is referring to
Dante's employment of coded writing in which he shares 'an ineffable sum
of mental experiences' with 'his initiated friends' (GC 18), as one reads the
poem in light of the intertext it becomes apparent that McGuckian is
alluding to Montale's appropriation of both Dante's style and content to
encode and work through his unrequited love for Irma Brandeis, a translator
and student of Dante whom he met in 1932, is represented in his own
poetry as 'Clizia', a latter-day Beatrice.[69] She is the 'cloaked girl' of the
second stanza: 'cloaked' both literally, since this is Dante's vision of Beatrice
in the famous opening of the *Vita Nuova*, and figuratively, as Brandeis is
figured here at several removes. The stanza records the tension between her
status as a real, 'all-too-human' woman and as an imaginative construct, a
'lady of the mind'. The latter is a necessary and self-protective construct:
Montale conceives of her as 'his mind's moated bride' because he had
married someone else.

The third stanza presents a tension between the desire to communicate
and the deliberate withholding of information. When McGuckian writes
that the 'seraph's second wing' is said to reverse 'the needle of happiness /
at the wrist', she conjoins two quotations from very different sources. Within
Dante's schema, when love is aimed at the object of desire it is said to be
'the needle of happiness in the compass of the soul' (GC 63). However,

McGuckian writes that this needle has been 'reversed'; desire is directed elsewhere. There is perhaps an inference of male self-pleasuring since the 'needle of happiness' is reversed 'at the wrist'. Hence, there is both a denial of the desired object and sublimation. The image of the 'seraph's second wing' being 'reversed at the wrist' is taken from *The Medieval Craft of Memory*, a study of medieval memory images. The particular image referred to is a drawing from the Beinecke Library, MS416, fol. 8, based on Alan of Lille's mnemonic treatise on penance. While the first wing is the 'self-accusing demonstration of sin' (MC 94), the second wing is 'reparation', namely 'the full execution of the penance imposed, or the appropriate rebuke and reform of sinners' (MC 97). The wing is 'reversed' so that it can more easily be read and not hidden. In a stratagem that is characteristic of 'Sealed Composition', therefore, the reparation is openly declared (via the mnemonic), but only to those who know the code. The self-denying poet is represented as snapping 'his helmet shut on his face', an image interpreted by Cambon as being a 'mask of otherness' and 'the price for self-isolation' (GC 172).

The final stanza's image of 'going up / and down another's staircase' (from Dante's *Paradiso*) can be taken to signify the habitation in and journey through another writer's *oeuvre* (Montale through Dante, McGuckian through both via Cambon's critical study). But where does the journey lead? One reading suggests a narrative of arrival: 'he' and 'she' finally come together as 'they' 'on the reached shore'. While 'lips' connotes both sensuality and communication, they are 'dry' and, in the intertext, 'silent'. That the line refers to the disembarking of spirits on to 'Purgatory beach' (GC 92) is perhaps significant since throughout the poem the male figure has been keeping his desires at bay and attempting to atone for his sin. Hence, he has not reached Paradise nor found peace with his Beatrice.

Editing this collection of essays with Richard Kirkland, I found myself constantly 'going up / and down another's staircase', being surprised and delighted in turn by the contributors' insights and reading strategies. I hope that the essays will enable the reader to gain a new appreciation of what Clair Wills aptly terms in her 'Afterword' McGuckian's 'strange and wonderful work'.

1

Speaking as the North:
Self and place in the early poetry of Medbh McGuckian

MICHAELA SCHRAGE-FRÜH

Medbh McGuckian ranks among the most prolific and original contemporary poets in English. She is, moreover, the only female poet to have gained international renown alongside an almost exclusively male generation of Northern Irish poets. Surprisingly, however, despite her Northern Irish background, the majority of critics have tended to label McGuckian's poetry as apolitical, not at all rooted in her native soil, thereby routinely excluding her from discourses of Northern Irish identity. At the same time, her supposed avoidance of political, public and national issues has often been deemed evasive, if not escapist, in a Catholic poet who was born and has spent all her life in Belfast, thus having experienced her share of the Northern Irish Troubles. Partly due to McGuckian's idiosyncratic use of domestic and nature imagery, critics have been disposed to categorise her early work as domestic and private, concerned exclusively with 'women's issues' such as pregnancy, childbirth and motherhood, while her notoriously dense, oblique and complex style has encouraged feminist readings in terms of *écriture féminine*. The following representative statements by McGuckian critics may serve to sketch the extent to which McGuckian's work, especially her early poetry written throughout the 1980s, has been relegated to the realm of the private. Thus, in a review from 1985, Christopher Benfey claims that McGuckian

> hasn't followed Seamus Heaney in searching for ways to be true to one's own private experience while registering the public strains of the North [. . .] To scan her poems for allusions to sectarian violence would be as fruitless and naive as to sift Emily Dickinson's poems for references to the Civil War.[1]

According to Michael Allen, in an article from 1992, there are '[t]wo related issues [that] confront the reader of Medbh McGuckian's poetry. The first is her obscurity, the second her female identity. It is only in passing from one to the other that one needs to mention her Irishness.'[2] Finally, as late as 1999, Jonathan Hufstader maintains that McGuckian's first four collections of poetry are, in core, 'nonpolitical (in any sense of the word)' as well as '[e]rotic, domestic, sensitive to detail, and private'. And he concludes: 'To be born a poet in Ulster, as Heaney long ago pointed out, does not require that one have a microphone at one's lips. When McGuckian talks about responsibility, she means motherhood.'[3]

In this chapter I will argue that a concern with Irish identity is at the heart of McGuckian's early poetry. This concern, however, is complicated and at times obscured by the conflation of woman and land/nation in Irish cultural and literary discourse. Thus, in the Irish cultural imagination, both the Irish land and nation have been traditionally envisaged as female, with Erin as a young maiden in distress, about to be ravished by imperial male England; as a harlot, about to collaborate with the coloniser; or as a mother bemoaning the suffering of her children. In Irish literature, the trope of Ireland as a woman appears in various guises, as Dark Rosaleen, Erin, Hibernia, the Shan Van Vocht or Mother Ireland, and, most famously, as Yeats's Cathleen Ní Houlihan, the old hag who turns into 'a young girl [. . .] with the walk of a queen'[4] when young men sacrifice their lives for her.[5] That these gendered representations are by no means limited to nineteenth- and early-twentieth-century colonial discourse is confirmed, for instance, by Seamus Heaney's poem 'Act of Union', published in his 1975 collection *North*. Here, the poet depicts Ireland as a woman raped by 'imperially / Male' England, presenting Northern Ireland as the 'bastard child' originating from an enforced 'act of union'.[6] Similarly, his bog-poems continue the conflation of woman and land in his invocation of pagan fertility rites. As Clair Wills aptly puts it, 'the representation of the Irish land as a woman stolen, raped, possessed by the alien invader is not merely one mythic narrative among many, but, in a literary context, it is *the* myth, its permutations so various and ubiquitous it can be hard to recognize them for what they are'.[7] Thus, the Northern Irish female poet's sense of self is inevitably shaped not only by her immediate socio-political environment, as well as by her everyday experiences of the Troubles, but by prevailing national, cultural and religious images of femininity and her need to come to terms with, adjust or revise these images. What is more, the neat distinction that some critics appear to perceive between 'private' and 'public' fails to take into account the ways in which these spaces blur in a place like war-torn Belfast, where, as McGuckian has put it, the home provides at best an illusory sense of security, since 'a man can come into your house and shoot you'.[8] Ultimately, despite Hufstader's implied claim that McGuckian's concern with motherhood is non-political, in a culture so dependent on religious and national images of the mother, the subject of female sexuality and motherhood is itself highly politicised.

A much-needed critical reassessment of McGuckian's *oeuvre* in terms of national and political consciousness has only begun, and has so far predominantly focused on the poet's more recent and more overtly 'political' work, from her fifth collection *Captain Lavender* (1994) onward. In this chapter, then, I would like to highlight McGuckian's early work, focusing on *The Flower Master* (1982), *Venus and the Rain* (1984) and *Marconi's Cottage* (1991).[9] As my close reading of selected poems from these collections will show, McGuckian's early poetry characteristically interweaves the private and the public, viewing the violence of the Troubles through the lens of the female body, through her elaborate domestic and nature images as well as through more or less oblique intertextual dialogues with Irish (and non-Irish) writers, texts, genres and motifs. In a cultural environment and literary tradition in which myths of a suffering Virgin Mary and a militant Mother Ireland still have currency, the poet creates spaces in which to interrogate and redefine conventional images of woman and/as nation. McGuckian's poetry, then, provides a highly original and relevant female perspective on Irish identity and the Northern Irish Troubles.

Internalising the Troubles

The short poem 'That Year', consisting of four unrhymed four-line stanzas, was the opening poem of McGuckian's first book-length collection, *The Flower Master* (1982). A slightly modified version was republished under the title 'Eavesdropper' in *The Flower Master and Other Poems* (1993). Although arguably one of McGuckian's more readily accessible poems, its intricate use of rhetorical devices and images is exemplary of the poet's multi-layered style. The poem explores a girl's confusion at the onset of her first menstruation, presented as an identity crisis in which the speaker discovers her 'otherness' in terms of both sexual and national consciousness. The poem, then, exemplifies McGuckian's characteristic mode of creating multiple levels of meaning by interweaving images of female and national identity. It also illustrates the way a hostile environment affects and pervades a person's sense of self to the extent that a conflict like Northern Ireland's sectarian division and its resultant violence are internalised:

> That year it was something to do with your hands:
> To play about with rings, to harness rhythm
> In staging bleach or henna on the hair,
> Or shackling, unshackling the breasts.
>
> I remembered as a child the red kite
> Lost forever over our heads, the white ball
> A pin-prick on the tide, and studied
> The leaf-patterned linoleum, the elaborate

Stitches on my pleated bodice.
It was like a bee's sting or a bullet
Left in me, this mark, this sticking pins in dolls,
Listening for the red and white

Particles of time to trickle slow, like a wet nurse
Feeding nonchalantly someone else's child.
I wanted curtainings, and cushionings;
The grass is an eavesdropper's bed. (*FM* 15)

This poem conjures up the image of a pubescent girl faced with the confusing changes of her body, starting to 'play about', i.e. to experiment with
jewellery ('rings'), the colour of her hair ('bleach or henna'), her first bra
('shackling, unshackling the breasts'). The terms 'playing about' and 'staging'
both imply the girl's sense of alienation from herself, suggesting that she feels
like an actress, dressing up and rehearsing her unfamiliar role as an adolescent. On the other hand, the terms 'harness' and 'shackle' contrast sharply
with this sense of experimental playfulness by suggesting foreign control and
captivity. Ultimately, the onset of puberty terminates the child's playful
freedom.

While in the first stanza the speaker addresses her former self (the pubescent girl) in the second person singular, from stanza two she adopts the first
person singular: '*I* remembered as a child the red kite / Lost forever over our
heads, the white ball / A pin-prick on the tide' (my emphasis). The time-shift
occurring here is also noteworthy, as the (by now adult) speaker recalls a time
(puberty) in which she remembered her lost childhood, symbolised by the
kite 'lost forever over our heads'. The pronoun 'our' suggests a lost community, while the image of a 'pin-prick on the tide' indicates disorientation, as
well as a teasing pain, echoing the vocabulary of violence introduced in
stanza one. Menstruating for the first time, the girl feels injured, associating
this experience with a 'bee's sting', 'a bullet / Left in [her]', or a 'doll stuck
with pins'. Her pain seems to be caused by external forces rather than originating within her own body and self. Accordingly, she feels estranged from
herself as she directs her attention first to the 'leaf-patterned linoleum' of the
bathroom floor, then to the 'elaborate / Stitches of [her] pleated bodice',
probably trying to sort out her confused emotions and thoughts. Menstruation is further suggested by the image of 'a wet nurse / Feeding nonchalantly
someone else's child'. This image, however, may just as well refer back to the
mysterious slow trickling 'red and white / Particles of time' the speaker
listens for. '[R]ed and white' serve as a recurring motif in the short poem, as
suggested by the 'bleach' and 'henna' of the first stanza as well as by the 'red
kite' and the 'white ball' referred to in the second. Rather conventionally,
white and red symbolise purity and innocence on the one hand, and blood,

menstruation and loss of innocence on the other. While the girl's awakening sexuality made her dream of romantic 'curtainings and cushionings', she now has woken up to the sobering realities of a woman's life, realising that '[t]he grass is an eavesdropper's bed'. For a girl, growing up is not a bed of roses as she realises the traditional path mapped out for her.[10] Tellingly, the 'linoleum' of stanza two evokes domestic chores, 'elaborate stitches' and 'sticking pins in dolls' suggest needlework, and 'feeding [a] child' hints at mothering – the three tasks a woman has traditionally been supposed to 'master' in her life.

To a girl, then, puberty means becoming aware of restrictions and a sense of otherness. Accordingly, menstruation is perceived as a mark, a curse, a punishment – ideas which are directly connected to the poem's title. Thus, a child's eavesdropping on a grown-up conversation and gaining forbidden knowledge indicates premature initiation into adulthood. The disillusioning and painful fall from grace thus implied is further suggested by the poem's title, 'Eavesdropper', which puns on the name Eve as well as on the idea of 'dropping', i.e. 'falling off the eaves'. The girl's sexual awakening, then, is represented as a child's paradise lost. Moreover, a Catholic girl for the first time 'eavesdropping' on her body's involuntary changes could easily feel tainted and associate her sexuality with Eve, whose transgression caused the Fall. There are, however, different possibilities of interpretation. A 'bee's sting', 'a bullet / Left in me [. . .] sticking pins in dolls' could just as likely denote the speaker's deflowering, and thus her actual loss of virginity and initiation into womanhood and sexuality. Moreover, as Alexander Gonzalez suggests, the reference to 'rings', the colour white and a 'wet nurse / Feeding nonchalantly someone else's child' may denote the young woman's wedding and early motherhood so that the poem would portray a young wife and mother, disillusioned by the realities of married life or perhaps suffering from postpartum depression.[11] To Thomas Docherty, the stitches on the speaker's bodice suggest a Caesarian birth.[12] Of course, these alternative options are inherent in the central motif of menstruation, whose onset all too often maps out the course an adolescent girl's life is bound to take. At one level, then, the poem stages an identity crisis initiated by the girl's first awareness of her sexuality and gender.

On a second level, the poem abounds with allusions to the political conflict. In her essay 'Drawing Ballerinas', McGuckian herself points out the significance of red and white as two colours of the Union Jack flag.[13] There are, however, two further colours implied in the poem. Green, the colour traditionally associated with Ireland, is evoked by both the 'leaf-patterned linoleum' and the 'grass' referred to in the final line. A faint allusion to blue, the third Union Jack colour, is provided by McGuckian's implied references to the sky and the sea, which serve as backdrop to the 'red kite' and the 'white ball'. Significantly, blue is also the colour associated with the Catholic religion and the Virgin Mary. While red and white, the colours of her official status as a Northern Irish citizen, visibly stand out in the poem, green and blue provide hidden and officially unacknowledged backdrops. The uneven combination of the colours red, white, green and blue, then, indicates the Ulster Catholic girl's split or blurred sense of identity. Moreover, the numerous references to violence, imprisonment and blood reflect the hostile environment of the Troubles, which the speaker internalises, as most poignantly suggested by the central image of 'a bullet / Left in me'. Finally, a faint echo of Heaney's representation of Ireland as bastard child ('Act of Union') is provided by McGuckian's reference to 'a wet nurse / Feeding nonchalantly someone else's child', an abandoned child like Northern Ireland, fostered by uncaring strangers. Even though the analogy may be neither particularly original nor historically apt, in an interview McGuckian uses a similar image to illustrate her emotional view of the relationship between the Republic and the North: 'It's like they're both bleeding, like there was a mental surgical slice in two. It's like a mother who has had her child cut away from her, and she's unhappy and miserable and the child is unhappy as well, but they cannot find each other.'[14]

While the speaker's ambiguous sense of her own sexual and national identity results in a confusing pattern of images, this very pattern points to the third component of the speaker's emerging identity: the artist's. The images employed in the poem are mostly taken from domestic life, referring to women's traditional occupations. An interest in clothes, jewellery and one's hair is suggested, while the images reflect domestic surroundings (the linoleum floor), needlework (elaborate stitches) and nursing (the wet nurse). In this early poem, then, McGuckian hints at what will emerge as some of her major metaphors of poetic creation: women's traditional craft and motherhood. Moreover, to harness *rhythm*, to study a *pattern*, and *elaborate* stitches all suggest artistic creation. The poem itself, in its use of an intricate pattern of rhetorical devices and images, particularly in its abundance of alliteration and internal rhyme, can be read as the creative outcome of a demanding existential situation in the young girl's life. Since the poem focuses on the female poet's emerging identity in the specific Northern Irish context, it might well be read as McGuckian's poetic response to a poem like Seamus Heaney's 'Digging', which touches upon similar themes from a male perspective. Trying to come to terms with one's sexual and national identity triggers the artistic process out of which the poem emerges.

Gender Trouble

In order to assert a sense of self and find a voice, a Northern Irish woman poet first needs to revise her traditional national representation as passive object and symbol of the land. This aim is most effectively achieved by modifying traditional scenarios such as the colonial marriage or rape trope. In the poem 'The Soil-Map' this endeavour is, moreover, coupled with a playful reappropriation of formerly occupied space. The poet is depicted as a trespasser in masculine disguise, while the central motif of a house and its violation is described in terms both gendered and sexual. The first stanza reads:

> I am not a woman's man, but I can tell,
> By the swinging of your two-leaf door,
> You are never without one man in the shadow
> Of another; and because the mind
> Of a woman between two men is lighter
> Than a spark, the petalled steps to your porch
> Feel frigid with a lost warmth. I will not
> Take you in hardness, for all the dark cage
> Of my dreaming over your splendid fenestra-
> tion,
> Your moulded sills, your slender purlins,
>
> The secret woe of your gutters. (*FM* 36)

From the first line, the reader is bound to assume a male speaker addressing an objectified woman or a feminised house, since the one hint at characterisation regarding the speaker is: 'I am not a woman's *man*' (my emphasis). However, while the poem's very first line seems to determine this reading in terms of a male invader taking possession of a maiden in distress, the final line comes as a surprise, when the speaker, like an Irish version of Virginia Woolf's Orlando, changes her gender by expressing her impatience 'for my power as a *bride*' (my emphasis). The idea of a bride is evoked earlier by the reference to 'clearing its [the house's] name' (*FM* 36). Traditionally, a bride, too, 'clears' her name on her wedding day by adopting her husband's surname. Moreover, the allusion to houses and their female names is again dwelled on in the last stanza, where the speaker discovers the houses' names on the 'soil-map': 'Annsgift or Mavisbank, / Mount Juliet or Bettysgrove' (*FM* 37). The speaker implies that she will change the name of the house she is about to move to as a bride, but, contrary to the tradition, she will not give it her own or another woman's name. Instead, she argues, addressing the house:

> they should not
> Lie with the gloom of disputes to interrupt them
> Every other year, like some disease
> Of language making humorous the friendship
> Of the thighs. I drink to you as Hymenstown,
> (My touch of fantasy) or First Fruits,
> Impatient for my power as a bride. (*FM* 37)

A number of hints in the poem suggest that, besides describing the house as politically contested space, McGuckian is simultaneously addressing an architectural version of the woman as Ireland trope – which is not surprising given the fact that the house is another popular symbol of Ireland, used for instance by Yeats in his play *Cathleen Ní Houlihan*, where Cathleen complains about '[t]oo many strangers in the house'.[15] Among other things, the feminine representation of Ireland is evoked by McGuckian's hint at her own mythical namesake Medb, Queen of Connacht, of whom it is said that she never had 'one man without another waiting in his shadow'.[16] This statement testifies to the fact that Medb is a forerunner of the nationalist *Cathleen*-figure; as a humanised Celtic goddess representing the land, Medb is mated to whoever happens to be King of Ireland. Moreover, the terms 'woe' and 'dreaming' evoke the young maiden appearing to an eighteenth-century Gaelic poet in a traditional *aisling* (dream vision) as another feminine allegory of Ireland, while the terms 'derangement' and 'collapse' conjure up the sovereignty goddess roaming the wilderness in madness because no king is left to mate with her. Finally, in stanza three, the speaker explains how 'anyone with patience can divine / [h]ow your plasterwork has lost key, the rendering / [a]bout to come away' (36). Metaphorically, this description may well point to the outdated status of the conventional feminine allegory of Ireland. On a literal level, though, it suggests the decaying state of the house the speaker is about to make her home, which is actually the house McGuckian inhabits in Belfast. As she has explained in an interview,

> 'The Soil-Map' is a[n] autobiographical piece. On a geographical map the good land is occupied by the English and the planters, the poor land by the natives. I am in the poem addressing the house I am now actually writing this in, before we moved in, so *I* was the rapist as it were. As I said, the map of Belfast was changing and Protestants who could afford to leave were also leaving and Catholics moving into their areas. So a Presbyterian house never before occupied by Catholics is the focus of the poem. It is a very cynical poem, since it was a kind of scorched earth policy, in that only when the soil was exhausted and the house beyond repair would it be abandoned. I say that my house is like a whore, really, and the innocent relationship between land and owners can never be recovered.[17]

Consistently, the names of the houses the speaker finds on the soil-map are compounded of English-sounding female names. Interestingly, notwithstanding her initial invocation of Queen Medb – whose name is never explicitly given in this poem – the speaker moving into the house, as it were retrieving her rightful place, refrains from replacing the unambiguously English names with unambiguously Irish ones such as Medb. Instead, she suggests the names 'Hymenstown' and 'First Fruits', alluding to the bride-to-be's anticipated wedding night and the conception of her first child. This could be interpreted as an attempted move away from the 'gloom of disputes' to a reconciliatory vision based on love and procreation, or even the recovery of the original role and function of the ancient Celtic goddess, which was to bring prosperity to her people and fertility to the land. The term 'power' in relation to the bride would tie in with this, although there is certainly an ironic ring to the idea of a powerful bride. Exposing women's traditionally powerless and objectified status which cuts across sectarian divisions, the poem, then, repudiates the 'gloom of disputes' in favour of a more optimistic vision. Presenting the reader with a third alternative of naming the house ('Hymenstown' or 'First Fruits', rather than an English or Irish female name), it disrupts binary coloniser/colonised representations as well as playfully deconstructing women's traditional passive and silent role as an object and national symbol. This guardedly optimistic vision, however, is overshadowed by the speaker's doubtful pondering in the third stanza, in which she wonders whether it is really possible to discard one's roots and overcome socio-political divisions simply by moving house:

> So like a rainbird,
> Challenged by a charm of goldfinch,
> I appeal to the god who fashions edges
> Whether such turning-points exist
> As these saltings we believe we move
> Away from, as if by simply shaking
> A cloak we could disbud ourselves,
> Dry out, and cease to live there? (*FM* 36)

It seems as though the cultural, even the geographical, environment is again internalised by a speaker who likens herself to a 'rainbird' and carries her Northern Irish Catholic origins with her wherever she goes.

Revising the Rising

The poem 'The Rising Out' from McGuckian's second collection *Venus and the Rain* (1984) reverberates with literary, cultural, political and personal allusions. These allusions need to be unravelled carefully to bring to light the poem's political resonances, inextricably entwined with its gender concerns. In an interview, McGuckian has pointed out the gendered significance of the term *rising out* in an Irish context, explaining that

> *éirí amach* is the Irish for rising out. In the tradition, when a woman married, it was the transition from her father's home to her new home, her husband's home or to her husband's people. [It was] a peasant tradition that when the woman of one tribe or one family was transferred through marriage and through the bargaining and through the dowry

and all of that negotiation, there was this very definite voyage or journey which she had to make. [. . .] It's actually a very ambiguous poem in that sense in that the woman never had a moment of herself. She either belonged to this man or belonged to that man. She never had a rising to herself.[18]

Besides this specific cultural subtext, the title 'The Rising Out' inevitably conjures up not only the Easter Rising of 1916, but also its most famous poetic treatment, Yeats's elegy 'Easter 1916', which was written shortly after the failed uprising had taken place. Allusions to Yeats's poem are scattered throughout McGuckian's first stanza:

> My dream sister has gone into my blood
> To kill the poet in me before Easter. Such
> A tender visit, when I move my palaces,
> The roots of my shadow almost split in two,
> Like the heartbeat of my own child, a little
> Blue crocus in the middle of a book, or the hesitant
> Beginning of a song I knew, a stone-song
> Too small for me, awaiting a drier music. (*VR* 36)

Here, McGuckian takes up fragments from Yeats's poem, reassembling them and imbuing them with different meaning. 'Easter 1916' can indeed be termed a 'stone-song', as the poem's central image is the stone:

> Hearts with one purpose alone
> Through summer and winter seem
> Enchanted to a *stone*
> To trouble the living stream.
> [. . .]
> The *stone's* in the midst of all.
> [. . .]
> Too long a sacrifice
> Can make a *stone* of the heart.
> O when may it suffice?[19]

McGuckian, however, rejects the 'hesitant / Beginning of a song I knew, a stone-song / Too small for me, awaiting a drier music'. Words used by Yeats, such as 'shadow', 'cloud', 'child' and 'dream' reverberate in McGuckian's poem, and the 'weatherly remarks' she mentions in the second stanza correspond with Yeats's reference to 'polite meaningless words'. While these echoes suggest that McGuckian's poem might be a rewriting of or response to the earlier text, there is all the same a striking discrepancy regarding the representation of motherhood. In Yeats's poem, motherhood is clearly related to death:

> That is Heaven's part, our part
> To murmur name upon name,
> As a mother names her child
> When sleep at last has come
> On limbs that had run wild.
> What is it but nightfall?
> No, no, not night but death[.][20]

Moreover, Yeats employs the image of birth in order to convey his central claim that '[a] terrible beauty is born'. The ancient image of the hideous old hag becoming young again through blood sacrifice shines through this metaphor. In contrast, the 'dream sister' of McGuckian's initial line seems closely related to 'the heartbeat of my own child', and in McGuckian's metaphorical frame of reference the idea of a 'familiar closing of the unseen room' is bound to be read as the onset of pregnancy. In interviews McGuckian has repeatedly commented on her inability to create poetry during some of her pregnancies, a circumstance which helps explain how her 'dream sister' could threaten to 'kill the poet' within her.[21] McGuckian has also pointed out how much she longed for a daughter, a wish that was to remain unfulfilled until her fourth pregnancy. The term 'dream sister' might express exactly this wish. In an interview, McGuckian has helpfully elaborated on her own biographical situation at the time of writing 'The Rising Out':

> You want to be a good mother, a good wife, a good daughter, you want to play all these roles that you have to, but your main need is to be the poet. You have to keep all these things in little compartments within your mind, and when one dominates over the other, then there's a crisis. So I try and try to keep these parts of myself operating. It's like different pieces or different selves and it was very, very difficult to me.[22]

The 'expectant' mother at first tries to continue working 'on [her] arm-long / "Venus Tying the Wings of Love"', a title which suggests highbrow poetic work, but in the course of the poem she becomes more interested in Lewis Carroll's children's tale *Alice in Wonderland*: 'In my mind, / I try and try to separate one Alice / From the other, by their manner of moving' (*VR* 36).[23]

Despite her allusions to Yeats and the associations of the 1916 Easter Rising created by featuring the terms 'rising' and 'Easter' in the same poem, McGuckian's version, then, moves in a completely different direction. Once more, her speaker seems to internalise the political conflict with '[t]he roots of [her] shadow almost split in two'. In the course of the poem, however, it soon becomes clear that the major conflict is between her two competing identities of poet and mother. At the beginning of the poem she is not yet sure whether the 'tender visit' she senses is 'like the heartbeat of [her] own *child*' or 'the hesitant / beginning of a *song*' (my emphasis). Both comparisons suggest creative acts on the speaker's part, which can, at first, hardly be told apart – actually, the image of a 'blue crocus in the middle of a book' combines the spheres of nature (birth) and art – and which, halfway through the poem, seem to become mutually exclusive. As the speaker's actual pregnancy proceeds, her poetic impulse weakens, 'weatherly remarks' replacing her 'arm-long' lyric. In the final stanza, however, the conflict between mother and poet seems to be resolved, as it becomes clear that the poet is reborn by giving birth to her child. The stanza carries allusions to Christ's crucifixion and resurrection and remains characteristically prophetic in its, at first glance, enigmatic imagery:

> If she had died suddenly I would have heard
> Blood stretched on the frame, though her dream
> Is the same seed that lifted me out of my clothes,
> And carried me till it saw itself as fruit. (*VR* 36)

In this final stanza McGuckian turns from Anglo-Irish to German poetry by appropriating some phrases from Rainer Maria Rilke's 'Requiem für eine Freundin [Requiem for a Friend]'. In this poem, addressed to the painter Paula Modersohn-Becker, the German poet mourns Paula's death after childbirth and, according to Sarah Broom, depicts 'Paula's death as tragic proof that women, being forced through pregnancy and other social demands to be "fully in the world" and to open themselves to others, cannot maintain the inner separateness and degree of tranquillity that Rilke believes is essential for the artist'.[24] In his 'Requiem für eine Freundin', Rilke writes: 'Und sahst dich selbst zuletzt wie eine Frucht, / nahmst dich heraus aus deinen Kleidern, trugst / dich vor den Spiegel' ['And at last, you saw yourself as a fruit, / you stepped out of your clothes and brought your naked body / before the mirror'].[25] The words of the English translation unmistakably echo in McGuckian's final lines: 'though her dream / Is the same seed that lifted me out of my clothes / And carried me till it saw itself as fruit'. If 'her dream' refers back to the 'dream sister', and thus the child, the reader may conclude that it is not only the mother who conceives, carries and finally gives birth to her child, but that the child, too, 'carries' and creates the mother. Unlike Rilke, who is 'lamenting the fragmentation that he imagines took place within Paula as a result of pregnancy',[26] McGuckian's poet speaker is defined by and cannot be separated from her identity as a mother. Although the woman physically and mentally experiences the fragmentation of her body and self, and, on a metaphorical level, temporarily internalises the division of her nation, her tension is resolved in the end. She neither dies nor is she a Mother Ireland-figure who sacrifices her children so that 'a terrible beauty' can be born. Rather, she bears a child whose existence may temporarily prevent, but ultimately inspires and moulds her poetic work.

Death, Birth and Rebirth

The Northern Irish Troubles provide an important subtext in McGuckian's fourth major collection, *Marconi's Cottage*. Sectarian and sacrificial implications are frequently implied by means of religious symbolism. Throughout the volume, traditional Christian images are associated with war, violence and death. Thus, Christmas is evoked in 'No Streets, No Numbers', which belongs to a group of poems that trace unnatural, untimely and violent deaths as opposed to the natural cycles of life and death explored elsewhere in the collection. According to McGuckian, 'No Streets, No Numbers' is about a miscarriage caused by the child's violent father, which serves as a 'metaphor for the horror in Ireland [as] life itself was being killed in the womb before it could happen'.[27] The poem evokes a place of complete confusion, a place without streets or numbers to provide orientation, '[s]and-ribbed and troubled, a desolation / That could erase all memory of warmth', a place 'where all the colours are wrong' (*MC* 39). Images of bruised fruit, knife-wounds and 'the drawing-room with the wall / Pulled down' (*MC* 39) conjure up a desolate, dejected atmosphere in which there seems to be no life worth mentioning in the interval between the '[d]ouble knock of the stains of birth and death' (*MC* 39). At the centre of the poem is the most horrible, surreal image of the smashed embryo:

> [. . .] That dream
> Of a too early body undamaged
> And beautiful, head smashed to pulp,
> Still grows in my breakfast cup;
> It used up the sore red of the applebox,
> It nibbled at the fortnight of our violent
> Christmas like a centenarian fir tree. (*MC* 40)

The 'breakfast cup', the vessel that holds the image of the embryo, can be read as yet another religious symbol since '[t]he most frequent symbolic sense of cup, one's portion or bit in life, is biblical; it is usually God who fills the cup'.[28] A reference to a '[m]asterless and flagless' (*MC* 40) house reinforces the reader's sense that this poem is about the political predicament of Northern Ireland as much as it is about an individual woman's loss of her unborn child and that, again, McGuckian explores the political tragedy of her country through the lens of personal loss and suffering. The death of a child or the failure to conceive a child are clearly images for the horrors of war, such as in 'The Invalid's Echo' where '[t]he long autumn / Has scattered its poisonous seeds, / So I will have no October child' (*MC* 13).

However, the ending of 'No Streets, No Numbers' expresses a vague future vision which implies that hope is embodied by 'the voice reserved for children' (*MC* 41). Accordingly, pregnancy and birth provide a positive counterbalance in the collection. A number of poems in *Marconi's Cottage* deal with the birth of McGuckian's daughter, Emer Mary Charlotte Rose. In many of these poems the speaker expresses her sense that by giving birth to her daughter she has somehow outwitted death: 'we poised together / Against the crevice formed by death's forefinger / And thumb' (*MC* 84). In 'Charlotte's Delivery' she expresses a similar idea: 'In the wrecked hull of the fishing-boat / Someone has planted a cypress under the ribs' (*MC* 83). The cypress as a symbol of life and birth is not only 'sacred to all nature and fertility goddesses',[29] but, as an evergreen tree, traditionally 'associated with funerals and tombs', it 'naturally suggests eternal life'.[30] Finally, in 'The War Ending' the pregnant speaker even feels as if 'the war [. . .] has gone / Into us ending' (*MC* 82). The threats of death, decay and war are all assuaged, even redeemed, by the birth of the long-wished-for daughter. In 'Drawing Ballerinas' McGuckian elucidates her reasoning behind these images:

> There is probably a deep religious questioning hidden in the sensuality of this book [*Marconi's Cottage*], culminating in the almost mystical daughter-poems at the end. The child within redeems the outer world's gratuitous slaughters. She was born around August 1989, when the country had been under martial law for twenty years and people were beginning to seek change with a guarded optimism. Maybe this new feminine self will not have to grow up under the hazards and constraints and abnormality that we have endured as a generation, and our parents before us, who were born in the Civil War, even more so.[31]

Indeed, *Marconi's Cottage* is full of allusions to a new kind of *female* saviour. In 'The Partner's Desk' the speaker describes a dream in which she and a composite father/husband figure 'took a walk across loose stones, / And he took my hands and stretched them out / As if I were on a cross, but not being punished' (*MC* 71), thus revising the image of Christ's crucifixion by replacing sacrificial implications with erotic and pleasurable ones. Similarly, the 'world's [imagined] redemption' (*MC* 85) is achieved by her daughter's (impending) birth, 'one discarnate shadow / [being] worth a whole generation' (*MC* 85). Likewise, the birth of her daughter enhances the speaker's sense of identity. Whereas in McGuckian's earlier collections pregnancy usually resulted in a state of internal division, fragmentation and a split sense of identity, the pregnancy and daughter-poems of *Marconi's Cottage* bear witness to a new sense of wholeness and unity. In one of these poems, 'Sky-Writing', the pregnant speaker describes her new condition in terms of 'sky-writing' or, rather, 'sky-*riding*':

> Being seen like this by you,
> A steeply perched, uplooking town,
> Am I the same in a more strengthened way?

Can another afternoon belong
To such a morning? When will the evening
Be itself again, and who?

What can I do against this room
I was obliged to let grow and grow
In the new space all through the winter?
October dawns seeking the distance
Of their unfolding are startled
By a vessel so restricted holding them.

I forfeit the world outside
For the sake of my own inwardness,
I am so at one with the scent of its many wills:
Its inexhaustable innocency
Lapses past me like a future not lived strongly,
I abandon myself to its incubative weight.

I am on the point of falling
Like the essence of rain or a letter
Of ungiveable after-love into the next degree
Of spring, its penultimate tones:
Shall I ever again be caught up gently
As the rustle of a written address by the sky? (*MC* 79)

The speaker experiences her pregnancy in terms of a brand-new beginning as implied by the images of 'morning', 'October dawns' and 'spring'. There is no doubt that the speaker is changed, but I disagree with Clair Wills's claim that the 'fragmentation of the woman's body in the poem mirrors the disruption of the fabric of the poem itself; the body within the body is not only a double, but a foreign body which disrupts any sense of self, and the possibility of saying "I"'.[32] While this interpretation is cogent with respect to earlier pregnancy-poems like 'The Rising Out', in 'Sky-Writing' the speaker suggests that, rather than being alienated from her self, she might be 'the same in a more strengthened way'. She also, rather paradoxically, admits that she is 'at one with the scent of [the] many wills' of her 'inwardness'. Even though the speaker 'forfeits[s] the world outside / For the sake of [her] own inwardness', she compares this internal world to a sky wide enough even to hold 'October dawns'. Moreover, despite abandoning herself, the speaker seems thoroughly to enjoy her state of quiet harmonious drifting. Only when she, 'on the point of falling', is about to give birth, is there a tinge of sadness at the possibility that this might have been her last pregnancy: 'Shall I ever again be caught up gently / As the rustle of a written address by the sky?'

The fact that the speaker of 'Sky-Writing' addresses a 'steeply perched, uplooking town', presumably Belfast, suggests the idea that the poem's significance, once more, surpasses the merely individual level. While the title's reference to writing clearly alludes to the poet, the speaker could also be viewed as a version of Ireland herself speaking, meditating on her own redeemed future. In view of the sky imagery, there may even be a faint allusion to the eighteenth-century genre of the *aisling*, the Gaelic dream vision poem, in which the bardic poet encounters the *spéir bhean*, or sky-woman, and asks her a number of formulaic questions until he learns that she is *Éire*. In McGuckian's version of an *aisling*, however, it is the sky-woman herself who addresses the town and poses numerous questions, all of which defy a simple answer. In an interview, McGuckian has confirmed that, at one level, often the 'I' in her poems is 'speaking as the North of Ireland [. . .] the country itself',[33] and with reference to the collection's last poem she has offered a similar metaphorical reading:

> 'On Her Second Birthday', the last poem from *Marconi's Cottage*, has the image of a mother talking to an infant daughter which is really used to give voice to the broken nature of Ireland addressing a future new Ireland. The poem operates on these levels simultaneously and I want it to. My contours are at once my own physical boundaries and the political shape of the 'Six Counties'.[34]

The final two stanzas of this poem indeed suggest a political dimension, when the speaker refers to 'the imperfection of the union' and talks about 'flower[ing] again / More perfectly' (*MC* 108). More than anything else, though, the mysticism of 'On Her Second Birthday' implies a concern with spiritual life and religious meanings, and without the poet's explanations it would probably be difficult to arrive at an interpretation of this poem in terms of a renewed Ireland.[35] However, a number of poems in *Marconi's Cottage* both intend and succeed in conveying the metaphorical connection between mother/child and nation, thereby revising the one-dimensional Mother Ireland trope at the heart of Irish representations of nationhood. This revision entails a re-appropriation of the maternal body, by means of which McGuckian not only renegotiates women's authorial position and representation but also redefines the concept of nation. This becomes particularly apparent when McGuckian employs the image of the rose. The poet has explained her attraction to this image by arguing that 'the rose cannot be appropriated'[36] while there are at the same time manifold and at times contradictory associations attached to it. Thus, the rose 'is, in essence, a symbol of completion, of consummate achievement and perfection'.[37] Its symbolic connotations include love and passion, virginity (the Virgin Mary as the Mystic Rose), the Wars of the Roses (1455–85) and the English rose.

Lastly the rose has served to represent the Irish nation from the mid–nineteenth century on, not least of all in the allegorical figure of 'Róisín Dubh', which translates as 'Black Rose' or 'Dark Rosaleen'. The rose, then, is a version of the female representation of Ireland so that the very title 'Open Rose' implies a simultaneous revision of the image of woman and nation. In *Marconi's Cottage* and after, McGuckian's poems abound with references, more or less prominent, to all kinds of roses. In many of the *Marconi* poems, the rose is clearly used as a symbol of pregnancy or the pregnant woman's condition.[38] Most obviously, this connection is established in the poem 'Open Rose', in which McGuckian once more explores the themes of pregnancy, poetry and national identity:

> The moon is my second face, her long cycle
> Still locked away. I feel rain
> Like a tried-on dress, I clutch it
> Like a book to my body.
>
> His head is there when I work,
> It signs my letters with a question-mark;
> His hands reach for me like rationed air.
> Day by day I let him go
>
> Till I become a woman, or even less,
> An incompletely furnished house
> That came from a different century
> Where I am a guest at my own childhood.
>
> I have grown inside words
> Into a state of unbornness,
> An open rose on all sides
> Has spoken as far as it can. (*MC* 80)

At one level, this poem focuses on the speaker's impending motherhood. This is suggested, for instance, by the moon's 'long cycle / Still locked away', which alludes to the fact that a woman does not menstruate during pregnancy. Moreover, the speaker grows '[i]nto a state of unbornness', which indicates the child's impending birth, 'unbornness' being a circumscription for not yet born or not having given birth yet. Giving birth, then, is equated with opening up.

On a second level, the poem is about the female poet as suggested by the various references to writing and speech. The speaker clutches the rain '[l]ike a *book*' to her body; she refers to writing *letters*, and, most importantly, claims to 'have grown inside *words*', while the open rose has '*spoken* as far as it can' (my emphases). In the context of women's writing, the 'moon' associated with the speaker's body suggests her identity as a woman poet, one which she aims to express in her writing. Accordingly, the rain in its double role as fertiliser in both a creative and a procreative sense is likened to a *dress* as well as a *book* clutched to the speaker's *body*. In the second stanza, '[h]is head' which is 'there when I work' is suggestive of the male writer's overpowering presence in a male-dominated literary tradition, an influence which the female writer needs to escape so as to develop her own voice. The 'question-mark' with which he 'signs [her] letters' expresses both the male writer's inability to understand her feminine way of writing as well as her own insecurity. However, she continuously resists his hands which 'reach for [her]', letting him go to 'become a woman, or even less, / An incompletely furnished house'. Her writing is 'incompletely furnished' in the sense of being open, unfinished, ambivalent and in continual progress. Indeed, McGuckian's style has often been regarded as a kind of *écriture féminine* characterised by multiplicity, elusiveness and flux, which enables her to deconstruct traditional representations of women as static one-dimensional and allegorical figures.[39] In an earlier poem entitled 'Hotel', for instance, she dreams of 'a name / With a hundred meanings, all of them / Secret, going their own way' (*VR* 37), which she would like to bestow on the damsel in distress, traditional stock image of the *aisling*-genre. McGuckian's purpose, however, is not only to disrupt patriarchal language and nationalist discourse, but also to create a language that is 'un-English' and, thus, subversive of the colonisers' tongue as well. Interestingly, McGuckian has never made a conscious attempt to recover her lost Irish mother tongue, but, rather, in Joycean fashion, she creates what she herself calls 'a specialised language of my own, fairly private, which is not English, less than, more than English, which subverts, deconstructs, kills it, makes it the dream language I have lost'.[40] Moreover, English, the language of the coloniser, becomes 'Europeanised' as well as 'Hibernicised', as McGuckian incorporates the translated writings of, for instance, Russian or German poets into her own works, placing them in active dialogue with Irish themes.[41] Her poems, then, change into what in 'The Dream-Language of Fergus' she calls 'a seed-fund, pressing out the diasporic snow' (*OBB* 57), thereby dissolving binary oppositions. According to Breda Gray, 'the notion of "diaspora" suggests an inclusiveness that allows for different geographical locations and ways of living out Irishness. Diaspora, therefore, has the potential to expand Irish identity and may contribute to a more open and fluid notion of that identity'.[42] By evoking this idea, McGuckian destabilises both the sense of an insular homogeneous identity and the focus on a binary relation between Ireland and England. In the wider context of McGuckian's *oeuvre*, then, the 'open rose' signifies an opening up in terms of gender as well as in terms of external (cultural) influences. It represents the writer who practises a poetics of multiplicity, who absorbs and is in dialogue with a multitude of intercultural texts and voices from various centuries and whose writing refuses to be pinned down to one particular position or theory. Simultaneously, the open rose symbolises a concept of Irish identity characterised by intercultural exchange and dialogue, so that binary oppositions like Ireland and Britain or Protestant and Catholic are effectively disrupted. The 'state of unbornness', then, comes to denote the numberless options of an as yet unborn Ireland. Moreover, this state marks the speaker's triumphal transcendence of her one-dimensional representation as woman in Irish literature: Having 'grown inside words / Into a state of unbornness', the speaker, rather than dissolving her own identity, celebrates the fact that neither her own identity nor the identity of her unborn child is predictable, predetermined or prescribed. Rather, it is like 'An open rose on all sides / [speaking] as far as it can'.

In *Captain Lavender* (1994), McGuckian chooses a quotation by Picasso to precede her fifth major collection of poetry: 'I have not painted the war [. . .] but I have no doubt that the war is in [. . .] these paintings I have done.' Although this telling epigraph refers to the poet's more openly political *Lavender* poems, it can certainly be read as emblematic of her work prior to that collection. Although Jonathan Hufstader claims that *Captain Lavender* marks 'McGuckian's poetic entry into the Troubles',[43] this chapter has highlighted the early poems' continual engagement with Northern Irish politics and has adumbrated the complex ways in which daily violence, fear, tension, sectarian division and historical consciousness are inextricably intertwined with this Northern Irish woman poet's search for a female poetic voice and identity.

2

A Gibbous Voice:
The poetics of subjectivity in the early poetry of Medbh McGuckian

CATRIONA CLUTTERBUCK

During the period in which Medbh McGuckian was establishing her authority as artist – from the early 1980s up to her fourth volume, *Marconi's Cottage* (1991) – that authority was configured through a process of confirmatory self-displacement: resistance to expansionist ego as the means of delivering the subject. There is a paradox in claiming such a procedure for a poet whose gender, in the retrospective light of the *Field Day Anthology* debate, can be expected to have curtailed her opportunities for excessive ego-enlargement as artist in that period. However, this inimical context was exactly the point of departure for McGuckian's task of self-definition in terms seemingly pliable to, yet also precisely subversive of, the gendered norms of that task.

McGuckian's work can be aligned to Eavan Boland's in that, by the early 1990s, both poets had very visibly embarked upon a project of rebalancing the recognised sources of aesthetic authority in the Irish poetic tradition. This tradition was identifiable then as now for its peculiar concern with its own mimetic yet interventive, collusive yet redistributive power of engagement in various Irish political and cultural status quos. Through very different textual effects, McGuckian and Boland were each engaged in disclaiming the over-elevated power of poet-representative of socio-political realities which was at that time under delimited offer to them as aspirants to the Irish canonical upper ranks. They did this in order to reclaim status for the under-recognised and inclusive power of poet-participant in those same realities (their roles as primary care-givers of children focusing in a particular way their calling to be so engaged). Their impulse was to rebalance power relations between the artistic ego and the historical circumstances to which it attends, through incorporating renewed awareness that poets are subject to, as well as mediators of, the worlds represented in their texts.

This movement, while more definitively enacted in McGuckian and Boland than in most, was neither gender-specific nor unusual in contemporary

Irish writing in the period under review. Irish writers in the 1980s and early 1990s understood in a particular way the foundational urgency of alertness to the claims of the artistic ego as a task that affects the ethical register of the artist's voice in the world. This project of self-reflexivity can be said to have characterised the integrity at the heart of the creative enterprise at a time when the crises of territorial political stalemate in the North and of harshly divisive sexual politics in the South were driving towards centre stage the question of the ethics of representation in Irish culture more generally. If the feint-and-duck mode of the Northern Irish poets signalled their earlier recognition that their own position of authority in relation to their material was a major aspect of their response to historical circumstance, it was later complemented by the more head-on sweeper-mode of their Southern peers in addressing this same concern. The subtlety in each body of work inheres in the challenge of the task undertaken rather than in any one cultural context's claims – whether place- or gender-based – to generate a superior poetic voice.

My argument in the present essay on Medbh McGuckian is as follows: through her early work's prominent concern with the push-and-pull of ego-displacement and ego-regeneration, she is both a contributor to, and definer of, the Irish lyric poetry tradition as a cross-generational community of readers and writers concerned with the release of aesthetic energy through what can be called a double 'nuclear' process of self-reflexivity. This is the process whereby, upon each encounter with the poem, the untidy fission of experiencing and interpreting selves that occurred during a preceding act of producing or receiving the text (and its antecedents) casts a shadow upon the neater fusion of public and private selves under current attractive offer in the poem. This haunting of the unified self called into being as an effect of the 'finished' poem, by the self disunited from its own experience through an earlier act of writing or reading it, is an important feature of the Irish lyric. It is central to the capacity of this lyric to become the codifier and transmitter of a sense of troubled connectivity between the individual and a more general destiny. For McGuckian, the question of the split or unified self at the heart of this self-reflexivity has a particular urgency, as the displacement of ego it suggests is pre-installed in the hard drive of her identity as a Northern Irish Catholic woman poet. This essay will argue that McGuckian overcomes the determined and delimiting nature of such culturally conditioned loss of self, by investigating the possibility and value of ego-resistance as choice. The result is a poetics of subjectivity through which this poet can present a quest for individuation that is truly capable of modelling the ethics of witness in the public political arena.

McGuckian's contradictory claims in the early 1990s that 'I don't talk about myself, or I erase my experience',[1] but also that her work is 'almost totally autobiographical',[2] confirm the presence of the private self within the poem while leaving its availability in question. The tension between these two positions drove the early reception of McGuckian, as critics – positive and negative alike – refused McGuckian's challenge to hold both together in the same space of understanding. Instead, their readings privileged either the present or the hidden self of this artist. On the one hand, critics lauded a 'real' private McGuckian concerned with female identity-assertion to the exclusion of public politics, who fulfils this aim by superseding the representative function of art – whether she is loved or hated for that semantic obscurity. On the other, critics privileged in her poems the 'secret' McGuckian as a teasingly offered, but deliberately unreal, private zone which functions as stalking horse for assumptions of the coherent subject and its communicability – assumptions which serve political intransigence. The expression of this 'hidden' McGuckian in her poetry's semantic obscurity was assumed to have the aim of either refusing outright an irredeemably corrupt public realm[3] or of challenging that public realm to make the positive political changes of which it is deemed capable.[4]

The notion that a focus on female subjectivity *ipso facto* relieves a poet from responsibility to engage with political life and its assumed correlative in clear discourse, exemplified by (among others) Michael Allen, James McElroy and Alan Robinson in relation to early McGuckian,[5] is easily challenged, based as it is on McGuckian's supposed revelation of an 'ethical superiority [. . .] in the marginalized feminine subject position'.[6] Their respect for the superiority of this position can conveniently relieve such critics of the possibility of engaging fully with her work. Alan Robinson so excuses himself (before going on to offer readings which, in their proper ambition to understand this poet, are at odds with this self-imposed limitation): 'it must be recognized that my analytic explications as a (male) critic working within the Symbolic order are unavoidably at odds with McGuckian's affective, intuitive discourse.'[7] Clearly, this is a position that only consolidates the gendered binary thought it appears to criticise. The problem with such approaches is that they wrongly assume that McGuckian's complexity serves the truth, when her focus from the outset has been on the processes of arriving *at* the truth. Even when this posited essential female identity is regarded as uncertain, or provisional, or in process, as in Neil Corcoran's more nuanced reading of the poet,[8] in its status as an identity-in-waiting rather than an identity-in-creation (in which latter form it would itself be characterised by active agency), it still cannot be interrogated, only encouraged or refused. An identity-in-waiting cannot voice itself, only be voiced or silenced.

An uninterrogatable, un-self-voicing identity has as its correlative an uninterrogatable and un-self-voicing politics that is both dangerous and ultimately ineffective, no matter on which side of the Irish politico-cultural divide it locates itself. A given identity, even if unknowable or unknown, will always align to a given politics, despite declarations to the contrary. This truism is demonstrated by the mid-eighties debate in Ireland on the Fifth Province of the Imagination. The term derives from the old Irish word for province, *coiced*, meaning a fifth, implying the presence of an unknown central province, the idea of which was adapted to give a symbolic home to what Richard Kearney called 'the whole realm of aspirations [. . .] where one can free oneself from the particular and prejudiced associations of reality as it exists [. . .] in the sense of projecting from this fifth province of intellectual disposition, new possibility, new notions of unity and reconciliation'.[9] The Fifth Province, for Seamus Deane, would ground 'an obligation to create an equivalent centre from which the four broken and fragmented pieces of contemporary Ireland might be seen as in fact coherent'.[10] Advocated here is investment in a pre-existent unity so as to overcome differences, an idea which resonates with the notion of identity-in-waiting underpinning many readings of McGuckian's aesthetic in the same 1980s period. They both suggest the possibility of skipping the difficult practical work of coming to terms with real differences, as would be required by the alternative understanding of identity-in-creation. The absent centres both of the Fifth Province and of McGuckian's attributed poetics, from which can be projected a notional coherence of being, represent a utopian neutral gear in cultural self-location. But this realm of the imaginary can as easily host monolithic as genuinely transformative concepts of identity. Neutral gear, after all, is useful only as the release mechanism to choice of another active position: as Kearney said, 'The idea is to translate the fifth province into reality, to bring it to bear on reality.'[11] The realisation of the transformative as opposed to the retroactive potential both of the Fifth Province and of McGuckian's poetry is conditional upon understanding the neutrality associated with each, as transitional rather than destinational: neutrality does not in itself grant purchase for progress.

The concept of identity-in-waiting underpins the dual conditions of uninterrogatability and disarticulation on each side of the unionist/nationalist political divide, which facilitated the larger politics of violent stasis endemic in Northern Ireland during the early period of McGuckian's writing career. The international literary academy can be said to have contributed, however unwittingly, to this politics of stasis through readings of McGuckian's obscurity as a natural function of her gender. These are readings that see 'the difficulties of her syntax and diction [as] necessitated by their intrinsic foreignness to the culture in which they are articulated'.[12] We see such politics of stasis operate, for example, when McGuckian's 'compulsive imaginative fluidity' is naturalised in service to the idea that 'the poem [should] write the poet',[13] rather than the reverse. This proposal by Peter Sirr

idealises the act of what he calls 'submission'[14] – that is, of the poet uncriti-
cally yielding interpretative authority, such yielding being proposed as the
proper means of subverting establishment authoritarianism.

This idea bears interesting relations to that of Harold Bloom, the highly
influential theorist of literary canonicity, as analysed by Moynagh Sullivan in
her ground-breaking 2004 article on McGuckian. In that work, Sullivan
investigates tropes of birth in modernist canon-formation which exclude the
presence and agency of the female.[15] She quotes Bloom thus: "'a poem is
always the other man, the precursor, and so a poem is always a person, always
the father of one's second birth.'" Sullivan comments: 'The linguistic second
birth is explicitly appointed as the origin of poetic identity, and as such the
pre-oedipal period and the original material birth are expunged from the
symbolic landscape.'[16] Sullivan's larger argument allows a reading of Sirr's
requirement that the poem write the poet as implying that McGuckian is
recoverable for a male-identified canon by means of her surrender of her
own authority to that of language. This subtext of Sirr's valorisation of
McGuckian's supposed 'compulsive imaginative fluidity' is consonant with
his simultaneous objections to what he calls 'patronizing views' of 'female
poets [as] less rational than male ones'.[17] This is because the authority of language, so prioritised, serves reason, which in Sirr's formulation is still upheld
as the ultimate criterion of success. Sullivan's psychoanalytical reading of the
politics of authority in Irish poetry facilitates deconstruction of this position:
because McGuckian is a woman (thereby identified irredeemably as lack in
Bloom's Lacanian system), her 'submission' as above-praised can lead in
McGuckian only to a semiotically constituted 'compulsive' obedience to the
symbolic order rather than full participation in its power. In other words, full
identification of the poet with language's authority – an authority which in
this thinking is understood in monumental terms – is precluded. As a result,
co-occupancy with her male peers of the position at the top of the canonical
pyramid can never be open to McGuckian: in this critical economy she and
her work can only ever aspire to a place further down the pecking order,
however valued be the work associated with that station.

The impoverished nexus of critical assumptions under description here
rallies form as much as content in order to make sacrosanct an unconscious
McGuckian whereby the public world is collapsed into a private one through
the splitting of an essential female self in the poetry from the possibility of the
poet's real, public, political relevance. A central plank of this arrangement was
removed by Clair Wills at the end of this early period in McGuckian's reception, in her timely reminder that female subjectivity is intrinsically bound up
with the political domain in Ireland through the iconic status in this country
of woman-as-nation, so that 'public political discourse and notions of private
ownership and personal identity' do not part company but, rather, 'precisely

[. . .] interpenetrat[e]' on the site of 'representations of the female body'.[18] McGuckian herself best answers these readings of her evasion of politics. Two of her key early prose comments on stylisation indicate the crucial difference between *suggesting* the availability of meaning, and *asserting* its substance, either as concrete presence or as identity-in-waiting:

> The poems are to cover and warm empty spaces like rag-rugs or quilts with primitive colours, they stem from the same protectively decorative animal instinct. They are more to be admired than useful to others, but primarily useful to me for clothing the raw or bare consciousness. They shield me from basic harsh reality, which they jazz up and present as food is arranged or flowers vased. The pleasure is in the arrangement or the vase, though this is often its own statement.[19] [. . .] Every poem is a whirlpool around me to protect the inner inwardness [. . .] There must always be this inner inviolability to it. The language is just spinning around all the time, and it's never going to be 'this is what happened'.[20]

McGuckian here argues that her focus on form is a means of self-conservation in her relation with harsh reality. However, this does not mean that hers is an escapist aesthetic; rather, her remarks indicate that such self-protection safeguards her capacity for response to the external world. The 'raw or bare consciousness' described here is one that, by definition, is *not* indelibly engraved with an epistemology of prejudice – such prejudice being imprinted through the operation of a strictly defined symbolic order of coherence. Instead, protected by the loose clothing of the associative imagery in her poems, where authority is shared with, though never ceded to, the reader, the raw consciousness preserves its capacity for acting, in the senses both of agency and theatre. In short, McGuckian refuses the 'real' as publicly given in calcified interpretation, and thereby faces the power that in large part generates reality: the human action of (re)choosing to understand in one way rather than in another. She highlights this power to (re)make the real through her focus on form. Thus, her 'arrangement' of reality is not a way of avoiding reality, but a way of 'softening [the] blows'[21] it delivers in its damaging incarnation as rigidified meaning. McGuckian's 'spinning' language enacts a de-calcifying interventive mimesis of interpretative action, of that sorting of experience which proceeds in the experiencing psyche: a mimesis that defamiliarises given responses and thereby rebuilds the potential for communication through language. In this manner, the paradox in McGuckian's thinking about violent external events – apparent when we place the above comments against her remark that 'poetry shouldn't be a surgical bandage over miscarriages and mutilations'[22] – is resolved. By safeguarding her capacity for response through their defensive function as shield, her poems focus renewed, live attention back on the real situations from which they are derived. Thus, the following crucial remark:

> What inspires me are the things that happen and how you cope with them, or how you make sense of them. What I tend to do is gloss over them, or use poetry to control horror and evil, to make them, not less important, but to put them into their overall context. That's what I'm trying to do, not trying to cover it up but to understand it, especially violent death, death imposed upon one human being by another. It's very difficult to do. It's a game of not facing reality, but if I didn't have it I would be insane.[23]

However, the subtlety of the distinction McGuckian's poems make between protective privacy as disabling and as enabling was not realised by the two early critics of this poet who did take seriously her public political import. Thomas Docherty and Clair Wills each valuably problematised the private biographical zone in McGuckian. Docherty's dissolution of the private sphere is essential to his early-nineties reading of McGuckian's 'refus[al of] the principle of monotheological Reality'.[24] For Docherty, this happens through McGuckian's refusal of reality itself by means of a language that approximates 'the postmodern simulacrum'.[25] In Docherty's memorable formulation,

> Throughout the verse, it is precisely at the moment of taking root, or of finding a single place from which to understand a poem, that it melts away again into ambivalence and ambiguity [. . .] Each poem is, as it were, a threshold inviting the initiation of its readers into some meaning; yet it also denies that meaning at the very instant of its perception.[26]

However, if meaning – which is associated with identity – 'melts away' at various points in the McGuckian poem, it no more disappears than does Docherty's analogue here, frozen water; rather, it changes form, demanding that the reader widen the 'single place' from which he or she understands the poem. These expanded spaces exist in potential and demand to be activated.

Co-dependent with the absolutism in his work on semantics in McGuckian is the over-limited choice between a stable persona and a vacant/absent persona that Docherty sets up in his postmodern reading of this poet. For Docherty, the 'I' in McGuckian's poetry is dissolved, and 'all we have is a potential of personality, a voice which cannot yet be identified'.[27] But Docherty's unending identity-in-waiting is surely instead an identity-in-*formation* within the text, as, following the poet, we as readers agree to identify the 'I' provisionally every time we interpret one of her poems (as does this critic himself in the essay under discussion).[28] Docherty asserts that McGuckian replaces the concept of power, and by extension 'essence', with 'a notion of mere interrelation. [. . .] The form this takes is one of seduction . . . [that is], the play of forces, attraction and repulsion, which enables such relation. The resulting tension *produces* the entity. [. . .] The important thing is that the forces come first; there is no essence.'[29] But McGuckian's work suggests that the idea of a play of forces depends just as much on an idea of 'essence', as the reverse. Rather than assuming that the difficulty of attributing meaning invalidates that which can be referred to in language, her disassociative poetics invites us to recognise that the meaning understood in language is never the *same* as that which is referred to, which remains private. This is the case, even though such meaning necessarily proceeds as though it could so match its object. The presence of this private referent is what guarantees both the sustained effort towards meaning and the continued troubling of any result. (The difference in language as used by McGuckian is that these two functions operate in counterpoint, as allies rather than enemies in the act of communication.) Without this fact of truth in text, there would be nothing at stake in the act of interpretation. Far from regarding the individual consciousness as absent or irrelevant, therefore, McGuckian's poetry instead focuses on it consistently, through holding out the possibility that meaning can be got right. It is exactly that faculty of consciousness that is the main focus of interrogation and support throughout her early aesthetic.

Rather than Docherty's dissolved self, Clair Wills in her 1993 book *Improprieties: Politics and Sexuality in Northern Irish Poetry*, promoted a *hidden* self as the focus of McGuckian's obliquity: 'The poems offer a private language whose rationale is in part the maintenance of secrecy.'[30] But McGuckian's secrecy resides far more in the provisionality of the understandings which she nevertheless requires her readers to seek than in the refusal of those readers. This is because McGuckian, like her readers, is engaged in the process not of understanding her life as a distinct if hidden entity (an object of knowledge),[31] but, rather, of comprehending her experience of her life as a lived process. Wills touches on this when she accurately observes that 'the disassembled veiled "self" presented in the work is often an analogue for something quite different from autobiography'.[32] The veiled self is the self in process, rather than the self as a finished archaeological find. In this light, McGuckian's self-reflexive versions of the private realm cannot be said to 'parod[y] the very idea of [this] private or intimate domain', as Wills in *Improprieties* holds;[33] rather, they explore the participatory apprehension of that private domain. This parody reading is an attempt by Wills to bridge the gap between her own reflex distrust in the efficacy of subjectivity, and her simultaneous defence of the power of private reference. Wills acclaims the manner in which in McGuckian's aesthetic, '[t]he personal narrative becomes a metaphor for a public and political one',[34] yet regards as a 'danger' the manner in which a poem may 'subjectivize [. . .] political events, thereby emptying them of their historical significance'.[35] But McGuckian's work shows that the subjectivisation of political events realigns, rather than empties, those events of their historical significance: rather than the fight to the death between the private and the public domains for attention and authority as locus of history, in McGuckian, private and public are in co-equal relationship as that locus, *in* their difference.

And Clair Wills knows this. In contrast to Docherty, she defends 'the elements of representation'[36] in McGuckian, or, this poet's 'belie[f] in the efficacy of the individual lyric voice',[37] arguing that '[t]he refusal of communication, the resistance to interpretation, the parody of privacy through secrecy is directed outwards'[38] towards 'question[ing] the grounds for reaching consensus and the boundaries of the public sphere itself'.[39] Yet Wills treads a very thin line between rejecting and defending the lyric voice being upheld. At the heart of her chapter on McGuckian in *Improprieties*, Wills argues that this poet's language – and, by implication, identity – can be read in the light of a Mandelstamian transplanting and condensing method whereby meaning must be constructed 'in between' the textual layers.[40] She spells out clearly the political implications of this method, namely, the recognition that '[h]istorical continuity is predicated on dissonance'[41] rather than on a homogeneity of origin. This conclusion clearly suggests that McGuckian's poetic method promotes a politics of non-conditional and non-appropriative comprehension of otherness. However, Wills risks contradicting her own authoritative argument on behalf of McGuckian's political relevance here through her inclination to reject the 'I' who is the subject and agent of this same politics of inclusiveness.

The danger common to all of these early critical responses is their committing of McGuckian to an over-essentialised privacy (either of the subject, or of politics, or of language/image work), *whether or not* the personal realm in her work is seen as real and her poetry is read as 'directed outwards' towards meaning.[42] The poem 'Venus and the Sun',[43] from McGuckian's second collection, arguably anticipates this delimiting hidden consensus in its suggestion that McGuckian's power as writer ('Venus') is one that, despite appearances, is patronisingly granted by the critical tradition ('the sun'), rather than being autonomously claimed: however much she 'order[s] [the] curved wash' of 'shifting stars', still 'I am the sun's toy – because I go against / The grain I feel the brush of my authority'. Although that authority's 'ripples stray[. . .] from a star's collapse', she recognises that 'the stars are still at large', and that her challenge renews rather than undermines their control: 'they fly apart / From each other to a more soulful beginning; / and the sun holds good'.

The present essay argues instead that the mystery pertaining to early McGuckian's foregrounding of a private self that is also refused is solved by understanding that she constructs self-reflexive, rather than either authentic *or* parodic, versions of the private realm. The title poem of her second volume, 'Venus and the Rain' (*VR* 32), can be read as a more confident anticipatory critique than is offered in 'Venus and the Sun', on the failure of the criticism of her poems, then only beginning to develop, to recognise the unwitting collusion it would require between the authentic and parodic McGuckians it variously was to present. In it, McGuckian foregrounds her own elliptical self-reflexive presence as a challenge to such an underlying consensus in her reception:

> White on white, I can never be viewed
> Against a heavy sky – my gibbous voice
> Passes from leaf to leaf, retelling the story
> Of its own provocative fractures, till
> Their facing coasts might almost fill each other
> And they ask me in reply if I've
> Decided to stop trying to make diamonds.

'Making diamonds' implies the forcing together of a single material into an unfracturable substance, which is the assumed effect of her work's resistance to practical interpretation, even while this recalcitrance itself takes up acres of print space and is the required condition of her status-to-be as object of love or hate in Irish poetry criticism. But McGuckian sagely remarks: 'What clues to distance could they have, / So self-excited by my sagging sea, / Widening ten times faster than it really did?' She indicates here that the assumption by critics of unbounded fluidity in the meaning of McGuckian texts functions to resist her aesthetic's presence-oriented version of self-reflexivity – what she calls here her 'gibbous' protuberant voice that is emergent from the 'hollow body' of her incomplete, fractured and imagined – but never illusory – subjecthood. The final stanza of 'Venus and the Rain' warns that these various 'conflicting' streams of interpretation in her critical reception have a propensity to run alongside each other in restoring the authority of an existing canon whose entertainment it is to celebrate such poetry's 'icy domes' of impenetrability. The canon does this by distracting attention (through its oppositional critic-emissaries' work of worrying at her textual 'rind') from a possible actual meaning in her texts, to an abstract and gener- alised 'depth understanding' of the author's larger import. Such a critical procedure leapfrogs individual poems and in the end has the effect of 'unstitching' her poetry's impact by diverting it as exotic affect through the main reception areas of the literary tradition:

> Whatever rivers sawed their present lairs
> Through my lightest, still-warm rocks,
> I told them they were only giving up
> A sun for sun, that cruising moonships find
> Those icy domes relaxing, when they take her
> Rind to pieces, and a waterfall
> Unstitching itself down the front stairs.

The relative dearth of whole-poem readings of McGuckian in existing criticism of her work – the lack of engagement with the single poem as a crucial unit of reading, in favour of offering interpretation based on a combination of isolated imagery and the whole McGuckian as the critic's ambit of evidence – underlines the aptness of the poet's critique here of the dissolution of her effect in responses to her work.

Of course, this avoidance of the poem unit by McGuckian critics is encouraged by the work itself in this early period. Epitomised by the semantic gap between her introductions to her poems at her public readings and the subsequently delivered text, McGuckian would regularly indicate that, although each poem had its own particular occasion and background, this context was suppressed in its final effect. This is seen in her remarks, 'There's usually one special person the poem is a *private* message to' (my emphasis),[44] or, 'when I pick up a poem I know who it was for; each poem is associated with a person or a place or an event or a time. It's a very specific occasion *but only for me*' (my emphasis).[45] Yet she could also claim: 'I don't mind if a part of the poem remains elusive, but most of it, with attention to the actual meaning, should yield a definite meaning.'[46] She states: 'I invest certain things with my own associations, but generally what a word brings to mind is what I mean by it.'[47] The only way that the paradox in this last remark makes sense is to understand that she is both privileging the importance of the reader's own personal associations with any given word, and assuming the possibility of crossover between her own associations and those of that potential community of readers. This has large-scale implications for the oft-discounted public nature of her early work. McGuckian links herself to her readers in this comment, not in a complacent elision of differences amidst her audience and between herself and them, but in an extraordinary act of faith in the power of language in poetry, not so much to communicate given content as to be the occasion of communication between given individuals in relation to the existence of given, but finally un-confirmable, thematic substance, 'As if someone had cried a message to you, / In one word, once, and would not repeat it.'[48] In this economy, meaning can be offered to, and shared with, a community of readers without the imputation of an objective rightness or wrongness in any one member's decision to accept or reject that co-created meaning, but also without releasing that person from their responsibility to claim and ground this decision to (mis)understand.

Critics (including myself in this essay) have been too anxious to safeguard credentials of disinterestedness in order to fully take up McGuckian's challenge to find a definite meaning in her poems in this manner: that is, to find a meaning on the critic's own terms, as terms which might – but also might not – be acceptable to others. This reluctance is perhaps never more evident than when such critics are theorising the value of subjectivity in

McGuckian. Her challenge to readers is to discover a solid meaning in poem units in which, typically, meaning comes about as an irregular and unpredictable unfolding where each element catalyses its fellow, meaning arising interpenetratively rather than sequentially in time. This unsettling arrival at the meaning of an individual poem models the creation of a community of readers in McGuckian: any one whole-poem reading, like the meaning of any one image in an individual poem, can stand independently of other readings, but offers itself to those other readings and readers (one of whom is the poet herself) as an element in the range of all possible understandings. Through this emphasis on the capacity to re-contextualise, her aesthetic emphasises the individual interpretation of experience by a readership that is necessarily various, but which ideally forms a whole society: 'I think my poems travel on a spectrum, and what would mean one thing to a child of ten would mean another thing to a farmer of forty or an academic at sixty.'[49] Inherent here is McGuckian's conviction that a sharable meaning is available in her texts, which she speaks of in terms reminiscent of the theology of the Eucharist; for McGuckian, the reader and the text cannot remain rigidly separated. The reader must allow himself or herself to be drawn into the world of the poem and must in turn take in the text to themselves as the host is taken into the body and broken down: 'I hope my poems will draw the reader into the particular mesh of thoughts and nexus of feelings, but I hope in the end to have spelled something out clearly. If the poem is swallowed whole it won't be digested. I want it to become part of the person.'[50]

As both example and comment on the sharable but unconfirmable nature of meaning in McGuckian, the 'waterfall / Unstitching itself' in 'Venus and the Rain' can refer equally to the dissolution of a single reader's certainty about any one reading he or she has developed of a McGuckian poem (such as my own one earlier, reading 'Venus and the Rain' as meta-criticism), and to the dissolving of seemingly solid readings as they are passed on to new readers who adapt the elements of these interpretations to new purposes. Thus, the 'gibbous voice' of the poet is like rainfall being 'Pass[ed] from leaf to leaf' of an ongoing series of critical understandings. Clair Wills's and Shane Murphy's pioneering analyses of McGuckian's borrowing and adaptation of external literary sources[51] support this vision of a non-exclusive community of readings and readers as central to McGuckian. At the heart of this vision is the assertion that meanings – like the human subjects who form and transform them – can be impermanent *and* definite at one and the same time. This is the basis of McGuckian's dual accord with and challenge to postmodernity, in the analysis of which Moynagh Sullivan's application of object-relations theory is foundational.[52]

In McGuckian, the temporary objectivity achieved by any one reading in its effort to discover the original subject of the poem – its provisional yet definite claim to understanding – signals the condition of identity itself. In 'For the Previous Owner' (*VR* 39), the text that hosts any coherent reading of a McGuckian poem can relate to its actual original subject only as do

> Sheaths so immune to the several atmospheres
> Of your perfectly positioned body, [that] when I
> Turn back the hood I can see the baby's
> Breath [. . .]

Bracketed here by the linked images of the sheath (which in this context suggests a condom) and the baby, these lines intimate that the text blocks so much of what the reading assumes is represented there, that the blockage itself turns, in the reader's mind, to a highly active imagining of that subject which is denied visible life, like a child imagined in the traces left on a contraceptive device. In Sullivan's terms of argument, this imaginary child connotes the presence of the mother who is denied representation within an Oedipal poetic economy that speaks through her rather than of her.[53] In this reading, the 'baby', in its absence in real terms (as that which has been contra-ceived), refocuses attention on the mother as the hidden ground of the poem's truth. It does so in its role as an imaginary real that calls us to profess (though not prove) the actual truth basis in the poem's material. This re-creation of the subject is possible because of, not despite, 'the freed doubt [that] awakens / All the room's shortcomings, its / Inefficient joins'.

   The imperfect structure of any one understanding of a McGuckian poem signals that meaning and identity are, for her, entities at once imaginatively self-sufficient *and* indebted to a real source, the unavailability of which need not matter ('So the weather of your leaving changes / Little'), so long as the validity of both that source and the proactive doubt it stimulates is acknowledged. Thus, the reader is figured as an amanuensis who, in his copying of a manuscript, dare not 'enhance the Prussian blue you / Set the sea to', because such a purely defined sea deliberately foregrounds itself as the unreliable sign of a reality which cannot be finally captured.[54] In this way, McGuckian's defence of the text as a traditional sign is predicated on a reversal of the more common contemporary understanding of its limitation, as she emphasises the value over the danger of the falsifying sign. The delicacy of this suggested state of value is beautifully captured in this poem's concluding image, 'If a woman's / Stiffness after labour made way for persons who never were.' The ambiguity of the 'person who never was' being potentially a new subject ('never was before'), or a figment of the imagination ('never was at all') – of the poet or reader giving birth to a new identity or to an illusion of identity – is an equivocacy forced to hold.

   Meaning in McGuckian requires a temporary, but secure, dwelling place – a balakhana, as she explores in the poem of that title (*OBB* 36), connoting the room in which nomadic travellers are put to pass the night.[55] Paradoxically, the temporary nature of its occupancy by a definite meaning allows the verifying of that place as significant: 'A town will never draw your mind to it / Like a place where you have camped.' 'Place' here refers to all the entities invested in the possibility of such meaning: the reader, the individual reading and the cultural and critical tradition that enables that reading. These entities understood as a balakhana allow the dual tenuousness yet tenacity of such meaning to be recalled in the act of reading: 'You will remember the very curve / Of your wagon-track in the grass / Where the ring swayed and was broken, almost.' The balakhana is the host or campsite of a meaning that is real yet destined to change and move elsewhere because this place cannot hold it, 'As if someone had cried a message to you, / In one word, once, and would not repeat it.' As this unstable holding ground, the balakhana paradoxically becomes more empowered than it would be as final destination of meaning. The capacity of reader, readings and cultural/critical traditions (figured here as this temporary dwelling place) to adapt to a variety of semantic occupants – in other words, their acceptance that they themselves are subject to the displacement of being deconstructed and redeveloped through the mutability of the meaning that can accrue to them in the act of reading – enriches them beyond measure:

> That flap of earth leaned against the sun
> As women lean their faces to the wall
> Giving birth. Its mountains stretched
> And spread and strangely took shape
> From the smells that ran among them,
> Their deeply responsible pauses and heights
> Striking sphere after sphere of sparks.

McGuckian's thinking on inspiration – her sense that she is spoken through rather than speaking in her best work – fits well into this model of necessary self-displacement as means to self-empowerment. The reader of 'Balakhana' is asked to link ('Compare') a number of 'metallic' man-made sounds created by the human effort to move from one place to the next – elevators, cars, aeroplanes. These sounds are analogous to human language that also represents the desire to break through the shell around the individual, through communication with another. This impetus towards communication ('The door I found / So difficult to close') is deliberately paralleled by the idea of community between nations, the opened door representing the special speech and response – that of art – that 'let in my first / European feeling which now blows about, / A cream-coloured blossom, with a blue vigour'. Hence, the politics of porousness between nations is associated, for McGuckian, with art's sensitising of the borders between individual consciousnesses. This does not

involve the breaking down of these borders but the contrary – the separateness of selves, of nations and of cultures within nations is confirmed by the
very effort of movement across the multiple membranes they share. It is this
effortfulness which McGuckian focuses on in her celebration of the balakhana or the one-night campsite – the effort to give birth to one's meaning
on the uninscribed lines of passage between identities, represented in particular (for the McGuckian of this early period) by the changing shape of the
reproductive female body.

From an exploration of the breakdown of hermetic and homogeneous
forms of identity in terms of place and language to an interrogation of the
political expression of that ideal in republicanism is an obvious step; it is one
taken by McGuckian in 'On Ballycastle Beach' (*OBB* 61). Here, the poet
addresses herself to the tradition of republicanism in Northern Ireland originating in the 1790s and at that time, in theory at least, inclusive of the full
range of religious traditions there. But in this poem she attends to its contemporary heir, a separatist politics in need of its forebears' enlightenment.
Personifying that politics as her addressee, the poet declares her intention to
use her language to guide it towards the realisation that the ideal of demo-
cratic self-government demands the embracing of a paradoxical loss of
control (signified by meaning in language) since control flows through the
many and not through the one:

> If I found you wandering around the edge
> Of a French-born sea, when children
> Should be taken in by their parents,
> I would read these words to you,
> Like a ship coming in to harbour,
> As meaningless and full of meaning
> As the homeless flow of life
> From room to homesick room.

The 'homeless flow of life' links back to 'Balakhana' and its ideal of a
nomadic shelter for identity *and* meaning in language. The idea of a home,
a secure border or any form of proffered and available selfhood, is consistently undermined in this poem through the agency of words. Here, cities
disappear to regain their language, words are traps to cause missteps, the
undue expansion of 'pockets' in the continuum of self contains unexpected
texts and, finally, the largest body of meaning surrenders its agency: 'Even
the Atlantic has begun its breakdown / Like a heavy mask thinned out
scene after scene.' That sea that is the ideal of republicanism is being
'thinned out' like the ideal of virginity being eroded, as suggested by the
woman who gradually lengthens her pre-wedding dress. Yet McGuckian
suggests that it is, ironically, the very process of recognising the unreliability

of language and of the political ideal it represents, which alone conserves
the original power of each:

> But, staring at the old escape and release
> of the water's speech, faithless to the end,
> Your voice was the longest I heard in my mind,
> Although I had forgotten there could be such light.

In *Marconi's Cottage* (1991),[56] however, McGuckian acknowledges that this
vision of a non-exclusive community is precluded in a critical economy
where radical vision is carefully contained. Despite the strenuous defences of
her autonomy in her earlier poetry ('Don't put me into your pocket: I am not
/ A willow in your folly studded garden / Which you hope will weep the
right way' ['Vanessa's Bower', *VR* 12]), McGuckian's effective designation as
symbolic 'poetess' in her early reception – whether this criticism centred or
decentred the subject in her work – made her complicit with the colonisation
of expression effected by the didactic 'colour-by-number' understandings of
art that underpin the acceptability of literature in the Irish political establishment. She explores this situation in 'A Small Piece of Wood' (*MC* 31): 'I
closed the top / Of my lesson-filled inkwell, / A she-thing called a poetess, /
Yeoman of the Month.' The poem probes how the disassociated 'appliquéd'
overall picture of McGuckian in her early reception is facilitated by a tradition where male and female 'rivers' of insight run parallel and to the same
end, but never meet. In a critical community where gender difference remains
essentialised and unproblematised – exemplified in particular in the Ireland of
the late 1980s and early 1990s when this poem was written – the available
conflicting interpretations of her poetic do not ground her authority; rather,
they scatter it: 'The sweepings of my study / Seemed all spoiled remnants / In
which the colour had run.' The amorphous mass of monotone pigment produced as the result is quite different to what McGuckian herself, later in this
poem, advocates as the sign of a successful aesthetic: a series of distinct shades
which blend into each other at their borders in order to form a meaningful
unit ('my numberless blues / Have neither end nor beginning, / Arranged
like a tribe of lovers / In a circle'). Indeed, McGuckian has described 'poetic
truth' as a 'shading of the boundaries' of 'what other people would see as
truth'.[57] Yet, McGuckian astutely recognises that any establishment is more
likely to confirm rather than revise itself by allowing the presence of such a
wilder fringe. She satirises the strategic value pertaining to the literary radical
from the point of view of the literary mainstream, by highlighting the fact
that, in the eyes of an objective assessor of their import, the 'tribe of lovers' of
her ideal art are dressed not in their own clothes but in the clichéd guise of
the female pioneers of the American Wild West: '— my headdress / A flaxen
wig, a velvet bandeau, / A beaver hat, with a plume of feathers.'

McGuckian is acutely conscious of the danger of being the radical darling of the literary establishment. Her alertness to the threat of any such falsely stabilised self-image was clear from the outset of her career. One of her earliest poems, the short piece 'Spring',[58] describes its female speaker as a would-be artist, implicitly at a point during adolescence and expectant of sexual initiation: she rises from the bed she shares with her sister 'To stare at the February moon'. This is the act of a poet trying to engage with otherness, but her purpose is frustrated by her own intervening 'frozen' presence:

> The curtains slit at my hand,
> My breathing marbled the pane:
> There was my face at the window,
> Frosted, so hard to see through.

This poem explores the difficulty of seeing through the false promise of coherence of identity by way of art – especially for a woman artist tempted by essentialist versions of femininity. This is figured here in the speaker's dislocation of self as she falls into the narcissistic trap of enthralment with a mimetic mirror image. That '[f]rosted' face at the window blocks access to the outside world and the more enabling, because independent and nonmimetic, version of herself that is found there: the moon. The moon is a body whose agency, like hers, is secured through reflecting the light of others rather than fusing with them. In 'Painter and Poet' (*VR* 23), McGuckian uses it to describe her resistance to that collapse of difference between reality and representation that characterises a blind critical culture: 'Unallegorically, I wanted his quenched eyes / To feel as well as see how the moon and we / Do not amalgamate.' Working against such a foreclosing impulse in 'Spring' (*FM* 13), McGuckian avoids the temptation either to wipe the pane clean to transparency in order to claim access to the real, or to elevate the iced-over unreal self as its total substitute. Instead, her aesthetic privileges a selfreflexive privacy in which the stability of the personal is grounded (not undercut) *in* the very instability of representations that continually test the 'I' that they porously shelter.

Through this procedure, McGuckian can realise the radical potential of a vision that is also under containment by the establishment agendas with which it is inevitably interwoven. For McGuckian, this task involves using the very constraints of the tradition and of the appropriation of her voice, to free up that voice: for example, in 'The Book Room' (*MC* 46), Yeats's famous female-occupied room in Lissadell catalyses for McGuckian an anxiety of influence regarding the curtailment, rather than inheritance, of an autonomous female authorial presence in the Irish literary tradition:

> I know this room so well
> I can't walk through it.

> Three deep windows, all south,
> Their shapes dark clots on the carpet.

In this room, her own radical presence seems diluted to decorative function: 'A boy-like, thin, soprano line of soulless bone / Like a bangle round the hand of the ceiling.' Yet this containment is not as all-encompassing as it seems; rather than a solid blockage, it can also operate as

> a balustrade
> Threaded through with sea, like thread–
>
> Gloves or sand shoes. A letter breaking
> The bounds of letters.

McGuckian challenges herself here to recognise the affinities within the given tradition with her own aesthetic project – the radical content hidden within its conservative aspect – so that this room can be co-occupied by herself and the Yeatsian inheritance in a relationship that may be uneasy, but which can become complementary:

> I lie on my right side
>
> And put my hand up to my forehead,
> While he looks out of his window,
>
> And I look out of mine.

In McGuckian, as Moynagh Sullivan has argued, the ego-competition of Bloomian anxiety of influence *vis-à-vis* poetic forebears, predicated as it is upon the 'muting' and appropriation of the maternal voice, is altered to a relation of acknowledged interdependence of identity which is based upon the visible autonomy of the facilitating feminine.[59] In this light, the Yeats of 'The Book Room' becomes McGuckian's child as well as forebear, as her poetry gestates a new understanding of the subversive potential of the Irish literary inheritance to accommodate radicalism, in relationship *with*, rather than in absolute contradistinction *to*, its own conservatism: 'The roots of my shadow [are] almost split in two, / like the heartbeat of my own child' ('The Rising Out', *VR* 36). This conservatism should be contextualised in terms of McGuckian's understanding of the limitations imposed by non-artistic responsibilities in the life of the working poet. McGuckian has always declared for the value of such limitations in her external life to facilitate her creativity, celebrating rather than decrying the impositions of her role as wife and mother upon her writing life: 'In order to be free in the poetry I had to be tied in the life';[60] 'I only write under those constraints that are pulling me away from the inner inwardness that is there, this core, which is like a seed, and all the other things around it [constraints] are the flesh that actually nourishes it.'[61] Constraints generate for McGuckian the experience of

otherness, the 'not–I' to which she is required to respond, and in this sense
nourish her identity development. In this way she seems to come to terms
with the duplicity of a cultural establishment which exoticises and contains
her radical female presence. If she is framed as the earth mother in this
economy, then, as she says in the conclusion of 'A Small Piece of Wood' (*MC*
32), 'Every apple is a feather-room / For seed's infectious star': every act of
collusion Eve performs allows an equivalent act of creation and independence. The paradox of openness being dependent upon closure is more
directly suggested in 'The Time Before You' (*OBB* 43), where it is figured as
'the movement / Of an accordion which closes / On one side and opens /
On the other'. McGuckian's aesthetic demands an embracing of those inimical conditions that restrict her independence in order to achieve a voice that
challenges these same restrictions. This paradox is most powerfully expressed
for the early McGuckian through the relationship of mother to child. Hence,
in a poem exploring this relationship – the rightly famous 'On Her Second
Birthday' (*MC* 107) – she concludes:

> It seems as though
> To explain the shape of the world
> We must fall apart,
> Throw ourselves upon the world,
> Slip away from ourselves
> Through the world's inner road,
> Whose atoms make us weary.

A number of poems in early McGuckian prefigure the celebratory conclusion of *Marconi's Cottage*, from where this poem is taken, by similarly
examining the role of an un-free maternal figure in facilitating the growth of
a daughter. In Yeatsian terms, this connotes the function of the anti-self in
bringing about the development of self. In these earlier poems, however,
there is not yet achieved the mutual creativity between mother and child
found at the close of this 1991 volume. In 'Sabbath Park' from *Venus and the
Rain* (*VR* 53), for example, McGuckian's *unheimlich* maternal self is essentialist ('absolute') in its devotion to a concept of inherently sinful purgatorial
female identity:

> My absolute address is Sabbath Park
> And the traditional light blue of its
> Paradise Lost room, which I took to be
> My mother.

'Light blue' is associated with Mariology and the impossible ideal of perfection represented by the Virgin mother; the mother figure, as represented in
this Victorian house and its ghostly occupant, emerges as an enabling version

of McGuckian, who asks rhetorically, 'Whether the bird learns to build its nest / Like that — a perfect nest from such arthritic wood'. She claims the mother's Victorian house as the essential anti-self, allowing her own power as artist: 'I feel the swaggering beginnings / Of a new poem flaring up, *because* the house / Is dragging me into its age' (my emphasis).

It seems clear, then, that from the beginning of her career, the loss of self that is involved in accepting external constraints in McGuckian is made up for by the gain of self generated through the manipulation of those restrictions to serve individual vision. It is only in the later work to date, however, that that loss and gain can be experienced by the same person, in equal relationship with another. In McGuckian, therefore, we can say that art's subversive potential is centred around the development of the ego – defined by the *OED* as 'that part of the mind which reacts to reality and has a sense of individuality'. In her work, the ego is made present through the power of the aesthetic, in the act of representation, to frame the clash between the competing determinisms of the 'I' as blindly experiential *id*, and the 'I' as interpretative *superego*. She indicates the urgent need for such a frame in her 1989 remark: 'There's a forgetful and regressive clash between the will of nature and the will of the mind over the body, so we fail to paint poetically the ultimate stretchings. Something pulls the edges together quickly again.'[62] The damage caused by conflict between female and male visions of the world, when those visions are mutually exclusive, is suggested in this critique of warfare between instinct and intellect which fails to recognise the 'ultimate stretchings' – the birth of a new liberatory vision through the interaction of these separate male and female world visions. This is not the privileging of anti-logic over conventional logic, as so many critics ascribe to McGuckian as main aim and achievement. Rather, this is the generation of a new form of logic that draws both on instinct and intellect, the semiotic and the symbolic orders. This is a poetics, therefore, that begins to answer the challenge of Kristeva's third generation of feminism. In McGuckian's words:

> It's absolutely opposite tensions [. . .] one is the physical, sensual, instinctive knowing thing – [. . .] to be the home, and the womb, and the woman [. . .] And the other is the mind, the brain, not totally the brain, but the spirit as well. It's two different kinds of creativity, pulling against each other, and almost destroying each other. Polar opposites. But at times they gel, and when they gel, I'm happy.[63]

Without this complementarity of subjective (female) and objective (male) visions, there is only stalemate between conflicting determinisms: from the outset, McGuckian's vision has consisted in the apprehension that *id* and *superego*, female and male, each taken in isolation, can only block the progress allowed by their interaction.

In 'Rowing' (*VR* 34), these two forms of poetic authority are represented as 'two kinds of light'. One is male, artful, detached, moralistic: its authority is 'perfect / Inside, pear-coloured, shedding that cool / Classical remorse over the angered field'. The second is female, romantic, 'authentic', involved, interventionist:

> gifted with an artlessness too
> Painful to live with, like a spur
> Eloping from the room below, its nurtured
> Discipline of dark tobacco golds.

The poem suggests that both kinds of artistic authority – artful and artless – are co-dependent in supporting cultural imperialism – one by classically apologising for it, the other by romanticising resistance to it:

> Just
> From watching how these circles call
> Towards each other, fitfully, whole-
> Heartedly, across the slightly
> Parted sky, recalls to me the egging tide
> That could not parallel its distant
> Claim upon the beach, the broken
> Line it had created earlier.

The 'egging tide' attempting the beach is a figure for the production of meaning in a text (water is always linked to meaning in McGuckian). The incoming 'egging' sea trying to match the 'broken line' of its visionary aspiration suggests the early claims for this poet's authority of representation which cannot be fulfilled due to this collusion of artfulness and artlessness, the recognition of which conducts the 'pain that wires / Its sour honey through my flush' – the flush of her premature triumph in the achievement of her art. The poem emphasises the fate of deconstruction that awaits such a limited understanding – a fate prefigured in the painted head with 'all its sutures / In the offing', or in Yeats's dualistic rough beast returned to its elemental form – 'the sand unhindered / Thickening with marble dust': the same 'sand' of the beach of text in stanza one upon which the 'distant claim' of the 'egging tide' was futilely made. This 'marble dust' suggests the disintegration of the authority of these two established pillars of aesthetics – classical and romantic – upon which McGuckian's revisionary eye is focusing.

What is left when their authority is gone? The process of development from pessimism to optimism in her thinking on the larger culture's failure to 'paint poetically the ultimate stretchings' in the relations between the instinctual *id* and the rule-bound *superego* can be seen in two key poems from McGuckian's third book, *On Ballycastle Beach*. 'For a Young Matron'

(*OBB* 38) presents two models of poetry text – text as womb and as aeroplane. The speaker is advised by a male poet friend to abandon a feminine form of creativity in favour of a masculine version:

> Why not forget this word,
> He asks. It's edgeless,
> Echoless, it is stretched so,
> You cannot become its passenger.
>
> An aeroplane unlike
> A womb claims its space
> And takes it with it.
> It says, Once it wasn't like this.

In the model of text as aeroplane, representing McGuckian's inherited poetry tradition, the word takes the self in as its passenger, the self being free to enter or exit an unchanging interior space in the poem that is unaffected by such movements since it itself is what moves, through phallic forward projection in space.[64] In contrast, text as womb grows with the self that it contains. The poem has no opened space of its own; instead, the self (of poet and reader) shapes the word, growing within the text, which expands to meet its development. But the fit between word and meaning in this normative maternal model may be too neat: text as womb lacks the element of replaceable identity and the momentum of forward movement that is accruing to the male model. Yet the male model is also lacking: whereas the male model of the poem asserts, through its independent forward movement, that *development* in its subject is a fact – 'It says, Once it wasn't like this' – the female model of poem as womb suggests that once it wasn't at all – in other words, that the subject of the poem is *created* rather than merely transported through its embodiment in text. In the male model, the function of the aeroplane-text is to carry an essentially pre-formed meaning or subject or self to new ground where they may operate in a new way but are not themselves affected by their vehicle of words. In an aeroplane, the conditions inside are strictly regulated to simulate those external to it; in the watery closeness of a womb the conditions are the inverse of those in the external world.

But the new self engendered by the poem-as-womb is also threatening: in poems at the start of *Marconi's Cottage*, McGuckian fears that she 'forfeit[s] the world outside / For the sake of my own inwardness' and worries that 'I have grown inside words / Into a state of unbornness'.[65] The threat of 'inwardness' in art is, therefore, the threat of the reversal or collapse of time itself. This movement into 'a state of unbornness' forces the eradication of the individual as subject in favour of an essential multiple identity. The poems of the concluding quarter of *Marconi's Cottage*, inspired by the birth of her daughter, suggest a resolution of this anxiety about the consistency of individual identity within a maternal model of creativity. As Sullivan has argued, the underlying principle of these poems is the release of one identity from inside another in such a way as to confirm the host, rather than bringing about the eradication of that host identity by a textual incubus.[66] This development is facilitated by incorporating key aspects of the male model of creativity into that maternal model. We see this development explored in possibly the most famous poem in early McGuckian, 'The Dream-Language of Fergus' (*OBB* 57). As Clair Wills has shown, this piece explores the relationship between a text's antecedent languages, the pro-duced text and the effect of that text in the world. The poem explores how the loss of the name (representing that clear identification or sourcing of meaning in language which McGuckian's poems continually disrupt) becomes part of the action of the effective text:

> So Latin sleeps, they say, in Russian speech
> So one river inserted into another
> Becomes a leaping, glistening, splashed
> And scattered alphabet
> Jutting out from the voice [.]

McGuckian describes this gibbous effect – the sense of meanings stretching beneath the surface of the poem until they scatter forth through that surface – using the image of an aeroplane that 'in full flight / Launched a second plane'. The aeroplane here incorporates the action of a womb giving birth – one plane launching another. It therefore converges the male and female models of creativity that opposed each other in standoff in 'For a Young Matron' (*OBB* 41). We saw that McGuckian's reservations regarding the womb model derived from the absence of the element of outward thrust, of movement to new contexts of understanding that she associated with the aeroplane model. Now she combines the two, and declares the positive effect of the ideal poem to be the result of such birth-in-flight: 'The sky [. . .] stabbed by their exits / And the mistaken meaning of each.' This poem with its linguistic focus suggests that the creative dissolution and reformation of identity are performed in a McGuckian poem by the perforation of meaning in language due to its re-appropriation in new contexts. Thus, Latin sleeping in Russian speech is an image for the latent, yet active, position of not only poem inside poet, but the poet inside her poem, and, likewise, of all possible readings of the text inside the poem, and the poem inside all such possible readings, transported and changed by each. By association, this androgynous model for the formation of ego from within the interaction of *id* and *superego* describes the flexible, evolving position of one political tradition inside another. The continuing disparity of the separate identities that form these contracts is an essential element of their capacity to enter and give birth to each other: 'Conversation is as necessary / Among these familiar campus trees / As the apartness of torches.' Just as torchlight is most effective when spread out, so the separateness of identities – linguistic and political – is the necessary condition of their interaction. The final four lines of the poem are crucial in pinpointing the primary elements of this complex relation:

> No text can return the honey
> In its path of light from a jar,
> Only a seed-fund, a pendulum,
> Pressing out the diasporic snow.

McGuckian asserts clearly here the irrecoverability of the source identity and experience in its re-embodiment in the poem. But if the text by itself cannot re-trace the path of its own sources, its imaginative effect in the world is a 'seed-fund' that is equivalent to a conceptual pendulum swinging in and out of that experiential base. It is this dual movement – towards origin and away from it – that is the basis of a poem's effect. That effect or action of the poem is referred to throughout McGuckian using the terminology of time. A pendulum's swing figuratively sets time in motion, measuring simultaneously both the loss and return of the recognisable self; the poem, for McGuckian, also sets time in motion.[67] Here, McGuckian presents the poem/pendulum 'Pressing out the diasporic snow'. The loss of origins experienced on a wide-scale level by whole cultures in the Diaspora is imaged as snow that is pressed into the ground as water. But this water, by losing its initial definition, both allows growth in the world and renews itself, re-entering its own cycle.[68] Similarly, the loss within the text of the original experience or the original self that gave rise to the poem or the new community of meaning is a condition of both the poem's positive agency in the world and the re-creation of that origin. This duality of outward thrust and return, even more than semantic ambiguity, may be what McGuckian indicates when she describes herself in 'The Dream-Language of Fergus' as 'a threader / Of double-stranded words'. One strand describes the loss, another the return, of the signified; one strand is in conversation with the other like a double helix building the genetic code of the subject of the poem and, by implication, of the new political community. This aesthetic-cum-political symbiosis is the basis of McGuckian's re-structuring of the source of authority in art.[69]

McGuckian's description of the process of her poetry's engagement with reality indicates this stretching of boundaries in her negotiation of a middle passage of self-reflexivity between *id* and *superego* that will support the development of the ego. Developing a theory of fantasy, she says that her poems 'don't so much translate fact as build fantasy on fact'.[70] 'Fantasy' is a self-consciously fictive means of confronting and realising experience, one

that seeks both to respect primal instinct (commonly regarded as the feminine input), *and* to shape or control it (commonly regarded as the masculine
input), in a form that, as a result, can be at once subjective and sharable.
McGuckian's election of fantasy as central to the operation of her art draws
her work into significant alignment with the Irish oral cultural theories
developed by Angela Bourke in her ground-breaking essay, 'The Virtual
Reality of Irish Fairy Legend', first published in the same year as both
Marconi's Cottage and the first three volumes of *The Field Day Anthology of
Irish Writing*.[71] Bourke's analysis of the capacity of Irish fairy legend, in both
its content and form of transmission, to 'provide fictional characteristics for
otherwise anomalous or unknowable places',[72] resonates strongly with the
capacity of McGuckian's poetics to excavate liminal states of being within a
polarised political culture. Bourke's description of the function of fairy
stories could as easily be applied to McGuckian's art: 'they [. . .] use the gaps
in the known environment for the elaboration of an imagined world where
all those things that are in Heaven and Earth and yet not dreamt of in
rational philosophy may be accommodated'.[73]

It is at the point of contracting for active and conscious faith between
storyteller and audience, poet and reader, that the dynamism both of Irish
fairy legend and a McGuckianesque aesthetic takes effect. Bourke writes:

> just as fairies are alive and yet not alive, so people can both believe in
> them and disbelieve. Some legends recount events that are merely odd,
> while others are downright preposterous, yet it is difficult to say when
> the boundary from reported fact to inventive fiction is crossed. It is partly
> in this ability to reconcile the impossible with the unexceptional that the
> legend-teller's skill lies [. . .] The story is impossible to believe, yet we
> have been sucked in; but neither we nor the original audience have any-
> thing to gain by protesting, 'That is a lie!'[74]

Angela Bourke focuses here on how credulity between the teller and the listener of the fairy tale is consciously stretched and is under continuous
renegotiation in the act of storytelling,[75] in order to bring the listener to
accept – on terms the listener has agreed provisionally to admit – the possibility of a new aspect to the reality under exploration in the tale. This
conscious stretching and renegotiation of an audience's credulity aptly
describes the experience of reading McGuckian. This poet, as we have earlier
seen, elects a related motif of 'stretching' of faith across the gap between 'the
will of nature and the will of the mind over the body' to describe the major
challenge for positive change in Irish culture. This challenge is addressed in
McGuckian's understanding of the practical contract of creative renegotiation of meaning that exists between herself and her reader. In this
contract, it is agreed that meaning arises through the individual's personal

filtering of experience. This filtering, by which poet or reader 'takes' meaning from experience or text, is a confirmation of his or her identity in, and understanding of, the world. It is also agreed, however, that the version of reality so created can only be useful to that individual if it is allowed to be open to adaptation through the questioning and input of the perspectives of others. The space for this adaptation of meaning ideally is generated in the same work of art through which that original understanding was propagated: the story, the poem, the painting, the song. In other words, the artwork is a site for active fictionality that is aware of its own limits through opening to others the power it claims to make up what may also be real.

Medbh McGuckian's and Angela Bourke's celebration of the efficacy of self-reflexive active fictionality stands in opposition to a more dominant position promoting scepticism of such fictionality, which emerged in the 1990s in an Irish critical culture riven by the exposure of major institution- alised corruption. This was a corruption seen to be facilitated by the façade of rectitude that was assumed by the Irish political and religious establish- ment — a façade traditionally allowed by the Irish people as necessary, even if it was not always credible, in order to secure the coherence of the nation- state. The critical position that arose as part of the collapse of this faith in public uprightness was expressed in analyses of literary form that held that unadulterated suspicion of narrative is the only way to secure the release of new stories in the Irish national self-understanding. It is exemplified in Luke Gibbons's 1999 essay, 'Narratives of the Nation: Fact, Fiction and Irish Cinema', which was collected, along with Angela Bourke's essay above, in Claire Connolly's influential 2003 reader for students of Irish culture, *Theo- rizing Ireland*.[76]

Gibbons's essay critiques simulations of the real in the genre of docu- drama, or 'faction', in international cinema. This critique is proposed through his assessment of Irish film's undermining of authenticity and naive audience faith in the fiction before their eyes, through its deliberately obtru- sive use of 'factual' elements which signal a 'radical divergence between story and setting, narrative and history'.[77] Angela Bourke's work, in contrast, pro- motes the opposite — the *con*vergence of story and setting, narrative and history — but in a self-conscious mode where responsibility is assigned to an audience well capable of it. That tolerating self-consciousness is not allowed for in Gibbons's thought.

In Bourke's Irish fairy story, as in Gibbons's Irish cinema, the line between credulity and scepticism is deliberately strained; however, while in the former this is to allow the previously unthought to become credible, in the latter it is to discredit as mere fiction what claims to be real. Which of the two is the more enabling position for Irish cultural self-revisioning? I elect Bourke's, because in Gibbons, credulity is stretched only to be broken. Once this belief is broken – as in the Irish obtrusive variant of cinematic faction that Gibbons celebrates – the authority to assign meaning becomes re-confined to the originator of the cultural artefact (here, the film-maker). In Bourke's position, in contrast, credulity is stretched in order that it be tested both for its possible dangers *and* usefulness, the authority to decide which and to what extent these qualities operate, resting with the artefact's consumers who thus become its co-creators. The operation of good faith – which has as its main requirement awareness of the potential for bad faith – marks Angela Bourke's vision; Gibbons's is based on an exposure of bad faith alone.[78] The protuberant 'gibbous voice' (*VR* 32) of McGuckian's aesthetic has far more in common with Bourke's vision than with Gibbons's, although her early critical reception – discussed at the start of this essay – would align her with him. Good faith, as a term which combines meanings of co-creativity, responsibility and imaginative vision, describes both the achievement and the challenge of Medbh McGuckian's poetry, as this essay in its focus on her career up to the early 1990s has sought to show.

3

'Poetry must almost Dismantle the Letters':
McGuckian, Mallarmé and polysemantic play

HELEN BLAKEMAN

It may initially seem incongruous to make a connection between Medbh McGuckian and Stéphane Mallarmé and yet, despite differences of time and place, the *oeuvre* of each poet demonstrates the instrumentation of what, in reference to Lacanian theory, can be termed 'polysemantic play'. This is not to say that what *motivates* each poet to utilise such polysemantic play is identical. For Mallarmé, deliberately obfuscated referentiality is an attempt to realise an ideal 'other world', while McGuckian interrogates the polyvocal condition of the signifier itself. For McGuckian, language has become devitalised and her poetry interrogates the possibility of 'upset[ting] the normal process enough'[2] in order to create new meaning through fracturing linguistic norms and employing semantic play. Within this chapter, I shall explore the theory of Symbolism in reference to Mallarmé in order to ascertain the similarities and differences between his concept of a 'purified language' and McGuckian's own poetic indeterminacy. My analysis will culminate in a brief consideration of the participatory role of the reader in the construction of meaning.

In his study *The Symbolist Movement in Literature* Arthur Symons stated that elements of French Symbolism could be seen, 'under one disguise or another, in every great imaginative writer'.[3] In view of the amount of critical writing dedicated to the Symbolist aesthetic, and its influence on both past and present writers, this comment proves more insightful than exaggerated. What constitutes Symbolism, however, cannot be strictly defined, as the term embodies a 'host of complex and contradictory aesthetic tendencies',[4] incorporating aspects of the decadent movement and the related *fin de siècle*.[5] Influenced by romanticism and the merging of the external landscape with 'the individual sensibility', the poet Charles Baudelaire became an important precursor and, indeed, executor of Symbolism. For example, his sonnet 'Correspondences' intuits a metaphysical perspective of the world. As the title intimates, Baudelaire formed correspondences 'between physical and spiritual realms and between the different senses',[6] promoting a poetry based on symbols and synaesthesia. Founded on a platonic belief in the 'ideal' form of things existing beyond the shadow of the 'real', Baudelaire's 'forest of symbols' evoked a transcendent world which the poet, as visionary, must call forth. Despite a steadfast belief in the beauty and harmony of the 'ideal world', however, Baudelaire felt disillusioned with Parisian life and the 'fear, revulsion and horror'[7] it provoked led him to disclose the 'strange, the bizarre, [and] the abnormal'[8] within both the external world and the self. This amalgamation of beauty and despair, order and disorder, became a characteristic of what was known as a decadent sensibility, in which experiences were 'permeated by a sense of loss, by a sense of life shrinking, being ever more colonised by the *profanum vulgus*'.[9] Thus, aspects of decadence and Symbolism converge and diverge; the former's morbidity does not entirely dissipate, yet it gives way to a greater preoccupation with the metaphysical search for the 'ideal' and the possibility of its Symbolic expression.

Although the Symbolist movement was not formally recognised until 1886, when Jean Moreas published the Symbolist manifesto in *Le Figaro*, the ideas that characterised the movement were already in existence. Despite modulations and divergences, therefore, it is still possible to locate the main tenets of thought that constituted the Symbolist aesthetic. The word 'symbol' derives from the Greek verb *symballein*, meaning to 'throw together', its noun *symbolon* denoting a mark, emblem, token or sign. Thus, in it its most basic form, Symbolism can be defined as 'an object, animate or inanimate which represents or "stands for" something else'.[10] This definition, however, can equally be applied to all language, thereby linking Symbolism with post-structuralism and the analysis of literary signification. Of all the Symbolist poets, Mallarmé in particular attracted the attention of post-structuralist theorists such as Derrida and Kristeva, as his linguistic fragmentation and semantic indeterminacy anticipated their own interrogation of traditional codes of order and univocal meaning. As Michael Temple states in his introductory essay to *Meetings with Mallarmé in Contemporary French Culture*, Mallarmé's verse 'appears totally modern' and his prose 'preempts so much of what we might call the "theory of our times"'.[11]

Despite Mallarmé's subversive appeal, such extreme indeterminacy and polysemy can make the poems appear impenetrable to even the most dedicated of readers. As Edmund Wilson states, Symbolism 'sometimes had the result of making poetry so much a private concern of the poets that it turned out to be incommunicable'.[12] Thus, Symbolism is often considered an esoteric form of writing, one in which the ideas of the poet are heavily disguised, leaving the reader with only partial access to what is being expressed. Similarly, the poetry of Medbh McGuckian is regularly criticised for its esoteric qualities, her characteristically oblique and occluded style leaving many readers bewildered and frustrated. For many critics, McGuckian's veiled language and enigmatic symbols leave the poetry completely incomprehensible; the texts' secrecy, for them, is less than seductive. The use of symbols in Mallarmé's and McGuckian's poetry, however, both conceals *and* reveals; although both poets challenge univocal meaning, this does not entail, as Kristeva states, 'a free flux, lacking all definition'.[13] As this chapter will attest, both poets promote indeterminacy and nurture connections between disparate things in order to provoke a reassessment of language, or, as George Craig claims, to engender 'the revaluing of the word'[14] rather than eliminate sense completely. How this is achieved will be discussed in relation to Kristeva's notion of the semiotic, an instinctual aspect of language linked to pre-verbal forces and unconscious drives. According to Kristeva, the semiotic draws on repressed energy and corporeal drives associated with the infantile fusion of mother and child before the child's symbolic separation into language and the social order. Thus, the recovery, or *memory*, of the semiotic constitutes a subversive threat to the status quo as 'maternal rhythms, melodies and bodily movements'[15] breach the symbolic code, destabilising accepted notions of both signification and subjectivity. In her work *Revolution in Poetic Language*, Kristeva considers poetry as a privileged site of contact with semiotic modalities, perceived primarily through semantic indeterminacy and linguistic disruptions. Significantly, Kristeva maintains that '[T]he transformation of poetic language *at the end of the nineteenth century* is fundamentally a practice in which the semiotic can be seen to tear at and transgress the syntactic stability and constructions of identity proper to the symbolic' (my emphasis).[16]

The work of Mallarmé is considered illustrative of how the semiotic forces of language fracture the signifying process, revealing 'an irrepressible heterogeneity of multiple sounds and meaning'.[17] The 'musicality' of language pertinent to Symbolist poetry melds with Mallarmé's convoluted images, resulting in an impressionistic style of writing that ruptures the symbolic in order to create 'its own modality of meaning which does not conform to the requirements of univocal designation'.[18] In this chapter I will focus predominantly on Mallarmé's poem '*Ses purs ongles*', regarding it as, in Kristevan terms, a 'genotext', a 'heterogeneous domain' that is 'at the same time verbal and of the nature of drives'.[19] According to Kristeva, the genotext constitutes a *process* through which the semiotic modalities are released 'and inscribed within the phenotext',[20] the structural element that conforms to accepted rules of communication and categorisation. In *Revolution in Poetic Language*, Kristeva states that to locate the genotext within the text involves

> pointing out the transfers of drive energy that can be detected in phonetic devices (such as the accumulation and repetition of phonemes or

rhyme) and melodic devices (such as intonation or rhythm), in the way semantic and categorical fields are set out in syntactic and logical features, or in the economy of mimesis (fantasy, the deferment of denotation, narrative etc).[21]

It is, therefore, these features of '*Ses purs ongles*' that require exploration before I consider McGuckian's affinity with both the Symbolist movement and aspects of the semiotic.

Ses purs ongles très haut dédiant leur onyx,	Her pure nails very high up dedicating their onyx,
L'Angoisse, ce minuit, soutient, lampadophore,	Anguish, this midnight, holds up lamp-bearing
Maint rêve vespéral brûlé par le Phénix	Many an evening dream burned by the Phoenix
Que ne recueille pas de cinéraire amphore	That no funeral amphora gathers
Sur les crédences, au salon vide: nul ptyx,	On the buffets, in the empty salon: no ptyx,
Aboli bibelot d'inanité sonore,	Abolished, knickknack of sonorous emptiness,
(Car le Maître est allé puiser des pleurs au Styx	(For the Master has gone down to dip tears from the Styx
Avec ce seul objet dont le Néant s'honore).	With this sole object through which the Nothingness honors itself).
Mais proche la croisée au nord vacante, un or	But near the vacant casement to the north, a gold
Agonise selon peut-être le décor	Agonizes according perhaps to the decoration
Des licornes ruant de feu contre une nixe,	Of unicorns kicking fire against a nixe,
Elle, défunte nue en le miroir, encor	She, defunctive nude in the mirror, while
Que, dans l'oubli fermé par le cadre, se fixe	In the oblivion bounded by the frame, is fixed
De scintillations sitôt le septuor.	Of scintillations at once the septet.[22]

Described by Robert Greer Cohn as Mallarmé's 'first truly hermetic poem',[23] the sonnet '*Ses purs ongles*' evokes a disturbing sense of absence, anguish and transformation, and yet nothing is overtly stated or described as 'Mallarmé allows the verbal play to take over'.[24] As Craig notes, there is no specific title, address or theme, and ideas are conveyed visually and audibly through the semiotic effects of 'intonation, sound-play [and] repetition'[25] rather than through semantic or syntactic continuity. Throughout his *oeuvre*, Mallarmé searched for a purity of expression by 'yield[ing] the initiative to the words'[26] themselves and yet, for the poet, this 'sacrificial opening up to language'[27] must resist what he termed 'universal reportage', as he believed that 'to name is to destroy, to suggest is to create'.[28] True creativity, for Mallarmé, 'involves no longer describing something that already exists'. Thus, his poetry embodies the art of 'evoking an object little by little'[29] in the search for the 'absolute'. The term that encapsulates Mallarmé's aesthetic, therefore, is *suggérer* (to suggest), which Wallace Fowlie defines as 'first to awaken, to indicate without specifically naming or defining, to propose a meaning without dogmatically imposing it', and then 'to incite and prolong an emotion on the part of the reader'.[30] Victor Shklovsky's declaration of the 'purpose of art' proves informative here, as he states:

> The purpose of art is to impart the sensation of things as they are per-
> ceived and not as they are known. The technique of art is to make
> objects 'unfamiliar', to make forms difficult, to increase the difficulty and
> length of perception because the process of perception is an aesthetic
> end in itself and must be prolonged.[31]

Shklovsky's concept of 'defamiliarisation' and the prolonging of perception succinctly describe the poetry of Mallarmé, in which objects as well as
words are rendered equivocal, thus constituting a complex network of indeterminate associations akin to Freud's exposition of condensation and
displacement in his analysis of dreams. As '*Ses pur ongles*' illustrates, objects
become mutable and acquire complex metaphysical value, thereby contributing to the overall opacity. The 'pure nails', for example, symbolise, for
Cohn, 'the distant cold stars which seem to be an organic part, a projection
of the universal anguish';[32] yet 'nails' and 'anguish' are not grammatically
contiguous, and nothing can be definitively deciphered or firmly identified.
It is interesting to note here that translations of '*Ses purs ongles*', such as
Cohn's, interpret this initial image as '*Her* pure nails', but the gender remains
indeterminate in French grammar.[33] By assigning the pronoun 'her', the allusion to a woman's fingernails is augmented, and a desire to disambiguate the
text is exposed.[34] Furthermore, as Craig suggests, the defamiliarisation of
what is known becomes even more disturbing than the inclusion of the
mythical or enigmatic, as 'we accommodate faster the strangeness of the
strange than the strangeness of the presumed familiar'.[35] It is the very act of
presumption that Mallarmé undermines through a '*verbal* strangeness'[36] that
allows 'the metamorphosis of one object into a number of other symbolic
referents',[37] leaving nothing intact. Indeed, 'nothing' proves an apposite Mallarmean signature and it is specifically pertinent to '*Ses pur ongles*', a text
which is imbued with signifiers of 'nothingness': '*aboli*', '*vide*', '*vacante*', and
'*Néant*' (also translated as the Void), which is capitalised for emphasis. Objects
equally serve to signify this pervasive vacuity, and the concomitant process of
transformation and dissolution, as the window and the mirror 'reflect' what is
simultaneously both present and absent, the 'oblivion bound by the frame'.

In relation to Kristeva's semiotic, Cohn provides an interesting, if problematic, reading of the 'occult' mirror and the enigmatic 'ptyx'. He
maintains that the ptyx represents 'the simplest container of reality (or
nothing) a sort of womb developed from the merest bend or concave shape,
the fundamental female Rhythm'.[38] For him, the mirror embodies the 'feminine essence'[39] of the 'nixie'. Despite the gender assumptions inherent in
Cohn's interpretation of the ptyx as a 'sort of womb', embodying 'the fundamental female rhythm', I believe he makes a pertinent, if unintentional,
link with Kristeva's concept of the semiotic Chora. The Chora is defined
by Anne-Marie Smith as 'a non-expressive in the sense of non-verbal

totality underlying language; a non-spatial, non-temporal receptacle of energy and drives'.[40] Significantly, the definition of ptyx remains undetermined and has been comprehended in different ways by various critics.[41] Interpretations of this enigmatic word include objects such as a table, vase or (sea)shell; yet, ptyx has also been construed as an amorphous fold or coil, thereby signifying a shape, or indistinct space, rather than an identifiable object. Whether object or ambiguous spatial entity, such readings concur in their interpretation of ptyx as a form of container, a *receptacle* able to receive or emit a substance or force.[42] Such extreme semantic ambiguity, however, can equally render *all* meaning absent for, as E.S. Burt maintains, while the above definitions 'are plausible and even attractive, the *ptyx* is first of all a group of letters that means nothing'.[43] Thematically, the ptyx as a signifier of 'nothing' collocates with the many references to 'nothingness' discussed above, but in Burt's terms, ptyx lacks *any* signified, it 'stands alone'.[44] Due to a lack of any specific referent, the ptyx can thus appropriate significance from neighbouring words and images, allowing it to enter an endless play of signification. As Burt states, 'it sets in "motion" the surrounding words, demanding to be related to them while at the same time installing a nonreferentiality, an impossibility of certain meaning at the center of the poem'.[45] It is this lack or *suspension* of any 'certain' meaning that characterises Mallarmé's work, creating a layering of equally viable readings that can be neither privileged nor discarded. Hans-Jost Frey employs the metaphor of a 'bi-furcated fish tail' to refer to such 'undecidability of ambiguity'[46] which, he insists, cannot be 'solved', but remains perpetually suspended. An analogy with Freud's dream analysis, or more specifically, his concept of 'condensation', will help elucidate this simultaneity of various meanings. As Freud states: 'one is inclined to regard the dream thoughts that have been brought to light as the complete material, whereas if the work of interpretation is carried further it may reveal still more thoughts concealed behind the dream.'[47] Each element of the dream is related to a vast number of associations that exist beneath the surface, and, thus, what is manifest connects to a wealth of symbolic relations. Similarly, in Mallarmé's poetry, no signifier relates to a specific or fixed signified, but rather discloses a tissue of discrete and even dichotomous possibilities that do not unfold sequentially but, rather, simultaneously.[48] Through the compelling non-referentiality of the ptyx Mallarmé suggests the unstable condition of all signification.

Despite the disruptive force of the ptyx, aspects of the semiotic in '*Ses purs ongles*' are primarily perceived through the phonetic *rhythm* evoked within and between words, such as through the rhyme scheme that opposes the harsh consonantal sound of 'yx' with the more mellifluous vowel sound of 'or'. Such sounds work in conjunction with syntactic and semantic discontinuity to challenge expectations and evade referentiality for, as Frey states, 'the subject becomes more and more obscure, replaced by word games, a phonetic and orthographic ballet'.[49] Kristeva's understanding of the 'phoneme' is essential here, as she reminds us that it is not 'simply an element of the word, but a signifier in itself' which 'can thus be read in terms of its pulsional significance or its semantic associations'.[50] The 'yx' (ix) and the 'or' sound, therefore, are not just part of the words in which they are pronounced, but contribute their own 'supplementary meaning'[51] and musical nuance to the text. The jarring 'yx' sound relates to the underlying thematic emptiness, as in French it intones the letter 'x', which is commonly employed as a symbol for something unknown or incomprehensible. That both the phoneme 'x' and the 'yx' rhyme occur in the words 'phoenix', 'styx', 'ptyx' and 'nixe' thus augments the mythical and mystical element of the poem through a subtle layering of semantic connotations and phonetic effect. The contrasting 'or' sound proves equally multivious: softer than the vocally awkward 'yx' sound, the 'or' promotes a mellifluous rhythm that creates a radical contrast in tone from line to line. Significantly, Edgar Allan Poe chose the word 'Nevermore' as the most adequate 'close' to his poem 'The Raven' as he believed it evoked the melancholic tone he wished to create. Poe states that 'Such a close, to have force, must be sonorous and susceptible of protracted emphasis [. . .] and those considerations inevitably led me to the long o as the most sonorous vowel, in connection with r as the most producible consonant.'[52] Anticipating Shklovsky's desire for prolonged perception, Poe refers to the effect of 'protracted emphasis' which, he infers, can be achieved through the apposite employment of sound. The repetition of the word 'sonorous' is also interesting as '*sonor*' features frequently in Mallarmé's poetry, often creating indeterminate meaning through syntactical and grammatical play.[53] The work of Poe greatly influenced the Symbolist poets, and specifically Baudelaire and Mallarmé, both of whom adopted Poe's search for 'pure poetry'. At age eighteen, Mallarmé was already translating Poe into French and incorporating his doctrine of composition into his own work.[54] Furthermore, as Charles R. Lyons reminds us, 'Mallarmé and Manet collaborated on an edition of *The Raven*, in which Mallarmé translated the poem and Manet provided the illustrations'.[55] 'The Raven' is also considered exemplary by Kristeva, who claims that Poe is 'perhaps the first writer in the modern era to have founded his text on negation', the 'Nevermore' constituting 'a refrain which is never the same as itself'.[56] Negativity, as Ffrench notes, 'becomes psychoanalytically redefined as the "semiotic"',[57] and it is Mallarmé who, Kristeva maintains, 'was one of the first to understand' and 'was the first to have formulated its theory as well as its practice'.[58]

Apart from such specific graphemes as 'yx' and 'or', individual letters throughout '*Ses purs ongles*' contribute to the rhythmic effect. Within the line '*Aboli bibelot d'inanité sonore*', for example, the repeated b's, o's and i's create a melodic rhythm that is vocally pleasurable to read. As Cohn notes, however, in conjunction with the rest of the poem the o's and the n's reinforce the thematic emptiness and sense of negation, while the i's 'support the lucid quality of the rhymes in *i*-sounds'.[59] Each individual letter, as well as word, therefore, *enacts* the 'Mallarmean doctrine of *suggestion*, of undecided allusion'[60] which suspends univocal interpretation. Furthermore, in terms of the 'genotext', the 'transfers of drive energy that can be detected in phonetic devices',[61] such as repetition and rhythm, are exemplified.

Mallarmé's instrumentation of such phonetic effects is not restricted to '*Ses purs ongles*' but pervade his entire *oeuvre*, reflecting his belief in the auditory power of words. As Cohn states, Mallarmé was 'extremely patient and meticulous in choosing his words' as he was aware that 'they saturate the air with overtones which emerge when they marry the overtones of other terms'.[62] This notion of a sonic 'marriage' between words is accentuated in '*Prose (pour des Esseintes)*' in which 'two words melt into one or two discrete phonic units become a phonic continuum'.[63] In the middle quatrains, for example, Mallarmé not only employs cross-rhymes, but separate words in the first rhyme conjoin in its partner rhyme, thereby creating an audible *rime riche*. In the sixth stanza '*de visions*' rhymes with '*devisions*' and in the seventh stanza '*se para*' becomes '*sépara*', thereby eradicating the gap that creates semantic differentiation. Malcolm Bowie considers this latter rhyme to be significant for he states that 'The singularity of the "*se para*"/"*sépara*"/ rhyme is that it catches up between the members of the rhyme-pair the very word, the most *juste* of *mots justes*, needed to characterize gaps of this kind: lacune.'[64] Bowie considers the importance of the word *lacune* thematically within the poem, and also in relation to 'the non–adequation between metre and syntax' which, he maintains, becomes 'in the word *lacune* a self-naming and autotelic verbal event'.[65] It is Bowie's consideration of syntax which interests me here, as, according to Kristeva, a further component of the 'genotext' concerns irregular 'syntactic and logical features', such as anomalous grammar, ellipsis and the disruption of linear structure. Through the fracturing of these features the semiotic can, once again, puncture the symbolic, and disrupt the signifying function of language. Bowie reads '*Prose*' alongside Lacan's discussion of *se parare/separare* in '*Position de l'inconscient*', claiming that both are 'intellectual performances of great subtlety that willingly take chances with sense', and furthermore, he maintains that both writers 'allow a pre-articulate, pre-semantic babble'[66] to pervade their work. For Derrida, such disruption of syntactic continuity pulls the reader's attention in different, and often opposing, directions, thereby suspending any decision between alternative interpretations. Frey's notion of the 'undecidability of ambiguity', therefore, is not attributed to 'the richness of meaning', but rather 'it is a certain play of the syntax'.[67] Derrida significantly illustrates this syntactic *play* in Mallarmé's poetry through 'the syntax of the short word for *or* [which] is sometimes calculated to prevent us from deciding whether it is the noun "gold", the logical conjunction "or" or the adverb of time, "now"'.[68] Thus, grammar is also implicated in Mallarmé's 'game' playing as words are positioned in such a way as to problematise their grammatical function. In '*Ses purs ongles*' for example, the line '*Elle, défunte nue en le miroir*' proves problematic as '*défunte nue*' may be read as 'naked dead one', or alternatively, 'dead cloud', depending on how the syntax and grammar are interpreted. This ambiguity, in turn, problematises the referent of '*elle*', such indeterminacy creating a ripple effect throughout the rest of the poem, as 'doubt strikes forward as well as backward'.[69] As Burt suggests, then, grammar 'shows its capacity to manipulate the meanings of the terms that it relates' and, as such, it 'threatens simultaneously with an excess of sense [. . .] and with a lack of sense'.[70] These notions of excess *and* lack are symbolised in '*Ses purs ongles*' by the final image of the constellation of stars, the '*scintillations sitôt le septuor*', an expansive cosmic image that, for Mallarmé, simultaneously epitomises the emptiness or void behind all existence.

Mallarmé's fragmentation of linear syntax is equally important to Kristeva, who, as I have mentioned above, considers such structural disruption as a feature of the semiotic. In his article entitled 'Revolution in Poetic Language? Kristeva and Mallarmé', Patrick Ffrench claims that, for Kristeva, '[s]hattering and starring, correspond to the key elements of Mallarmé's poetic language: the transformation of syntax and musicalization by way of work on the phonic level'.[71] If '*Ses purs ongles*' closes with a symbolic 'starring', his exemplary poem '*Un Coup de Dés*' enacts a (visual) 'shattering' of language and sense. Semiotic pulsions traverse the surface of the page through Mallarmé's 'shattered' configuration of words, thereby challenging the symbolic structures of language and order. Concerned with its own instability and displacement of meaning, the scattered black marks accentuate the gaps (the lacunae) between words that are conventionally overlooked to ensure a continuous reading process. This continuity, however, is part of the *illusory* stability of the symbolic order that is disrupted by the pulsional processes of the semiotic. Like Derrida, Kristeva maintains that Mallarmé's complex syntax is related to his 'undecidability' to the extent that 'the recovery of linear sentences with subject, verb and object is disallowed'.[72] Through the progressive elimination of syntactic and grammatical conjugation, therefore, '*Un Coup de Dés*' epitomises Mallarmé's attempt to free language from the 'tyrannical aspect of the sentence'[73] and pluralise meaning. '*Un Coup de Dés*' similarly closes with an image of the 'Great Bear', thus providing an intertextual link with '*Ses purs ongles*', and yet the referential function of language has collapsed even further in this extraordinary poem that appears to leave all meaning to 'chance'.

In the following section, I aim to apply this analysis of Mallarmé and the crisis of referentiality within a modernist episteme to the contemporary poetry of Medbh McGuckian.

'To Make the Stone *Stone*'

As I have suggested above, despite writing a century apart, both Mallarmé and McGuckian promote the heterogeneous possibilities of language and frustrate univocal meaning. Through the (semiotic) interrelation of sound-play and word-play, both poets renounce pure description in order to give primacy back to the word, and yet, despite elements of striking congruity, their poetry is by no means identically structured or motivated. Mallarmé generally employs the sonnet form, thereby binding his semantic play to formal features such as line length and rhyme scheme. '*Ses purs ongles*' provides a salient example as the rhyming of etymologically strange words accentuates the formal composition of the poem. Although Mallarmé's referential indeterminacy remains the pervasive feature of his poetry, therefore, the more evident surface play is clearly perceptible. In comparison, McGuckian provides few such structural footholds through which the reader may procure a sense of stability, and yet as Peter Sirr states: 'There is an exact if paradoxical relationship between the "yielding imagination" and a preoccupation with form, with the liberating potential of shape and rhythm and space pushed out as far as they will go.'[74] Thus, McGuckian pushes the *limits* of form rather than abandon such restrictions completely, her idiosyncratic style producing an intricate orchestration of linguistic and semantic play that skilfully appears to transcend the poetic restrictions within which she works. Alongside her 'yielding imagination', Mallarmé's desire to 'yield the initiative to the words' is equally shared by McGuckian, who aspires to be 'at the mercy of language itself'.[75] However, the impulse behind each poet's work radically differs. Mallarmé's preoccupation with symbols and the self-directive potential of language derives from his belief in an ideal world that can be penetrated through the manifestation of 'pure poetry'. McGuckian, however, is concerned with language itself as she endeavours to free words from their historical accretions. Recognising that (in Bakhtinian terms) 'there are no neutral words', as all language carries the weight of previous contexts and 'inflections of meaning',[76] McGuckian asserts that 'the responsibility the poet has, is to revive, to wash the words'[77] in order to promote their non-verbal sensual quality. This is what Kristeva terms '*jouissance*'. For Kristeva, '*jouissance*' is linked to the maternal, the semiotic and the erotic, aspects of the genotext that pervade McGuckian's *oeuvre*. Thus, her poetry discloses the heterogeneous domain of emotional affect that disrupts the stability of the symbolic order.

Once again Shklovsky's essay 'Art as Technique' proves pertinent to my discussion, as his explication of the 'economy of perceptive effort' articulates McGuckian's own aesthetic concerns. Shklovsky maintains that 'as perception becomes habitual, it becomes automatic', and as such 'all of our habits retreat into the area of the unconsciously automatic', resulting in abridged or indistinct speech and 'an "algebraic" method of thought'. An object is consequently perceived 'in the manner of prose perception', and is thus insufficiently cognised to the extent that 'even the essence of what it was is forgotten'. Conversely, Shklovsky maintains that 'art exists that one may recover the sensation of life; it exists to make one feel things, to make the stone *stony*'.[78] This conviction is echoed by McGuckian, who claims that 'poetry exists because the way we use words when we are talking to people is so inadequate',[79] and, thus, 'poetry must almost dismantle the letters'.[80] For Kristeva, such 'dismantling' involves a necessary 'cracking, stretching, and subverting of language' in order to 'revitalise a discourse' that, in recalling Shklovsky and McGuckian, 'is always prone to automaticism'.[81] As with Mallarmé, McGuckian thus explores the polymorphous nature of language through the use of symbols and verbal play, and yet, unlike Mallarmé, McGuckian does not enact a search for perfect expressions or 'ideal' forms, but, rather, promotes a reassessment and revaluing of the word.

A consideration of a McGuckian poem such as 'Time-Words' best illustrates the affinity (and disparity) between McGuckian and the Symbolist aesthetic and her incorporation of the semiotic.

Time-Words

I am a debt, soon I will be added,
As words wither away with the things they describe,
As clouds may catch each other up,
As now is overtaken and tomorrow is an 'I'

Saying 'we' is dangerous, like time-words without soul
I must have met them yesterday and loved their
hunger.
The sea lives in the present so the present exists
In its waters like a heart not made to be broken.

Light is wider than time, it is I love,
It gives up being everything to become a view,
Like an emerald uncreating itself
To be green predominating in a skirt.

And the kiss is to turn the light back,
As though burnt or exhausted by its touch;

It is the theft when it has vanished,
And dark feels, what part of it was loved?[82]

From her collection *Marconi's Cottage* (1991), 'Time-Words' encapsulates some of the main tenets of Symbolism and yet equally exemplifies McGuckian's individual and idiosyncratic style. The title itself marries two distinctive concerns: language and an exploration of existence through a contemplation of 'time'. Replete with ambiguity and uncertainty, 'Time-Words' rejects an empirical view of reality to evoke a world imbued with contradictions and metaphysical qualities. Light and dark, reality and dream, become fused and presence and absence coalesce as McGuckian undermines oppositions, borders and thresholds. The reader must relinquish any expectations of transparency for McGuckian, like Mallarmé, has perfected the use of compression, connotation, allusion and suggestion. Such linguistic and semantic instability also constitutes the topic of much of Mallarmé's poetry, its self-referential critique engendering 'a speaking that is no longer concerned just with what is said, but with itself'.[83] 'Time-Words' similarly refers to its own interrogation of signification, making its displacement of univocal meaning a thematic as well as semantic aspect of the poem. Within the first stanza, the speaker claims that 'words wither away with the things they describe'. This ambiguous line tentatively alludes to the impermanence of language as, although it could feasibly refer to the phonetic transience of the spoken word, it equally, and more radically, refers to the signifying function that constitutes language itself. The signifier thus 'withers away' alongside the terms it creates, rendering *both* signifier and signified, the 'word' and the 'thing', unstable.[84] A sense of dissolution also occurs audibly through both the alliteration of the 'w' and the elongated vowel sounds which slow the sentence down, imitating the withering action of the words. When voiced, the line splits into two rhythmic six-syllable parts, thereby enabling it to fold in on itself, uniting the signifier and signified ('words' and 'things') and coupling 'describe' with 'away'. The repetition of the 'I' also pervades the poem as both a phonetic unit and personal pronoun, the two subtly interconnecting in stanza three, which begins 'Light is wider than time it is I love'. The assonance of the vowel 'I' enacts the widening that ends in the actual pronoun 'I', yet the pronoun's position renders the sense of the line ambiguous. The 'I' can be read as both modifying the love, or, alternatively, as a form of ellipsis, leaving exactly *what* the person loves unspoken. Throughout 'Time-Words', all references to an 'I' or 'we' are given weighted significance and accentuated through the use of quotation marks, the pronouns forming part of a discourse in which 'multiple layers of meaning and numerous associates suggest both a deconstructed language and a deconstructed self'.[85] As Kristeva maintains, the semiotic frees the energy within language that engenders a multiplication of meaning and provides an alternative understanding of subjectivity that is 'rhythmical rather than linear in development'.[86] This undermining of linearity is pertinent to 'time-words' in which the speaker interrogates the connection between the past, present and future. Time cannot be reduced to a measurable stretch, but consists of a temporal unfolding understood in terms of different rhythms.

As I stated above, Mallarmé was aware of the scrupulous care and consideration needed when placing words together and this is similarly true of McGuckian, who maintains that each word becomes part of an 'axis' and, as such, it is affected by what precedes and succeeds it. For example, 'debt', 'describe', 'dangerous' and 'dark' are linked through the sounds of *deh* and *da*; furthermore, the words thematically connect to suggest how language, freed from the restraints of instrumental communication, is often considered with hesitancy and even suspicion. As Frey states of Mallarmé's texts, 'since they don't communicate anything tangible, they are considered to be dark';[87] a comment equally applicable to McGuckian. The linking of words in this semantic web also brings the semiotic once more to the fore. Kristeva claims that an insurmountable *debt* is owed to the mother who acts as a 'bridge to speech, culture and separation',[88] without which there remains a *dangerous* 'maternal fusion'[89] with the semiotic realm of pulsions and drives which renders all *description* unstable. Furthermore, the semiotic not only ruptures the signifying process but also creates a crisis of subjectivity reflected in the assertion that 'saying we is dangerous' in opposition to the repeated 'I', reinforcing the notion of a 'split subject'. Indeed, another phonetic and thematic group of words links 'being', 'become' and 'be' alongside 'broken', 'back' and 'burnt', the harsh 'b' sound conjoining subjectivity with an implicit sense of loss or lack accentuated in the final poignant and convoluted stanza:

> And the kiss is to turn the light back,
> As though burnt or exhausted by its touch;
> It is the theft when it has vanished,
> And dark feels, what part of it was loved?

The emphasis here rests on what is taken, as 'burnt' works in conjunction with 'exhausted' to culminate in 'vanished'. To burn is to consume energy, and a feeling of fatigue pervades the end of this poem, that closes with the question, 'what part of it was loved?' The 'it' of the final two stanzas retains an anonymity and ambiguity which, consequently, renders the 'it' of the question equally indeterminate. McGuckian appears to be playing with the most basic grammatical sentence 'it is it' and asking the reader to elaborate. Thus, the poem once again alludes to its own processes, to the act of writing, and its instability. Equally, in relation to the semiotic, sound and sensation are privileged above semantic cohesion or any discernible meaning. The proximity of the words 'kiss' and 'is' creates an echoing effect that serves to extend the kiss and emphasise its gravity. Yet its origins are withheld. The use of ellipsis features throughout 'Time-Words' as what is left *unsaid* becomes as pertinent to the poem as what is said. The assertion that 'dark feels' can be read as one such ellipsis, as exactly what the dark feels remains unstated. However, it can also be read as a complete clause, evoking a semiotic space of instinctual *jouissance* that remains ultimately inexpressible in language. The indeterminate use of 'it' is, thus, appropriate, as both speaker and reader are returned to the semiotic threshold in which feeling, rhythm and sound oppose the regulations of the symbolic order. As with Mallarmé's poetry, 'Time-Words' 'dwells on the metaphysics of [its] own creation' whilst creating symbolic 'correspondences between physical and spiritual realms and between the different senses'.[90] Drawing on this sense of being 'between', it seems that an apposite symbol for 'Time-Words' is the hyphen that rests between 'Time' and 'Words', the space between the symbolic and the semiotic, language and silence; the borders of speech.

Tangled Paths

As my comparative reading of Mallarmé and McGuckian exemplifies, oral and intuitive aspects of language permeate both poets' *oeuvres* and, as such, Kristeva's definition of the semiotic as 'musical, anterior, enigmatic, mysterious and rhythmic' provides a valuable means of exploring their work. As I noted above, however, although both Mallarmé and McGuckian promote the semiotic through 'undecidability' and 'polysemantic play', such linguistic and semantic subversion does not eschew *all* elements of structure and order. Furthermore, Kristeva maintains that such a feat is ultimately unrealisable (or risks psychosis), for she states that 'because the subject is always *both* semiotic *and* symbolic, no signifying system he produces can be either "exclusively" semiotic or "exclusively" symbolic, and is instead necessarily marked by an indebtedness to both'.[91] In his comparative study of Mallarmé and Lacan, Bowie maintains that the cultivation of word-play ultimately constitutes 'the speaking subject's optimistic riposte to the simple fact of being trapped inside a language that she/he did not create and whose rules she/he has no real power to affect or mitigate'.[92] Despite the allusion to the subject's 'optimistic riposte' this is a rather bleak analysis, one that my above reading of Mallarmé and McGuckian works to contest. Although neither poet can *completely* break the symbolic contract, their suspension of referentiality and indeterminacy engenders only the *potential* of meaning, thus *affecting* the very function of language. As Ricoeur states in an interview with Richard Kearney, although 'creativity is always governed by objective linguistic codes', it 'continually brings [them] to their limit in order to invent something new'.[93] Although this may be applicable to all creativity, McGuckian not only *brings* such codes to their limit, but consciously pushes them further, her indeterminacy constituting a deliberate act of obfuscation through which she involves her readers.

Finally, therefore, I wish to consider the role of the reader in this invention of 'something new', an invaluable consideration in relation to both Mallarmé's and McGuckian's poetry. As Fowlie states in his curiously entitled study 'Stéphane Mallarmé: The Poet and the Clown', Mallarmé, through his title *Divagations*, warns us that his work will 'turn the readers' minds from their usual ways and channels' since his art constitutes an 'arduous exercise for the mind and a testing of the sensibility'.[94] McGuckian is equally aware of the 'arduous' task her poetry presents for her readers, for she states: 'I do think that I demand an awful lot of patience and I demand an awful lot of . . . love, the reader would have to really love going along the path that I lay out for them because it is so bloody tangled.'[95] The poetry of Mallarmé and McGuckian, therefore, constitutes a linguistic challenge, for the reader is given no certainties but rather must *participate* in the reading process, creating chains of associations and forming interpretations depending on what connections are privileged above others. As Burt aptly states regarding '*Sonnet en yx*', 'if both the terms and the relationships are ambiguous, our own reading is at the same time necessary and necessarily misleading'[96] as the reader is drawn to make his or her own conclusions. Such 'open' interpretation, however, raises pertinent questions regarding the issue of authorial intention and the concomitant act of 'communication' between poet and reader. Indeed, Phillip Sollers states how 'one of the essential postulates of [Mallarmé's] thought' concerned 'the necessary impersonality of the author',[97] a sacrificial act which entailed 'the death of the poet as personality' in order to ensure that 'the communion of the reader with the text [. . .] remain[ed] undisturbed by voice'.[98] Mallarmé aimed to create poetry in which the reader's engagement with the text remained free of any authorial intervention, the poem, thus, constituting a polysemic space within which the reader negotiated his or her *own* interpretation. Once again, Mallarmé proved himself ahead of his time, as it is possible to read his petition for poetic impersonality in relation to Derrida's more radical notion that *every* 'mark [is] cut off from its alleged "production" or origin'.[99] In his essay 'Signature, Event, Context', Derrida contests the classical notion of 'communication', as he argues that a message transmitted by the addresser does not inherently correspond to what is received by the addressee, for 'something like a law of undecidable contamination' can always 'divert an intention or cause it to go astray'.[100] Due to the repeatable and iterable nature of language, *all* writing, states Derrida, continues to function irrespective of the presence, and *absence*, of the author (and the addressee) and their 'intention-to-signify'. To write, therefore, 'is to produce a mark that will

constitute a kind of machine that is in turn productive, that my future disappearance, in principle, will not prevent from functioning and yielding, and
yielding itself to, reading and rewriting'.[101] In Derridean terms, the work,
once written, no longer 'belongs' to the author, but becomes susceptible to
an 'essential drifting' which may lead the text in entirely new directions.

Unlike Mallarmé, who wished to exclude all trace of (his) voice from his
poetry, McGuckian states that her poems are predominantly concerned with
people or events in her own life, and often involve someone that she has had
'a fairly tempestuous relationship with'.[102] As Peter Sirr states, however, 'hers
is a poetry of occasion whose occasions are meticulously withheld',[103] for
despite McGuckian's affirmation of the 'confessional' nature of her poetry, her
deliberately obfuscated language dislocates her poems from the original
impulse, experience, person or event. Obscurity, for McGuckian, constitutes
the crux of her work, and she is aware that, in terms reminiscent of Derrida,
'the poems drift',[104] yielding multiple interpretations that may conflict with
her own 'intention-to-signify'. McGuckian is equally aware of the academic
interest in her work and unlike Mallarmé, who wrote poetry in order to penetrate an 'ideal world', McGuckian employs 'polysemantic play' as a means to
draw the reader into the poem whilst simultaneously withholding any
coherent meaning. In a *comhrá* with Nuala Ní Dhomhnaill, McGuckian states
that 'if anyone did actually deconstruct the whole poem, the poem is dead,
the poem is killed'.[105] Here, then, is a clear expression of her anxiety towards
the very act of interpretation that her own poetic indeterminacy engenders.

Although what motivates Mallarmé and McGuckian to utilise polysemantic play may differ, the reader of both *oeuvres* is doubly removed from any
authorial intention due to the indeterminate nature of their poetry *and* the
'essential drifting' that attends every text. Once again, I am not advocating a
complete lack of meaning; rather, the indeterminacy augments the role of
the reader in its creation as 'you are just kind of *pointed* in a direction'[106]
which is composed of many 'tangled' paths. As Barthes states, 'the work does
not stop, does not close. It is henceforth less a question of explaining or even
describing, than of entering into the play of the signifiers'.[107] In relation to
the semiotic, this may evoke 'more deeply rooted forms of experience' for
the reader.[108]

4

Signs of encounters in Medbh McGuckian's Poetry

ELIN HOLMSTEN

All speaking is an enigma.
– Emmanuel Levinas, *Basic Philosophical Writings*, eds. Adriaan
T. Peperzak, et al. (Bloomington: Indiana University Press,
1996), p. 73.

And what is a sign? Is it a signal? Or a token? A marker? Or a
hint? Or all of these and something else besides?
– Martin Heidegger, *On the Way to Language*, trans. Albert
Hofstadter (New York: Harper & Row, 1982), p. 61.

The complex issues of the nature of signs, speaking or representation generally, as commented on by Heidegger and Levinas above, have been
extensively debated in contemporary philosophical discourse and aesthetic
practices. In this respect, Medbh McGuckian's poetry is no exception, since
many of her poems deal with representational acts such as writing and
painting. This feature has been much discussed by critics of McGuckian,
especially with regard to her departure from rational, conceptual representation or, as Eileen Cahill puts it, her 'concern with dismantling the letters'.[1] A
common argument suggests that McGuckian's poetry is engaged in a linguistic rebellion which is motivated by post-structuralist sensibility or
feminist intentions, and critics frequently compare her work to that of theorists in these areas. Susan Porter, for instance, argues that 'there are similarities
between her poetry and the writing of the contemporary philosopher
Jacques Derrida',[2] and Thomas Docherty proposes that McGuckian's poetry
is 'aligned with the postmodern thinking of Deleuze, Baudrillard and
others'.[3] Another suggestion is that her poetry is propelled by French feminist zeal, since, as Cahill suggests, it 'approximates both Hélène Cixous' *parler
femme* and *écriture féminine*, achieving a female *langage-parler*',[4] and 'resonates
the feminist linguistic theory of Luce Irigaray'.[5]

84

It cannot be denied that there are features in McGuckian's works that are similar to ideas about language expressed in post-structuralist and French feminist theory. I believe, however, that there is more to McGuckian's concern with representation than a wish to 'disrupt structures of meaning' and 'fragment the linguistic order'.[6] The often quoted comment by McGuckian on dismantling the letters, for instance, runs in its entirety: 'Language has been devitalized by advertising and news; poetry must almost dismantle the letters.'[7] This comment suggests that one of the driving forces behind McGuckian's style is not a wish to take the letters apart for the sake of sabotage, but for the sake of revitalising language in order to make it say more than the everyday chatter of advertising and news. Thus, this chapter will examine the meta-representational poems by McGuckian in a wider context, and suggest that the 'dismantling of letters' allows for speaking differently, which opens towards encounters with otherness. To this end, I will examine how McGuckian's poetry brings the spatial and temporal gaps of language to the fore, and suggest that it is through these gaps that otherness is allowed to enter. The post-structuralist and French feminist perspectives on language will be used as points of reference to see how the view of language in McGuckian's poetry complements or contrasts with these perspectives.

The Hotel of Language

One poem which illustrates the strong concern with language and representation in McGuckian's poetry is 'Hotel'.[8] O'Connor sees this poem as part of McGuckian's project to 'upturn syntactic conventions' by being 'deliberately obfuscating'.[9] Indeed, this poem can be said to unsettle conventions, but such unsettling widens the frame of meaning rather than simply 'obfuscating' meaning. A deconstructive impulse can be seen already in the first stanza:

> I think the detectable difference
> Between winter and summer is a damsel
> Who requires saving, a heroine half-
> Asleep and measurably able to hear
> But hard to see, like the spaces
> Between the birds when I turn
> Back to the sky for another empty feeling. (*VR* 36)

These lines clearly show an insistence on difference located in the in-between, which is a favoured site of feminists and post-structuralists alike.[10] The idea of difference presented in 'Hotel', however, differs from post-structuralist theories, since it goes beyond the formal concept of difference as a structural abstraction, which, as Derrida expresses it, 'is not a present-being

[. . .] in any form'.[11] In contrast to Derrida's presentation of difference as non-presence, difference takes on concrete form as a 'damsel, / who requires saving' in 'Hotel'. Although the damsel of difference is 'hard to see, like the spaces / Between the birds', and almost seems incorporeal as the speaker turns '[b]ack to the sky for another empty feeling', the embodying of difference as someone in need of saving makes it impossible not to take notice of her.

Personifying difference as a damsel also suggests, conversely, that human beings can be thought of in terms of difference, which indicates a heterogeneous self which cannot be framed by unequivocal concepts. This idea that human beings overflow the univocality of concepts is central to McGuckian's poetry. This overflow is also hinted at in the first stanza of 'Hotel' since the damsel fits neither of the opposites of 'winter and summer', nor can she be seen like the birds flying through the sky, but is somewhere between or beyond these concepts. Avoiding framing the damsel's otherness, the speaker gives her

> a name
> With a hundred meanings, all of them
> Secret, going their own way, as surely
> As the silvery mosaic of the previous
> Week, building itself a sort of hotel
> In her voice, to be used whenever
> The tale was ruthlessly retold.
>
> And let her learn from the sky, which was
> Clever and quiet, the rain for its suddenness,
> Yes on its own can be a sign for silence,
> Even from that all-too-inviting mouth. (*VR* 36)

The speaker's assertion that the damsel 'requires saving' in the first stanza is given an explanation in the two concluding stanzas cited above, which reveal that she needs saving from having her 'tale ruthlessly retold', that is, from being appropriated in representations which are oppressive or inadequate. The consequence of such ruthless retelling, the speaker suggests, is that what cannot be expressed clearly and unequivocally risks being silenced. Thus, even though unambiguous statements such as 'Yes on its own' may be compelling, they exclude alterity and otherness, such as the 'difference / Between winter and summer', as the concluding lines of the poem show: 'Yes on its own can be a sign for silence, / Even from that all-too-inviting mouth'.

Against the risk of ruthless representation, the speaker in 'Hotel' inserts undecidability as a means to unsettle easy access to meaning, giving the damsel 'a name / With a hundred meanings, all of them / Secret, going their own way'. This multiplicity of meaning is then likened to 'the silvery mosaic of the previous / Week, building itself a sort of hotel / In her voice'. The fragments of the previous week indicate a discontinuity in time which makes it difficult to pin down the damsel in the present, a circumstance which is accentuated by the 'hotel / In her voice', since a hotel is a temporary rather than permanent abode. Both the hundred secret meanings and the discontinuity of time contribute to building not a 'house' of language, as in Heidegger's famous phrase, but a 'hotel' where difference is granted refuge. 'Hotel', hence, suggests that there is a way of speaking which is open to otherness and difference, and which consequently can surpass the categorical concepts and strict linearity that logocentric discourse entails.

The concern with being silenced, seen in 'Hotel' above, recurs in many of McGuckian's poems, such as 'The Sailor', where the speaker says:

> I fear you might eliminate,
> Abbreviate me, tiring of my mild fingers,
> Clear as a telegram, at work below
> Your silvery breasts; in this subdued light
> I track you like a submarine,
> Your night-born murmurings [. . .][12]

What risks being abbreviated or eliminated here is a message, or meaning, which eludes straightforward representation, as this message is conveyed by 'mild fingers [. . .] at work below / Your silvery breasts'. This message appears 'Clear as a telegram' to the speaker, who appears to belong to the sphere of otherness, in this case the unconscious, as suggested by the images of 'subdued light', the submarine and 'night-born murmurings'. The paradox of presenting 'clearly' what eludes rational representation is also echoed in 'Circle with Full Stop', in the lines 'When sleep flings its inkstand, everything / is a few degrees clearer'.[13] These lines suggest that when writing, or 'flinging' the 'inkstand', emanates from an unconscious state ('sleep'), everything becomes clearer. A parallel can also be drawn to 'A Different Same', where the speaker says that '[m]oonlight is the clearest eye: / Moonlight as you know enlarges everything',[14] suggesting that the subdued light of the moon, often associated with the unconscious or the darker side of the psyche, brings a wider perspective, 'enlarg[ing] everything'.

Thus, 'Hotel' and 'The Sailor' indicate that the dismantling of the letters in McGuckian's poetry is connected to a widening of language, letting the other speak and, consequently, become 'detectable' and 'able to hear', as the speaker puts it above.[15] Thus, McGuckian's poetry suggests that silence is not the only alternative to 'ruthless retelling' since it is possible to speak differently by making room for otherness and difference. As Ricoeur argues: 'Language, indeed, is constituted in such a way that it does not condemn us to the choice [. . .] between the conceptual and the ineffable.'[16] McGuckian's poetry, as discussed below, finds an alternative to the conceptual and the ineffable by opening the spatial and temporal gaps in representation, where otherness enters.

Gaps

> Between living and recounting, a gap – however small it may be – is opened up.
> – Paul Ricoeur, *From Text to Action: Essays in Hermeneutics II*, trans. Kathleen Blamey and John B. Thompson (Chicago: University of Chicago Press, 1991), p. 5.

Although 'Hotel' and 'The Sailor' suggest that there is room for difference and heterogeneity in language, these poems also hint at the difficulties involved in representation, and to the elusive, fragile character of what is represented. The latter is a major concern in McGuckian's poetry, and her meta-representational poems often thematise the inadequacy, or difficulty, involved in representing aspects of existence not easily expressed in words. One such poem is 'Querencia',[17] whose title suggests both homelessness and the process of being on the way home, since the Spanish word '*querencia*' means 'homesickness', 'homing instinct', 'lair' and 'home ground'. The theme of exile is also seen in the first stanza, where the unnamed 'she' is in a liminal state, not being fully at home either in the unconscious realm of sleep or in waking consciousness:

> Her hands come awake from the apple-green shutters
> Of sleep. She clasps the end of her leather belt tightly,
> As if she can no longer speak for herself, or only
> With telephone distortions, the meaning of a row
> Of black spinal buttons between sender and receiver. (*OBB* 25)

The first lines of this stanza suggest a transgression between the states of sleep and wakefulness. The 'apple-green shutters', however, indicate that there is a border preventing any uninterrupted flow from sleeping to being awake. Such a boundary is also visible in language, the speaker suggests, since coming awake is seen as analogous to speaking or attempting to convey a message: it is '[a]s if she can no longer speak for herself or only / With telephone distortions'.S The image of the telephone distortions is continued in the last lines of the stanza, as the message is seen to be 'the meaning of a row / Of black spinal buttons between sender and receiver'. The spinal buttons, suggesting vertebrae, in conjunction with the telephone metaphor, evoke an image of nerves transmitting signals up and down the spine. However, there is clearly no immediacy of self-understanding; instead a sense of distance is emphasised, causing the telephone distortions 'between sender and receiver'.

A gap is thus revealed between what is felt and what is said, between 'living and recounting', as Ricoeur puts it above, between the body or the unconscious sending signals and the receiver, that is, the conscious mind attempting to interpret these signals. This gap is frequently brought to the fore in McGuckian's poetry. As in 'Querencia', the poem 'To Call Paula Paul' (*MC* 16–19), for instance, similarly uses the metaphor of the telephone to show the distance between sender and receiver: 'I hear her voice like a telephone / Torn from the wall by lightning / Where she is telephoning endlessly' (*MC* 18). As is the case of 'the meaning of a row / Of black spinal buttons' discussed above, only the act of telephoning, that is, trying to communicate something, is seen in the poem, not what is said, as 'her voice' is dramatically disconnected, 'like a telephone / Torn from the wall'.

A similar theme is explored in 'The Sitting' (*VR* 15), where the issue of representation is dealt with more directly. This poem is from McGuckian's second collection, *Venus and the Rain*, in which double selves in the form of dream- or half-sisters are numerous. Here, one of these double selves approaches the speaker to have her portrait painted:

> My half-sister comes to me to be painted:
> She is posing furtively, like a letter being
> Pushed under a door, making a tunnel with her
> Hands over her dull-rose dress. (*VR* 15)

The half-sister's furtive posing, 'like a letter being / Pushed under a door', indicates the mysteriousness and elusiveness of her character. Further, the image of the door recalls the shutters of sleep discussed above, since it marks a limit between the half-sister and her message on the one hand, and the speaker attempting to represent her on the other. This divide between representation and the represented is further accentuated as the poem continues:

> Yet her coppery
> Head is as bright as a net of lemons, I am
> Painting it hair by hair as if she had not
> Disowned it, or forsaken those unsparkling
> Eyes as blue may be sifted from the surface
> Of a cloud [. . .] (*VR* 15)

Here, the speaker is painting the half-sister's head 'hair by hair', which can be read as the precision aimed at in rationalistic representation. This meticulous style of painting, however, fails to capture the half-sister's 'coppery / Head', since she appears to have disowned both her hair and her eyes. Interestingly, this disowning occurs in connection with the speaker's activity of painting, suggesting that something may be lost in trying to represent it. This is also indicated in the metaphor of sifting blue from a cloud, evoking an image of the painter filtering the blue colour from the half-sister's eyes in order to paint the portrait, leaving the leached eyes of the sister 'unsparkling'.

Thus, 'The Sitting' brings the selective nature of representation to light. As can be seen in the continuation of the poem, the half-sister casts doubt on the images the speaker selects to represent her: 'she questions my brisk / Brushwork, the note of positive red / In the kissed mouth I have given her'. At the end of the poem, the half-sister's initial doubts become outright dismissal:

> she calls it
> Wishfulness, the failure of the tampering rain
> To go right into the mountain, she prefers
> My sea–studies, and will not sit for me
> Again, something half-opened, rarer
> Than railroads, a soiled red–letter day. (*VR* 15)

This poem calls attention to the inadequacy of representation for fully capturing the object to be represented, suggesting that it is only 'wishfulness' to believe that the 'tampering' activity of the speaker-painter can penetrate and reveal the essence of the furtive and mysterious half-sister. The image of the 'tampering rain', in connection with the painting of hair, recalls the poem 'Blue Sky Rain', where 'a small-bodied / Shadow asked me what I painted – / It was her own superb sienna eyes', and where 'some blue sky rain / Exploited her still living hair' (*OBB* 24). In 'The Sitting', by contrast, the representational exploitation of the sister and her hair is deemed a failure, and the poem is, thus, only 'half-opened' to the mysterious half-sister, who is seen to be 'rarer / Than railroads, a soiled red-letter day'. These last lines, which conclude 'The Sitting', further reinforce the idea of inadequate representation, suggesting that the portrait of the half-sister is similar to a smudge of paint staining a holy day in a calendar.

Again, we see that McGuckian's poetry marks a divide in representation. Paradoxically, however, by revealing the inadequacy of her portrait, the speaker does not restrict the poem's meanings; rather, she widens the frame to draw attention to what is normally beyond representation. This technique of suggesting the excess beyond representation by emphasising the failure of attempting to capture what is beyond the immediate grasp of concepts is common in McGuckian's works. In 'Vibratory Description', for instance, the speaker points to what is beyond explanation in words, in the following: 'The soul being a substance cannot explain / Just that red as felt in the room or bed.' However, by suggesting the failure of explanations to carry the substance of the soul, the words of the poem paradoxically succeed in 'disrobing / The more with which we are connected' (*MC* 95).[18] In other words, by pointing out the gap between 'living and recounting', representation can put the speaker or reader in touch with the excess – the 'more' – of living.

A similar technique is used in 'Story Between Two Notes' from *Captain Lavender*.[19] As the title suggests, the story told is not in the actual words themselves but between them. The poem begins by addressing the other:

> You are the story I can't write.
> Every page of you
> has to be torn out of me.
> Even after your death when you are alone
> your mysteriously-suppressed
> name-sickness
> will weave itself into all I see. (*CL* 16)

The speaker here says that the other's 'story' cannot be written, yet a story is nevertheless told, albeit with difficulty, as suggested by the pages that are torn from the speaker. As the remainder of the stanza suggests, by writing this impossible story, the words succeed in bringing about the other's presence in the 'name-sickness' weaving itself into all the speaker sees. This name-sickness can be read in two ways: first, in the sense of being sick of names, which is in line with the initial statement that the other's story cannot be written; second, 'name-sickness' can be read as longing for names, as people long for home when they are homesick, which implies that the speaker experiences that the other desires to have his or her story told. The second stanza further reinforces the idea of the strong presence of the other experienced by the speaker:

> It is as if you already listen
> from the adjoining room, earthly wagon
> harnessed to unearthly horses;
> the red years have just failed
> to take you out of the world
> which looks like another world. (*CL* 16)

Although the other here is experienced as close by, 'already listening', the other's presence is modified by several metaphors which point to the separation and difference between speaker and other: the other is in another room, and the relationship is likened to an 'earthly wagon' drawn by 'unearthly horses'. The concluding lines of the stanza show the hermeneutic effect this experience has on the speaker; interacting with the other, the world appears to have changed, 'look[ing] like another world'.

The following stanzas continue the motif of difference, this time between language and the other:

> Nobody has ever seen
> the true shape of your lips.
> You are walled round, a too-well-laid-out path.
> You detour round the language
> like a wound closing wearily.
>
> But now, when this music is playing between us,
> though I never dream meaning into it,
> this winter-quiet that loses itself
> completely in sound seems the active beginning
> of a normal, if still secret, name. (*CL* 17)

The first of the stanzas quoted above recalls the speaker's initial attestation that the other's story cannot be written, as well as the pain involved in writing this impossible story, as the other here is 'walled round', detouring 'round the language / like a wound closing wearily'. The second stanza above, however, changes tone, as indicated by the words 'But now'. The line 'But now, when this music is playing between us' refers self-referentially to the poem itself – 'Story Between Two Notes' – and to the act of writing, which is likened to music, an interplay between the 'notes' of the speaker and the other. The lines that follow suggest the hermeneutic transformation that writing entails for the speaker. As the 'winter-quiet', which can be interpreted as the absence of the other and the other's own words ('Nobody has ever seen / the true shape of your lips'), 'loses itself / completely in sound', that is, in the words of the poem, there is an 'active beginning / of a normal, if still secret, name'. Significantly, the name which could potentially pin down the other remains secret, and the speaker 'never dream[s] meaning into it'. Rather, the door remains 'half-opened', as in 'The Sitting' above, and it is precisely this half-opened door, the gap that both separates and connects self and other, that allows for this open-ended sense of communication with otherness to take place.

McGuckian's poems not only disclose a gap between representation and the object of representation, as seen above, but they also mark a divide between speaker and speech. This can be seen, for instance, in 'The Sofa', which begins with an image of postponed communication:

> Do not be angry if I tell you
> Your letter stayed unopened on my table
> For several days. If you were friend enough
> To believe me, I was about to start writing
> At any moment; my mind was savagely made up,
> Like a serious sofa moved
> Under a north window [. . .] (*FM* 19)

The moving of furniture here both indicates the preparations undergone in order to start writing, and hints at the dislocation that writing will imply. As the speaker prepares a poetic reply, the addressee 'ask[s] for some − / About nature, greenery, insects, and, of course, / The sun'. The image of the sun stands in contrast to the place of writing prepared by the speaker, which is '[u]nder a north window', that is, a place where direct sunlight does not enter. This discrepancy between the speaker and the wishes of the addressee is further emphasised as the type of poetry asked for is rejected on the grounds that 'surely that would be to open / An already open window?' Refusing the 'already open window', and 'of course, / The sun', that is, matters that are self-evident and already illuminated, the speaker then offers alternative images:

> If I could
> Interest you instead in his large, gentle stares,
> How his soft shirt is the inside of pleasure
> To me, why I must wear white for him,
> Imagine he no longer trembles
>
> When I approach, no longer buys me
> Flowers for my name day . . .(*FM* 19)

The lines that the speaker offers the addressed 'you' here are deeply personal in nature, in contrast to the verses on 'nature, greenery, insects, and, of course, / The sun' above. The ellipsis following 'no longer buys me / Flowers for my name day . . .' suggests a pause, perhaps waiting for the message to reach its destination, or being lost in personal thoughts. However, what follows this attempt to communicate personal emotions is a scattering of the self:

> But I spread
> On like a house, I begin to scatter
> To a tiny to-and-fro at odds
> With the wear on my threshold. Somewhere
> A curtain rising wonders where I am,
> My books sleep, pretending to forget me. (*FM* 19)

These lines draw attention to the difficulty of expressing the self in language, since the effect of speaking is shown to be a dislocation of the self. One sees clearly here that the signs that would express the speaker's experiences do not coincide with the self, as the speaker is scattered, 'at odds / With the wear on my threshold'. Furthermore, the 'curtain rising' is suggestive of a theatrical representation, which in this case would present the speaker's emotions. As the curtains are drawn, however, the speaker is nowhere to be found and, thus, the distance between the speaker and representation is emphasised. Similarly, a sense of distance is articulated in

'Theatre', where the speaker asks to be told '[h]ow I live in poems, or how / Far away I was / In the bad light, on the stage of the summer theatre' (*FM* 46).

One of the reasons why it is difficult to express the self in language is, of course, because language cannot be totally singular and personal, but depends instead on the meanings and connotations it acquires as it is used by countless other speakers. As Derrida puts it: 'As soon as I speak, the words I have found (as soon as they are words) no longer belong to me.'[20] This is hinted at in 'The Sofa', where writing seems to have a life of its own, external to the self, as the speaker's 'books sleep, pretending to forget me' (*FM* 19). However, although this peculiarity of language is sometimes seen to be problematic, there is no attempt to ignore the exteriority of signs in order to make them reveal, transparently and directly, the interior ideas, thoughts and emotions of the self. Instead, McGuckian's poems frequently depict language as exterior to the self. One of the poems where this is seen most clearly is 'Harem Trousers' (*OBB* 43), which begins by separating poem and speaker: 'Asleep on the coast I dream of the city. / A poem dreams of being written / Without the pronoun "I".' The poem is then likened to a river, flowing freely through the landscape:

> The river bends lovingly
> Towards this one, or that one, or a third.
> [. . .]
>
> It straightens, stands, it walks
> Timid and incongruous
> Through roadblocks and breadlines.
> It holds the hundred and first word
> In its fingers and tears it apart,
>
> So the openness within the sound
> Is forced to break, dislodging
> Its already dove-grey music. (*OBB* 43)

These lines give an evocative illustration of how poetry, when liberated from the intentions of an 'I', is free to go wherever it wishes, bending 'towards this one, or that one, or a third', even breaking through 'roadblocks and breadlines'. This type of poetry does not simply 'open an already open window', but 'tears' the word apart to dislodge its 'music', thus giving access to perspectives beyond the already known and the intentions of the speaker, recalling Merleau-Ponty's statement that '[m]y own words take me by surprise and teach me what I think'.[21]

As the poem continues, the speaker ponders whether to enter this river of language:

An extreme and simple feeling
Of 'What if I do enter?' –

As I run to fetch water
In my mouse-coloured sweater,
Unkempt, hysterical, from
The river that lives outside me,
[. . .]

Your room speaks of morning,
A stem, a verb, a rhyme,
From whose involuntary window one
May be expelled at any time,
As trying to control a dream
Puts the just-completed light to rest. (*OBB* 43)

These lines indicate that language is seen as a resource external to the self, as the speaker goes to 'fetch water from / The river that lives outside me'. This resource is not there, however, to be exploited by the speaker at will. Language provides the speaker with a 'window', that is, a certain perspective from which to see the world, but this window is one from which the speaker '[m]ay be expelled at any time', especially when trying to master or restrain it. The commonsense notion that language is a tool at people's disposal is rejected, recalling Heidegger's reversal of the asymmetrical view of the relationship between speaker and speech: 'Man acts as though he were the shaper and master of language, while in fact language remains the master of man.'[22]

The consequence of attempting to control language is suggested in the last lines of the poem, where 'trying to control a dream / Puts the just-completed light to rest'. The fact that the light is put to rest in the last words of the poem, together with the movement of the river of language, suggests that this movement stops when one tries to control it. Thus, the creative process is shown to involve a renunciation of authority, which implies that one refrains from imposing one's preconceived ideas and meanings on language. As Derrida expresses it in a discussion of Edmond Jabès's poetry: 'To be a poet is to know how to leave speech. To let it speak alone, which it can do only in its written form. To leave writing is to be there only in order to provide its passageway, to be the diaphanous element of its going forth.'[23] In McGuckian's poetry, such 'going forth' can also be seen in the metaphor of the journey, as will be discussed next.

'Forever on the Road': The way of language

For perhaps we are always on the way to language, though language itself may be the way.

> – Paul Ricoeur, *The Conflict of Interpretations: Essays in Hermeneutics*,
> trans. Willis Domingo (Evanston: Northwestern University Press,
> 1974), p. 96.

Up to this point, the discussion has centred on the spatial metaphor of a gap
in representation, seen in the section on gaps above as the distance between
representation and the represented, and between speaker and speech.
However, the issue of time is as important as that of space in this context,
since McGuckian's poetry also marks the divide in representation by
pointing out temporal discontinuities. The idea of language as a journey
aptly suggests the dislocations in both time and space in McGuckian's poetry,
where, as in 'The Aisling Hat', 'to speak / is to be forever on the road' (*CL*
47). The metaphor of the journey is also frequently used in McGuckian's
poetry. This is, in itself, not remarkable; it would be difficult to find poets
who do not employ the journey as metaphor in one way or the other. What
makes the journeys in McGuckian's poetry significant in this context is that
they are journeys without return to the point of departure, which can be
related to Levinas's concept of the Abrahamic journey.

Levinas sees the journeys of Odysseus and Abraham as symbolic of two
distinct modes of thought corresponding to two different ways of
approaching the other. In Levinas's view, Odysseus' adventures are emblematic of the tendency of Western thought to assimilate the other into
consciousness, or to treat the other as a mere detour which the self takes only
to define itself and thereby secure its identity.[24] As Levinas puts it, 'the
autonomy of consciousness, which finds itself again in all its adventures,
return[s] home to itself like Ulysses, who through all his peregrinations is
only on the way to his native island'.[25] In the Abrahamic journey, on the
other hand, Levinas sees a movement towards the unknown with no possibility of return. Levinas thus refigures the story of Abraham as an ethical
journey towards otherness, which avoids reducing and normalising the alien
world of the other in pre-existing schemes of thought. Hence, the Abrahamic journey is seen as a mode of thought in which, as Levinas puts it,
'movement unto the other is not recuperated in identification, does not
return to its point of departure'.[26] This latter approach is, it will be argued,
similar to how McGuckian presents the theme of the journey in poetry.

One poem suggesting this Abrahamic journey is 'Elegy for an Irish
Speaker' (*CL* 42–3). The journey without return is not only suggested by
the death of the other, who is now in '[t]he undiscover'd country, from
whose bourn / No traveller returns',[27] as Hamlet would have it, but also by
the lingering words of the other, capable of 'bypassing / Everything':

> Most foreign and cherished reader,
> I cannot live without

> your trans-sense language,
> the living furrow of your spoken words
> that plough up time.
> [. . .] Bypassing
> everything, even your frozen body,
> with your full death, the no-road-back
> of your speaking flesh. (*CL* 43)

The lines above suggest the dialogic mode of the poem, since the addressed other, whose 'speaking flesh' animates the poem, is also a 'foreign and cherished reader', so that the speaker and the other are, in effect, both speaker and addressee. The difference between speaker and other, of course, is that the other is experienced as a presence beyond the grave, hence the 'trans-sense language'. The other's language, however, is experienced as a 'living furrow' of words 'that plough up time', suggesting that although the other may be departed, his or her words, perhaps as they linger in the speaker's memory, are a strong and enriching presence which bypasses 'everything', even the other's 'frozen body', with its 'full death'.

Another poem in which 'the no-road-back' of 'speaking flesh' is seen clearly is 'The Dream-Language of Fergus' (*OBB* 57–8), which gives an evocative illustration of how the passing of time makes exact meanings impossible. The first stanza outlines an image of stillness and silence preceding speech, as not even 'the rudiment / of half a vanquished sound, / The excommunicated shadow of a name, / Has rumpled the sheets of your mouth' (*OBB* 57). This stanza also indicates a mood of expectancy as the 'tongue has spent the night / In its dim sack as the shape of your foot / In its cave' (*OBB* 57). After this image of pregnant silence, the second stanza gives a clear picture of open-ended Abrahamic movement as two different languages mingle, that is, when

> [. . .] one river inserted into another
> Becomes a leaping, glistening, splashed
> And scattered alphabet
> Jutting out from the voice,
> Till what began as a dog's bark
> Ends with bronze, what began
> With honey ends with ice;
> As if an aeroplane in full flight
> Launched a second plane,
> The sky is stabbed by their exits
> And the mistaken meaning of each. (*OBB* 57)

The 'excommunicated shadow of a name', together with the title, 'The Dream-Language of Fergus', recalls the mythical story of Fergus, exiled king in the Ulster cycle, and W.B. Yeats's depiction of this king in 'Fergus and the Druid'.[28] In Yeats's poem, a druid offers Fergus a 'little bag of dreams', and tells him to '[u]nloose the cord'. In so doing, Fergus sees his 'life go drifting like a river / From change to change'.[29] Similarly, in 'The Dream-Language of Fergus', the tongue which was inertly sleeping in its cave in the first stanza is set loose, as the second stanza depicts the uncontrollable movement of language through time. The images all suggest the instability and fragility of language, which also implies that no stable self-sameness between word and thing, or the speaker and her speech, exists. However, there is more to this poem than popularised notions of Derridean *différance*, or post-structural questioning of presence, because this stanza suggests that language, by its very unstable nature, has the potential to go beyond the horizon of the known and consequently towards the other, as suggested by the idea that 'the sky is stabbed'. An important, but often overlooked, aspect of McGuckian's poetry is this celebration of the capacity of language to disrupt stereotypical and habitual ways of thought, and consequently its ability to open towards new insights and experience. Hence, language in itself is seen as a vehicle for a quest for widening insight and experiences; a journey where, to borrow a line from McGuckian's poem 'The Carrying Ring', 'no word closes our quest' (*MC* 88).

McGuckian's texts frequently comment on this capacity of words to open pathways towards new ways of seeing and thinking, often suggested by images of fertility and growth. This can be seen in 'The Seed-Picture', for instance, where the speaker asserts that '[t]his is my portrait of Joanna' (*FM* 23). However, this is clearly no conventional portrait, first because the speaker seems uncertain how to go about painting this portrait: 'I wonder where to put them, beautiful seeds, / With no immediate application'. Second, as in 'The Dream-Language of Fergus', words, here represented by the seeds, go beyond the intention of the speaker:

> the clairvoyance
> Of seed-work has opened up
> New spectrums of activity, beyond a second home
> The seeds dictate their own vocabulary,
> Their dusty colours capture more than we can plan [. . .] (*FM* 23)

These lines suggest that the temporal dislocation occurring in language, indicated by the 'clairvoyance / Of seed-work', is what provides possibilities for new perspectives and meanings, 'open[ing] up / New spectrums of activity, beyond a second home'. Hence, as this poem shows, it is by virtue of its non-coincidence with intentionality or the signified that, as Derrida puts it, 'language [is] always richer than knowledge [. . .] always capable of the movement which takes it further than peaceful and sedentary certitude'.[30]

Such movement beyond peaceful certitude can be seen also in 'Turning the Moon into a Verb', a poem which highlights the connection between temporality and language:

> A secret year, a secret time,
> Its flight is a written image
> Of its cry, its capacity for sound
> I call spring, the experience
>
> When the sky becomes a womb,
> And a vision of rivers slanting
> Across the doubly opened page
> Of the moon turns her into a verb. (*MC* 76)

Here, language, 'the written image', is described as the flight of 'a secret time', recalling 'The Dream-Language of Fergus' above, where the time–language relationship is compared to 'an aeroplane in full flight'. Here, too, the flight of language is understood as the possibility of new meanings and new ways of seeing, as it is likened to 'spring', 'the sky becom[ing] a womb', and a 'vision of rivers'. The concluding line where the moon – a frequent symbol of fertility – is turned into a verb further reinforces the idea of language as growth.

This idea of the fertility of language, seen in both 'Turning the Moon into a Verb' and 'The Seed-Picture', is also present in the last stanza of 'The Dream-Language of Fergus', which similarly suggests transformation and growth:

> Conversation is as necessary
> Among these familiar campus trees
> As the apartness of torches;
> And if I am a threader
> Of double-stranded words, whose
> Quando has grown into now,
> No text can return the honey
> In its path of light from a jar,
> Only a seed-fund, a pendulum,
> Pressing out the diasporic snow. (*OBB* 57)

The image of the seed-fund suggests the rich potential of language, which is further strengthened by the etymological roots of 'diaspora', deriving from the Greek *dia*, meaning 'through'/'across', and *speirein*, meaning 'to sow'. Thus, this poem shows an open-ended Abrahamic movement from the stillness and pregnant silence at the beginning to 'a seed-fund, a pendulum, / pressing out the diasporic snow' at the end. Allowing this semantic growth in poetry lets language 'capture more than we can plan', as in 'The Seed-Picture' above, or, as Roland Barthes expresses it: 'Each poetic word is thus an unexpected object, a Pandora's box from which fly out all the potentialities of language.'[31]

The progression from stillness to movement in 'The Dream-Language of Fergus' can also be seen in 'From the Weather-Woman' from McGuckian's collection *Shelmalier* (*S* 33). *Shelmalier* commemorates the tragic events which occurred during the rebellion of the United Irishmen in 1798, which suggests that the addressed other is an other from Ireland's past. The poem begins by evoking the silence of the other:

> Not even a dead letter
> a pseudohope from your pseudohome.
>
> You are dissolved in me
> like the death of the century. (*S* 33)

The absence and inaccessibility of the other are here acknowledged; there is not even a 'pseudohope' of communication, as the difference in time – 'the death of the century' – makes direct communication impossible. The next four lines indicate that the speaker longs for and needs the other:

> I need your summer movements
> as the spirit needs the world,
>
> my non-world the inner
> gospel of your letters. (*S* 33)

However, what follows stands in sharp contrast to the speaker's wishes for 'summer movements', since what arises 'from the unhardened nature / of the memories' is neither 'summer movements' nor any joyful 'gospel', but

> your prison
>
> look, that mood, that number,
> leads a road where nothing
>
> can unhappen, to the meeting
> of two opennesses: the one
>
> I write before the visit,
> the one you will write after it. (*S* 33)

Thus, this poem suggests an approach in which the visitation of the other overrides the needs of the self, because what catches the speaker's attention is not the needed 'summer movements', but the other's 'prison look, that mood, that number', evoking the suffering of an unnamed other. In other words, unlike Odysseus, who conquers and defeats what is other to him, the speaker here lets the other lead the way – much like Abraham, who goes forth into the desert, not as a result of his own needs and wishes, but, as Levinas explains, because he is following a command of the other. As the other gains primacy over the egocentric needs of the speaker in McGuckian's poem, the road on which 'nothing can unhappen' significantly leads to 'the meeting / of two opennesses: the one / I write before the visit / the one you will write after it' (*S* 33). These lines further suggest the speaker's unwillingness to assimilate and frame the other, since the other is not 'written into' the poem and we are left with two opennesses, that is, an open-ended encounter which allows the other to retain his or her alterity.

Encounters with Otherness

> my pen
> Beginning with a walk must
> End with a meeting [. . .] (*OBB* 54)

The temporal and spatial dislocations discussed above might recall Derrida's concept of the play of *différance*, that is, the theory of the sign as deferred presence and as the notion that signs gain their meaning by differing from other signs.[32] Indeed, the displacements occurring in McGuckian poetry resemble Derrida's idea of *différance*, with one notable exception. Derrida's concept primarily concerns the difference between, and deferral of, signifiers, and, as Michael Roth notes, '[t]here is no signified for Derrida. Rather, each signifier – in turn – signifies another signifier, which in turn continues this procedure without cease'.[33] McGuckian's work, by contrast, emphasises the difference between signifier and signified, speaker and speech.

McGuckian's poetry differs from the popular view of postmodernism as a practice blurring the distinction between text and world, representation and represented, and, consequently, presenting a world where '*[t]here is nothing outside of the text*'.[34] This view is the framework which Thomas Docherty draws on in his reading of McGuckian, and he thus comes to the conclusion that '[a]ll here is image, there is no presence, only representations'.[35] As seen above, however, this is clearly not the case, since McGuckian's poems constantly insist on the difference between representation and the object of representation, which, properly speaking, is not an 'object' at all. In 'The Sitting', for instance, the half-sister is not portrayed as a helpless victim of her portrait; instead, her activity of questioning, and finally dismissing, the speaker's representation of her turns her into a subject in dialogue with representation, rather than its object.

Similarly, the relation between speaker and speech in McGuckian's work does not support the frequent argument that postmodern writing does away with all notions of self outside of language, embracing the view that, as

Richard Rorty puts it, 'the human self is created by the use of a vocabulary rather than being adequately or inadequately expressed in a vocabulary'.[36] Again, Docherty's analysis provides a good example of this line of reasoning. While it is true that, as he maintains, there is 'a gap between what is said and the voice that says it',[37] it does not follow that the self is reduced to 'the vacuous Subject' of 'blank phenomenology'.[38] As seen in, for instance, 'Harem Trousers', by pointing out the gap between speaker and speech, McGuckian's texts place the human subject in a dialogic relation with language.

Also, in contrast to Derrida's view of *différance*, McGuckian's poems do not treat the temporal and spatial incongruities merely as a structural inevitability of language, which one tries to escape – albeit in vain, since, as Derrida maintains, there is 'no insurance against the risk of writing'.[39] Rather, the incongruities involved in speaking and writing are constantly sought by McGuckian's speakers. Why would one seek out 'the risk of writing' and affirm spatial and temporal difference, as McGuckian does in her poetry? One reason, mentioned above, is that such writing opens other perspectives, or, as the speaker in 'The Seed-Picture' puts it, '[n]ew spectrums of activity' (*FM* 23). Another equally important aspect is hinted at in 'Something Like a Wind', a poem dealing with the theme of time:

> Your lips were always a single line of time
> Flowing through a single place – day after day,
> Like kisses bestowed on both cheeks, they
> Fastened the years together, when I would like
> To have prised them, ever so gently apart. (*VR* 53)

This first stanza begins with a description of linear time, one which is straightforwardly and homogeneously '[f]lowing through a single place', comprised of years seamlessly fastened together. The speaker, however, would like to have 'prised them, ever so gently apart', thereby disrupting the flow of time. The reason for this wish is disclosed in the last stanza:

> For

> The silences immersed between the waves
> Were poor streets where women might present themselves
> As points of darkness only, things that happen,
> Good times [. . .] (*VR* 53)

As in 'Hotel' above, where the damsel of difference is 'hard to see', the 'women' mentioned in this poem reside in an obscure in-between state of silence 'between the waves'. The waves recall the flow of time in the first stanza; hence, these lines indicate that the speaker wants to prise the years apart to allow for otherness, here embodied as women, to 'present themselves', even if '[a]s points of darkness only, things that happen'. This poem thus suggests that the gaps in representation are pried open in order to make way for encounters with what is not normally seen, instead of 'open[ing] / An already open window', as the speaker in 'The Sofa' puts it above.

In 'Something Like a Wind', the opening of this gap also suggests an opening of the mouth, in contrast to the closed lips of the first line, which 'were always a single line of time'. Hence, as the mouth opens to allow for women to 'present themselves', speaking in McGuckian's poetry is seen to involve more than the act of naming and representing things; rather, the words uttered become the means of encounters with otherness. Another poem linking signs with encounters is 'The Witchmark', which begins:

> You paint, Miss Churchill? Pray go on.
> Then you would know a dangerous face.
> How spirit lusts towards us as we to it, like
> The play of different lights. Your body,
> That naked altar, how would you show
> Behind a picnic, gloves and violets, its readiness
> To be roused, its hopeless snow? (*FM* 39)

The quaint conversational tone of the line 'You paint, Miss Churchill? Pray go on' is abruptly followed by a statement indicating that representation involves more than an innocent depicting of, say, 'a picnic, gloves and violets', since painting could result in knowing 'a dangerous face. / How spirit lusts towards us as we to it'. Again, McGuckian's speaker lays bare a gap in representation, by asking how '[y]our body, / That naked altar', and 'its readiness / To be roused', connoting erotic desire, would 'show / Behind a picnic, gloves and violets', the picnic and gloves suggesting social entertainment, and the violets evoking unassuming shyness, images in stark contrast to the naked body's 'readiness / To be roused'.

Thus, the poem opens the divide in representation in order to encounter desire and otherness, that is, the spirit 'lust[ing] towards us'. Such lusting in connection with representation is a frequent element in McGuckian's work. For instance, in 'The Sitting' (discussed above), '[m]y half-sister comes to me to be painted / [. . .] posing furtively'. Similarly, in 'Woman with Blue-Ringed Bowl', an unnamed 'she' appears to desire poetry:

> Like a curtain opening a glade in a children's bedroom,
> Her fallen shawl unpins a brown and fallen breast.
> If I was possessed of a pen that wrote in four colours,
> I could patrol how differently each tree contains the sun.
> Hold me in the light, she offers, turn me around,
> Not the light controlled by a window, but the cool gold
> Of turning leaves after their short career in the sky. (*OBB* 58)

As in 'The Sitting', where the half-sister dismisses the speaker's meticulous and controlling 'hair by hair' style of painting, and instead 'prefers my sea-studies', the represented in this poem also has opinions about the kind of poetry she wishes to appear in. Thus, while she desires to be held in the light, she rejects 'the light controlled by window', which suggests a limiting and static field of vision. Instead, she wishes to be seen in 'the cool gold / Of turning leaves', and invites the speaker to 'turn [her] around', evoking a widening, many-sided way of seeing and representing, which would be more sensitive to her otherness and difference. Similarly, the autumnal image of the leaves' turning and 'short career in the sky' refers back to the pen that might write in four colours, thus reflecting the diversity of colours seen in autumn trees, or how 'differently each tree contains the sun'. The 'cool gold' of 'turning leaves' also suggests the leaves of poetry, which, unlike the author-itative 'light controlled by a window', could let the desiring 'she' of the poem be seen 'like a curtain opening a glade in a children's bedroom'.

In this context, it should be noted that the non-authoritative style of McGuckian's texts involves more than what many critics see as a 'feminist refusal' of patriarchal 'authoritative certainty',[40] as if the main concern was to rebel against the supposedly masculine tendency to control language by refusing to say anything clearly or with certainty. As Molly Bendall, for example, declares: 'What *is* working in the poems is a struggle to subvert what some feminist theories have named as characteristics of phallo-centric literature: a strict linearity and an affirmation of authority.'[41] Certainly, McGuckian's non-authoritative style departs from linear, logocentric dis-course. However, it should also be noted that, as seen for instance in 'Harem Trousers' and 'The Seed-Picture' above, by refraining from imposing oneself on language, other perspectives are allowed for, thereby letting what ordi-nary representation suppresses present itself and be encountered.

Thus, McGuckian's meta-representational poems challenge the hypoth-esis of many readings of her poetry, namely the argument that her dismantling of the letters is primarily or solely motivated by a wish to subvert logo- or phallo- centric language. By avoiding 'ruthless retelling', her poetry also seeks to speak differently, which will make room for encounters with otherness and desire. Hence, the departure from restrictive modes of writing cannot be seen merely as an escape from language and meaning, because, as Celan notes in response to complaints about obscurity in poetry: 'This obscurity [. . .] has been bestowed on poetry by strangeness and dis-tance [. . .] for the sake of an encounter.'[42] A similar idea is expressed in McGuckian's 'The Sky Marshal', quoted above, where the speaker's 'pen / Beginning with a walk must / End with a meeting'.

5
The Space that Cleaves:
The house and hospitality in Medbh McGuckian's work

SCOTT BREWSTER

The house in Northern Ireland has at times offered only partial sanctuary from turbulence 'outside': it is a physical and affective interior, a space of retreat and secrecy, yet it remains far from invulnerable to the history it must endure. The phrase 'safe house' paradoxically suggests both shelter and security, and also the harbouring of a threat within. The *unheimlich* house has been variously portrayed as damaged, under siege or constant surveillance, as something that shuts out the gaze. As such, it is treated either as a refuge from, or purely reflective of, the perturbed public realm. Shane Alcobia-Murphy has argued that representations of the house by Northern artists and writers, while self-aware and critical, 'convey a sense of being trapped in a hiatus, unable to progress'; they contrast sharply with depictions in the South, which demonstrate 'a positive, forward-looking engagement with outworn symbols'.[1] Alcobia-Murphy adduces the scarred house-wall in Victor Sloan's c-type print, 'House, Edenderry, Portadown': the inability of the viewer to look beyond the flat, mute surface of this wall at once memorialises violence and symbolises political impasse.

The invitation of home ground in the North can also be readily transformed into an economy of exclusion, silence and vulnerability rather than of shelter, custom and affiliation. In this refusal of the law of the *oikos*, and its obligations of hospitality to the stranger, doors can be shut, houses can be evacuated and streets can be cleared. While a number of male poets have explored alternative, future-oriented and more hospitable notions of dwelling,[2] it can be argued that women poets have traced most fully the intricate, enigmatic fabric of the domestic interior, and its sensitivity to social and historical change. The house is *of* the world and a shelter *from* the world. As Lucy Collins comments:

> At the beginning of the twenty-first century the house may enclose not a clearly defined unitary family but a series of relationships, some lasting,

some transitory. Through the image of the house the poet may explore a concept of belonging necessarily altered – and further alterable – by the disintegration of traditions and by social mobility.[3]

In each case, the specificity of the house operates as an index of something beyond its bounds. Such poetry does not merely transcribe or appropriate personal narratives of everyday experience: it acknowledges that the house obliges us to negotiate between the inside and the outside, the singular and the general.

Gerry Smyth reflects that poetry strains to a greater extent than other forms of writing 'under the weight of a supposed "special relationship" between place and Irish identity'.[4] Irish poetry has articulated the dwelling place predominantly in terms of landscape rather than the built environment. In contrast, the novel, and the critical vocabulary the form has fostered, shares an array of terms associated with domestic architecture (such as structure and aspect) that portray the house and the work of fiction as similar spaces.[5] As Kathy Mezei and Chiara Briganti observe, 'novels and houses furnish a dwelling place – a spatial construct – that invites the exploration and expression of private and intimate relations and thoughts'.[6] In this vein, Heather Zwicker sees Northern Irish fiction as at once affirming and affronting a traditional household economy. Its 'closely plotted novels [. . .] take place in narrow, domestic spaces; triumphs are tiny and misery is constant'. These domestic settings, however, do not 'corroborate or approve the division of spaces into public/masculine and private/feminine' but instead 'offer the most efficient site for critiquing patriarchy and colonialism simultaneously'.[7] For Collins, however, poetry constitutes an equally effective space for challenge and critique: 'For Irish women poets the house represents a material site, where their own roles as women can be explored, and an imaginative one, allowing them to structure the psychological explorations in their poems.'[8]

For Gaston Bachelard, the house is *primordially* poetic: 'the house image would appear to have become the topography of our intimate being.'[9] The sense of dwelling can be mediated by material objects, but it is also about feeling, remembering and imagining. It is the power of poetic imagination to transform our perception and disclose the world that apprehends most acutely the emotional investments and intimacies associated with the house. Bachelard contends that poetry opens up an 'immemorial domain [. . .] beyond man's earliest memory',[10] and through poetry, more than recollection, 'we touch the ultimate poetic depth of the space of the house'.[11] Poetry, rather than prose, utters the language of the house, transfiguring the phenomenal details of the everyday. Bachelard's poetics of the house comports with a view of the McGuckian poem as secretive and withdrawn: 'the house shelters daydreaming, the house protects the dreamer, the house allows one to dream in peace.'[12] Yet poetic homecoming is a matter of comfort and estrangement, of finding and losing a place. Our houses have resonances, and speak of other occupants, other affiliations that are not ours. To inhabit a house is often a matter of living with other stories, other memory-hoards, where many moments crowd for attention in the here and now. These familiar ghosts retain the power to defamiliarise our sense of presentness, and of our dwelling places. As such, the otherness of our 'own' place is always already inside. In a moment of historical transition, where optimistic visions of the future vie with the pain of the past, an experience of *unsettlement*, where proximity and distance, intimacy and strangeness mingle, may constitute a political and ethical necessity. Understood in this way, this essay considers the conditional hospitality offered by the house in Medbh McGuckian's poetry, and its relation to wider questions about the ethics and politics of settlement in Northern Ireland.

The interplay of concealment and exposure in McGuckian's poetry would seem to confirm poetry's *in*hospitability. While the house provides an essential, empowering creative space for Southern poets such as Vona Groarke and Eiléan Ní Chuilleanáin,[13] for McGuckian it is a space that must be confronted and carefully negotiated. In her charting of 'typically' feminine spaces – family networks, gardens, the body and domestic interiors – the identification with the private sphere is ambivalent. The house is lure and trap, a refuge and a site of containment, resistant to any synthesis of internal and external worlds. Threading silence and enclosure into its formal structures and thematics, and always alert to the threat of intrusion, her unsettling textual strategies render the domestic interior estranging and disquieting. As Patricia Haberstroh has commented, McGuckian's linguistic experimentation is 'anchored in houses'.[14] Doors, windows, shutters, frames and thresholds predominate, yet the syntactical shifts, cryptic scenarios and etymological resonances often seem to bar or withhold access. The poems appear to revoke their invitation to the reader, and there is an apparent fascination with what Bachelard terms an 'aesthetics of hidden things'.[15] Thomas Docherty discerns few home comforts in the typical reading experience of a McGuckian poem: 'Each poem is, as it were, a threshold inviting the initiation of its reader into some meaning; yet it also denies that meaning at the very instant of its perception.'[16]

'The Sitting'[17] plays out precisely such a discomforting, reluctant, uncertain invitation. The speaker's 'half-sister' – an unwilling visitor, suspicious of welcome – arrives 'like a letter being / pushed under a door'. She announces her resistance to the intrusion of the painter's 'tampering' gaze, questioning the imprecision, artifice and 'wishfulness' of visual art in its attempt to capture subjectivity:

> she questions my brisk
> brushwork, the note of positive red

> in the kissed mouth I have given her,
> as a woman's touch makes curtains blossom
> permanently in a house.

Yet the sitter merely voices the painter/poet's own unease with 'brisk/brush-work': each party is delimited by the frame of the painting, just as surely as the curtains solicit and constrain the 'woman's touch'. The imposition of the 'kissed mouth' is as equivocal in its impact as the delicate feminine touch that makes the 'curtains blossom': the sitting, like these domestic accomplishments, is a matter of inauthenticity, performance and unequal exchange.

To turn the house into the representative ground of femininity is a provocative gesture, of course. Although the focus by women poets on the internal spaces of the house may present an alternative to the public landscape charted by male poets,[18] and can attempt to politicise 'the "neutral" spaces of domestic geography which history has enforced upon Irish women',[19] the house remains a problematic, over-determined site for the woman writer. In 'The Soil Map',[20] read by Clair Wills as a parody of the *dinnseanchas* poem,[21] the house and the woman stand in for the motherland, as each is already colonised by representation, but the house is (in) a state of disrepair. The house is already entered, its feminised openness an affront to property rights, domestic security, rootedness:

> I have found the places on the soil map,
> proving it possible once more to call
> houses by their names, Annsgift or Mavisbank,
> Mount Juliet or Bettysgrove: they should not
> lie with the gloom of disputes to interrupt them
> every other year, like some disease
> of language making humorous the friendship
> of the thighs. I drink to you as Hymenstown,
> (my touch of fantasy) or First Fruits,
> impatient for my power as a bride.

While the poem can ironise and contest patriarchal claims to home ownership, however, its work of restoration must still operate within that name- and place-logic. It yearns for the grounding denied, as Luce Irigaray argues, to women in Western philosophical discourse. In conceptual and material terms, for the house to be seen as the woman's place merely serves to confine and efface the feminine: woman is used to construct the 'house of language' but then 'it is not available to her'.[22] The house that sustains the man makes the woman homeless. The figure of the house stands for the wider erasure of the female within philosophical tradition, where 'the / a woman fulfils a twofold function – as the mute outside that sustains all systematicity; as a maternal and still silent ground that nourishes all foundations'.[23]

While McGuckian's poetry suggests a reluctance to expose the woman in a domestic setting to scrutiny, since that figure has been such opened ground within Irish culture, she has stressed the centrality of the figure of the house for her poetics:

> 'The house is probably the poem itself often, or a symbol for the world of the poem. I feel a house is a very secure place, especially in Belfast [. . .] I am for houses. They're symbols of the protective – the protectiveness a woman feels about her personal life and her body and her history.[24]

The three categories that McGuckian emphasises here – the personal, the bodily and the historical – are central to the ways in which critics have interpreted the house in her poetry. For some, the house is the womb, or the maternal body more generally. Ann Beer sees the connection between body and text as seamless: 'McGuckian frequently uses the metaphor of the womb, the hollow inner space, the house, to remind her readers that poetry is like child-bearing and that child-bearing is a kind of poetic enterprise.'[25] In a similar vein, Mary O'Connor argues that when McGuckian 'presents her female speaker as the womb, the house, the enclosed space, then the reader must consider what precious thing is carried, nurtured'.[26] Yet McGuckian's poetry precisely complicates and often refuses the obligations of this metaphorical equivalence, exploring instead the sense of invasiveness, clutter and displacement bound up with the intimate sharing of space.

If the house is a metaphor for the womb, there is barely house room for the poem: the text is a crowded interior, its roof-timbers creaking under the symbolic weight. 'The Over Mother' is a striking example of this assailed interior:

> In the sealed hotel men are handled
> as if they were furniture, and passion
> exhausts itself at the mouth. Play kisses
> stir the circuits of the underloved body
> to an ever-resurrection, a never-had tenderness
> that dies inside me.[27]

If this is the maternal space, its passion is exhaustion, its articulation is cancelled, and it functions as a site of transit and transience to which 'men' endlessly return. The sealed hotel is yet another house infringed and appropriated, the rooms gone stale with occupancy. The inner space of the maternal body is far from 'hollow', and is not free from inscription and conscription. If the house is the womb, the enclosed space, what might be contained or sheltered? In 'Sky-Writing', the poem/house is an enclosure that does not contain, a space ineluctably open to otherness, to an outside that has already come inside:

> What can I do against this room
> I was obliged to let grow and grow
> In the new space all through the winter?
>
> [. . .]
> I forfeit the world outside
> For the sake of my own inwardness,
> I am so at one with the scent of its many wills:
> Its inexhaustible innocency
> Lapses past me like a future not lived strongly,
> I abandon myself to its incubative weight.[28]

Wills remarks that in the poem '[t]he body within the body is not only a double, but a foreign body which disrupts any sense of self, and the possibility of saying "I"'.[29] The foreign body suggests parasitical dependence but also reciprocity. Guinn Batten rightly notes that '[p]regnancy, in McGuckian's terms, is perilous for maternal–host and child–hostage',[30] but as 'Sky-Writing' demonstrates, the relation between host and hostage is not hierarchical. The unborn child needs a host who will become a hostage to its demands, but equally the child cannot exist independently of the maternal body that nurtures it. The maternal relation here is prey to an inwardness characterised by threat, obligation and responsibility.

At other times, McGuckian presents the house as a space of nurture and homely arts: children, flower-arranging, tapestry and decoration, where McGuckian places herself within 'a female artistic tradition by acknowledging her debt to the female heritage of domestic artistry'.[31] As Wills argued over a decade ago, 'feminine and familial "privacy" in Ireland is orientated towards a public and political domain',[32] and, at least for critics, this domain casts its shadow over such domestic artistry. We could alternatively see the house in McGuckian as 'a room of one's own' – a site that resists appropriation, offering a resistant poetics intent, in Hélène Cixous's terms, on 'changing the furniture'.[33] In this reading, the house is an arena in which to refuse, to invent and to nurture an alternative society. For all the emphasis on privacy, secrecy, seclusion and carefully delineated autonomy, however, there is a marked ambivalence towards the room of one's own. The house is both an open and closed space, textually, culturally, politically, historically, a representational trap for a writer conscious of a demand that still exerts itself for a woman to 'be' nation, mother, nature. The pull between definition and indefinition is captured in 'What Does "Early" Mean?'. The 'Happy house across the road' is a friendly intimate,[34] but its enigmatic recesses elude the speaker's 'study':

> None of my doors has slammed
> Like that. Every sentence is the same
> Old workshop sentence, ending

> Rightly or wrongly in the ruins
> Of an evening spent in puzzling
> Over the meaning of six o'clock or seven:
>
> Or why the house across the road
> Has such a moist-day sort of name,
> Evoking ships and their wind-blown ways.[35]

There is a mixture of freedom and frustration here: the poet puzzles over names and definitions, but the house cannot be claimed in language. Indeed, it is language that thwarts identification with the house. In this way, McGuckian's poems 'lack a fundamental ingredient of the refuge – a stable and secure centre, a grounding for the authenticity of personal experience'.[36] Even if this might be a welcome response in a situation where one's ground is forcibly declared, there is a residual draw in her work to capture and to piece together the interior.

As stand-off gradually moved to proximity talks in the 1990s, and Northern Ireland emerged tentatively from a moment in which the ground of home was overshadowed by claims to 'home ground', the welcome mat at the front of McGuckian's poetic house could be viewed differently. Interviewed in 2004, McGuckian returns to the door as both an ethical and a political threshold:

> The thought of the threshold is very frightening to me, because where I live, you always had to guard the door. All through the Troubles, you kept the front door locked, and if you were in a middle-class area, you'd have an inner door, and you'd keep them both locked all the time, even if you were in the house. When the cease-fire happened and the peace process began, we very slowly began to open the outer door, but still keep the inner door locked. That's the stage we're at in Northern Ireland: one door locked, but the other one tentatively open with a little gap.[37]

Bachelard claims that 'the door is an entire cosmos of the Half-open',[38] but to open the door to the unexpected knock in the North during the 1970s and 1980s in particular was fraught with fear, an act of utmost risk or exposure. For Emmanuel Levinas, however, it is precisely the experience of risk and vulnerability upon which the ethical relation is both predicated and inaugurated. The primordial ethical encounter is one in which we experience the otherness of the other. Ethics is grounded precisely in 'the questioning of my spontaneity by the presence of the other'.[39] To see the face of the other does not lead to a comforting recognition of sameness: the face provokes, but at the same instant arrests, hostility, since it commands our respect and responsibility for the other. Levinas stresses that access to the face is 'straightaway ethical': 'The face is exposed, menaced, as if inviting us to an act of violence. At the same time, the face is what forbids us to kill.'[40] Levinas's ethical encounter is, as Derrida suggests, a matter of welcome and hospitality (*ethos* means abode, or the customs of a place).[41] We are obligated to open ourselves to the other; the one (or more than one) who seeks admission may or may not share our values, may or may not share our experience of alienation or unhomeliness in the act of welcome, but she or he cannot be bound before arrival to our house rules. At the crossing-point of the outer door, the subject is both *hôte* – host and guest – and *otage* – hostage, with the mixture of vulnerability and responsibility this entails.[42] Levinas regards the maternal relation as the exemplary instance of this inaugural face-to-face encounter.[43] It is a form of hosting that precedes the law of the *oikos*, and is in marked contrast to the property rights associated with the patriarchal household.

The ambivalent embrace of hospitality is discernible in McGuckian's collections in the last decade, and in the ethical turn of the readings she has attracted. Perhaps the most notable is Erin Mitchell's celebration of McGuckian's 'postmodern' hospitality: 'In her images of elusive hostesses and uncanny, awry houses, McGuckian offers a postmodern, feminized (in)hospitality and asks whether and how the feminine split speaker welcomes and/or shuns the other(s).'[44] The relationship between gender and hospitality has been a matter of *oikonomia*, or household management, and its associations with the familial, the proper and the domestic. Forbes Morlock acknowledges what is lost by departing the house: the move away from the *oikos* in and beyond ancient Greece meant the gendering of public space, discourse and exchange as male.[45] Derrida has traced how Aristotle construes women as 'derivative or exterior' to the 'syngealogical cell' of familial friendship within the house,[46] and that patriarchy excludes women from hosting in the capacity of 'master' of the household. Thus, only unconditional hospitality that begins with 'the unquestioning welcome' has been possible for women.[47] Yet Nausicaa's indiscriminate welcome to strangers in the *Odyssey* suggests the dangers of hospitality that is not conditioned or 'properly' sanctioned.[48] The potential risks of hosting the foreigner are clear: the guest may become a parasitical host, bringing hostility into the home and disrupting the economy of hospitality.

McGuckian's recent collections reveal a progressive opening-up to the street; they leave ajar the door to a house that 'welcomes the other within and the other without despite the anxiety the other provokes'.[49] This shift is anticipated by the ownerless house in 'Marconi's Cottage': it receives radio waves from the utmost distance into the intimate interior of the home, showing how the law of private property can be transgressed even by invisible arrivals.[50] This cautious receptiveness to exteriority anticipates 'The Rose-Trellis' in *Shelmalier* (1998). No place in the 'anxiously protected room' is

> safe enough
> to close itself back
> over those still unused voices,
> that slide from music
> to soon-to-be-living words,
> and bring back a kind of weak spring,
> as if it had always stayed in the street.
> It is so completely back inside it.[51]

The house is a repository for resonant, secreted voices, and their occupancy constitutes potential rather than clutter. The 'warm housewinds' have forced open the voices and 'fallen into them'; this enfolding of the external by the house culminates in 'the dense sound that wraps up / the meaning of an act of love'. This openness can be set against the embattlement evoked later in the volume in 'Blue Doctrine', where hospitality would be shunned in favour of aggression, insecurity and retreat:

> For those who sit in the darkened
> doorways of their dwellings devoid
> of doors, the trouble-adding sound
> of bells can mean whatever you want
> to – mobilization, a warlike tempo,
> passive defence.[52]

'The Building of the "Hebe"' has the speaker lodged on a 'harbourless coast, my harbour / for the season', reflecting on the house as space of intrusion and often reluctant, but unavoidable exposure:

> You blanket the door with a faithless shuddering,
> having stripped off the entire bark of a tree
> while all the dew was on.
>
> We walk dry under its coverlet
> to the opposite hills with their different iron
> colours.
>
> Higher and higher the tearless grass
> opens a window under my feet,
> and quite across my mouth, leaving the smooth
> meadow where my house stands all entry,
> like a fungus, in a coarse snarl.[53]

The house at once abjures and absorbs the outside, the very management of its boundaries subject to a complex blend of hostility, closure and possibility. Eluned Summers-Bremner argues that the fungal contamination of the threshold 'posits entry or welcoming as inseparable from decaying growth.

[. . .] Without incorporation of the alien element [. . .] there can be no sanctification of, nor safety within, a culture founded on domestic space'.[54] Again, we can discern the reciprocity associated with the foreign body that accrues around the act of welcome. Summers-Bremner's 'culture' might alternatively be read in the medico-biological sense; the culture of hospitality grows, and is nurtured, as if under experimental test conditions. Rather than developing within the clinical detachment of the laboratory, however, this culture is nourished by an ambivalence tied to the maternal: the poem ends with 'the growing moon' glimpsed 'through rafters with the bark still on'. The house makes reparation, its roof-timbers that replace the stripped bark at the door acting as a compact, yet in doing so it opens itself to the risk of further entry.

This opening to the 'alien element', and the reluctance to sanctify the domestic, is strikingly performed in 'She Thinks She Sees Clarissa', from *The Currach Requires No Harbours* (2006):

> I patrolled the windows and the house,
> walking in front of the mirror in varying angles.
> If I stood too close I suffocated
> I was so very concentrated there,
> like a blood sample left standing
> without a breath of air.
>
> Every inch of its final yellow, slight shine
> had the radiant afterglow of the explosive
> if I touched it I was too easily inspired
> because it was touch itself which returned
> as a kind of ghost – I have learned to live
> in peace with what there is.[55]

The house is a protective but also porous surface, a privacy responsive to the call of the external. The house clothes its inhabitants like a skin but also touches the outside, as Carsten and Jones observe: 'The house is an extension of the person; like an extra skin, carapace or second layer of clothes, it serves as much to reveal and display as it does to hide and protect.'[56] The speaker is likened to 'a blood sample' – an index of health and the bonds of kinship – that cannot survive without air, without a permeable, breathable atmosphere. The windows of the house register the reverberation and aftermath of other histories from which its occupant cannot separate. The patrolling 'I' mimics the authority of the household master, but habitation in this space is a thinking or touching back through the mother, rather than an affirmation of patrilinear power. The speaker unravels ties to a maternal past – roses, pearls – in the attempt to articulate 'my differentness', but the final stanza muses

> how far then
> did I get away from the number of letters
> in my mother's maiden name?
> I admit I had not noticed them –
> when you scratch one name you discover others underneath.

The break with the paternal is only partial, as the maiden name returns to the father's name, yet the poem touches upon a notion of hospitality marked by inclusion rather than demarcation. The names discovered are not delimited by the paternal name. The uncovering of layers of identification, and the process of naming without asserting ownership, recalls Bachelard's strange evocation of the maternal house: 'The house clung close to me, like a she-wolf, and at times, I could smell her odour penetrating maternally to my very heart. That night she really was my mother'.[57] The house, a skin that returns the subject to itself and yet cloaks it in another's scent, subjects the singular 'I' to the paternal law of generation yet surrounds that 'I' with the insulation of the maternal. The house becomes part of me, but it exceeds my exclusive possession.

The intimate topography of the 'little gap' between inner and outer doors in McGuckian's poetry (and perhaps the exploration of desacralised dwellings and resistant interiors in Sinéad Morrissey's first three collections) suggest that to which the house cannot be reduced or give house room: determinism, completion, the programmatic. As Bachelard says, it is by remembering houses and rooms that we learn 'to abide within ourselves'.[58] To abide within ourselves, however, is less a matter of declaring or designating one's space than of recognising that the other already belongs, merits welcome, even if the nature of that other who approaches the threshold cannot be determined or anticipated in advance. This moment anterior to naming or categorisation constitutes for Levinas the immanence of ethical responsibility. This discussion has shown how the house has been a site demarcated, furnished, inventoried and occupied in advance for women, a space that has always called into question the singularity, the originality and the primacy of the female poet. The ethical encounter between the two doors that McGuckian describes, and the tentative response to the call of the other that takes place in the gap, can be seen as an opening rather than a breach in the house's defences, an invitation rather than a surrender of sovereignty, a sharing rather than an annexation of space. The house counsels resistance, but cautiously opens its door. McGuckian's house poems offer a fable of interlocution, where we overhear our own strangeness and yet remain capable of hearing, and responding to, *other* others. In McGuckian's work, the house is akin to the intimate neighbour. It is the space that cleaves, the *u-topos* or impossible dwelling that constitutes profound, originary attachment and a perpetual experience of separation. Such ambivalence cannot be thought without regard to the politics of gender, but it cannot be thought *only* in relation to sexual difference. It suggests, rather, the possibility of opening to the other who approaches the threshold of the home. This complex blend of invitation, obligation and responsibility represents the current stakes of thinking in the North, when, after a protracted period stuck on the threshold, exchange is finally taking place in the same room.

6
'Warding off an Epitaph':
Had I a thousand lives

CONOR CARVILLE

Questions of names and naming loom large in Medbh McGuckian's collection *Had I a Thousand Lives* (2003): the act of naming as a mode of control, as a means of change and renewal, and as a token of possession.[1] Most of all, however, naming appears in these poems as a practice of remembrance. In this sense one could argue that behind McGuckian's collection there remains one exemplary poem: W.B. Yeats's great work of naming, remembrance and renewal, 'Easter 1916'. As Yeats puts it there: 'Too long a sacrifice can make a stone of the heart / O, when may it suffice? / That is heaven's part, our part / to murmur name upon name / As a mother names her child'.[2]

Of course, Yeats's poem is itself an example of such murmured remembrance, particularly in its closing litany of those who were executed: 'I write it out in a verse: MacDonagh and MacBride / And Connolly and Pearse.'[3] And yet the poem is also something more, or something less, than that intimate, oral term 'murmuring' might suggest. For it is also a strident, rhetorical text, something implacably written and inscribed. It has, that is to say, the considered calm of the epitaph, as well as the keening quality of the lament, the stolidity of a monument, as well as the immediate, transfiguring power of performative speech. Indeed, the tension between these two aspects is part of the poem's powerful inner dynamic. And, as we shall see, this same tension between the oral and the written, the formal and the personal, the constative and the performative, is very much present in *Had I a Thousand Lives*.

One of the more deceptively immediate poems in the collection, 'A Religion of Writing', concentrates on a gravestone, or on some sort of commemorative structure:

> Despite the thicket, the writing
> is set low, half-empty lines
> with ivy leaves and fruits

acting as punctuation.
such unsteady capitals,

the backward *S*, the *L*
with its foot slanting sharply
downwards, the *B* with detached
loops, a *G* consisting of two opposing
curves, a *Q* with an extended tail

taken up inside, a long palm-like
Y. There are cuts reinforcing
the heads and the forking
of the uprights, letters of smaller
size placed inside others [. . .]

a death's head carved
with a human head inside it.[4]

It seems clear from the references to the 'thicket' that has grown upon or around it that this gravestone has not been raised recently. There is also the strong implication that its letters are fashioned in an archaic, dated way (the 'long palm-like / *Y*'), while the decorative embellishments of 'ivy leaves and fruits' might again suggest a relatively old grave. The headstone also seems to have been weathered to the extent that the lines written upon it are 'half-empty', and it is this sense of emptiness that the poem will concentrate upon, restricting itself to a description of the grave's appearance, and leaving the reader to conjecture as to the identity of its occupant.

At the same time, while doing all this, the poem is careful to insist, again and again, on the placing and act of inscription, on the physical incision of the tombstone. Significantly, however, the resulting capitals are referred to as 'unsteady', 'slanting', 'detached' and 'opposed'. What is more, the way in which the poem lists fragmented letters to create a kind of rebus, leaving us to infer the possible name or epitaph on the tomb, suggests a degree of imaginative freedom, of interpretation on the part of both the narrator and the reader. In this sense, 'A Religion of Writing' delicately balances those two aspects of 'Easter 1916' referred to earlier: the formal permanence of inscription, as against the intimacy of personal interpretation and remembrance. The ambiguity and balance between marmoreal immutability and human agency are beautifully conveyed in the final image of the human head inside the death's head carved.

In contrast to these reservations about naming, many, if not most, of the titles in McGuckian's collection explicitly invoke the proper name of a person or place: 'Slieve Gallion', 'Cathal's Voice', 'The Flower of Tullahogue', 'The Garryduff Bird', to list but some. Many others metaphorically christen a person or place: 'The Chimney Boys', 'The Mule Path', 'The Sleeping Room', 'The Grief Machine', 'The Pyx Sleeper'. This concentration on naming is perhaps inevitable given the ostensible subject of a book which its dust-jacket calls a 'memorial collection, honouring the bicentenary of the resistance organizers Robert Emmet and Thomas Russell'. Both men were executed in 1803, two hundred years before the book appeared. As McGuckian puts it, emphasising the mediated nature of historical knowledge, she is writing of events observed 'through a double roof two posts ago'.[5] Both men were also United Irishmen. In this sense, *Had I a Thousand Lives* extends the interest in the events of 1798 that McGuckian's previous collection *Shelmalier* had begun.[6] Having said this, however, the collection is also very varied, addressing, as the dust-jacket goes on to state, nineteenth-century Irish history, notably the Famine and the decline of the Gaelic language, alongside the Holocaust and the Northern Irish peace process. In the rest of this essay, however, I am going to limit myself to the collection's address to the ideology of commemoration in Irish nationalism, an ideology that in many ways Emmet's death, and the manner of that death, initiated.

Robert Emmet was tried for treason, then hanged and beheaded – what McGuckian calls, with some understatement, 'an assisted death'.[7] The very moment of that beheading is obliquely recorded at various points in the collection. Hence, in 'Low Low Sunday' we find reference to a 'ruined riverscape ferociously / on view, that rushes over a cropped opening – / my blindingly red but yesterday jet of poetry, / that fitted itself like magic into my intensive care –'.[8] This imagery is taken up in greater detail in the final poem of the collection, 'Forcing Music to Speak':

> A white cloud by his mouth,
> he stands on a platform left by ruins
>
> from the eighteenth century,
> before diving into the early nineteenth[9]

McGuckian goes on to compare the 'lifeblood' of the poem's central figure with 'a scarlet flood of sound', and writes of how 'A shock wounds his windpipe' while another 'splits his throat', so that 'his slit throat resounds'.[10] The poem ends:

> His severed head continues to sing
> As it floats down the Heber
> And is immersed in stagnant winter water
>
> To land on the island of Lesbos.[11]

Clearly we are not dealing here with the Robert Emmet known to the Ancient Order of Hibernians. Nevertheless, 'Forcing Music to Speak' does convey some of the power and passion that the Emmet myth aroused, and finds in the image of Orpheus' singing severed head a convincing figure for the extraordinary insistence of Emmet's last words. The poem is also a good example of the way in which this collection continually reflects upon monuments or representations of past lives rather than the lives themselves. The reference above to a figure standing with 'a white cloud by his mouth', for example, suggests a speech-bubble, with the poem voiced by a narrator who is looking at one of the many later cartoons of Emmet's speech from the dock.

Emmet's famous speech is, of course, one of the most quoted in Irish nationalist rhetoric, rivalling Patrick Pearce's graveside orations in both its mantic and mantric status. The condemned man ensures that his name will be remembered through the paradoxical refusal of its commemoration:

> I have but one request to ask at my departure from this world, it is –
> THE CHARITY OF ITS SILENCE – let no man write my epitaph,
> for as no man who knows my motives dare now vindicate them, let
> them and me repose in obscurity and peace, and my tomb remain unin-
> scribed, and my memory in oblivion, until other times, and other men,
> can do justice to my character. When my country takes her place among
> the nations of the earth, *then* and *not till then*, let my epitaph be written.
> I have done.[12]

This idea of the perpetuation of a name through the denial of its recording, the notion that we can more effectively honour the singularity of an existence through failing or refusing to represent it, is at the heart of McGuckian's 'Ring Worn Outside a Glove'.[13] This is a poem that acknowledges Emmet indirectly by approving his rejection of monumental inscription, which it radicalises to include all forms of symbolic coding.

The practice of wearing a ring outside a glove can be interpreted as vulgar ostentation, but also as a kind of flaunting of the symbolic, an over-investment in signs and images. The poem is suspicious of such confidence. This is clear from the less than positive diction of the lines I will quote directly below – 'kills', 'useless', 'shut eyes', 'wasted', 'wither', 'barbaric' – words which suggest a mistrust of the fixing of meaning in any single image or object. McGuckian also explicitly links an absolutist investment in the image with a misplaced fidelity to the past: 'Because we do not deny the image / Of a particular year, the first time / Is always once again.'[14] Thus, there is a criticism here of what we might call a commemorative complacency, of the sense that the historical event can be easily retrieved and represented. What is more, there is also the suggestion that such procedures not only fail to do justice to the complexity of the past, but actually enslave and corrupt those who adhere to such images:

> The picture
> kills the ones around its life
>
> with ropes of useless starlight,
> wasted heaven of last year's burned
> palm. They shut their eyes parading
> and taste themselves with the glittering
>
> pacifism of their tongues,
> as if they were really idols,
> and must wither to decoration,
> barbaric stone pillars we pass by.

The line 'The picture / kills the ones around its life', with its martial, iambic rhythm, could refer both to those who preserve and uphold an ideological image of the past and to the victims of such ideology. We can be more precise as to the identity of the former by attending to the 'ropes of useless starlight', the 'glittering / pacifism of their tongues' and the way in which '[t]hey shut their eyes parading'. As in a later and much more explicit poem, 'Crystal Night', we seem to have reference here to Northern Ireland's July marching season and the uses of historical imagery in Orange banners.[15] In this sense, the 'particular year, whose first time is also once again' could be 1690, and the more local occasion of this poem the annual confrontations at Drumcree in the mid-1990s. Yet the poem is a caution to anyone attempting to recruit the past to the present, and sees the dangers of doing so in terms of a fossilisation into dogmatism, a transformation into 'stone barbaric pillars', a loss of humanity. This reference to 'stone' introduces the notion of monumental commemoration once more, the idea that the worship of the past in the form of a fixed image turns the worshipper into a kind of monument, a testament to one's own death. We are reminded again of Yeats's 'Too long a sacrifice can make a stone of the heart'.

From the very moment of his death Emmet had an effect on major poets both in Ireland and in England. Thomas Moore, Coleridge, Southey, Shelley and others recorded their reactions in verse and prose. Indeed, Coleridge writes of him in a way which curiously anticipates more recent republican protests: 'Emmet = mad Raphael painting Ideals of Beauty on the walls of a cell with human Excrement'.[16] Yeats, too, reflected on Emmet and his legacy, and McGuckian uses some excerpts from his essay 'Emmet as the Apostle of Liberty' to frame her collection.[17] The surpassing, and most popular, response, however, is Thomas Moore's, which begins with a direct reference to praxis and the predicament of poetic naming itself:

> Oh breathe not his name – let it sleep in the shade,
> Where cold and unhonoured his relics are laid;

> Sad, silent and dark, be the tears that we shed,
> As the night-dew that falls on the grass o'er his head.
>
> But the night-dew that falls, though in silence it weeps,
> Shall brighten with verdure the grave where he sleeps;
> And the tear that we shed, though in secret it rolls,
> Shall long keep his memory green in our souls.

We might compare this poem with the first section of McGuckian's 'The Flower of Tullahogue', where, unusually, a strict rhyme scheme is used in conjunction with a fairly regular line length.[18] It is a form which suggests reference to Moore's verse in general, and deploys his customary palette of twilight and dimming, of weakening and failing, of water and the melancholy of memory.

The form of the second part of the poem is significant too, in that it evokes the ballad, the familiar metre being clearly there in the first two lines: 'I drove myself to Morrow Town, / a hundred towns away.' The ballad was, of course, one of the mainstays of the oral culture which preserved and perpetuated the event of Emmet's death in the absence of a more concrete memorial. These references to Moore and the ballad form initially suggest a self-conscious affiliation with popular tradition. As the poem goes on, however, we find the strident opening of the second section progressively undermined by the intrusion of less predictable rhythms and ideas. It is the last two verses that I want to concentrate on in particular:

> I walked there unwetted,
> willing the jewelled river
> to freeze stiffly facing south,
> its body to form a ring.
>
> Can it be that Spring
> parading before my eyes
> was warding off an epitaph
> by planting something stone?

There seems to be an overt reference to Emmet's final speech here, and his attempt to 'ward off', to defer, his own 'epitaph'. However, the references to jewellery and a ring, to parading and a stone, also echo 'Ring Worn Outside a Glove' and the concerns with dogmatism and the fetishisation of the image that we saw there. The effect, I suggest, is to locate the presence of such tendencies as much within nationalism as unionism. Here, McGuckian seems to allow the possibility that Emmet's refusal of inscription may have had consequences as lethal as the styles of over-investment described in the earlier poem. In other words, the refusal of a conventional gravestone may have resulted in a more metaphorical, but equally obdurate and ideological 'planted stone', similar to those barbaric stone pillars of 'Ring Worn Outside a Glove'. Yet such a reading is ultimately unsatisfactory, in that it neither accommodates the speaker's acceptance of his or her own desire to engage in such reification, nor avoids a platitudinous sense of any ideological commitment as inevitably doomed. Rather, the poem, not least in the full rhyme of 'Spring' and 'ring', seems to accept a much more dialectical relationship between flux and stasis, water and ice, the diachronic and the synchronic.

In teasing out these complexities, McGuckian's poems echo and complicate recent concerns in Irish cultural criticism. What seems particularly contemporary about Emmet to many critics is his prophetic sense of the power of the unrepresentable. To be specific, the way in which Emmet engineers his absence from his own memorial, and the subsequent notoriety of this absence, might be a metaphor for the manner in which Luke Gibbons, Terry Eagleton and others see Irish culture as being 'haunted' by events that were never properly symbolised. Eagleton writes of the Famine, for example, as an event so excessive as to defy representation, which has as a consequence shadowed Irish culture ever since.[19]

The theoretical template for Eagleton's analysis is, of course, psychoanalysis (via Jameson's *The Political Unconscious*), and, specifically, the idea that traumatic events must be narrativised, must be pieced together symbolically before they can be laid to rest.[20] The ritual of the funeral, with its prescribed actions and inscriptions, is one example of such a narrativisation or symbolisation. By refusing to allow his name to be inscribed in this sense, Emmet deliberately frustrates the processes of conventional remembrance. For Luke Gibbons, the breakdown of such processes results in alternative forms of remembrance, popular or unconscious memories that are not codified in official memorials.[21] Indeed, Gibbons sees such failures and disruptions of memorialisation as a means of preserving the import and impact of the original events in all their power and alterity. Indeed Gibbons sets up a binary opposition between these two types of remembering: official, inscriptive memorialisation is reifying and constrictive; allegorical, oral, popular remembering, even when 'traumatic', is somehow more authentic. It is one of the valuable aspects of a poem like 'The Flower of Tullahogue', and indeed of the book as a whole, that it resists such oppositions.

Yet, there are times in the book when McGuckian seems to flirt with this rather sentimental elevation of the oral and the communal as the authentic repository of historical truth. One example is the second poem in the collection, 'Slieve Gallion', which begins:

> That great central bone of mountain
> belittling the apple-shaped earth,

or the unhandled marble of its head-bone,
warmed me to the very eye-lids.

Find-spots of judas-coloured blossom
wove bird-lure and man-burning furnaces
on its high-quarried joy –
in a place not to be trodden[22]

Like 'Ring Worn Outside a Glove', this initially seems to be a critique of a cynical or complacent understanding and representation of the past. The landscape becomes a metaphor for historical knowledge, which is seen as a vast mountain, 'belittling [. . .] the earth', and spotted with various meta-historical hazards: traps for the unwary or careless (the 'bird-lure'); unreliable witnesses (the 'judas-coloured blossom'); the presence of ultimately unrepresentable horrors (the 'man-burning furnaces').

In the first stanza McGuckian writes: 'the unhandled marble of its head-bone, / warmed me to the very eyelids'. The crest of the mountain is here seen as composed of sepulchral marble, and this association with the funereal is strengthened by both the repeated metaphor of the bone and the sonic similarities between 'head-bone' and 'headstone'. It is important, too, that the marble is described and approved as 'unhandled', which I take to suggest that it is uninscribed, as opposed to a headstone that might bear a name and epitaph. Hence, there is the suggestion that the mountain holds its meaning in potential: like Emmet's gravestone, it is blank, awaiting its inscription. Furthermore, if the head of the mountain is 'unhandled', the mountain as a whole is 'not to be trodden'. And so to the lack of inscription is added a sense of reserve, a taboo against a trespassing that heightens the sense of the mountain as unmarked. The poem continues, however:

The neck-fetters of an asphalt smooth,
regrettably modern road paved the thread
of its voice – its breath-poem
into battle-letters, its mouth music

into a pocketful of women-nation-
voters.[23]

It might initially seem that what we have here is a continuation of the opposition between the blankness of the 'unhandled' mountain and its potential disfigurement; however, a closer look confirms that a subtle modification has taken place. The opposition is not now one between blankness and inscription, but one between voice and writing. Thus, we have the 'neck-fetters' of the 'regrettably modern road' displacing the fragile 'thread'-like voice. This opposition then modulates into the juxtaposition of the 'mouth-music' and 'breath-poem' of the landscape against the 'battle-letters', the alphabetical inscription, of encroaching modernity. In this way historical authenticity becomes associated not only with a landscape seen as 'unhandled' and untrodden, but also with the voice and the breath. Inscription, on the other hand, is related to captivity, modernity and the prosaic concerns of parliamentary democracy: 'a pocketful of women-nation-voters'. The effect is to privilege the spoken, and presumably Gaelic, word as natural, and the 'battle-letters' of English as a construct, a 'regrettable' and inauthentic imposition. It is perhaps this lost and unadulterated natural voice which McGuckian refers to as the absent 'monosexual' river in the final stanza: 'I looked fifteen times / for that monosexual, banished river / smell, for its unnailing.'[24] The fact that the narrator repeatedly looks for, and fails to find, this singular river suggests that it is never to be recovered, and these last lines of the poem thus go some way towards undermining its earlier somewhat nostalgic and sentimental elements.

Yet this association of Gaelic with nature and the cultural with English is, of course, a very familiar nationalist trope, and so, despite the equivocation of the last lines, the poem's central equation is still somewhat hackneyed. Yet it is an equation which runs through a number of other poems in the collection, perhaps most explicitly in 'The Mirror Game', but also in a poem like 'Asking for the Alphabet Back'.[25] At times, in other words, Emmet's deferral of inscription is radicalised into a suspicion not just of language and commemoration in general, but of the English language as a means of representing Irish experience. Thus, in 'Cathal's Voice', the narrator's 'native silence' is contrasted with 'All the rich juices of the first official language / bulged in the woody sequence of plants / along the hedge, where leaf / was at home with delicate-tongued / leaf'.[26] Here again the landscape seems to be sentimentally identified with 'the first official language', with the suggestion that the history this landscape conceals can only be accessed through Gaelic's 'delicate tongue'. Crucially, however, this poem concludes with a string of metaphors that infer, by turns, alienation, defensiveness and tentativeness:

> It took the feeble shape
>
>> of battlements around my lilac neck,
>> or a Hesitation valse through numb
>> furniture, the late returning traffic
>> of that completely bilingual, attempted embrace.

The reference to 'bilingualism' here forces us to reconsider the attachment to, and nostalgia for, Gaelic as an authentic or natural language detected earlier in the poem. It also stands in opposition to that 'monosexual' river which the narrator of 'Slieve Gallion' sentimentally and fruitlessly searched for. If the poem still laments the narrator's lack of facility in Gaelic – her 'native silence' – it also recognises that any 'traffic' with the past must be, in a sense, doubled. We can read this acceptance or advocacy of bilingualism as a call for, to slip into the language of the Good Friday Agreement, the acknowledgement of the 'two traditions'. However, a more interesting reading might suggest that the poem recognises the radical estrangement of the present from the past, the idea, in other words, that any responsible relationship with history will always involve a kind of translation from the language of the past into that of the present. The poem implies, in a sense, that the text of history can never be read in the original, so that the last line sees McGuckian's 'late-returning traffic' with the eighteenth century as still only an 'attempted embrace'. There is, thus, a further recognition here that the kind of judicious balancing that bilingualism suggests means there can never be a full possession of the past, in the same way that there can never be a perfect translation. Yet it is perhaps such a metaphorical bilingualism that allows a perpetual 'traffic', an exchange between present and past that would avoid the fossilisation out-lined in 'Ring Worn Outside a Glove' and 'The Flower of Tullahogue'.

The examination of such delicate balancing is present elsewhere in the collection. In the marvellous poem 'Reading in a Library', for example, we find descriptions of an interlocutor's moving from one language to another, and again it is around the question of the name that the issue crystallises:

> You wake me up with the name
> I carry inside me like a first
> language. It becomes needles
> on your lips, slightly grey, a waste
> of light I swallow like a syrup.
>
> A tree forks at the level
> of your eyes, it spreads my dark
> dipthong upwards like a cup,
> I place myself expectantly
> under your open hand.[27]

As many writers and researchers would attest, falling asleep in the library is something of an occupational hazard. Typically, however, McGuckian uses such an occasion as a metaphor for her own less than empirical historiography. Thus, although the main figure seems to be startled into consciousness at the beginning, I prefer to read this poem as having the narrator wake into a dream, to see it, in other words, as a kind of *aisling* or vision poem. By doing so, one can identify the figure interrupting the protagonist as an avatar, or ghost, of one of the historical figures whose life McGuckian has delved into for her collection. We also seem to have a meditation on the Irish language here, and, once again, as mentioned above, on the name and the process of naming. Hence, the reference in the first stanza to a 'name [. . .] like a first language' echoes 'Cathal's Voice', and its concern with the 'first official language', while the 'dark diphthong' of the second verse leads us to McGuckian's own name, 'Medbh', with its explicitly Gaelic orthography. Such a name is at once a 'first language' for the narrator, a primordial, intimate identity, and yet at the same time part of a 'first official language' (Gaelic) that she feels distanced from, one that she is unable to fully call her own. This double relation of self to name is reflected in the way the narrator describes it both in terms of 'needles' that might irritate, and of a medicine that can soothe ('syrup'). As the poem continues into the second and third verses, however, a slightly different tone emerges, though again it is the sense of doubleness that is emphasised:

> You talk with your hands
> like two people, you zigzag
> softly from person to person,
> rubbing my names together
> as if that were your goal,
>
> not pushing my thoughts into
> the space beneath the bed.[28]

If we take the interaction between the narrator of the poem and the other who wakes her by speaking her name as representative of the relationship between McGuckian and the historical figures she is writing about, we can see that the relationship here is more positive than in the previous poems we have considered. In 'Cathal's Voice' the 'traffic' between past and present was seen as belated, 'late-returning', and there was an emphasis on the absolute otherness of the past, the 'lupins like corpses', etc. The tone here is much more accommodating and positive. Although the historical object is still seen as elusive, 'zig-zagging from person to person', the common, everyday phrase 'talk with your hands' introduces a lovely intimacy which still retains a trace of the difficulties of interpretation, the need to elaborate and amplify the speech of the dead. The zig-zagging movement also belies the teleological, goal-orientated history criticised in 'Ring Worn Outside a Glove', replacing this with the more intimate, sensual and almost gratuitous action of 'rubbing names together'. It is also worth noting that the narrator assumes a stance of openness and receptiveness with the phrase 'I place myself expectantly / under your open hand', receiving the speech of the other rather than constructing a version of it: as in an *aisling* the image is thus not one that is summoned, but one which appears. Indeed, the poem as a whole does not attempt to interpret or reproduce the voice of the other figure, but is content to merely describe the forms of his or her speech. This adds to a general sense of plurality and possibility rather than the fixity of an image. Anxieties about a lack of proficiency in language, and a consequent lack of empathy with the past, are replaced by a sense of the possibility of interpretation. Such a sense of freedom is again, however, qualified by the end:

> I bring a sentence to your body,
> brimming like an island, I sit
> filled with that, as with a bible.[29]

One can read these lines in such a way that it is 'the sentence' 'brought to your body' that 'brims like an island', so that we find here an affirmation of the power and plenitude of the imagination. Yet one can also interpret the object of the main clause in line two as being the body of the poet herself: it is McGuckian that brims with the fruits of her own imagining. In this sense, the two-way 'traffic', the bilingual relation with the past of 'Cathal's Voice' is here reaffirmed. The active way in which the poet brings her words to the inert body of the past is balanced by the way that the past inhabits her own body. There is a further ambiguity in the final clause. On the one hand it could suggest that the poet's body is filled 'as with a bible', a phrase which again implies a passive religious possession, a deferral to the impersonal power of the Word. On the other hand, it also has connotations of the intense concentration of biblical reading and exegesis: thus, the poet sits filled with the sentences of her own imagination as if she were reading a bible. Again, the ambiguity here is beautifully balanced between activity and passivity.

And yet with all this, McGuckian also artfully insinuates a compelling undertone of judgement and violence by using that word 'sentence': there is the suggestion of a possible complicity here between poet, judge and executioner. By 'writing it out in a verse', as Yeats put it, by constructing this collection, McGuckian is still acutely aware of the possibility that she is betraying the singularity of the past, condemning it to death. Yet the subsequent reference to the bible, Scripture itself, seems to indicate a *rapprochement* with the idea of inscription. In this sense, I see the last lines of the poem as beautifully equating the ethical resources of written Scripture with the imaginative power of poetry. In conclusion, I would suggest that the ghost, or avatar, to which this poem refers is Thomas Russell, Emmet's friend and accomplice. Russell was bilingual in Gaelic and English, and was fascinated by scriptural matters, as so many of the radicals of the period were. In his final speech he asked for a few days' reprieve so that he could finish a study and interpretation of the Book of Revelation.[30] He was refused and, like Emmet, was hanged and beheaded. It is from the same speech that *Had I a*

Thousand Lives takes its title. McGuckian's collection allows us as readers to participate in a painstaking process of remembrance of that death by foregrounding the difficulties of such a commemorative enterprise. It is in the contradictions, ambiguities and opacity of these poems, the way that they restlessly stage the complexities of commitment, history and poetry, that Emmet and Russell have found perhaps their most profound contemporary memorial.

7

'That Now Historical Ground':
Memory and atrocity in the poetry
of Medbh McGuckian

SHANE ALCOBIA-MURPHY

> Remembrance shapes our links to the past, and the ways we
> remember define us in the present. As individuals and societies,
> we need the past to construct and anchor our identities and to
> nurture a vision of the future.[1]

When searching for ways to impose a meaningful order upon reality, we rely
on memory for 'the provision of symbolic representations and frames which
can influence and organize both our actions and our conceptions of ourselves'.[2] However, in the aftermath of the Belfast Agreement and the creation
of the Northern Ireland Assembly narratives produced by the media and
governmental institutions have been underscored by a pronounced and predominant process of selective forgetting whereby the awkward sectarian
complexities of the Troubles have been erased or archived. Hence, as Colin
Graham's recent research has documented, a recurrent trope has emerged in
Northern Irish culture of 'an ache which notices, knows, but can barely
comment on the cauterisation of the dark complexity of the past'; hence,
'the difficult and the embarrassingly recent past, or the irritatingly non-con-
forming present, is archived'.[3] Excessive remembrance may lead to madness,
but forgetfulness carries its own inherent dangers, and Northern Irish
writers and visual artists have consistently guarded against any politically
expedient embrace of amnesia. For example, contrary to those who wished
to forgive and forget amidst euphoric post-conflict jubilation, the poet
Michael Longley weighed in with prudent counsel, arguing that 'amnesty
isn't amnesia' and that '[i]n order to make sure it doesn't happen again', he
warns that 'you've got to remember it in great detail. Those who forget
history are the ones who are doomed to repeat it.'[4] This point is made graph-
ically in Jack Pakenham's large canvas *Lest We Forget*, painted following the
Downing Street Declaration. In his poetic commentary on this painting,
Pakenham declares:

> In their eagerness for Peace
> the dead were all forgotten
> the lies were all forgiven
> and someone said
> 'Let's pretend it never happened . . . .'[5]

Much of the recent cultural production from Northern Ireland retains a marked scepticism towards what Graham terms 'archive fever'. For example, Willie Doherty's visual artworks are often ghosted by history, preoccupied as they are by that which is unresolved. *Ghost Story* (2007), a single-channel video installation with a voiceover by Stephen Rea, presents a narrative that 'evokes memories of the dead and a sense of loss and foreboding, as their haunting presence is made palpable'.[6] More specifically, the speaker's first memory returns to 30 January 1972 and what he witnessed on Bloody Sunday:

> The scene reminded me of the faces in a running crowd that I had once seen on a bright but cold January afternoon. Men and women slipped on icy puddles as they ran for safety. [. . .] Troops spewed from the back of the vehicle as it screeched to a sudden halt. They raised their rifles and fired indiscriminately into the fleeing crowd. [. . .] The narrow streets and alleyways that I walked along became places where this invisible matter could no longer be contained. It seeped out through every crack and fissure in the worn pavements and crumbling walls.[7]

Since the Saville Report has not yet been published and the victims' families still have not received justice, Doherty's work demonstrates how the traumatic past still has a perniciously over-arching influence on the present. Similarly, David Park's most recent novel, *The Truth Commissioner* (2008), imagines what it would be like if a Truth Commission were established in Northern Ireland; rather than achieving satisfactory closure, each character is left haunted by the past, unable to lay their personal ghosts to rest.[8] Perhaps the starkest example of Northern Irish artworks which counter both amnesia and historical fixity is Eoghan McTigue's *All Over Again* (2004), a series of photographs documenting erased murals in loyalist and republican areas of Belfast. Loyalist and republican murals have had as their primary function the 'political mobilisation within their respective communities' and are intended as 'political education or reinforcement'.[9] Although the versions of history encoded within the murals of each community contend with one another for legitimacy and recognition, as artworks they are not intended as immutable or fixed; they are often painted over depending on the shifting Northern Irish political realities. While McTigue's images of whitewashed murals capture such moments of transition, they do not simply signal the erasure or over-writing of previous texts; rather, these 'spectrally suggestive shrouds of interred images and political slogans' have, as Aaron Kelly has argued, the status of 'blank or open signifiers' and 'attest to the dynamics of historical process, its continual renegotiation of both the past and the present, and the layering of evermore subsumed communal memories in its wake'.[10] The photographic images invite the viewer to acknowledge historical narratives as social constructs and to be aware (if not wary) of the hand that seeks to draw support for its own version of remembrance.

Each of the texts mentioned above suggests that peace should encourage self-reflexivity, not a negligent wholesale indifference to history. Renouncing the often propagandist reconstruction of the past which occurs in Northern Ireland, Longley advocates 'a mixture of affirmation, self-interrogation and mutual curiosity': 'To bring to light all that has been repressed can be a painful process; but, to quote the American theologian Don Shriver: "The cure and the remembrance are co-terminous."'[11] This is the approach adopted by Medbh McGuckian in a number of her later poems which seek to bring to light forgotten or neglected atrocities and matters of historical controversy. Her texts draw on the work of historians and cultural commentators who have striven to break the silence surrounding key historical events; she quotes from a variety of sources, including letters composed during the American Civil War, French literature produced within the Nazi prisons and concentration camps, interviews given by the children of Holocaust survivors, and documentary evidence detailing post-war abuse meted out to German civilians. Within each poem, there is a juxtaposition of intertexts which, once uncovered, forces the reader to meditate on the role of art in a time of violence and the ethics of poetic composition. Within many of the texts there is an implicit parallel made between Ireland and those other areas of conflict; indeed, when asked if she felt that there was 'a rush "to forget" the past in post-ceasefire Northern Ireland', and whether she makes analogies between other instances of historical silencing and that of her own time, she replied with a blunt, impassioned 'yes to all those questions!'[12]

In the opening stanzas of 'Corduroy Road'[13] the speaker refers to an unspecified 'historical ground' situated 'not far from Richmond'. The source text being used is David W. Blight's *When This Cruel War Is Over*, a study of a collection of letters from 1861–4 documenting the experiences of Charles Harvey Brewster, who served in the 10th Massachusetts Regiment during the American Civil War. Blight's analysis argues that those who fought in the Civil War experienced conflicting emotions, running 'from naïveté to mature realism, from romantic idealism to sheer terror, from self-pity to enduring devotion':[14]

that now historical ground (DB 158)	That now historical ground
growing wheat (DB 122); an Oatfield	of growing wheat, an oatfield,
not far from Richmond (DB 136);	a clover field, not far from Richmond,

a clover field (DB 134)	
faded into light green (DB 169)	is faded into light green,
ripe and suffering (DB 340)	ripe and suffering,
covered with dirt and pitch (DB 169)	is covered with dirt and pitch,
the sentimentalized blossoms	the sentimentalized blossoms
outlast the stench (DB 17)	outlast the stench.

The second stanza cites Blight's observation that combatants often mask ugliness and horror when writing about war, not only as a self-protective measure, but also as a means of shielding loved ones from atrocity: '[s]entimentalized blossoms so often outlast and even replace the stench of the dead and the vileness of war.'[15] Within McGuckian's text, the quotation extends Blight's argument to suggest that historiography and commemoration can equally render the reality of war as safe and distant for those in the present: the poem's word choice – 'covered', 'faded', 'outlast the stench' – confirms that the site of conflict has become 'that now historical ground' in the sense of being firmly relegated to the past. Yet the poem refuses to participate in the whitewash and insistently dwells on the psychological effects of war:[16]

the compass that had been built into me (DB 64)	It was a compass built into me,
militarization of thought (DB 368)	the militarization of my thought,
the crackling shots were to him like voices (DB 65)	their shots were to me like voices . . .

In the context of the American Civil War 'militarization of thought' refers to what Blight discerns as 'a male tradition deeply ingrained in American society, and one that common and less literary-inclined men like Brewster had helped to cultivate. Brewster's own manly compass sent him irresistibly off to war' (DB 64). Individual volition is negated due to the war effort, and Brewster's imagination is left, like Henry Fleming in Stephen Crane's *The Red Badge of Courage*, tormented by the sounds of battle; the 'shots' may be 'like voices', but they drown out *his* voice. The poem is, then, about different kinds of erasure: the consignment of an atrocious war to the realms of history; the neglect in historical scholarship of the suffering of ordinary soldiers in favour of analyses which treat the war 'as almost exclusively an affair of presidents and generals' (DB 4); and the enforced silencing of Blight's own voice due to codes of manliness and etiquette.

McGuckian's poem is not, however, specifically about the historiographical treatment of the American Civil War: not only is the source unacknowledged, and hence does not overtly direct the reader's interpretation, her choice of lexis in the following stanzas ('Caravat'; 'Hassidic sidecurls'), indicates contexts other than that of mid-1800s America. She is, in fact, incorporating quotations from two other historical studies of conflict and atrocity, namely Martin Gilbert's *The Boys: Triumph over Adversity*, an absorbing study of the experiences of 732 Jewish post-war refugees who came to Britain, and a collection of essays entitled *Irish Peasants: Violence and Political Unrest, 1780–1914*:[17]

'I would go outside and lie	I would go outside and lie
Naked in the dry sand' (MG 156)	naked in the dry sand
Caravat lips (IP 83)	for their Caravat lips, because they were
dry and tightly folded (DB viii); Hassidic sidecurls (MG 7)	dry and folded, for their Hassidic sidecurls.
I have just counted (DB 161)	I have just counted
rain of bullets [. . .] I felt the wind of them (DB 142)	the wind of giddy bullets
the first giddy days (DB 17); the woven bread (MG 9)	woven into my bread.

Textually, the intertexts become 'woven' together like the Jewish *challah* (woven bread) and the distinctions between contexts become blurred; the time of rest on the Sabbath is not kept separate from the time of conflict. The 'I' here becomes an amalgam of different participants/victims of war and the juxtaposition of intertexts asserts their commonality in suffering. First, we have Michael Etkind, a survivor of the Lodz labour camp, who attests to the hardship of camp life: '"At night we could not sleep because of the fleas. [. . .] I would go outside and lie naked in the dry sand. Anything was better than being stung by those jumping beasts that no one could catch"' (MG 156). The 'I' then morphs into a member of the Caravats (*Carabhaití*), a Whiteboy faction that took part in the agrarian unrest in Munster, 1802–11, until finally changing back into Charles Brewster as his experience of civil war is transformed from the 'giddiness' of his first days in the army (DB 17) to his more anxious acknowledgement of war's reality:

> Our loss in killed and wounded yesterday is reckoned at 300 though I suppose it is not known yet. I have just counted and their heavy guns are firing at a rate of 24 a minute, and whenever these big shells are falling at that rate, it is a very hot place to be in. (DB 161)

Towards the poem's conclusion McGuckian incorporates yet another source, Hélène Cixous's *Three Steps on the Ladder of Writing*,[1] and presents a meta-commentary on her own procedures, an artistic credo summarising the poem's intent:

others were spirited away (DB 19)	Others were spirited away
toward black freedom (DB 18)	to black freedom,
plunge into (DB 109); unburying (HC 6)	plunging into the unburying earth
the desired outcome (IP 124)	of the desired Ireland,
young, present, ferocious, fresh death, the	young, precious, ferocious, fresh death,
death of the day, today's death (HC 7)	death of the day, today's death . . .
there's breath; let's keep it (HC 4)	but there's breath, let's keep it,
this is what we are made of (HC 6)	till it's what we are made of.

At first, the reader assumes that the text is detailing a series of conclusions: the fate of the black slaves (which forms part of the rationale behind the American Civil War) who are 'spirited away' into freedom; the Caravats' aim at achieving 'the desired Ireland'; and the 'death' (thrice repeated) of so many young soldiers. Yet in what way is the earth 'unburying'? Each of the authors whose work is included in the poem have, as their mission, the aim of unearthing forgotten or neglected details about the lives of those who have been affected by war. For Cixous (and, by extension, for McGuckian), '[g]iving oneself to writing means being in a position to do this work of digging, of unburying' (HC 6); for the author, '[w]riting is this effort not to obliterate the picture, not to forget' (HC 7). This is the sense in which the writer *needs* 'ferocious, fresh death': it is the source material for writers. One can make sense of McGuckian's curious use of 'I' in her poem by referring to the key trope used by Cixous, the graphic symbol 'H': 'I have drawn the *H*. You will have recognized it depending on which language you are immersed in. This is what writing is: *I* one language, *I* another language, and between the two, the line that makes them vibrate; writing forms a passageway between two shores' (HC 3). McGuckian's poem bridges the gap between a multitude of 'I's and together they form the 'H', a symbol in which one hears (in French) both death (*ash*) and the instrument for clearing new paths ('*hache* [axe]').

It is often argued that the historian, in constructing a narrative of the past, must tentatively negotiate between the related imperatives to remember and to forget; that is, to avoid an intransigent, melancholic obsession with the past – what Kevin Whelan terms 'the entropy of the traumatic version of memory'[19] – yet equally avoid the destruction or erosion of 'traces'.[20] Yet there are times when the historian, for political expediency, deems it necessary to suppress evidence of traumatic events and participate in a state-sponsored culture of silence. As Dominick LaCapra notes:

> Even in Israel, the immediate aftermath of the Shoah was typified by denial and resistance as Israelis forged a concept of the redemptive nation and its heroic inhabitants that presented the Diaspora as a time of erring that culminated in catastrophe for nationless, hence powerless, Jews. Survivors were often constrained to adopt a new identity and be silent not only about the old one but about the way it was destroyed and devastated.[21]

Referring precisely to such Zionist efforts to establish and justify the new post-war state of Israel, Ronit Lentin, in her ground-breaking monograph on gender and the Shoah, describes how that state denigrated concentration camp survivors, actively promoting myths of their 'supposed passivity, weakness, pathology, and non-virility'; they became 'the Jewish other' in contrast

to the new 'virile' and 'heroic' Israeli society.[22] Lentin argues that, just as survivors were 'tutored in self-silencing during the Shoah' (6) – partly as a result
of what Primo Levi terms the Third Reich's 'Orwellian falsification of
memory, falsification of reality, negation of reality'[23] – so too were they
'silenced by pre-State and early Zionist narratives that privileged heroic
myths constructed around the partisans and around Erez Israeli youth' (6).
Such silence informed and shaped Lentin's own childhood and that of her
generation.

   McGuckian is alive to ways in which, as Huyssen argues, '[t]he place of
memory in any culture is defined by an extraordinarily complex discursive
web of ritual and mythic, historical, political and psychological factors'
(Huyssen 250), and she uses Lentin's study as the basis for 'She Thinks She
Sees Clarissa',[24] a poem of eight six-line stanzas, making an implicit analogy
between the deliberate erasure of memory post-Shoah and her own intimate
experience of 'forgetting' (the text on the left is from Lentin's *Israel and the
Daughters of the Shoah*):

And I patrolled the windows and the house (56)	I patrolled the windows and the house,
Walking in front of the mirror in varying angles (60)	walking in front of the mirror in varying angles.
If I stood close to the mirror (46); I was suffocated	If I stood too close I suffocated
when I wrote it (46); the text is very dense,	I was so very concentrated there,
concentrated, like . . . a blood sample which was left	like a blood sample left standing
standing (46); It hasn't got a breath of air (46)	without a breath of air.

   The poem's opening delineates a policing of space through sight, a
panoptic practice which, as de Certeau argues, 'proceeds from a place
whence the eye can transform foreign forces and objects that can be
observed and measured'.[25] The space is not described as homely or familiar,
nor is there a hint of secure proprietorship; rather, the house is viewed as
threatening or threatened. Hence, the speaker's actions constitute not an intimate haptic negotiation with her environment, but rather a distanced, optical
interaction, a quotidian reflex borne out of disquiet. Imposing a strict scopic
regime, the speaker describes how, in the past, she adopted a defensive
posture with regard to an unspecified exterior threat – 'I patrolled the
windows and the house' – one which is symptomatic of an interiorised guilt
or sense of danger that forced the subject to regulate her behaviour and self-
image, 'walking in front of mirrors in varying angles'. She could not
countenance an engagement with her reflection: the sight 'suffocated' her
when viewed too closely. To become the object of her regard, almost as if she
were 'a blood sample left standing', was too painful for her to bear and necessitated self-repression. Indeed, the act of figuring herself as a 'blood sample'
constitutes a deliberate attempt at estrangement. Paradoxically, then, her constant introspection was maintained to avoid self-reflection; she had, with due
vigilance, to remember to forget. '[S]o very concentrated' here connotes not

simply her mental activity, but also its resultant ambiguous effects: not only a sense of overpowering constriction, but also a welcome degree of protective self-containment. The image of a 'blood sample' – something which can be used to confirm one's identity or be used to diagnose a suspected illness – suggests, through a metonymic logic of association, a diseased subjectivity: she renders herself as 'other', as objectified, fragmented, ready (and needing) to be tested.

Lentin's patrolling of the house was a curious replication of her own mother's behaviour; in Freudian terms, it emerged as 'the unwitting re-enactment of an event that one simply cannot leave behind'.[26] McGuckian uses Lentin's text to embody and convey her own experience. The stanza uses quotations from Lentin's interview with the Israeli novelist Nava Semel who, like Lentin, belonged to 'the category of silent families' (33), but who 'had broken the silence about the Shoah in her own family and in Israeli society' (29). Much of the poem's opening uses excerpts that refer to Semel's debut collection of short stories entitled *A Hat of Glass*, which she wrote after learning of her mother's experiences in Auschwitz:

> *A Hat of Glass* was simply an investigation, myself in front of the mirror, therefore the text is very dense, concentrated, like, pardon the analogy, like a blood sample which was left standing and began congealing. It has many congealing factors, this book. I cannot read it today, I find it very difficult, very difficult. It hasn't got a breath of air. I was suffocated when I wrote it, but I didn't realise how suffocating it is to read. Therefore I cannot read it today. [. . .] I mean, if I stood close to the mirror for *A Hat of Glass*, in the other books a process of distancing begins and I look at the reflection from other angles too. (46)

Using Semel's tropes, McGuckian is also breaking silence with her own text since it was written following her mother's revelations about what it was like growing up during the Second World War and in a sectarian society: 'The key informant is my mum [. . .] She does not discuss her violent past but refers obliquely to being burnt out and in the Blitz. She rosy coloured everything so we would not be aware of being second class citizens.'[27] Both the poem and Semel's collection, then, involve painful journeys of self-discovery for their respective authors.

The trajectory of Semel's narrative of self-discovery is plotted as follows by Lentin:

> Semel's narrative is clearly organised and channels to one central the-matic field, which occupies the final part of the narrative, the trajectory from (a) what Semel describes as 'the position of the rejected', the embodiment of the offspring of the diaspora Jew, the survivor, the 'lamb to the slaughter'; to (b) learning 'to live with in peace with what there is'.

In other words, a trajectory from being a silenced child of survivors, living with the secret world of the 'code word "Auschwitz"', in an Israel which internalised, yet repressed, the memory of the Shoah, to an adult writer who is using her writing as the 'closing of circles'. (Lentin 30)

Such a structure finds its parallel in the opening stanzas of McGuckian's text as it moves from 'without a breath of air' to being 'in peace with what there is' (both lines occur at the end of their respective verses and both stand out as they are written in iambic trimeter):

'every inch' (R 35); 'final yellow' (R 170); 'slight shine' (R 169); 'radiance is the after glow of the explosive (R 169); 'too easily inspired' (R 162) 'now touch itself returns as a ghost' (R 169) learning 'to live in peace with what there is' (Lentin 30)	Every inch of its final yellow, slight shine had the radiant afterglow of the explosive if I touched it I was too easily inspired because it was touch itself which returned as a kind of ghost – I have learned to live in peace with what there is.

However, the 'peace' in McGuckian's poem is an uneasy, almost resigned one at this stage: silence prevails here, with the speaker unable or unwilling to identify the twice-mentioned 'it'. The past has returned as a 'ghost' through the speaker's bodily engagement with her environment; an index perhaps of a return of the repressed with which the speaker pointedly refuses to engage in her writing for ethical reasons ('too easily inspired'). Yet just as the penultimate line's enjambment renders the 'peace' ambiguous (either enforced or embraced), so too does the stanza's intertext.

Five of the lines are taken from a collection of essays on the American abstract expressionist Mark Rothko (who was also from a Jewish family that suffered persecution),[28] and the juxtaposition of sources here works ekphrastically: the stanzas made up of different sources mimic Rothko's signature style (symmetrical rectangular blocks of opposing, yet complementary colours). The source book emphasises that 'the success of a Rothko painting hinges not just on the details of pigment present on canvas but somehow extends to the nature of the viewing encounter itself' (R 1). Just as Rothko's art can be viewed as serene, mystical, transcendental or tragic, depending on the way in which one views it, the meaning (and experience) of a McGuckian poem shifts according to both one's knowledge of its sources and context, and one's perception of its poetic effects. Indeed, many of the phrases used by McGuckian refer to the varying experiences that occur when one encounters a Rothko:

There is a slow unfolding of the apperception of these works – of the thickening and thinning of the paint, of the tightening and loosening of the strokes, of the furrows tracing a shape, of ghostly skeletal shapes that fix the picture as an uncanny afterimage. Here 'radiance is the after glow of the explosive,' as Rothko recorded in a notebook. Rothko had always

liked the effect of shadowy vestiges, but now touch itself returns as a
ghost. (R 169)

McGuckian, in registering the conflictual dimension of his art, is alluding to
Rothko's belief in "'the tragic irreconcilability of the basic violence which
lies at the bottom of human existence and the daily life which must deal
with it'" (R 4). Hence, in two stanzas characterised by stillness, she incorporates unsettling images – 'patrolled', 'suffocated', 'blood sample', 'explosive',
'ghost' – which intimate the tragic reality underlying the seemingly
mundane.

I remember a real mention (33)	I remember a real mention
a 'key informant' (29); in my head,	by my key informant: in my head
I added two and two (34); That means	I added two and two, which means
that five years were missing (35)	that five years were missing.
It took me years to unravel all those roses	It took me years to unravel all the roses;
because they were embroidered very tightly	they were embroidered tightly, those pearls,
these pearls (44)	
there were different weights of	with their different weights of memory
memory (43); senses here differentness (45)	in which I sensed my differentness.
I was breaking something [. . .] seemingly	I was breaking something seemingly on purpose;
on purpose (45); I had a picture in my head	I had a picture in my head of me
of me doing it and my mother watching	doing it, my mother
and saying nothing (44)	watching me, saying nothing.

In the third and fourth stanzas we witness the revelation of a concealed
past, termed by Lentin as 'a black hole in her [mother's] biography' (35)
caused by a necessary dissociation from a traumatic past. The momentous
uncovering of a secret about one's family's past can have the effect of rendering one's world unreal or uncanny. Speaking about his own family's past
as outlined in his novel *Reading in the Dark*, Seamus Deane stated:

> The first effect is to make everything phantasmal. Everything you
> thought was secure and actual has now become almost ghostly and
> haunting, and yet at the same time, the very moment it becomes that, it
> becomes super-real: it is the reality that puts the quotidian, one that you
> thought was secure, out of court.[29]

In McGuckian's poem, however, everything becomes less phantasmal as the
speaker is finally able to rationalise her own 'differentness'; disclosure is here
marked as 'a real mention'. The images of 'roses' and 'pearls' come from
Lentin, referring to an evening purse of black velvet, embroidered with
pearls and tapestry-style roses, which had belonged to her mother and which
was the only physical reminder of her hidden past that she had in her possession. Due to their indexical relation to the past, such material objects can
carry too many traumatic memories so, just as Vladek in Art Spiegelman's
celebrated graphic novel *Maus* strives to silence the traumatic past by

burning his wife's notebooks,[30] Lentin's mother allows her daughter 'to unravel this thing for years, to ruin it, until it fell apart with my childhood things' (44). The image and verb choice are fortuitous as they indicate that writing is instrumental to the recovery process. To 'unravel' means both 'to undo a woven fabric' and to free a text (*textus*: tissue of a literary work, literally that which is woven) from intricacy or obscurity. However, while such writing may lead to closure eventually, here it is figured as a process and a coping strategy; 'pearls' and 'roses' still displace 'the real' as the story remains untold. Indeed, the structure of Semel's *Hat of Glass*, to which McGuckian alludes, demonstrates this fracturing and fractured experience: 'The researcher [. . .] noted that *I was breaking something* which is structured as a novel into short stories, but which I am turning *seemingly on purpose* into short stories' (45, emphasis added).

That was the end of its life (44)	That was the end of its life, no one
no one ever said a word (44);	ever said a word. But how far then
How far did I get away (51)	did I get away from the number of letters
	in my mother's maiden name?
I admit I had not noticed it (45)	I admit I had not noticed them –
when you scratch the Israeli	when you scratch one name you discover others
names [. . .] you discover Yiddish	underneath.
names (50–1)	
The root is not clear, but it is	The root is not clear, but it is probably
probably one of the versions of *Or*	one of the versions meaning 'light'
['light' in Hebrew] (51); Here	in the pre-language. Here again I stop her flow,
again I stop her flow (55);	saying she has renamed herself,
She was given exactly three	she was given exactly three minutes
minutes to change her name [. . .]	to change her name to the first that came to mind.
the first name that came to her mind (50)	

The suppression of the Shoah victims' experience was compounded by the erasure of family names and the pressure to adopt a Hebrew name: 'when you scratch the Israeli names of the 1950s', says Semel, 'you discover Yiddish names' (50–1). This re-naming has its corollary in McGuckian's biography and allows her to empathise with Semel's account: 'The fact that I spell my name in Irish is significant, because it's a re-Gaelicized version of what was previously anglicized. In a way I'm an English poet, trying to reverse into an Irishness that is an impossible dream. I was christened "Maeve".'[31] For McGuckian, the change of name is a political act of resistance, an assertion of her Irish identity within a British state; with Semel (and her mother), however, re-naming entails a dislocation (if not repression) of memory.

she refuses to see or read (47);	She refuses to see or read, although she thinks
thinks she sees Clarissa (45);	she sees Clarissa. It is important
it's important for her to fortify	for her to fortify herself
herself (47); exist by remote	so that she can exist by remote control.
control (48); the pills by the bed	The pills by the bed and the glass of water.

and the glass of water (46); Is it
already ten? Is it already eleven? (213)

Is it already four? Is it already five?

he dealt with the before, or the
after (54); it is a world based [. . .]
not on remembering (50); there
was a feeling of war at home all
the time (74); memory that was
too big for us (50); on a Day of
Independence eve (48)

She deals with the Before and the After,
the confection of belonging in reverse
to a world based on not remembering
there was a feeling of war at home
all the time, a memory far too big
for us, on a Day of Independence eve.

The poem's concluding stanzas reinforce the reader's sense of the difficulty of dealing with 'a memory far too big': the speaker's mother can confront 'the Before and the After', but not the unspeakable period spent under Nazi rule. To live in 'a world based on not remembering' is safe; one can 'exist by remote control'. Yet the poem insists on the importance of memory (linked here to 'independence'). Conjoining quotations that refer to two of Semel's fictional narratives, McGuckian presents two opposing coping strategies. The first comes from *Gershona Shona* (1988), in which the heroine meets a blond-haired boy whose name (Nimrod) and life-story convey an Israeli identity. In the course of the narrative the heroine 'refuses to see or read' the tell-tale signs that he is, in fact, a Shoah survivor: 'it is important for her', says Semel, 'to fortify herself within this [Israeli] identity' (47). However, this wilful refusal to confront the truth is opposed by the second strategy which is taken from the opening of *A Hat of Glass* in which the unnamed protagonist is walking in Tel Aviv and 'thinks she sees Clarissa' and says 'the truth is pieces of . . .' (45). The 'truth' may be fragmentary, but can be faced within writing that itself adopts a fragmented structure. 'Clarissa' – which has its roots in the Latin form of *clarice*, a medieval French diminutive of the Latin and English feminine form of *clarus*, meaning 'bright' or 'clear' – is linked to the other images of enlightenment that run through the poem ('mirror', 'slight shine', 'afterglow', 'picture in my head', '"light" / in the pre-language'). That McGuckian entitles her poem 'She Thinks She Sees Clarissa' is perhaps the clearest hint that for her the 'unburying' function of literature must prevail.

'To write about the Holocaust, and to write criticism on a text, any text, that acknowledges the Holocaust', argues Robin Sibergleid, 'is necessarily to engage in a conversation about literature and ethics.'[32] McGuckian may champion the idea of 'unburying', yet within Shoah studies it is not always clear whether this is deemed either possible or ethically correct:

[A]nything written now about the Nazi genocide against the Jews that is not primarily documentary, that does not uncover new information about the history of that singular event, requires special justification. Other writing about the same subject [. . .] serves too often as a rhetorical incentive for memory, assuming a role of surrogate in which voice substitutes for conscience so that the need to feel displaces reflection, or substitutes even for feeling itself' [. . .] [L]iterary representation imposes artifice, a figurative mediation of language, and the contrivance of a persona [. . .] on the part of the writer.[33]

The objection here is that the very idea of genocide is *unthinkable* and therefore *unrepresentable*. As another writer on the Shoah has put it, [n]o symbolic universe grounded in humanistic beliefs could confront the Holocaust without the risk of being shaken to its foundations'.[34] Art is said to render genocide knowable, its formal strategies containing and aestheticising the suffering. Narrative may offer closure, yet such atrocity resists being closed off. Yet documentary realism and historical scholarship are not the only valid approaches, particularly as 'history is never only "history of" but is also "history for", not only in the sense that it is narrated with a certain ideological aim but also that it is narrated for a specific public'.[35] As Lentin has shown, historical writing has been guilty of ideological bias and systematic erasure of social memory. But can art offer redress? Some critics argue that an artistic representation contains an inherent element of 'barbarism', that it violates the victims by offering up depictions of suffering for our voyeuristic entertainment. Adorno famously developed this line of reasoning in his *Notes on Literature*:

> [The] artistic representation of the naked bodily pain of those who have been knocked down by rifle-butts contains the potential – no matter how remote – to squeeze out pleasure [. . .] Through aesthetic principles of stylization and even through the solemn prayer of the chorus the unimaginable ordeal still appears as if it had some ulterior purpose. It is transfigured and stripped of some of its horror and with this, injustice is already done to the victims.[36]

However valid such reservations may be, an artist within his or her text can remain vigilant against stripping atrocity of its horror; indeed, as Ezrahi contends, '[i]t may be precisely in its *resistance* to conceptual abstraction, to psychological reductionism, that art as a version of historical memory can provide form without fixing meaning, insight without explanation, for the recovered events'.[37]

In 'The Stone-word'[38] McGuckian uses two intertexts, Ash Amin's *Cities: Reimagining the Urban* and Gary D. Mole's *Beyond the Limit-Experience*, a monograph on French poetry written during the Holocaust,[39] to create a poem which is intensely self-reflexive, yet ultimately affirmative, about representing the Shoah in art:

a finer-grained time (C 96); time lies thicker on
the ground (C 94); take out the warm lining of   A finer-grained time lies thicker on the ground.
overcoats and replace one sleeve with the sleeve of   We take out the warm lining of overcoats,

a different color (M 95); beyond the slower times (C 83); the city dreams of itself (C 122); the city's dreams of itself (C 106); 'Alarm all night' (M 81); a kind of weather (C 83); 'Nothing to read [. . .] There was a walk but not for me' (M 81); 'sick without books' (M 43); 'sad day [. . .] I wasted you' (M 95); the sun 'young, strong, demanding' (M 106); 'useless in the shadow of the sheds' (M 55); a small abandoned notebook (M 48) doubts concerning words (M 54); 'two heart fingers' (M 170); the sight of the end of the platform (M 90); 'A very long perfume' (M 161); ease of gathering (A 120); 'ceiling is blue like an eyelid' (M 175).

replace one sleeve with a sleeve of a different colour.
Beyond the slower times the city dreams itself,
dreams of itself, its footprints, the nightwalk,
alarm all night becomes a kind of weather.
There was no walk, not for me, nothing to read,
sick without books, day, I wasted you,
the young, strong demanding sun, the unwounded leaves.
Useless in the shadows of the sheds, I invented
a small abandoned notebook of doubts concerning words, held it between my two heart fingers.
And the sight of the end of the platform
loosened a very long perfume that had ease
of gathering into my ceiling blue as an eyelid.

The poem's opening, taken from *Cities: Reimagining the Urban*, refers to the ways in which we experience and represent time: the invention of the watch meant that human beings could 'construct finer grained time', and the multiplicity of times and spaces depicted in the city meant that in the urban space what we term 'everyday life' becomes increasingly more complex ('time lies thicker on the ground'). Yet while the text contends that we can readily conceptualise our experience of time, the poem presents a context which challenges this assumption. The image of someone taking out 'the warm lining of overcoats' and replacing 'one sleeve with a sleeve of a different colour' metonymically represents the stripping bare of what we call 'everyday life': here 'alarm' becomes the new 'weather'; daily life becomes characterised by loss and deprivation ('There was no walk, not for me, nothing to read'). The subject is out of her element: anthropomorphising nature, the sun becomes 'strong, demanding' and while the leaves are 'unwounded', it is assumed that the speaker has been less fortunate. Literature is not only presented as an absent panacea, it is the condition on which the speaker's survival depends ('sick without books').

That the poet is constructing an argument about the value of literature in a time of violence is hinted at by the poem's title which alludes to Pierre Macaire's '*Je suis parti comme on s'endort*', a text in which the speaker's thoughts become contaminated by 'stone-words':

> I flow silently
> My thoughts are circles
> Born and expanding
> To my surface
> They come from the bank
> Of the words of others who are on it
> And who throw at me
> Stones which are words. (M 53)

While the poem is written 'as an antidote to this violence', Mole argues that the poetic word is penetrated by the 'stone-word' (M 53) and confirms the author's linguistic doubts and hesitations. McGuckian's speaker states that 'I invented / A small abandoned notebook of doubts concerning / Words', implying here that the act of writing is coterminous with, yet produced despite, her own misgivings about aesthetic representation. 'Invented' may suggest a pose, that such 'doubts' are not sincerely felt, yet it also affirms *poeïsis* (the making of poetry) as an antidote to feeling 'Useless in the shadows of the sheds'. McGuckian's text is here juxtaposing two contrasting poetic responses to the Shoah: the first is André Ullmann's '*Pont au change*' in which the speaker, finding himself 'alone amid the corpses of words' (M 55), is '"trampling intertwined images / Useless in the shadow of the sheds"' (M 55); the second quotation asserts the contrary impulse, that of Yves Eyot, writing from Dachau, whose '"main occupation was to write in this note-book"' (M 48). The juxtaposition neatly condenses the twin polarities of Gary Mole's study, which investigates the context in which the resistance to representation becomes the subject of representation; in the concentration camps, artistic representation meets 'its most forceful challenge in a limit-experience that did indeed seem to *prevent* its own representation, one that had *blinded* its eyewitness, and beyond which art either could not or should not go' (M 2). Rather than be blinded, McGuckian suggests that the artist withdraws into the self, into dream, and can confront real life there while at the same time imagining alternative futures. The concluding image of her 'ceiling blue as an eyelid' is taken from Christian Pineau's '*Les Élements*', a meditation on the omnipresence of death in the camps and which shows how relief (however 'fugitive') can be achieved in dreams: 'the withdrawal into the realm of sleep and dream is [. . .] suggested by the ceiling being blocked out by closing eyelids behind which prayers, thoughts, memories can circulate freely even as bodies are motionless and death continues to hang in the air' (M 175). Dream time, with its 'ease of gathering', depicts a lyrical stasis. This 'finer-grained time' is not an escape from but a resistance to atrocity.

If 'The Stone-word' seems hopeful in its lyricism, then 'Notice',[40] a more recent poem on the treatment of post-war prisoners, is in many respects fractured, sardonic and unpoetic even though, paradoxically, it is about order ('orders' and 'ordering'). Stanzas 1, 3 and 5 are taken verbatim from a list detailing the key principles of the funerary landscape, its properties, attributes and symbolic motifs.[41] The first part of the list, constituting the poem's opening, is as follows:

> Architectural inscription in the site,
> Centred on, emphasized by, the vegetation
> (Solemnity), or drowned in vegetation

(Integration, disappearance, discretion);
A command of volumes: the horizontal (rest),
The vertical (resurrection), a combination
Of both (opposition, reflex action).

As a taxonomy of the funerary landscape, this list exudes order and exactitude; as a stanza in a poem, it is metrically disjunctive, sonically dissonant
and, despite the insistent end-line rhyme, it is chaotic due to the paratactical
arrangement and constantly interruptive parentheses. The poem conveys
(and resists) the restitution of order after a person's death. What is remarkably
clever about 'Notice' is the way in which she juxtaposes this taxonomy with
two texts (also taken verbatim) from James Bacque's *Crimes and Mercies*.[42]
Stanza 2 is a 'notice' issued by the District Administrative Commission of
Kraslice ordering the expulsion of Germans after the war, and begins:

People selected for transport must leave their homes
In complete order. One piece of luggage
Weighing sixty kilograms, and hand baggage
Of a maximum of ten kilograms, will be allowed
Per person. . . .

Reading without the source, one could surmise that it is mimicking the
insidious efficiency and inscrutability of the Nazis' dehumanising discourse;
indeed, the first line's enjambment calls attention to the way in which, by
attempting to achieve 'complete order', the notice is in fact 'incomplete' (it
is as if no one is responsible since the notice's opening sentence does not
identify who is undertaking the selection). In reality, the text is written by
those who opposed and fought against the Third Reich and who seem here
to be perpetuating the cycle of atrocity, displacing (and ultimately robbing)
German civilians. Stanza 4 is similarly taken from an order, this time a letter
dated 9 May 1945 and issued to the highest district official in Bad
Kreuznach:

The military has requested me to make it known
That under no circumstances may food supplies
Be assembled among the local inhabitants
In order to deliver them to the prisoners of war.
Those who violate this command and nevertheless
Try to circumvent this blockade
To allow something to come to the prisoners
Place themselves in danger of being shot.

Bacque (and by extension McGuckian) is not only unearthing evidence
about forgotten victims and calling attention to the hidden crimes of the
Second World War (namely the Allies' policy of imposed starvation and

enforced deportation), he is highlighting the aporias in historical texts written by the victors and showing how depersonalising rhetoric is used to mask the brutal reality of revenge. Just as the funerary landscape can sanitise the reality of death, so too does the rhetoric which effectively orders such death.

In the context of post-ceasefire Northern Ireland, McGuckian has written poems which focus on the dangers of forgetting and on the ideological biases of historiography. The letter cited in 'Notice' advises the official to 'explain to the local inhabitants in suitable terms about the facts of the matter'; in her poems, McGuckian scrutinises what is meant by 'suitable terms' and sets about 'unburying' the past while at the same time questioning the terms in which this is to be achieved.

8

Medbh McGuckian and the politics of minority discourse

The difference between minorities and majorities isn't their size. A minority may be bigger than a majority. What defines the majority is a model you have to conform to: the average European adult male city-dweller, for example [. . .] A minority, on the other hand, has no model, it's a becoming, a process. One might say the majority is nobody. Everybody's caught, one way or another, in a minority becoming that would lead them into unknown paths if they opted to follow it through. (Gilles Deleuze)[1]

The church and the school receded when I was 18 and also the troubles started when I was 18. So there was a very dark period where I had nothing. Well I hadn't nothing, I sort of had Marxism, a mixture of Marxism and sex I think, but it wasn't very satisfying and for 10 years I had nothing. (Medbh McGuckian)[2]

The creation of human subjectivity is a necessarily endless process. Described by Gilles Deleuze as a 'becoming', it is a condition that constantly looks towards a final goal, a homecoming, but that destination is always deferred, always held out of reach. To understand and live within this is a difficult art, one that requires a particular sensuousness and a sensitive apprehension of flux. The poetry of Medbh McGuckian is exemplary in its demonstration of these qualities, and it is no coincidence that it is this subject, the inevitability of becoming and the duties that this places upon us, that is the major theme of her work. This is not simply to observe that McGuckian's poetry describes provisional shifting states of becoming (although this is the case), but also to recognise that it demands a reading practice that is similarly dynamic. As Peggy O'Brien observes of the sometimes unsettling experience of reading a McGuckian poem, 'to stare too long at a single, still intractable word [...] is to become paralyzed, and whatever accumulated meaning we might have been carrying topples with the jolt of suddenly arrested movement. Motion is critical.'[3] Understood in these terms, then, McGuckian is a kind of sorcerer, but only because, as Deleuze and Félix Guattari observe, 'sorcery always codifies certain trans-formations of becomings'.[4] Which, in turn, is as good a definition of a spell as I can recall.

In Deleuze's work becoming is the defining condition of what he terms minority status, a mode that does not describe a fixed identity but rather indicates a way of living, a continual process. In turn, its opposite, the majority, is not necessarily a verifiable or material entity, but rather exists as a standard, something to be judged against. As a result of this relentless posi-tioning it can be seen that what has been termed the politics of minority discourse are an inevitability as one always finds oneself occupying a space in relationship to an abstract other, and living that relationship in an active, con-stitutive way. As such, the minority becomes what Deleuze and Guattari describe in *A Thousand Plateaus* as 'a potential, creative and created becoming'.[5] To put this more bluntly, we have no choice but to take the 'unknown paths' that Deleuze speaks of.

The implications of this awareness in Deleuze and Guattari's work are considerable. Although, as they assert, the majority position is abstract, a prin-ciple of judgement and power rather than a verifiable state, it is at this chimerical location that the discourses of identity politics lodge themselves. The assumption of rights and aspirations depends upon a stable, achieved, identity position, a status that can be weighed in the balance, and the worth of its claims assessed. Conversely, as they insist, 'there is a universal figure of minoritarian consciousness as the becoming of everybody, and that becoming is creation'.[6] Most importantly, this figure takes a specific form as 'an amplitude that continually oversteps the representative threshold of the majoritarian standard, by excess or default'.[7] As such, minorities have to be seen through a number of perspectives: as 'objectively definable states, states of language, ethnicity, or sex with their own ghetto territorialities', and con-comitantly as 'seeds, crystals of becoming whose value is to trigger uncontrollable movements and deterritorializations of the mean or majority'.[8] The very absence of identity enables minor creativity, a process that can be understood as an experiment or innovation with life that at no time settles into a stable position. This is a necessarily political practice in that it speaks of (rather than speaks *as*) an alternative mode to the majori-tarian, and thus it carries with it an implicit and inevitable critique.

These negotiations can operate at the level of the word or the individual utterance. As Toni Negri, the interviewer in the conversation quoted at the start of this essay, makes clear, Deleuze's comments on minority status have to be seen in the context of three kinds of power: 'sovereign power, disciplinary power, and above all the control of "communication" that's on the way to becoming hegemonic'.[9] It is the latter mode – which Negri glosses as 'the most perfect form of domination, extending even to speech and imagination' – that concerns us here. For Deleuze, 'the quest for "universals of communication" ought to make us shudder', as it is through this process that power is particularised at the level of the individual and can achieve a totalitarian currency. As he observes:

> Maybe speech and communication have been corrupted. They're thoroughly permeated by money – and not by accident but by their very nature. We've got to hijack speech. Creating has always been something different from communicating. The key thing may be to create vacuoles of noncommunication, circuit breakers, so we can elude control.[10]

This distinction between creativity and communication strikes me as a productive way of apprehending some of the complexities of McGuckian's poetry, and it is a conflict that many of her poems dramatise. Indeed, McGuckian herself has invoked this opposition when describing her own sense of the writing process, dismissing the importance of 'ideas' to the art of writing a poem and emphasising the difficulty of 'trying to think communicatively rather than creatively'. As she notes, 'when I begin to think creatively, ideas take a back seat'.[11] It is, perhaps, as a result of this general uneasiness about communication that there is a sense in which the poetry speaks reluctantly, that her art is one of concealment. Alongside this, however, it is also important to recognise that, as Peter Sirr notes, 'one of the surprising aspects of McGuckian's work, given its density and its habitual state of cool reverie, is the directness of the poem's address. Again and again they engage a "you" whose identity is never clarified, but whose presence impels the poem.'[12] As few of her poems resolve this opposition it is ultimately the tension between the two registers that becomes the work's most important aspect. Her early poem 'On Not Being your Lover',[13] for instance, narrates a complex internal drama which locates tension between the necessity to clearly address the 'you' that obsesses the poem, and the creativity which must be held back and kept private:

> In a far-flung, too young part,
> I remembered all your slender but
> Persistent volume said, friendly, complex
> As the needs of your new and childfree girl.

To return to Deleuze and Guattari, the nature of McGuckian's linguistic sorcery here lies precisely in the manner in which the poem's spell codifies a transformation of becoming. The distinction between address and creativity, or art and artfulness, stands out all the more clearly in this example because of the persistence elsewhere in McGuckian's poetry of a kind of dialectical method, whereby all terms are enfolded with their opposite in order to create new wholes and epistemological understandings. As in, for instance, the recent poem 'Charcoal Angel':

> Sky as hard as a wall.
> Sea drowned in the sand.
>
> Two knowledges, one face upon another,
> Newly created rose, though the sea-forms
> In a squall are not repeated:
> He has too much moss upon his temples.[14]

To speak through silence, to force apart creativity and communication, to trace in a word its violent opposite – these are the acts of minoritarian consciousness. Seeking to 'elude both established forms of knowledge and the dominant forms of power', for Deleuze this consciousness is distinguished by a 'rebellious spontaneity',[15] a phrase that can describe the experience of reading many of McGuckian's poems with some precision:

> They set the whins on fire along the road.
> I wonder what controls it, can the wind hold
> That snake of orange motion to the hills,
> Away from the houses?
>
> They seem so sure what they can do.
> I am unable even
> To contain myself, I run
> Till the fawn smoke settles on the earth.[16]

McGuckian's early poem, 'Smoke', dramatises what is ultimately a political conflict between majoritarian and minoritarian discourse. The first work in her *Selected Poems*,[17] the primacy of its positioning is appropriate as it sketches in microcosm a theme that many of the later poems will explore with greater ambition and complexity. In its eight lines 'Smoke' enacts a drama played out between the forces of the 'They' on one hand – that which is fixed as a model to which one should conform and the majoritarian command of containment and control – and the 'I' which is in process, on the run, and 'unable even/to contain myself'. In the face of this certainty, the 'I' can offer nothing other than its own form of 'rebellious spontaneity'. As such, it remains in a Deleuzean state of becoming that is incomplete and unsatisfactory – the fawn smoke that settles on the earth referring us also to a young deer that has collapsed from exhaustion and will presumably die. The precise positioning of the Ulster-Scots vernacular word 'whins' in the first line locates the poem in the North, but it is as a parable of artistic self-consciousness in the face of violence that 'Smoke' gains its considerable power.

The shifting ways in which McGuckian's poetry has engaged with this theme during the last thirty years have been tracked by a literary critical practice distinguished by sudden leaps of intuition, periods of intellectual retrenchment, and a surprising amount of internecine squabbling. This body of criticism has also been noticeably homogeneous in that it has tended to read McGuckian's work in terms of a relatively limited number of primary concerns. This might be because of the degree to which McGuckian's poems appear to demand particular critical readings: as her poem 'The Seed-Picture' observes, 'the seeds dictate their own vocabulary'.[18] Certainly early criticism of McGuckian's work was preoccupied, like the poetry itself, with the analysis of self-representation and the question of writerly authority.[19] This concern was frequently delineated through comparisons with the poetry of Eavan Boland – a habit which could tend towards the banal and which inevitably served to underplay the significance of McGuckian's developing achievement. With the publication of *Captain Lavender*[20] in 1994 and the lessening of what Shane Murphy has referred to as 'the fear which drove her to disguise her political convictions prior to the IRA ceasefires',[21] McGuckian's greater willingness to allow something of Irish history and the recent violence in Northern Ireland into her poetry set critics of her work a series of new tasks. Although prior to this collection such criticism had been wary of orientating her work to the matter of political violence in Ireland,[22] and was particularly anxious to avoid any straightforward correlation between poetic image and historical event, poems in *Captain Lavender* such as 'Flirting with Strangers', 'The Albert Chain' or 'Dividing the Political Temperature' demanded that such contexts be addressed. As in the recent doctoral work of Leontia Flynn,[23] this has provided an invigorating intellectual momentum to readings of McGuckian's poetry. However, the suspicion remains that the necessary emphasis on delineating the terms of McGuckian's exceptionalism has sometimes inhibited considerations of the ways in which her work has always been recognisably part of a wider field of Northern Irish poetic discourse – a reticence that is all the more surprising as Clair Wills began tracing the contours of this lexicon as long ago as 1993 in her study of Northern Irish poetry, *Improprieties: Politics and Sexuality in Northern Irish Poetry*.

By my reading, Wills's analysis of McGuckian's poetry in this book constitutes one of the two major epistemological breakthroughs in the interpretation of her work. Following a politically nuanced reading of the early collections, Wills concludes by asserting that McGuckian's poetry has to be seen in the context of the 'transformed relation between public and private registers [. . .] the result of historical factors peculiar to the colonial and post-colonial experience'.[24] As a result of this, McGuckian emerges as a poet whose writing intervenes in the social realm of discourse and thus disrupts fundamentally bourgeois distinctions between the private and the public realm. In these terms, her poems are not necessarily 'about' privacy but instead should be understood as 'allegories of privacy'.[25] Wills's analysis established the template which much subsequent criticism would follow although the specific intellectual and political imperative suggested by the idea of allegory in McGuckian's work is an insight that has yet to be fully developed.

The second major development in criticism of McGuckian's poetry came with the intervention of Shane Murphy, a critic with a long-term interest in her work. Murphy's often exhaustive literary archaeology has revealed the striking extent to which McGuckian's poetry frequently consists of what he calls 'concealed quotation',[26] fragments of other texts reordered and juxtaposed with no reference to their original source. While Wills's reading of 'The Dream Language of Fergus' in *Improprieties* identified the extent to which the poem was 'almost entirely constructed out of quotations from his [Osip Mandelstam's] essays',[27] Murphy's criticism has gone further still and has discovered the existence of what he terms 'labyrinthine networks of intertextual relations' criss-crossing the poetry.[28] With this in mind, Murphy's 1998 essay '"You Took Away My Biography": The Poetry of Medbh McGuckian' effectively puts McGuckian's work on trial for plagiarism. While he ultimately acquits her of the charge,[29] there is something uneasy about his analysis and a sense that doubts remain. As he comments in relation to McGuckian's working papers, 'sources are *never* included on these sheets or anywhere else on drafts, copies or final versions'.[30] Little wonder, then, that he poses the question, 'is it possible for the critic to use the term *poet* when referring to a writer whose texts consist mainly of literary borrowings?'[31] Murphy's subsequent contribution to the *Cambridge Companion to Contemporary Irish Poetry*,[32] which demonstrates how the fractured images of McGuckian's civil war poem 'The Truciler' consist of little more than phrases taken from Tim Pat Coogan's biography of Michael Collins,[33] is, in many ways, even more devastating. Certainly, such criticism makes McGuckian's own description of her writing technique as one of 'build[ing] the poem from [. . .] scraps of language'[34] look quite disingenuous, although she has more recently acknowledged the existence of what she terms her 'sources', while referring to what she sees as the 'wild extremes'[35] of Murphy's detective work. However, despite some of the unsettling aspects of his discoveries, Murphy remains perhaps McGuckian's most persuasive advocate and most convincing critic.[36] As a result of his work, future criticism of McGuckian's poetry will have to take cognisance of what appears to be its overwhelming textuality because with this knowledge a very different poet emerges. Similarly, Murphy's work has a retroactive force in that it casts a long shadow over much of the criticism that preceded it.

Any discussion of minority discourse and the process of self-formation in McGuckian's writing needs to be cognisant of the insights of both Wills and Murphy. In my reading of McGuckian's autobiographical prose I want to respond to Wills's sense of her work as a series of 'allegories' by emphasising the extent to which it stages both the incipient possibility of 'becoming' and the inevitable failure to ever finally 'become'. As such, McGuckian's diaries can be understood as persistent attempts to construct narratives of self-formation through the available generic models. These narratives allegorise – albeit in a complex manner – the possibility of a nascent political state. Alongside this, and I think in a complementary manner, I want to recognise the intertextuality that Murphy has explored. This is necessary not simply because her prose work, like her poetry, is a fundamentally intertextual procedure, but also because, in a more fundamental way, the very idea of 'becoming' is a textual process. Finally, I want to allow for that which Flynn has described as the poetry's 'flirtation with outrageousness and nonsense which invite and flout literary critical interpretations'.[37] When reading McGuckian the presence of that which remains unknown is at least as important as that which can be guessed at.

Central to McGuckian's interest in self-formation are two diary essays she published in 2000 and 2001, 'Rescuers and White Cloaks',[38] and 'Women are Trousers'.[39] 'Rescuers and White Cloaks' begins in January 1968 with McGuckian aged seventeen and contemplating a university career, and concludes at the end of 1969. 'Women are Trousers' follows on directly, and takes the narrative up to June 1973, as Northern Ireland collapses into ever more extreme violence. Certainly the two pieces should be read together, although McGuckian provides no prefatorial comment to the later piece to indicate that it has a predecessor. Kathryn Kirkpatrick's summary of 'Women are Trousers' as 'a young woman's coming to writing amid the voices and violence of a male world of politics and texts'[40] describes both pieces well. McGuckian, in turn, articulates this process in one entry as the desire 'to use language, not study it or how others use it. I want it alive in my mind.'[41] This is vividly demonstrated by the manner in which she interleaves her record of events, both public and private, with what Kirkpatrick calls 'solemn canonical voices'.[42] These literary quotations are drawn from a variety of sources (although the predominance of women writers is notable) and have a complex relationship to the entries. Sometimes they mark a staging post in McGuckian's artistic development, sometimes they function as a warning, and sometimes a necessary rejection. Emily Dickinson's poetry and letters increasingly dominate (indeed after a period she is referred to simply as 'Emily') and constitute particularly important markers in the process of self-formation. As McGuckian has commented elsewhere, Dickinson's poetry 'managed to say things that I thought could not be said in language'.[43]

The reasons why McGuckian chose to publish these accounts when she did are worth reflecting upon. Flynn has argued persuasively that they are 'a strategy of critically rooting her poetry to place and event, at a time when it seems ever more abstracted and its systems of representation more complex'.[44] In these terms, the diaries have a contrapuntal relationship to the poetry – a means of 're-placing' the work in time and space. Alongside this, it is significant that their appearance coincided with a period when both McGuckian's poetry and her statements in interview demonstrate an increased sympathy with both cultural and political elements of Irish republicanism.[45] As such, the diaries demonstrate the formation of a political consciousness that is seeking an identity appropriate to its material and historical circumstance. This urge for selfhood is, as I will argue, frustrated, but the *structure* of its quest allows McGuckian's artistic development to be seen in parallel with that of Northern male poets such as Seamus Heaney, Seamus Deane, Michael Longley and Paul Muldoon, figures for whom this period was similarly constitutive. Ultimately her narratives of selfhood are expressed in the discourses of Catholicism, republicanism and the formation of the poetic self. It is, however, the eventual failure of these narratives to achieve a stable identity position that is important.

The dramatic social and historical changes described in the diaries should be placed in the context of McGuckian's perception of Northern Irish society before 1968, the period of her adolescence. Something of this can be glimpsed in her critical discussion of 'Tractors', an early poem by Seamus Heaney, in which she describes 'the hapless flaccidity of rural, Catholic, mid-century mid–Ulster, its disenfranchised gloom'.[46] The hopelessness of this vision is, of course, highly specific: it encapsulates the exclusion of Northern Catholics from the institutions of the Northern Irish state, the failure of Irish nationalism in the 1950s and 1960s to mount an adequate opposition to that state, and the concomitant increase of the social and political role of the Catholic church in the life of its community. Her early poem, 'Curtains', also reflects upon this political mise-en-scène, and poses a pertinent question:

> Who in their right mind would go back?
> Beyond the invisible repairs shop,
> The transistor hospital, the speedy cleaners'
> Iron curtain, airy as sex, generous as sleeping.[47]

As Ashley Tellis has observed, the poem 'rumbles with a subterranean resentment against the structure of what Edna Longley calls "the repressive force of Ulster patriarchies"'.[48] Indeed, such is its tone of weary denunciation that it bears surprising comparison with the polemic poetry of Tom Paulin, and specifically his contemporaneous collection *The Strange Museum*.[49] Certainly, in terms of McGuckian's autobiographical consciousness this period is, to use a phrase of Paulin's, 'before history', a time before the potential of 'becoming' is able to make itself known. When such history is absent intuitions and premonitions predominate, and so it is fitting that McGuckian's early entries in 'Rescuers and White Cloaks' articulate a sense of ominous apprehension in a manner reminiscent of Heaney's first collection, *Death of a Naturalist*.[50] In February 1968 she records that 'I smelt a terrible smell everywhere all day – a sickly, putrid smell, as of death or sin',[51] while in June 1968 'there is a strange stillness, a shadow over everything'.[52] The self that can exist under such conditions is necessarily pre-formed, an entity marked not by the assertion of identity, but rather by the particular timbre of its absence. As McGuckian has described in interview:

> I know being a woman for me for a long time was being less, being excluded, being somehow cheap, being inferior, being sub. I associated being a woman with being a Catholic and being Irish with being from the North, and all of these things being not what you wanted to be. If you were a woman, it would have been better to be a man; if you were Catholic, it would have been a lot easier to be Protestant; if you were from the North, it was much easier to be from the South; if you were Irish, it was much easier to be English. So it was like everything that I was was wrong; everything that I was was hard, difficult, and a punishment.[53]

When articulated in these despairing terms, 'becoming' can be understood as an act of will, a journey along Deleuze's 'unknown paths', and ultimately a mode of survival.

McGuckian's interest in self-formation during this period was shared by other Northern Irish poets in strikingly similar ways. In 1975, the year in which she had her first poem published, Seamus Deane was speaking of the 'Northern poets' as a group particularly well able to respond to the fact that 'the fixed situation of past years has become fluid again':

> It is in this connection that the Northern poets have their importance as a group. They are not articulating change. They are articulating what it is like to have been changed, to have undergone that process; and in such articulation, the existence and development of a political sensibility is inescapable. For many people, the future has already arrived. What politics is labouring to produce, poetry senses has already come.[54]

Deane's emphasis on the centrality of 'change' as a means of constructing an idea of Northern poetry at this time is important, not least because it allows the preoccupations of McGuckian's work to be understood as archetypal rather than anomalous. It is, after all, difficult to think of another poet from the North who has had such a prolonged fascination with the idea of process, or of charting shifting conditional states. McGuckian's diaries are also anxious to stress the extent to which her artistic development took place within a community of Northern poets, what Heaney has referred to as the 'play within the play'.[55] Indeed, the rescuers of 'Rescuers and White Cloaks' might be said to be the poets she encounters who give her life shape and purpose. McGuckian has spoken of these writers in this period as 'very supportive [. . .] father figures',[56] with Heaney and Muldoon, who are frequent presences in the diaries, playing particularly important roles. For McGuckian the experience of being taught by Heaney at Queen's constituted 'the big change for me in my evaluation and discernment of how to live through and survive what was happening around me, never mind understand it',[57] while elsewhere she describes his role in her life in essentially religious terms:

> I remember going to a poetry reading in Belfast, I was about sixteen, and around that time – 1966 – Heaney's *Death of a Naturalist* came out, and I was amazed that somebody from Derry could be an acclaimed poet. The poetry reading was like a secret society meeting – no other woman in the room – and I remember this feeling of 'I am here', like going to Mass. I decided that the second-best thing to becoming a priest would be to become a poet. This is something I can do though it is nearly as difficult but it is not actually unlawful. So it was only when I went to Queen's and Heaney was teaching there – in my final year, '72, I had him in a seminar, and he was just a wonderful mediatrix.[58]

McGuckian's diaries accord with this sense of belonging, of becoming part of a poetic community. Indeed, despite what I have described as McGuckian's exceptionalism, early criticism of her work interpreted her emergence as centrally placed in the predominant political aesthetic discourses that had shaped much of twentieth-century Irish poetry. As Edna Longley remarked in 1981 when reviewing a pamphlet of McGuckian's early poems: '*Single Ladies* conveys the exciting impression that Cathleen ni Houlihan, that much-abused muse, has found a voice of her own.'[59]

As might be expected given such observations, a major structural template for McGuckian's diaries is provided by James Joyce's *Portrait of the Artist as a Young Man*, and specifically Stephen Dedalus's diary in that work's conclusion. In this can be seen the extent to which received narratives of specifically Catholic self-formation are prioritised in McGuckian's artistic consciousness, although, as with *Portrait*, this centrality does not mean they cannot also be heavily subverted. Certainly many of the similarities between Stephen and the young Maeve McCaughan (as she was then) are obvious: both are preoccupied by sex, live life very intensely, construct experience via literary quotation, gain a form of unorthodox political awareness, fret over the English language, and take themselves too seriously. The structure of the diaries follows *Portrait* in being heavily influenced by the confessional urge of Catholic spiritual autobiography, an aspect most clearly revealed in their attitude to sexual desire. As Flynn notes, both texts feature 'elliptical accounts of a relationship',[60] and indeed, while McGuckian describes the circlings and restlessness of her desire at some length, its object (or objects) remains uncertain and frequently amorphous. It is certainly the case that the specifics of McGuckian's love life are much less important to the text than the effect it has upon her developing consciousness. In turn, the erotic charge that is never far from the surface of the diaries derives to a large degree from a barely suppressed sense of sexual guilt that re-emerges in different and often unexpected ways. This can take the form of a shameful recollection ('I could not recapture that party-love for him. His psychophantic methods awaken no spark in me. I should not have succumbed if I had not been intoxicated'),[61] while at other times it functions as the moment of repression ('I was on fire for him inside but it had to be quelled').[62] Ultimately, however, the major method of containment appears to be the deployment of a particularly stern dualism as a result of which 'sex oppresses me with its narrow unexpressiveness. My mind revolts against its blatancy, I felt I was stuffing things in where there was no room.'[63]

As the diaries gain in momentum there is a sense of increasing intellectual progress, a quickening of the movement towards art that again echoes the trajectory of Stephen's diary. The entry for April 1969 is particularly indebted to *Portrait*:

> Father Walsh said I had a great wee brain – there's an Irish lie for you. The streets were stark naked and stripped and openly ugly, a wasteland. My throat hurt after the fog, but the dawn was pastel as a shell, the sun feathered the trees, the wind tore blue holes. I was trembling with love and fright. My dreams were about nuclear war and American planes and a sense of silence. I dreamt of a thousand lost things and people. I remembered my schoolgirl devotion and that park with its breathing maiden promise. And resumed my lonely struggle with the mind.[64]

As images, fears and memories coalesce, so the mind synthesises new unities. In this the diary reveals a developing consciousness that is quite distinct from the 'schoolgirl devotion' with which McGuckian had armed herself on her arrival at Queen's. Should this process seem too idealistic, however, the pomposity of the final sentence suggests she also has something of Stephen's self-absorption and lack of self-knowledge – an indication that her journey is still far from complete.

Another element that McGuckian's developing consciousness shares with Stephen's is the extent to which her perception of what Deane terms 'a political sensibility' is interwoven with the fabric of lived experience. As such, the structure of 'Rescuers and White Cloaks' emphasises the links between the local and the multinational, and between the individual institution of Queen's and the wider institutional structures of the Northern Irish state. As this is the period in which Northern Ireland re-enters the world of international politics, so the diaries are peppered with (usually unmediated) references to the Vietnam War, the Cold War, American politics (particularly Bobby Kennedy) and commodities. As she notes sardonically (and, perhaps, prophetically), 'If I drink Pepsi I will come alive, the drink of my generation.'[65] This preoccupation with self-formation also shapes McGuckian's engagement with Irish politics and her interest in republicanism, an ideology frequently dependent on conversion narratives for its political efficacy. If nationalism frequently dreams of itself as instinctual, something born fully fledged into the world and convinced of the obviousness of its cause, republicanism, by contrast, requires a process of enlightenment. Its political claims are therefore based around stories of self-formation, the various lessons, temptations and rejections that must be experienced in order to achieve consciousness. This tendency explains something of republicanism's peculiarly close relationship to the practice of life writing. Irish republicanism in the twentieth century has generally been dependent on such narratives, but in the contexts of McGuckian's developing sense of political selfhood the specific model is the autobiography of the Northern politician and republican Bernadette Devlin, *The Price of My Soul*.[66] Written, according to the author, in order 'to explain how the complex of economic, social, and political problems of Northern Ireland threw up the phenomenon of Bernadette Devlin',[67] the major preoccupation of the book is the tension that exists between the acquisition of a political self – in other words, an identity position equivalent with the political and historical contexts that formed it – and the cost that this exacts in terms of the loss of other forms of more fragile or ephemeral selfhood. McGuckian, too, mobilises this opposition as a means of understanding her own life, and Devlin (who is in fact always referred to as 'Bernadette', as was the tendency at the time) becomes one of the major characters in her diaries, a figure whose political manoeuvres are detailed in the midst of more quotidian concerns: 'I am really happy in the green life. I can't always not be blue here just because he's gone. Bernadette lost her appeal. There was a huge cloud of smoke from buses on fire down town. I bought Tampax but am scared to use it.'[68]

The insistent gynocritical logic of the opening to 'Rescuers and White Cloaks' immediately indicates the diaries' focus on the possibilities and frustrations inherent to self-formation:

> It's 1968, over thirty years ago. I am seventeen, near the age of my eldest son. I have a Queen's University student diary of my brother's which he is not using and makes me feel more confident about passing the forthcoming entrance exams. But it is a world I do not know, a world of

royalty and men. Under 'Officers,' the first title is 'Visitor, Her Majesty the Queen.' The Chancellor is Sir Tyrone Guthrie, whose house I will myself incredibly visit. Pro-chancellor is the Right Honourable Lord McDermott of Belmont. All are male, the President, the Treasurer, the Bursar, the Librarian.[69]

As the pre-formed self is constructed through its absence, so the foundational text of the diary is inscribed primarily as an institutional object, demarcating its own time and imposing a particular disciplinary logic. That the book belongs to McGuckian's brother and that she, in turn, calibrates her age by that of her son merely emphasises the relational power structures inherent to the 'world of royalty and men' that she is entering. It will be McGuckian's task to write through and over this text, positioning her own nascent language between the official languages of authority. As such, the diary's bilingualism describes the tension between majoritarian discourse – which describes that which has already come to pass through its lists of achievements and titles – and McGuckian's attempt to write from a minority position as a linear voice caught in its own endless process of becoming. This tension eventually constitutes what we have previously encountered Deleuze describing as 'an amplitude that continually oversteps the representative threshold of the majoritarian standard, by excess or default'.

The form of the two diaries suggests that at some point there has been an intense cutting and reordering of narrative material close to the process that Murphy has identified as a central aspect of McGuckian's poetry. In this technique, individual phrases from an orthodox or linear text are reused, twisted, placed in new juxtapositions and stripped of context. As a result, the narrative of the original text might be reversed, or a new logic created by the symbolic correspondence of colour or sight image. Hence an entry for July 1968 reads:

> I worried all night about my literary medium, but Seamus will sort me out. I watched the death of the moon over the hill. Read *The Moon and Sixpence* by Somerset Maugham – colorsure, human, but not profound. Heavy white clouds with blue slits. We sat in the one-shilling-and-sixpence rows at the pictures. I washed my hair in milk flakes at great length. Dylan Thomas frightens me. The sunset was a crystal-clear wound. There was an immortal moth in the kitchen.[70]

While this passage connects to images elsewhere in the diaries, it also develops its own internal logic and suggests a specific strategy of reading. For instance, the description of watching the moon wane leads to a recollection of reading *The Moon and Sixpence*, which in its reference to currency triggers the memory of the 'one-shilling-and-sixpence rows' at the cinema. In turn, the 'blue slits' of the clouds impel the 'crystal-clear wound' of the sunset, while the moth drawn to the light of the kitchen returns us to the image of McGuckian herself drawn to the light of the dying moon. The associative technique is modernist in orientation if not in effect. Beyond these linguistic affinities, we are invited to make other connections. The reference to Maugham's *The Moon and Sixpence* appears to offer a clue to McGuckian's preoccupations at this stage of her life and indeed its subject matter – the extreme lengths artists will go to in order to pursue their vocation – indicates something of her own state of mind. The extract also reaches into the future; to Heaney, the figure who will indeed sort McGuckian out as the inspirational teacher she is searching for, and – in its reference to 'heavy white clouds with blue slits' – to the opening image of her poem 'Venus and the Rain',[71] a work yet to be written but an indication that her search for a vocation will be ultimately successful.

The second diary, 'Women are Trousers', is dominated by three shattering events: McGuckian's sister having some form of emotional and physical breakdown, the 'Bloody Sunday' murders of 30 January 1972, and the death of her friend Ann Owens in the Abercorn restaurant explosion in Belfast on 4 March 1972, a bombing that killed two people, injured 130 others, and was described by the coroner as 'pathological murder of the most depraved kind'.[72] As this suggests, the tone of this later diary is darker as it becomes increasingly apparent that the political possibilities inherent to the civil-rights movement in the North are not going to materialise. Instead, there develops something close to civil war, with troops on the streets, mass burning of houses and nightly explosions. Alongside this violence, however, other changes are apparent, and the masculine/unionist world of stifling disciplinary control described by the Queen's University diary of 1968 has begun to tilt on its axis. The opening entry for 1971 is glossed by a meta-textual commentary that notes: 'Now my own diary reads: Happiness is ring-shaped. There are Gaelic hurling pitches and Irish handball courts on the university campus. There are restaurants open on Sundays and cafés after midnight. Decimal currency came in on February 15th and Aer Lingus's telephone number is listed.'[73] The process that involves taking possession of her 'own diary' also appears to include the 'greening' of Queen's campus, and the gradual loosening of some of the more repressive elements of social life in Belfast. 'Women are Trousers', then, recognises that the experience of living through the modern is double-edged, that it includes the ever-escalating violence as 'Belfast gets uglier in the sun',[74] alongside the positive reform of sclerotic institutions. In this there is the seed of a dialectical political consciousness, the possibility of seeing how things might be other than they are.

Despite this, there can ultimately be no satisfactory conclusion. By the end of 'Women are Trousers' in June 1973, the self remains unformed, still lost in its dream of becoming, and the encircling political violence shows no sign of abating. For these reasons, the diary's despairing ending might be more appropriately described as an abandonment. This is encapsulated by the penultimate quotation that McGuckian cites, an extract from Maria Edgeworth's famous letter to her half-brother Michael Pakenham from 1834:

> There is literally no reign of law at the moment to hold the Irish and through the whole country there is what I cannot call a spirit of reform but a spirit of revolution under the name of reform; a restless desire to overthrow what is, and a hope – more than a hope – an expectation of gaining liberty or wealth or both in the struggle; and if they do gain either, they will lose both again and be worse off than ever – they will afterwards quarrel amongst themselves, destroy one another, and again be enslaved with heavier chains.[75]

The cadences of Edgeworth's sentence capture the enfolded terms of hope and despair implicit to revolutionary energy that McGuckian's own diaries display. The 'rebellious spontaneity' that she describes carries its own exhilaration, but its outcome is left frustrated. In an important way this accords with Helen Blakeman's perception about the experience of reading McGuckian's poetry, in which she notes that it is not the 'recurrent declarations of a fractured identity' that disturb so much as 'the regular *dissolution* of identity'. As a result, 'the persona of the poem is not only rendered unreliable but can merge into objects, and even experience synaesthetic dissolution'.[76] Endlessly fascinated by the process of shifting forms, McGuckian's poetry can be characterised in terms of its preoccupation with staging these allegories of dissolution. In this, the 'restless desire to overthrow what is', which Edgeworth finds in nineteenth-century Irish politics and which McGuckian's diaries translate to 1970s Northern Ireland, describes also McGuckian's relation to inherited aesthetic forms. This is, perhaps, where the ultimate significance of 'Rescuers and White Cloaks' and 'Women are Trousers' resides. Their appearance alongside what is becoming a formidable poetic achievement attempts to mediate between two forms of rebelliousness, and thus navigates just one of the unknown paths that can be taken in the movement from life to art.

9

'They Come into It':
The muses of Medbh McGuckian

Borbála Faragó

The most enigmatic participant in the performance of inspiration is the imaginary subject who, in one way or another, exerts authorial influence on the completion of the work. Whether imagined or real, this person, the muse, functions as the created projection of the work's singularity. In simpler terms, he or she becomes an essential participant in the performance of inspiration. This chapter concentrates on the figure of the muse in Medbh McGuckian's poetry, and looks at its different guises as women, men, angels and readers. The ancient, pre-Platonic (and plural) muses embodied the power of language, which is their 'gift' to humans. Because the human mind at that time was conceptualised as a receptor, rather than as the originator of language, the muses were credited with creativity and expression. They had authorial power, which they exercised through love. Situated at the threshold of the unattainable divine and the empirical human spheres, they metaphorically represented the ambiguity inherent in desire. The desire of the human mind to apprehend divinity is the driving force behind most of the ancient articulations of creativity. Because desire plays such a fundamental role in human creativity, it is not surprising that there is often a phantom participant in the performance of inspiration. Whether functioning as a subject or as an object of desire, the 'spectre' of another person usually accompanies poetic expression, and this is particularly true of Medbh McGuckian's work. She says:

> Nuala Ní Dhomhnaill and I would talk about this Muse figure. The first thing I would say when I meet her is 'How is your Muse?' We might not always have this figure that we need to encounter, but certainly it's a very big advantage to have one, or at least one, and then one to fall back on when the major one dies or ceases to attract. It is a lodestone. [. . .] I would have this colloquy, often with a male, sometimes a female, and often with a dead person, for example with the young boy that I didn't know, who suddenly became the Muse for the period of the poem. It is a funny process, that there is this other person, who you can't actually

speak to in real life, but you can in this space that you create. They come into it, or you pull them into it, and sometimes they pull you into it, and it's not something you can control.[1]

In this essay, which offers a thematic exploration of the muse's diverse manifestations in McGuckian's work, I argue that 'this other person' in her poetry is not only recognisable as someone of personal significance to the poet, but also as a modern-day manifestation of both a pre-Platonic and post-romantic figure of the muse. What differentiates it from other subjects appearing in her poems is its direct influence on the creation of the work. Whether passive or active, male or female, divine or human, visible or invisible, these figures unequivocally participate in the performance of poetry-making.

'Sigh for Liberation': McGuckian's female muse

The imagined 'other' of the creative process has most commonly, and most conveniently, materialised in the body of a woman throughout the ages; conveniently, that is, because for the male poetic imagination the female simultaneously represents comfort and enticement. The urge to create emerges as sexual, and indeed sometimes filial, desire, and gains fulfilment in the creative output of representing this desire. The muse, this beautiful, inert and distant woman, embodies the maternal origin and sexual target of the male poetic imagination. However, for the female creative mind she is neither straightforwardly maternal nor (simply) erotic. In fact, in McGuckian's poetry, if she is a woman, she is complicated, moody and never inert.

For a woman writer, engaging with the female muse involves an exploration of feminine agency. The individualised, embodied subject of the female muse disrupts conventional identity categories open to women within the context of poetry writing. McGuckian's poetic liberation of the restricting figure of the muse reinforces a linguistic reimagining of a female poetic self. The figure of the muse retains her emblematic characteristics, insofar as her direct influence on the performance of writing is explicitly acknowledged. What McGuckian questions and reformulates are the poetic and social attitudes surrounding and forming the muse. In this context, the explicit appearance and naming of the muse in McGuckian's poetry cannot be considered as a progressive utilisation of a cultural 'icon' in her work, but rather as a means by which the poet is enabled to question and circumnavigate cultural expectations surrounding her role as a poet. This explains the linguistic abandon with which the figure of the female muse is evoked. Unlike the romantic muse, she rarely stands alone and distant, and her role and position in the creative process are exposed to continuous challenge and an occasional *coup d'état*.

'The Seed Picture',[2] for example, from her debut collection *The Flower Master*, portrays McGuckian's female muse as the separated partner of a relationship who has left behind poems, the 'children' of the liaison:

> This is my portrait of Joanna – since the split
> The children come to me like a dumb-waiter,
> And I wonder where to put them, beautiful seeds
> With no immediate application[3]

Although Joanna, the muse, has withdrawn from the relationship with the poetic self, her absence continues to have a profound effect on the poet's creative performance, albeit a negative one. Distanced from the muse, the work takes on a life of its own and detaches itself from all authorial influence:

> The seeds dictate their own vocabulary,
> Their dusty colours capture
> More than we can plan,
> The mould on walls, or jumbled garages,
> Dead flower heads where insects shack
> I only guide them not by guesswork
> In their necessary numbers
> And attach them by the spine to a perfect bedding[4]

The second part of the poem attempts to explain why the 'split' has happened. Here, we get a glimpse of a more conventional positioning of the muse:

> Was it such self-indulgence to enclose her
> In the border of a grandmother's sampler,
> Bonding all the seeds in one continuous skin,
> The sky resolved to a cloud the length of a man?[5]

The answer is implied in the question: it seems that it is, in fact, the 'self-indulgence' of 'enclosing' the muse which leads to her abandonment. However, this is not to say that poetic creation cannot happen without her. On the contrary, 'The Seed-Picture' paints the muse in her absence and develops the 'split' as the backdrop against which the poem is written. In other words, this poem is 'unwriting' the stereotypical set-up of a presumed distance between poet and muse. Although separated, what is emphasised is the relational context in which muse and poet operate. The male poetic imagination seems to be unperturbed by the muse: she has no input into his work, and her only function is to reflect or absorb the creative performance. The muse of the woman poet, on the other hand, is an intrinsic participant in the creative process, one who refuses to be ignored. Present even in her absence, she 'makes women / feel their age, and sigh for liberation'.[6]

Rather than considering the muse as a figure in need of new attire, McGuckian enters into a dialogue with her, which leaves neither participant unaltered. This new relationship is the topic of many of her poems focusing on the female muse. One of McGuckian's early poems, 'Ode to a Poetess',[7] is especially instructive in describing and summarising the poet's methodology of rewriting the female muse. The title suggests that this poem is self-reflexive and will present a more or less straightforward imaginary construct of the speaking subject. In other words, the reader expects this to be a poem written either to another female poet, or to the poet herself. However, the relational context set out in the first part of the poem complicates this assumption:

> What survives of our garden is held together
> By the influence of water, as if we could only live
> In the shelter of each other, and just leave the matter
> Where we must leave all the doors that matter.
> How clear and beautiful and hard to bear,
> The shutters of these full delaying months,
> Like a window not made to open, or a house
> That has been too long to let, my dark woman's
> Slope.[8]

If there is a distance between two separate entities here – as a prerequisite of intersubjective communication – this is more like the distance that Robert Brazeau calls 'self-difference' visited upon a woman as a result of pregnancy.[9] The speaker and the addressed self can only exist 'in the shelter of each other'. The suggestive imagery about pregnancy of 'the full delaying months' and of the 'house let too long' implicitly deals with the sense of 'self-othering' experienced by a woman through pregnancy.[10] In terms of poetry, where childbirth becomes poem-birth, the split sense of self within the poetic persona corresponds to the imaginary presence of a contributing participant, a kind of midwife-muse, who, as the other half, 'half' shares in the pangs of creative labour:

> Half real, half-dreamed,
> Untouched, untouchable, the yet-to-be-born weather,
> Distempering me as lips disturb the vespered worlds
> Of grapes, this onset of a poetess and her
> Persuasive bones sending me and my life away.[11]

The 'onset of the poetess', recalling the onset of labour, simultaneously becomes the poetic performance and its instigator. The speaking subject persistently blurs with the 'spoken' subject, maintaining a tension within the female poetic self. This becomes explicitly registered at the beginning of the second part of the poem where the (compound) speaker says: 'I will not write her name although I know it.'[12] The act of naming would inevitably bring about separation and dissociation, eliminating the creative frustration inherent in this union. However, the poem suddenly destabilises the parameters of speaker-within-speaker (the 'I' talking about the 'she' inside) by directly addressing the muse:

> Now you are in a poem of your own cold
> Making, on your second fret, your life knit
> Like a bird's, when amid the singing
> Of the Sparrow Hills you yourself could not sing.[13]

The muse's agency lies in her own creation. Similar to the pre-Platonic muses, she is the giver of language that makes her come alive. She cannot sing, but gives the song which sings her. However, the speaker-subject reflects on the pain and frustration inherent in this process. Lacking in the erotic gratification often experienced by male poets when relating to their muse, 'Ode to a Poetess' focuses on the dissatisfying self-distancing and self-othering the female poetic speaker undergoes. The female muse of a female poet has a profound effect on the construction of the poetic self, and the collusion of the two is often portrayed as a threat to self-coherence. 'Ode to a Poetess' aptly captures this sense of danger when it surmises about the muses that 'what they ask of women is less their bed . . . than to be almost gone'.[14]

The Domesticated Male Muse

If McGuckian's female muse is interpreted as the projection of feminine poetic agency that threatens as well as assists in the performance of poetry writing, her male muse certainly subverts readerly expectations of this creative partnership. The men who appear in her poems as possible aides rarely fit stereotypical descriptions of masculinity. Her male muse is an imaginary construct that cannot be separated from his feminine originator. He is not a man, but a woman-made man. If we appreciate the limitations of the traditional figure of the female muse as a male imaginary construct, then the same holds in the case of the woman-made male muse. This has crucial implications for reading McGuckian's poetry in a cultural and political context. Creating a male muse is not only a subversion of the sexual determinants of a 'muse-tradition', but it is also a comment on the nature of gender as seen by McGuckian. The act of creating a poem becomes intertwined with creating sexualities: the performance of writing reflects on the performance of gender. McGuckian draws critical attention to the interconnectedness of performing her identity as a woman and as a poet, and her male muses provide the opportunity to demonstrate an increased awareness of discourses of gender in her poetry.

An early poem, 'Open Rose',[15] offers an accomplished exploration of this idea. The masculine pronoun that appears in the second stanza provides a startlingly clear image of the male muse:

> His head is there when I work,
> It signs my letters with a question-mark;
> His hands reach for me like rationed air.[16]

The first line places the male muse in a somewhat conventional position. 'His head' is 'there', somewhere out of reach of the poet, at a distance, from which inspiration could arrive. However, instead of divine stimulus, the muse provides the poet with a 'question-mark' and then leaves his place, reaching out to the poet in existential hunger ('like rationed air'). In terms of creating a connection between the performances of poetry and gender, the male appears as a fundamental participant in the process of writing, profoundly influencing the identity of the poet-speaker. Now the relationship is seen from the speaker-subject's point of view:

> Day by day I let him go
>
> Till I become a woman, or even less,
> An incompletely furnished house
> That came from a different century
> Where I am a guest at my own childhood.[17]

The construction of womanhood is seemingly inseparable from the process of discarding an interfering masculinity. However, the poem suggests that without the male muse the female poet is incomplete: she is a woman but not a poet. This line of thought has a strange resonance with what Toril Moi terms 'social magic'. She says that 'social magic is a socially sanctioned act which attributes an essence to individual agents, who then struggle to become what in fact they already are declared to be'. Summarising this argument, she states that 'to cast women as women is precisely to *produce* them as women'.[18] The 'letting go' of a possessive male muse produces a lack in the feminine which reinforces the 'essence' of a subdued second sex. The poetic subject appears as 'less than woman'; she is a woman of past centuries who does not have control over her own life, being merely a 'guest' at her own development.[19] It seems, however, that the most significant symbolic capital[20] of the speaking subject, the ability to write the poem, remains in the woman's control:

> I have grown inside words
> Into a state of unbornness,
> An open rose on all sides
> Has spoken as far as it can.[21]

The imagery of pregnancy serves as an ultimate exclusion of a masculine presence. However, the completion of the poem paradoxically remarks on its own incompletion ('unbornness'). It seems, then, that the conclusion of the poem acknowledges the assumed masculinity with which it opened. It is left open to interpretation whether the male is a necessary contributor in the creative reproductive process, or whether he is a hindrance. McGuckian seems to circumvent a straightforward declaration of ideological positioning in terms of gender politics. Her male muse in this poem seems to be an extension of the self whose existence, even if it creates an obstacle to ful-filling an ideal of 'womanhood', suggests creative completeness. However, this is less a manifestation of androgynous creative powers than a demonstra-tion of how the two genders perform one another. In 'Dovecote' McGuckian says that 'you cannot reproduce in your own shade'.[22] In 'Open Rose', however, she seems to be doing just that.

'The Potter'[23] in *Shelmalier* is especially instructive in reinscribing the role of the male muse from a feminine point of view. Called the 'word spouse', the male muse is reinvented as a writing subject who has lost the iconic woman as his inspirer:

> To my word spouse
> I was not Eve nor Helen,
> Not Mary nor Sophia,
> But the fool of the house.[24]

Stripped of her traditional attributes, the feminine poetic subject is formed in tandem with the masculine. The inspiring 'breath' does not originate from the muse or travel into the writing subject; on the contrary, it comes from the 'I' and is extinguished by the 'he'. ('He followed my breath / and left it in the face / of one who was pronounced dead / by the history of faith.')[25] His effect on the woman poet is simultaneously damaging and constructive. The poem is an explicit commentary on the type of lyrical discourse that assigns the female muse her conventional roles, and it is meant to highlight the unsustainable poetic reality when these roles are reversed. The male muse is domesticated and familiar; he communicates with the 'fool of the house',[26] and it is merely his imaginary (constructed) presence that influences the per-formance of inspiration in this poem. The speaking subject positions herself in 'the lotus of courtly love',[27] the traditional space reserved for the muse, and from there strategically denies a masculine influence:

> and deny that he is
> all spices commingled,
> with my entire body sown,
> deny that he is light.[28]

However, as the subject of 'The Potter', the male remains a significant reality that assists in the formation of a feminine identity. The title of the poem strategically directs our attention back to Plato's potter, who strives for perfect roundness in making his plate in imitation of the divine. Similarly, the feminine subjectivity in this poem is the imperfect imitation ('not Eve nor Helen, / not Mary nor Sophia'), whose actuality contains the masculine.

McGuckian's male muses challenge profoundly the enduring mythology of the female lyrical muse. There are several women poets who offer polemical responses to this tradition.[29] However, McGuckian's writing draws critical attention to 'woman's' embeddedness in societal and psychological gender-constructs. In other words, the masculine is present not only as an alienated 'other' against which the feminine is formulated, but also as the familiar 'other' integral to the writing-woman's identity construct. 'I had cried out my promise in his unconscious', says McGuckian in 'Dear Rain',[30] reflecting on the fundamental interconnectedness of masculinity and femininity in her work. She calls her male muse 'my active, operative germ of self',[31] and wittily comments that 'his mind is the moon that I am selling land on'.[32] In her later collections she calls 'Him' a 'domestic muse',[33] a 'mere muse',[34] and in *The Face of the Earth* we see the most explicit account of this relationship. She says, 'I have drowned in him'[35] and 'I wrote letters by him to myself'[36] and 'he was my ambition, my wildly carved harp'[37] and, as a strange conclusion, she remarks, 'he no longer lays his ear to the weapon of my lips'.[38]

The Angel Muse

In her later poetry, McGuckian introduces angels as agents of poetic perception. Angels are arcane spiritual beings, whose personalities hover between celestial perfection and human frailty. Similar to the muses, their characters inhabit our literary and religious consciousness. In literature, whether considered as messengers of God or translators of human prayer, their main role is to mediate the eternal discourse between humans and the other world. But deeply embedded as traditional touchstones of the Catholic faith, what role can angels play in the *oeuvre* of a contemporary, and in many ways unconventional, Belfast poet?

McGuckian has remarked that 'Catholicism is simply a part of the way my mind thinks [. . .] There is a spiritual dimension with Catholicism which sometimes influences the way you see things like nature.'[39] This explains the complexity in appearance and attitude of her angels. The attraction of these creatures for McGuckian seems to be their position as perpetual outsiders to both human and divine realms. Their purpose in 'life' is analogous to poetry's function in McGuckian's view. They are not there to take sides; they are there to assist communication and mediate between segregated facets of the divide, whether this is political, religious or personal. One could argue that McGuckian, by reviving the figure of the angel in her work, reverts to romantic notions of affinity between poetry and religion.[40] However, in most cases her poems are devoid of prophetic urges.

Another significant characteristic of McGuckian's angels is their speech, or, on occasion, the lack of it. Linguistic indeterminacy is a well-known feature of McGuckian's work. However, the ambivalence of the speaking subject in most of the angel poems further complicates a straightforward resolution of meaning. McGuckian's speaking subjects seem to strive to challenge meaning and establish ambiguity as a means of communication. Problematising their integrity as subjects, McGuckian allows her angels the freedom of incoherence; in other words, she focuses on the processes of linguistic exchange, rather than its outcome.

The mythic figures of angels embody several facets of the human consciousness. In *The Book of the Angel*,[41] a collection dedicated to angels,[42] McGuckian reconsiders issues of religion, spirituality, identity and, perhaps most significantly, the linguistic erosion of prayer and death. In Part Two of the volume, there are nine poems written in honour of the nine muses. The muses are differently portrayed as angels, Christ, Mary or a saint; their only constant is their characterisation as mediators between the secular and the divine. The Gospel narrative, which frames this part of the book, takes centre stage in 'A Chrisom Child'.[43] The title refers to a child who dies before s/he is a month old, but the poem depicts the Annunciation, the moment when Gabriel offers his good news. Or, to be more precise, we see the moment when 'it is impossible to tell [. . .] whether he has already spoken'.[44] Gabriel, as an angel, carries in him the ambiguity of divine happiness and human sadness, the joy of eternal life and the despair of death:

> The cushion plays such a very ambiguous
> role, and the fall of his hair
> may be compared to a crucifix
>
> that previously disfigured the sky.
> The wood, cherry, that within so short
> a radius, carried death at its heart.[45]

Thus, the Annunciation also becomes the news of death. Christ, the chrisom child, carries his death at the moment of his conception. The relevance of this to poetic creativity is complex. Gabriel is the messenger of both life and death, and a poem about his image becomes a standpoint from which to contemplate the origin and purpose of writing.[46]

'Saint Faith',[47] the last poem of this sequence, positions the poetic self back in the lines, exploring its position vis-à-vis the divine agents who have dominated the previous pages:

> All in all, there were too many spires
> and waves, more than my own footsteps.[48]

The method of portraying angels as works of art (paintings, sculptures), freezing them in a moment, paradoxically results in capturing their transience: what we see is the *lack* of a smile or a movement. This absence of animation highlights the angels' inherent desire for life and reflects upon humanity's entrapment in the still finality of existence. The angel, portrayed here as 'summer', eventually breaks out from its statuesque immobility. However, significantly, this takes place within the poetic consciousness:

> Summer stood nude, as alone as the rain,
> her family smile absent, as many sleepless
> eyes on her body as she has feathers.
>
> I heard a roar of wings, a darker flesh,
> and started walking, lest the mountain
> should soar right out of the book,
>
> then kneel down inwardly
> over a holy organ such as a feather.[49]

The 'book' gives birth to the monumental image of the angel, who 'inwardly' encounters him/herself. However, this spiritual union happens only in the conditional. The poetic self walks away, hearing, but without ever actually coming face to face with, the angel. This is because the only possible encounter is in 'saint faith', where both entities communicate. The immobility of the angel is in stark contrast to the walking image of the person, and it is the 'book', or poetic imagination, which eventually propels an imaginary meeting between the divine and the secular faiths of this poem. Thus, as a fitting conclusion to the nine poems of this sequence, 'Saint Faith' captures a frozen moment in the 'life' of a divine identity, creating an atmosphere of unease about the finality and fragility of human existence.

The angels, who occupy these poems and accompany the reader on a spiritualised journey, remain ungraspable, shapeless, and in most poems genderless, yet lovingly humanised transient creatures: 'Words remain on the shore, but when the angel / falls in love, with his different prayer movements, / he is the perfect human.'[50] 'Kaddish',[51] a poem from her most recent volume, *The Currach Requires No Harbours*, offers another instructive portrayal of the angel. A Jewish prayer of mourning, Kaddish is a form of thanksgiving for the life of the deceased. This poem is the closest the reader gets to McGuckian's angel: her hand, face, spine, eyebrows and hair are poetically described in the first four stanzas. However, the description fits a corpse more than a living being: 'her eyebrows sewn in a line / in the afternoon, without looking'.[52] Is this the angel of death? Simon Critchley argues that 'the representation of death is always a mask — a *memento mori* — behind which nothing stands'.[53] In fact, the angel of this poem is significantly distanced from the speaking subject, set 'away from my door'. Her ethereal beauty is contrasted with the claustrophobic and depressing setting of the human heart in the stark shadow of the concentration camps:

> My heart that burns like an oven
> where the dead are locked
> till cold or warm memory
>
> lengthens out their shadow
> or buys them prayer.[54]

Prayer becomes the space which allows the interaction to take place between the angel and poetic self. However, whereas in the poems of *The Book of the Angel* the language of prayer is portrayed as the desire of humans, here it is the angel who internalises desire, 'coveting' the speaker's 'indigo skirt'. This transformation confuses the direction of communication: 'her desiring left its mark / on the child like glass in her womb'.[55] The glass reflects a perplexing human incapability for interaction and the poem concludes with the denial of faith:

> Now I do not see any colourableness
> in empty winds that could be
>
> spirit-laced, the turning over
> of the world by ankle-bells'
> sheer fabric-lack.[56]

The poem mourns the angel of death and also mourns a failure of encounter between the sacred and the secular. However, it celebrates its own lack and says Kaddish for a dead angel, symbolising the ultimate deconstruction of the poetic language of prayer.

The angels' dichotomy as divine and secular imaginaries embodies the ambiguity of poetry as experienced by McGuckian. The figure of the angel, her 'winged muse', radically alters our preconceptions of human interaction. Alternating their position between sender and recipient, the angels fundamentally disturb routes of language transmission. The dislocated reader has no choice but to accept this dialogic relation to McGuckian's works, otherwise the poems simply get lost in the labyrinth of logical decoding.

'You are my Masterpiece': McGuckian's reader–muse

The figure and idea of the reader have been central to most scholarly discourses engaged in outlining what makes a text a work of art. It is obvious that, without reading, a published book remains a chance meeting between paper and ink. The reader therefore seems to be the omnipotent creator of the work. As Maurice Blanchot argues:

> What is a book no one reads? Something that is not yet written. It would seem, then, that to read is not to write the book again, but to allow the book to *be*: written – this time all by itself, without the intermediary of the writer, without anyone's writing it. The reader does not add himself to the book, but tends primarily to relieve it of an author.[57]

Derek Attridge also gives the reader a crucial role in literature. He argues that the 'inventiveness'[58] of a work is registered by the reader, and creative reading is a successful 'attempt to respond to the otherness, inventiveness, and singularity of the work'.[59] He states that the reader has a responsibility towards reading. This manifests itself as 'readerly hospitality', which is a readiness to have one's purposes reshaped by the work to which one is responding.[60] Thus, reading creatively involves a 'suspension of habits, a willingness to rethink old positions in order to apprehend the work's inaugural power'.[61] Reading, according to Attridge, is simultaneously an event and an act, which calls for 'sympathy'; it is a positive openness that characterises full responsiveness.[62] 'In a creative reading it is only as a singularity that I can respond to the singularity of the work,'[63] he argues, pointing to the obviously privileged position of the reader. Attridge also qualifies what he means by 'responsible' or 'proper' readerly response. He argues that this is based on a contradiction, whereby the reader is simultaneously required to understand, or 'repeat', the work in his/her mind, and produce something unique and 'creative' as a response. Attridge concludes that the reader's role ultimately is to 're-enact' the work.

However, while the above scholars testify to the crucial role a reader plays in the creative process, some of McGuckian's work seems inventively to reconfigure this proposition. The poems that this section examines challenge the assumption of authentic 'author' and 'reader' figures encountering and constructing each other in the process of reading. The fundamental hypothesis that the reader comes to life only *after* the work is finished and is being read is defied by McGuckian's preconfigurations of a readerly presence within her texts. Many authors have used their texts before to 'talk' to the readers. However, this rarely demonstrates a direct influence on the creative performance of the work. In McGuckian's poetry, however, the reader is an abstraction on a par with the author, and has a direct influence on the actual process of writing. In other words, the reader is not projected or presumed, but written into the text. It is for this reason that the reader is inventively reconstituted as an imaginary muse figure, the symbolic 'other' of the work.

'The Over Mother',[64] a poem that was written at a time when McGuckian was running a creative-writing workshop at the Maze prison, looks at the symbolic 'birthing' of the reader. The emotional frustration that precedes the appearance of the 'audience' is portrayed in the first stanza:

> Play kisses
> stir the circuits of the underloved body
> to an ever-resurrection, a never-had tenderness
> that dies inside me.[65]

The 'underloved body' is a composite image simultaneously referencing the abstinent prisoners ('passion exhausts itself at the mouth'[66]) and the poet-mother who is pregnant with her work. The 'play kisses' and the 'never-had tenderness' come from an audience which has limited access to a freedom of understanding. Thus, the audience is invoked as the cause of the emotional turbulence that triggers the poem:

> My cleverly dead and vertical audience,
> words fly out from your climate of unexpectation
> in leaky, shallowised night letters –
> what you has spoken?

The imprisoned readers are conceptualised in a somewhat shocking image of the 'dead and vertical' foetuses of the 'over mother'. They themselves are not burdened, having a 'climate of unexpectation', but still produce the 'words'. Put in a different way, the reader is carried by the author and is therefore incapable of consciously sharing in the experience of the creative process. However, this inability becomes a potential to create. The imprisoned reader 'leaks' the words of this poem to the page, and speaks: 'what you has spoken?' The severance of the two subjectivities, those of the author and the reader, is denied by disallowing a symbolic birth. This means that the moment of reading never follows the work, but accompanies it:

> I keep seeing birds
> that could be you when you stretch out
> like a syllable and look to me
> as if I could give you wings.

This 'as if' is a recurring phrase throughout McGuckian's work. It provokes the reader actively to reflect on the performance of a readerly identity through which the poetry is generated.

As demonstrated, the reader in McGuckian's poems is prefigured as a constructive subjectivity 'writing' the work. However, as a present 'other' within the work, the reader can also threaten authorial intentions. 'Breaking the Blue'[67] traces the creative, self-reflexive disruption that the readerly presence brings to the process of composition. The colour blue, a trope designating creativity in McGuckian's work, is 'broken' by the intrusive, 'unspeaking likeness' of the reader:

> Deluged with the dustless air, unspeaking likeness:
> You, who were the spaces between words in the act of reading,
> A colour sewn on to colour, break the blue.[68]

The imaginary space occupied by the reader is shared by a somewhat reluctant authorial presence. In fact, there seems to be a single 'body' inhabiting the two subjectivities:

> Single version of my mind deflected off my body,
> Side altar, sacramental, tasting-table, leaf to my
> Emptying shell, heart with its aortic opening,
>
> Your mouth, my dress was the scene that framed
> Your shut eye like hand or hair, we coiled
> In the lifelong snake of sleep, we poised together
>
> Against the crevice formed by death's forefinger
> And thumb, where her shoulder splits when desire
> Goes further than the sender will allow.[69]

Desire for creation usually materialises as desire for unity and harmony, which is achieved in the subsequent act of reading. Here, however, desire 'goes further' and results in a premature 'split' within the writing subject. The 'sender', the author, has 'allowed' her creative power to slip away from her control, and now the reader within seems simultaneously attached and severed, a 'womb-encased and ever-present mystery without / release'.[70] Because the writing subject encompasses both the author and the reader,[71] the resulting poem cannot represent wholeness or unity without a sense of inherent division. The simultaneous acts of writing and reading create a fissure in meaning, and produce inevitable fragmentation:[72]

> Fragments of once-achieved meaning, ready to leave
> The flesh, re-integrate as lover, mother, words
> That overwhelm me: You utter, become music, are played.[73]

The symbolic birth of 'meaning' accompanies the birth of the reader, who supersedes authorial subjectivity. What emerges at the end of the poem is the peculiar McGuckianesque writing subject, who, as the ultimate muse, Language, speaks and is spoken.

McGuckian's fascination with the reader permeates her work. The reader haunts her imagination and her poems. In other words, while the reader is performing the poem, the poem in turn performs the reader. Nevertheless, this is not aimless word-play by McGuckian. By dispensing with the myth of a presupposed static readerly subject, McGuckian demonstrates her scepticism about critical interpretations that dissect and fixate, but let the joke played on us go unnoticed. McGuckian's reader-muse is in a precarious position of simultaneous authorial power and powerlessness. S/he creates, but is also being created, rather like the rings suspended on Plato's magnetic chain, which, by being attracted, also inherit the power of attraction. In the context of inspiration, therefore, the reader is present at the commencement of the poetic performance, rather than being 'added' later on.

In conclusion, Medbh McGuckian's muses demonstrate the poet's intricate and multi-layered approach to subjectivity and language, which is simultaneously orthodox and subversive. It is orthodox in the sense that McGuckian displays a strong belief in a distinct entity that she calls 'muse' in her poetry, and she is unfailingly confident in talking about this. On the other hand, her portrayal of, and relationship to, these subjectivities profoundly subvert romanticised representations of the muse. In many ways, the pre-Platonic muses stand as precursors to McGuckian's reimaginings: her muses are also proprietors of language and desire, and, in several cases, take over authorial responsibility. However, McGuckian's muses are, indisputably, personalities, with their own sets of values and characteristics that are seemingly independent from those of their creator. McGuckian's enduring interest in muses does not stem from a literary quest to find the ultimate 'source' of writing. (In fact, sources are a surprisingly open concept for McGuckian, who freely 'picks' literary texts for her own work.) Rather, her muses seemingly assist her in pondering upon issues of identity. Thus, her female muses, with their direct involvement in childbirth, share McGuckian's concern for self-coherence, and their portrayed authorial power reflects on the poet's exploration of issues of her identity as a writing woman. The male muses, on the other hand, create a framework within which issues of sexuality can be assessed, and where the performance of writing becomes intertwined with the performance of gender. For their part, the angels allow for a more abstract investigation of the divide between the secular and the divine, and the function of language and communication within prayer and poetry. Perhaps the most complex of McGuckian's muses is the reader, the 'you' within the text, whose innate power and simultaneous powerlessness to create the poem disrupts critical anticipation of intellectual distance and literal decoding.

Re-assembling the Atom:
Reading Medbh McGuckian's
intertextual materials

LEONTIA FLYNN

I 'Meaningless and Full of Meaning': against 'descriptive and explanatory poetry'

The title poem of *On Ballycastle Beach* speaks of 'read[ing] these words to you [. . .] meaningless and full of meaning',[1] and may be taken as a description of the aesthetic which first brought Medbh McGuckian's work to critical attention. By the time of the publication of her third collection, however, the poet's meaningful meaninglessness, or meaningless meaningfulness, had begun to exhaust the patience of some of her readers. Patrick Williams's review of *On Ballycastle Beach*, indeed, has come to be seen as evidence of the kind of critical fury McGuckian's work can excite. Having cautiously welcomed her previous work, Williams now found his attitude (perhaps in an unconscious echo of the images of softness and hardness which permeate these poems) had 'hardened' and concluded that 'if lines are so arbitrary that they mean more or less anything, then necessarily they mean more or less nothing'. One of the only things he could find to recommend the 'verse' was that it 'has generally the sound of sense'.[2] And it was after reading *On Ballycastle Beach* that even McGuckian-advocate Michael Allen concluded that in order to validate the poet's work 'we must be able to explicate her gnomic tendency, prove that she is not writing nonsense verses or being wilfully obscure'.[3] Popularly McGuckian's defence on these matters has been a feminist one, relying on the argument that her sinuous and elusive work represents the subversion of a particularly *masculine* sense. Now, however, surprisingly concrete proofs against her 'meaninglessness' have been offered. Through extensive study of the author's papers, Shane Alcobia-Murphy has discovered that McGuckian's poems are composed in a 'montage effect',[4] drawn from various literary biographies and scholarly works. As yet, the critical verdict seems to be out on what this means for a re-reading of McGuckian's work. Is it the case that, with some investigative work, we can locate those meanings of which, previously, her work only *seemed* to be full? Do these sources provide – like a private, idiolectical Rosetta Stone – proof, finally, that the poet is not writing 'nonsense verse'?

Prior to Alcobia-Murphy's work, there had been only sporadic intimations of McGuckian's intertextuality. In 1989, Meva Maron, a Ukranian translator, wrote a letter to *The Honest Ulsterman* concerning the final lines of the poem 'Little House, Big House':

> Since our blood
> Is always older than we will ever be,
> I should like to lie in Tarusa under matted grass,
> Where the strawberries are redder than anywhere else.[5]

Aware that Marina Tsvetaeva had a summer residence in Tarusa, Maron suspected an unadvertised source here concerning the Russian poet. This, she wrote, 'does more than let one say "Aha, Tsvetaeva! I've solved the crossword!"' In a tantalising throwaway comment, the translator also suggested something of the origins of 'The Dream Language of Fergus', again from *On Ballycastle Beach*: 'there's nothing that insists on your finding Mandelstam's "Conversations about Dante", from which half of it comes'.[6] Yet, suggestive as her insights were, Maron had not quite solved the crossword. Nor, although Clair Wills earlier discussed 'The Dream Language of Fergus' in terms of McGuckian's borrowings from Osip Mandelstam's prose, does the story end there. Alcobia-Murphy's findings suggest more fully the extent of the poet's enterprise: McGuckian's appropriated language is both exact and circuitous in its routes/roots. Thus, the reference in 'Little House, Big House', he writes, is 'far more indirect than Maron suspects'. Tarusa and the strawberries are no casual allusion to Tsvetaeva, but a *direct quotation* from a memoir written by (less predictably) Olga Ivinskaya, who, within the frame of her account of life as Boris Pasternak's mistress, discusses Marina Tsvetaeva's suicide and burial in an unmarked grave in Yelabuga:

> In May 1934, while she was still in Paris, Marina had written: 'I should like to lie in the Khlyst cemetery in Tarusa, under an elder bush, in one of those graves with a silver dove on it, where the wild strawberries are larger and redder than anywhere else in those parts.[7]

McGuckian's poems, then, are often underpinned not by a single allusion but operate at another remove. They often contain specific words by a writer or translator speaking of another author, or they might have several interconnected sources.

The first thing to note about Alcobia-Murphy's findings is that he claims that the poems must now be interpreted in light of their original context. '"Little House, Big House" becomes, with reference to its sources, a tribute to

Marina Tsvetaeva.'[8] Here is one defence against Williams's charge of arbitrariness extended to the interlinear interpretation of these intertextual poems. The words of the poems only *seem* arbitrary if we are unaware of the figure or figures with whom McGuckian is in dialogue. Alcobia-Murphy also suggests that the obscurity of the materials which inform McGuckian's work – 'well beyond the scholarly ambit of her critics within Irish Studies' – goes some way towards explaining 'the lack of understanding with which she has frequently been received'.[9] The second thing to note (indeed, for a critic seeking to discuss this work it is inescapable) is the sheer complexity of tracing McGuckian's source material. It is not merely that the use of other texts is entirely *unsignalled*, but that, once uncovered, the texts she uses bleed into one another in a curious way. These points might be illustrated with reference to the origins of the language which comprises 'The Dream Language of Fergus' and 'Harem Trousers'. 'The Dream Language of Fergus' is, as Alcobia-Murphy has found, made up of at least twelve quotations found in Osip Mandelstam's *Complete Prose*, often hundreds of pages apart, but most often in his essay 'Conversation about Dante'.[10] More complex still, 'Harem Trousers' is drawn from at least *four* different works by or about Marina Tsvetaeva: the poet's selected prose, and her own *Art in the Light of Conscience: Eight Essays on Poetry* as well as Elaine Feinstein's biography of the poet and a study by Simon Karlinsky, *Marina Tsvetaeva: The Woman, Her World and Her Poetry*.[11] What this effectively means, it seems, is that from being deemed a poem in praise of a dreamlike postmodern sensibility ('Asleep on the coast, I dream of the city / a poem dreams of being written without the pronoun "I"'), the reader might (with some effort) now 'wake' to a referent to these words. The lines regarding 'the pronoun "I"', as well as a later line in 'Harem Trousers', 'An extreme and simple-feeling / Of "What if I do enter"?', are drawn specifically from Simon Karlinsky's book on Tsvetaeva. Here, Karklinsky describes how, at a reading given by women poets in 1920, Tsvetaeva felt compelled to read poems expressing her right to support the Tsar, for several reasons, which she lists:

> (1) seven poems by a woman without the word 'love' and *without the pronoun 'I'*; (2) proof that poetry makes no sense to the audience; (3) a dialogue with some one particular person who understood (perhaps a student); (4) and the principal one: fulfilling here, in Moscow in 1920, an obligation of honor. And beyond all aims, aimlessly, stronger than aims, *a simple and extreme feeling of: what if I do?*[12]

So whereas previously Thomas Docherty had suggested 'Harem Trousers' as a comment on McGuckian's 'blank phenomenology', how her poetry 'often reads as if the language itself, a language devoid of consciousness, were directing it',[13] now we are faced with the prospect that 'the personae in the poem are not as unspecified as he [Docherty] claims'.[14]

And yet does this knowledge make 'Harem Trousers' a very different poem and radically alter our reading of it? 'Harem Trousers', like *On Bally-castle Beach* as a whole, is filled with images of violent linguistic fragmentation and dispersal. 'It', in stanza three, 'holds the hundred and first word / In its fingers and tears it apart', while in the final stanza 'A Stem, a verb, a rhyme' might be 'expelled at any time' from a room's 'involuntary window'.[15] The 'Dream Language of Fergus' likewise concludes with the idea of a 'seed-fund' and 'diaspora', and seems explicitly to refuse a return to linguistic origins: 'No text can return the honey / In its path of light from a jar.'[16] Such imagery, like the 'littered' poetry of 'The Time Before You' or the 'nouns' in their 'scattered rooms' in 'A Dream in Three Colours' ('Where they sit for years unable to meet, / Like pearls that have lost their clasp'),[17] might not persuade us that the reconfiguration of vocabulary throughout these poems is anything other than random. Moreover, in the passage produced by Alcobia-Murphy, there is clearly an ironic dimension to what has been uncovered. If the Karlinsky text owes its relevance to our determination to 'solve the crossword', or find 'proofs' against McGuckian's nonsense, what we find instead here is Tsvetaeva's assertion of (point 2 on her list of reasons for reading a poem in support of the Tsar) 'proof that poetry makes no sense to the audience'. Clair Wills has already pointed out that that a similar irony accompanies the reader's exploration of the quotations which make up 'The Dream Language of Fergus'. Parts of the first stanza here, for instance, have been traced to comments in 'Conversation about Dante' which are, again, about the pointlessness of seeking straightforward explanations for poetry. McGuckian's poem begins:

> Your tongue has spent the night
> In its dim sack as the shape of your foot
> In its cave. Not the rudiment
> Of half a vanquished sound,
> The excommunicated shadow of a name
> Has rumpled the sheets of your mouth.[18]

One of Mandelstam's remarks which lies behind this poem is: 'where one finds commensurability with paraphrase, there the sheets have not been rumpled; there poetry has not, so to speak, spent the night.'[19] As Wills points out, this is the overall message of 'Conversation about Dante': a plea 'for a less scholarly, more immediate response to Dante's poetry'.[20] Mandelstam argues against critical pursuit of 'semantic equivalences', and against the kind of investigative digging which, in the context of seeking explication for McGuckian's poem, is only the reason we have arrived at his caveats at all. Indeed, at one point in the essay he describes an activity which sounds suspiciously close to our own: 'If a physicist, having once broken down an atomic nucleus, should desire to put it back together again, he would resemble the partisans of descriptive and explanatory poetry.'[21] Here, McGuckian's fragmented language, re-placed, 'scientifically' in Mandelstam's text, as with Tsvetaeva's, reveals less a possible, hidden interpretation of her poem than a reflection of our own (misguided) search for one. And once more, this ironical commentary on our activity as investigative readers would seem to be widespread in McGuckian's sources. In another text from which McGuckian has been found to draw, Clarence Brown's study of Osip Mandelstam, we encounter Tsvetaeva again commenting on her interpretation of Mandelstam: 'I do not know whether in general we need real life inter-linear translations for poetry [. . .] To what end? In order to bring us closer to the living poet. But surely he must know that the poet lives *in the poem*, while *in essence* he was far away.'[22] So too, finding ourselves reading these words after such extensive research reinforces the feeling that by seeking to interpret McGuckian's poem we have moved further away than ever from properly understanding it.

What Alcobia-Murphy's findings would suggest, in other words, is that there is a convergence among McGuckian's quoted sources on arguments that poetry actually 'makes no sense to the reader', and, thus, against interpretation or paraphrasable explanation. There is also a convergence on a (similarly self-validating) celebration of the mysterious 'aural' dimension in poetry and poetry composition. If one were to look for a reason for the presence – while certainly 'very far away' – of Tsvetaeva and Mandelstam in McGuckian's third collection, one might hazard a guess that Seamus Heaney's 'The Government of the Tongue' holds the key: Clair Wills has suggested such a nod to Heaney's essay in McGuckian's strange twinning of Russia with Ballycastle here, since Heaney focuses on Mandelstam's ideas about poetic speech, and 'Conversation about Dante' in particular. And indeed in 'The Government of the Tongue' Mandelstam embodies an argument for poetic autonomy and against, again, 'ready-made meaning' in poetry – against 'Bluff expositors in verse of arguments or narratives which could have been as well conducted in prose' or, what New Zealand poet C.K. Stead called 'poetry that made sense'.[23] Supporting the notion of *highly mediated* dialogue with Heaney on the nature of poetry is the further discovery that McGuckian has used other sources referenced in Heaney's prose. In another essay from *The Government of the Tongue*, 'Osip and Nadezhda Mandelstam', Heaney praises the 'indomitable memoir'[24] of Mandelstam's wife, which relates the hardships suffered by the couple when they had fallen foul of the Stalinist regime. And Alcobia-Murphy has found that the images of scattered and hidden poems in 'Yeastlight', 'those poems sewn / Into cushions, or pushed into saucepans or shoes', are drawn from Nadezhda Mandelstam's description of police searches of their apartment in 1934, during which Mandelstam's poems were concealed.[25] In addition to referring to Clarence Brown's study of Mandelstam (which Alcobia-Murphy has shown McGuckian uses for several poems in poems from *Marconi's Cottage*), in his final essay on Sylvia Plath Heaney invokes Robert Frost's ideas about composition. This is Frost's famous theory that poetry required a sensitivity to language and sentence sounds which are previous to 'content and articulated meaning'.[26] These ideas are contained in Frost's letter to his friend John Bartlett, and it is this collection of letters that – once more – has been discovered behind another of McGuckian's poems, 'Frost in Beaconsfield'. The poem begins:

> A voice beyond a door that cuts off
> The words was my coverless book to you,
> Myself the price of it.[27]

Alcobia-Murphy has found that this 'coverless book' has been appropriated from Frost's description of the unbound galley proofs of *A Boy's Will* which he sent his friend. As for 'A voice from behind a door that cuts off the words', this, Frost said, was the best place to hear the cadencing and sentence sounds – the 'vitality of speech' – needed for good writing. 'A voice behind a door' is the best place to hear 'the abstract sound of sense'.[28] Digging out the origins of McGuckian's poetic material here once again takes us away from the experience or intuitive understanding of the poems which the poet (now with some heavyweight commentators behind her) seems to be counselling. Yet, at the same time, this labyrinthine detective work simultaneously brings us *back* to her poems again. For, in fact, Alan Jenkins, reviewing *The Flower Master*, explicitly referred McGuckian's effects to Frost's 'sentence sounds'.[29] And 'the sound of sense', after all, is what even Patrick Williams acknowledges that her poems have.

One might begin to formulate a theory, then, that the intertexts at work in *On Ballycastle Beach* (and later in *Marconi's Cottage*) operate as a paradoxical, extra-poetical apologia, and in particular an apology for McGuckian's poetry. McGuckian's poems here repeatedly return to what is 'meaningless and recognisable' ('My Brown Guest')[30] – that is, to the qualities of 'dream speech', which communicates without being literally meaningful. Associating this with poetry, her work insists on the *patterning* of poetic language as its most important function:

> The sounds that shapes make in the air,
> the shapes that sounds make, matter [. . .][31]

In particular the poems of *On Ballycastle Beach* might be seen to test how far they can push the poem away from the language of ordinary communication and towards the musicality of its original impulse. It seems that in order to do this McGuckian has used particular materials which, if investigated, underpin her sensibility, and protest (whether to Seamus Heaney or to any reader who has undertaken the peculiar, self-martyring task of 'making sense' of McGuckian) that this mere '*sound* of sense' is, in fact, the quintessence of true poetry. McGuckian's poems suggest their affinity with the 'voice behind a door' (the pre-linguistic impulse of poetry) by using voices not *behind doors*[32] but within the covers of books, but which are, nevertheless, 'cut off'. The quotations which underlie McGuckian's work return, then, to the idea of the auditory. For Frost, for example, 'The ear does it. The ear is the only true writer and the only true reader';[33] Mandelstam was, according to Clarence Brown, 'an aural poet, he heard his lines and took them down';[34] Tsvetaeva's attack on *sense*, according to Alcobia-Murphy's findings, is due to her feeling that, overtaken by inspiration, she 'would obey, seek out with my ear some assigned aural lesson'.[35] And yet, precisely because of this, none of this uncovered material can be described as discursive *content* of McGuckian's poems. The reader does not need to follow the logic of Diaspora and transformation which litters McGuckian's poems to know this. If we look for them, the 'quotations' McGuckian has used tell us this. In another paradoxical discovery, Mandelstam writes in 'Conversation about Dante': 'A quotation is not an excerpt. A quotation is a cicada. Its natural state is one of unceasing sound. Having once seized hold of the air it will not let go.'[36] His point too is one about the hybrid process of poetic discourse 'which crosses two sound modes' and, in discussing Dante's *Inferno*, about the 'contentlessness' of poetic material:

> Poetic material does not have a voice. It does not paint with bright colours, nor does it explain itself in words. It is devoid of form just as it is devoid of content for the simple reason that it exists only in performance. The finished poem is no more than a calligraphic product, the inevitable result of the impulse to perform.[37]

Likewise, this material is not 'quoted' by McGuckian so much as her poem – her new, finished, performative product – is made *continuous* with it. In this way, then, McGuckian's sources, particularly for *On Ballycastle Beach*, may refer back to her own heady sense of the inspirational/aural origins to her work (which again dovetails with, say, Tsvetaeva's conception of composition as 'self-directing dream work [. . .] an almost complete analogy to dreaming').[38] But they also make a similar point about *text* to that made by Roland Barthes in 'From Work to Text':

> [The text is] . . . woven entirely with citations, references, echoes, cultural languages, (what language is not?) antecedent or contemporary, which cut across it through and through in a vast stereophony. The intertextual in which every text is held, it itself being the text-between of another text, is not to be confused with the origin of the

text: to try to find the 'sources', the influences of a work, is to fall in with the myth of filiation; the citations which go to make up a text are anonymous, untraceable, and yet *already read*: they are quotations without inverted commas.[39]

They tell us, that is, what we already know – even if we did not know we knew it.

II The 'Resurrective Voice': a question of origins

On first looking into McGuckian's 'sources', then, the reader finds what looks like a highly ironic and convoluted joke on 'partisans of descriptive and explanatory poetry', crossword-puzzle solvers and searchers for proofs of meaning. Thomas Docherty has written of the 'pleasurable pain of interpretation in McGuckian's poems', of how their meanings are revealed as illusions just as we seem on the point of understanding them.[40] A similar illusion of meaning – followed by refusal or deferral – seems to be offered by these 'deeper' materials. At second glance, however, another point seems to be being made in McGuckian's 'source' materials (simultaneous to, though separate from, the point being made in her poems) about poetic authorship, and the origins and destinations of poetic language. Origins and destinations are, of course, signalled overtly in the very title of *On Ballycastle Beach*. It offers a curiously specific location, for one thing, for poems which so often figure *dis*location, and are awash with foreign or Russian terms: 'Mazurka', 'Balakhana', 'Querencia', a 'French-born' sea, etc.[41] Yet this perhaps flags up the nature of the 'voice' here. For although Alcobia-Murphy has suggested that 'Little House, Big House' and 'Harem Trousers' are *about* or in dialogue with Marina Tsvetaeva, it would seem now that, on the most literal level, the language and voices are both McGuckian's *and* Marina Tsvetaeva's. The words are both those of the biographical McGuckian, who had recently purchased a house near Ballycastle, Northern Ireland (and thus might be 'asleep on the coast', dreaming of the city),[42] and Tsvetaeva, who had used some of them in a different context. The poems in 'Yeastlight' are secreted both by Nadezhda Mandelstam *and* McGuckian, in the sense that McGuckian had disguised or hidden Nadezhda's words. In their self-referential, elusive way, the poems offer the idea of a mutual language: a poem written 'without the pronoun "I"', or by what 'To the Oak-Leaf Camps' refers to as 'our shared portmanteau name'. 'Balakhana', indeed, declares 'Things of the same kind are separated only by time.' Likewise it now seems that this blurring of influence, originality and authorship in favour of *shared* language re-echoes through the source materials of the poems as well.

Indeed, if the concerns with 'sound' and 'sense' were found curiously refracted through McGuckian's intertextual materials, collapsing the distinction between poetic form and content or revealing 'content' to be an illusion, now the identities of the authors from whom she borrows are also multiplied and reconfigured like images in a hall of mirrors. The 'quotations' which form poems in *On Ballycastle Beach* alone have already yielded a strange shifting chain of authorship: Olga Ivinskaya discussing Marina Tsvetaeva in the context of her life with Pasternak in 'Little House, Big House'; Mandelstam discussing Dante in 'The Dream Language of Fergus'; Tsvetaeva discussing Mandelstam and Mandelstam discussing Tsvetaeva in both the Karlinsky book used in 'Harem Trousers' and in Clarence Brown's study, which is used in poems like 'Visiting Rainer Maria'; Nadezhda Mandelstam recalling her life with Osip Mandelstam in 'Yeastlight'; Frost in dialogue with John Barlett in a book of letters edited by Bartlett's daughter (all mediated in some way by Seamus Heaney), and so on. Before noticing the strong female cast in this particular literary history, another feature of the poetic identities to which McGuckian's poems gesture (invisibly, or notionally) is that often they seem to have become so merged with McGuckian's own poetic persona that one wonders where she ends and they begin. To return to the issue of inspiration, for instance, McGuckian has long claimed that her work is the product of inspiration or unknown forces. She has said that 'Inspiration works with me. It takes over, if it's a good one,' and that 'It approaches me, basically. I find that you can't force it. You have to be in the mood. You have to be almost in a religious [. . .] I guess I approach it passively.'[43] Leaving aside questions of how well an extensive fragmentation and reconfiguration of countless textual sources sits with a 'passive' inspiration, one notes that in these aids to the muse, the sources on Tsvetaeva, we meet an almost identical account. Alcobia-Murphy notes Tsvetaeva's description of receiving her assigned 'aural lessons':

> Things always chose me by the mark of my power, and often I wrote them almost against my will, all my Russian works are of this sort. Certainly things of Russia wanted to be expressed, they chose me. And how did they persuade, seduce me? By my own power.[44]

Indeed, McGuckian's Russian predecessor felt that in order for things to be expressed 'through her', this external force would select her very words: 'And it was not I who, out of a hundred words [. . .] would choose the hundred and first, but *it*.'[45] In turn, the external force which guides McGuckian's poetry has selected this very word 'it' for 'Harem Trousers': 'It holds the hundred and first word / In its fingers and tears it apart.' Roland Barthes has written of the text that in it 'everything is to be *disentangled*, nothing *deciphered* [. . .] the space of writing is to be ranged over, not pierced',[46] that it can merely be *run*, like a stocking. Here too, a twitch on one of McGuckian's threads simply leads to a different, similar point in the text, rather than to a point inside it. We know now that McGuckian's 'special language is very often that of others refracted within her own text, the quotations giving it the veneer of a dream language'.[47] But this 'language of others' also, it turns out, validates poetry as a 'dream language', offering us a continuity with that 'veneer' rather than a glimpse behind it. And if there seems to be a potentially endless sequence of writers and texts here, it is particularly the figure of Tsvetaeva who feels like a doppelgänger in the labyrinth. McGuckian's Russian forebear seems an unlikely explicator of her work when we learn, for instance, that she too was accused of writing only with *the sound of sense*. Karlinsky notes that she was dismissed as a producer of 'extremely melodious nonsense'[48] and of having no feeling for words as meaningful *logos*. In fact, in terms which directly echo Patrick Williams's criticisms of *On Ballycastle Beach*, Nabokov accused her of 'amusing herself with unintelligible rhyme-weaving'.[49] The gestures towards Tsvetaeva in McGuckian's work – 'presence' seems less than ever the right word – therefore often work to reflect back the figure of the poet. In the mutuality of their aesthetic, is Tsvetaeva a cipher for McGuckian, or is McGuckian the Second Coming of Tsvetaeva?

This question is less facetious than it might seem. McGuckian has explicitly said that she regards her poetic practice as a form of resurrection: 'I feel that actually every poem I write is a resurrection of some individual, it's a biography, a conversation, a reworking of someone's life. My words are just to rekindle some of their life that is spoken through me.'[50] This, therefore, justifies her appropriation of the words of these figures without signalling her practice: 'The words are given to me [. . .] and the authors, and the translators, especially if they're dead, they are very aware of me using them.'[51] Her mode of composition might further be seen to be supported by the fact that (and this is perhaps the single most significant feature of the sources in *On Ballycastle Beach* and *Marconi's Cottage*) she resurrects resurrectionists and appropriates from appropriators. That is, even McGuckian's attitude to her poetry cannot be said for certain to originate *with her*. Rather, her intertextual cast also tend to point to a similar-sounding appropriation of sources. The title of 'Visiting Rainer Maria', as Clair Wills notes, most likely derives from an unfulfilled pact between Pasternak and Tsvetaeva to go to visit Rilke. It is found in a series of letters, written in the summer of 1926, and exchanged between all three poets, in which Tsvetaeva writes: 'what would you and I do if we were together [. . .] we would go and see Rilke':

> Today I would like Rilke to speak – through me. In everyday language this is called translation. How much better the Germans put it – *nachdichten*! Following in the poet's footsteps to lay again the path he has already laid. Let *nach* mean follow, but *dichten* always has a new meaning. *Nachdichten*, laying a new path all traces of which are grown

over instantaneously. But 'translate' has another meaning: to translate not into (into Russian, for example) but also to (to the opposite bank of the river). I will translate Rilke into Russian and he, in time, will translate me to the other world.[52]

McGuckian's own poem, 'Visiting Rainer Maria', then, follows this example – it is one which has 'laid a new path' by following the footsteps of others, speaking through their words and images. Almost all of it, in fact, as Murphy shows, is borrowed piecemeal from Clarence Brown's study.[53] In turn, in Clarence Brown's study we learn that not only Tsvetaeva but Mandelstam too used sources in their poetry and sometimes failed to acknowledge them. Tsvetaeva, as her remarks on laying new paths would suggest, practised the appropriation and dislocation of 'inherited texts' in her poems, and was accused of refusing to supply the necessary clues to her readers.[54] Like McGuckian, she proclaimed a mystically personal relationship with the materials she borrowed: 'I myself am my sources,' Karlinsky records her saying of her 'Phaedra', an adaptation of the myths of Gustav Schwab, 'the sources are within me'.[55] Clarence Brown writes that Mandelstam also made use of earlier work in a way which is 'oblique, fragmentary and atmospheric'.[56] The most direct way to appropriate from the work of earlier writers, Mandelstam considered, was 'to translate the earlier writers' words into one's own language'.[57] Another way, as Brown notes, 'is to write as it were from *inside* the other work', to re-make it. Of Mandelstam's 'Phaedra', then, Brown asks: 'Is this Racine's Phedre, or Mandelstam's? The question is too limited. Why should one exclude the predecessors of Racine – Euripides and Seneca – from the question of proprietorship?'[58] We might now ask the same questions about the language in McGuckian's poem: is it McGuckian's or Mandelstam's? Or is it Brown's for that matter? McGuckian's 'sources' therefore do not just point to multi-authored texts (the triangulated Rilke/Pasternak/Tsvetaeva exchange is just one *literary* instance of recurring *ménages-à-trois*) but can also be found to assert that writing is inherently intertextual. Mandelstam even claimed that Dante worked in this vein:

> The secret of Dante's capacity resides in the fact that he introduced not a single word of his own fabrication. Everything sets him going except fabrication, except invention [. . .] He writes to dictation, he is a copyist, he is a translator [. . .] He is completely bent over in the posture of a scribe casting a frightened sidelong glance at the illuminated original he borrowed from the prior's library.[59]

Bent over McGuckian's sources, ranged along the shelves of the library, the reader now finds yet another 'quoted' image of the poet's own activity beneath or within her texts. The effect is of an ever-receding spiral of 'origins', in which the poet-as-author gives way to the figure of the copyist or translator – now merely one of many participating in the great self-renewing and *unoriginal* act of writing.

In this intertextual landcape, we investigative-readers are meant, no doubt, to notice the feminist implications of this disruption of *authori*ty and originality. McGuckian herself as suggested as much (perhaps disregarding Mandelstam's more scathing remarks on women poets) and concluding '*Comhrá*', a conversation with Nuala Ní Dhomnaill, with his words: 'There was a time when equals translated equals, contending only for the glory of the language, when translation resembled a graft of foreign fruit and a wholesome gymnastic exercise for the spiritual muscles.'[60] The vision of writing as enabling, egalitarian translation is also suggested by Pasternak in his description of his relationship with Rilke in the letters exchanged with Tsvetaeva in 1926: 'I always believed that in my own efforts, in all of my work, I did nothing but translate or write variations on his themes, adding nothing to his world, always sailing on his waters.'[61] (To this we might, if we had time, investigate another thread: Rilke's mystical ideas of poetic origins and of 'resurrective' verse, particularly in *Sonnets to Orpheus*.) Such mutual inspiration and exchange of language and ideas potentially disrupt the notion of the individual (male) poetic genius. Indeed, as Alcobia-Murphy himself astutely suggests, in those poems where McGuckian rewrites texts which concern father–daughter relationships, such as Tatyana Tolstoy's *Tolstoy Remembered*, what we are offered is an alternative to Harold Bloom's Oedipal model of the 'Anxiety of Influence': 'McGuckian's palimpsestic rewriting often centres thematically on the very notion of "power" and reconfigures the gender allocations of the original text.'[62] The image of the web, then, is a feminist one. As Julia Kristeva writes: 'Any text is constructed as a mosaic of quotations; any text is the absorption and transformation of another. The notion of intertextuality replaces that of intersubjectivity, and poetic language is read as at least double.'[63] Likewise McGuckian's language, her translated, 'double-stranded' words, make the language of others live again in a way which suggests that writing is *without hierarchy or centre*. They offer, that is, a sense of what Barthes called 'the *stereographic plurality*' of the text's 'weave of signifiers'. And they do this both in the poems themselves and the sources they rewrite – for if, as Barthes noted, 'etymologically the text is a tissue, a woven fabric',[64] for Mandelstam too, in fact, '[p]oetic discourse is a carpet fabric containing a plethora of textile warps differing from one another only in the process of coloration [. . .] It is an extremely durable carpet woven out of fluid.'[65] Again, too, the interwoven texts which McGuckian uses and the words she translates also converge on the notion of poetry as a 'sounding out through': they seem to approve the poet's opaque resurrection as an egalitarian, feminine, and even maternal function in poetry.

This can perhaps best be suggested, finally, by disentangling the 'translation' of other sources that is 'Visiting Rainer Maria'. As Clarence Brown noted of Mandelstam's use of other texts, McGuckian's borrowings are 'oblique, fragmentary and atmospheric', to say the least. The poem, from *Marconi's Cottage*, seems to begin with an encounter with (Rainer Maria) Rilke himself:

> He said he was just leaving
> As I was just arriving, in my blue
> Smock, yesterday, without meaning to.
> Though this first sentence would
> Have been equally suitable
> For the last, for a poem made
> From a kitchen conversation.[66]

In the penultimate stanza, moreover, the poet seems to signal her feminist intent in this literary encounter: 'I said, I must find it, / Using the feminine form of must, / What *you* want, what *I* want, what can be done.' In fact, however, as Alcobia-Murphy has shown, the source of the vocabulary is a letter, quoted by Clarence Brown, from Mandelstam to his wife. (This, Brown writes, is the first surviving letter from Mandelstam to Nadezhda, and 'It tells something of their life together that *the first sentence would have been equally suitable for the last* letter in 1938.') The letter is one in which Mandelstam describes hearing his wife's voice in the silence. As Tsvetaeva wanted Rilke to speak through her, Mandelstam recalls how his wife seemed to speak *through* him or he *for* her:

> Your little paw like a baby's, all black from the charcoal, your blue smock – it's all memorable to me, I haven't forgotten anything.
>
> Forgive me for being weak and for not always being able to show how much I love you.
>
> Nadyusha! If you were to turn up here right now I would burst out crying with happiness. My little animal, forgive me! Give me your forehead to kiss – your round little forehead, like a baby's! Daughter, sister, I smile with your smile and hear your voice in the silence**a**.
>
> Yesterday, without meaning to, I thought to myself 'I *must* find it' – using the *feminine* form of 'must' – for you, that is, you said it *through* me. We're like children, you and I – we don't look for big words but say whatever we have to.[67]

The triumphant final lines of the poem, then, also turn on translation: 'Because / The *it* of his translation may mean silence, / But the *she* of mine means Aphrodite.' And in fact by this stage it has been well documented that here McGuckian inverts a remark made by Clarence Brown about the difficulty in translating Mandelstam's poem 'Silentium'. 'Silentium' concludes with a plea that Aphrodite 'remain foam' and word 'return to music'. However, the problem here for Brown is with *Mandelstam's* words: Brown notes that the first word is differently translated by his friend, Richard McKane: 'The word is a Russian pronoun that can mean 'it' or 'she' depending upon the antecedent, which is of course the problem. The 'it' of my translation means silence; the 'she' of his meant 'Aphrodite'. Therefore, if Medbh McGuckian's poem is *speaking through* an existing text, making it new, the excavated sources to 'Visiting Rainer Maria' propose the following (entirely invisible) scenario: McGuckian appropriates language from Brown who translates Mandelstam who appropriates the voice of his wife Nadezhda, or hears it in the silence and allows it to speak through him. Silence is also, naturally enough, the subject of Mandelstam's poem 'Silentium', the first stanza of which, in Clarence Brown's problematic translation, is:

> It has not yet been born,
> it is music and the word,
> and therefore inviolably
> bonds everything that lives.[68]

Again this returns us to the idea of poetic origins and aurality – but if, for Mandelstam, silence is 'the limitless, the unfathomable and ubiquitous ambience against which speech has its momentary being',[69] McGuckian's silence, as well as her speech, has a peculiarly female character. That is, just as the texts to which McGuckian's poems gesture here concern women who might otherwise have remained *silent* in the story of literary history, so Nadezhda Mandelstam's silence might be said to metaphorically underpin the layers of translated sources in 'Visiting Rainer Maria'.[70] The simultaneous or mutual 'voice' in the poems from this stage in McGuckian's career contains the voices of the wives of poets (Nadezhda), as well as their daughters (Tatyana Tolstoy) and mistresses (Olga Ivinskaya); it resurrects the language of artists who were regarded as inscrutable or nonsensical and buried in unmarked graves (Tsvetaeva – and also, as Alcobia-Murphy has shown, Gwen John),[71] but who often are shown, in these texts, participating as equals in literary life. And the poems do this at the same time as refusing (as Osip Mandelstam does for Nadezhda) to speak *for them*, but rather gesturing to the phenomenon of men speaking through women, women speaking though men, in a utopian vision of the relationality of the text. While Alcobia-Murphy suggests, then, that her 'palimpsestic double-writing [. . .] allows McGuckian to insert herself into a poetic tradition from which she feels excluded',[72] it would be more accurate to say that McGuckian makes the intertextuality of her poetry a notional vehicle for collective female others. McGuckian's location at the time of the poems' composition, in the cottage in which

Guglielmo Marconi sent the first telegraphic messages to Rathlin Island, must have seemed an ideal one for these voices to clash, meet and become channelled through her own. Despite the poems' official silence about these women, and refusal to claim them as discursive content (her poems are the sites of their collective *unmarked grave*), the voices of women are woven, like a secret lining, into the very structures of McGuckian's poetry. McGuckian's texts refuse a chronology whereby these women are 'foremothers' and McGuckian literary inheritress, but in a way women are these poems' secret history.

III 'Most Foreign and Cherished Reader . . .'

As far as an examination of those uncovered sources goes, though, those discussed here represent merely the tip of the iceberg. I have dealt, indeed, with only a few of those discovered for *On Ballycastle Beach* and with fewer still at work in *Marconi's Cottage* – poems from a relatively early stage in McGuckian's career. Were time (and energy) to permit the examination of further of the biographies and studies which Alcobia-Murphy has discovered as intertexts in McGuckian's poetry, it seems that further ironic arrangements would emerge of literary figures counterpointing or echoing the persona of the poet. To take a few brief examples, in one of his early essays on the subject, Alcobia-Murphy considers whether McGuckian's poetic technique makes her guilty of plagiarism before going on to analyse her use of Winifred Gérin's biography of Emily Brontë in her poem 'Gigot Sleeves' from *Marconi's Cottage*. Winifed Gérin's biography, in turn, is also much concerned with whether Brontë might be considered a plagiarist. A 'sibyl' and a 'mystic', the Brontë of Gérin's account is ultimately unknowable – much like the reclusive figure of Gwen John in Susan Chitty's biography, vocabulary from which McGuckian uses in 'Road 32, Roof 13-23, Grass 23'.[73] If these women feel like covers for the self which is absent in McGuckian's poetry, or reflections back of her inscrutability as author, they also give way, again, to relational chains of authorship. Chitty's study of Gwen John relies on John's passionate letters to Rodin, re-echoing the correspondence between Tsvetaeva, Pasternak and Rilke, and Osip and Nadezhda Mandelstam (less so the Frost/Bartlett letters) – and indeed we learn that John was also acquainted with Rilke at this time. Another nexus of relationships might be, then, Gwen John/Rilke/Paula Modersohn-Becker – whose artistic and personal histories are also interlinked, as suggested by the footnote concerning Modersohn-Becker in to 'To Call Paula Paul' in *Marconi's Cottage*.[74] Alcobia-Murphy has also found that Anne and Samuel Charters's *I Love: The Story of Vladimir Mayakovsky and Lili Brik*[75] provides some of the vocabulary for, appropriately, 'The Man with Two Women', and so on. Whatever else we might be meant to infer from this proliferation of secret love lives and extra-marital affairs, these passionate accounts with their woman artists and muses reflect back the erotic turbulence which already abounds in *Marconi's Cottage*. The concern with female authorship then comes to its baffling cause-or-effect apotheosis in the discovery that McGuckian 'quotes' from Gilbert and Gubar's seminal study of women writers, *The Madwoman in the Attic*, in poems such as 'Journal Intime'.[76] Do we read McGuckian's poetry *in terms* of these feminist theories of female subjectivity and artistry – and if so, how does this sit with the fact this these theories have been used in the very *forms* of the poems? At points such as this, it becomes difficult to know whether we are reading McGuckian's poems or somehow writing them.

Where McGuckian's later, more political poetry is concerned, moreover, the intertexts discovered by Alcobia-Murphy are sometimes bewilderingly diverse. In her expansive and rapidly proliferating collections from *Captain Lavender* onwards, McGuckian has turned to Irish politics and history and Alcobia-Murphy has found some of this work to deploy language from various, very different histories: 'A Deserted Landing Stage on the Rhine', from *Had I a Thousand Lives*, for instance, incorporates words from contro-versial right-wing historian David Irving's *The Destruction of Dresden* alongside socialist Stephen Spender's *The Thirties and After*.[77] Other unlikely bedfellows in poems from *Drawing Ballerinas* include popular historian Tim Pat Coogan (whose biography of Michael Collins is used in 'The Truciler') and feminist academic Angela Bourke, whose *The Burning of Bridget Clearly* is referenced in 'Manteo'.[78] Whether McGuckian is translating new meanings out of old histories, or renewing exhausted ideological languages by inter-weaving them with studies of aesthetics (a book on Matisse delivers us the title poem of *Drawing Ballerinas*, and Elias Canetti's *The Torch in My Ear* is another intertext here)[79] requires examination. Likewise, we might speculate that, in its intertextuality, this poetry is always demonstrably contingent on, or porous to, other discourses: politics, journalism, McGuckian's own recy-cled criticism as well as rather disparate material. As an example of the kind of disparate, far-flung material used, Alcobia-Murphy has found that the texts used for 'Scotch Argus on Jerusalem Sage' are a journalistic source, a book about 'revolts which took place amongst the Highland Regiments during the mid-to-late eighteenth century', and (unexpectedly) a monograph about lepidopterology.[80] Tracing the sources of the incredibly technical vocabu-laries which litter the poet's more recent work, as well as reading different volumes of biography on Thomas Ashe and Roger Casement, Feuerbach, Aristophanes and Kierkegaard (keeping strange company with Gerry Conlon), is a task which now, more than ever, looks endless. Roland Barthes, indeed, wrote that the text could be distinguished from the 'work' by its exis-tence primarily in the process of demonstration ('the work can be held in the hand, the text is held in language') and by this very endlessness: 'It follows that the text cannot stop (for example on a library shelf); its constitutive movement is that of cutting across (in particular, it can cut across the work, several works).'[81] McGuckian's texts likewise seem to spread on unstoppably, extending beyond the reader's reach, gesturing to the library in its infinity. What I have offered in the preceding paragraphs, indeed, is just one path through the bookshelves.

What seems clear, though, is that while offering a glimpse on to bewildering intertextual vistas, and a commentary on its own forms, the meaning continues to elude us as far as interpretation of McGuckian's individual poems is concerned. The sudden spectre of underlying sources in McGuckian's work only seemed to offer the prospect of proofs or solutions: the disclosure of the poems' secrets confounds the idea of secret contents. Her poems have told us this already: 'It isn't *like* a blow, it's a secret' says the disembodied mouth and 'cry' in 'Mazurka'.[82] More telling still are the opening lines of 'The Time Before You':

> The secret of movement
> Is not the secret itself
> But the movement
> Of there being a secret[83]

That is, while 'the work closes on a signified [. . .] Either it is claimed to be evident (as in science) or else it is considered to be secret [. . .] and the work falls under the scope of a hermeneutics, of an interpretation,'[84] McGuckian's secret is only the *movement* of there being a secret. The poems seem to beckon us inside (into the interiority of McGuckian's world), yet once there we merely find 'Inside me everything was blurred/ like tea with smoked milk, the stone/ In the fruit, the meaning'.[85] Or, as the speaker of 'The Most Emily of All' puts it: 'If you call out "house" to me / [. . .] I answer "library"'.[86] While we seem on the threshold of the poet's private world, we are referred back to the collective world of language and writing. McGuckian is aware, like Barthes, then, that 'should a writer seek to 'to *express himself*, he ought at least to know that the inner "thing" he [sic] thinks to "translate" is itself only a ready-formed dictionary'.[87] And her poetry, finally too, clearly requires the kind of collaboration Barthes suggests. The text, he declares, requires us to 'abolish the difference between writing and reading, in no way by intensifying the projection of the reader into the work but by joining them in a single signifying practice [. . .] it asks of the reader a practica collaboration.[88] What Alcobia-Murphy's findings herald perhaps, then, is less the ultimate solution to the puzzle of Medbh McGuckian's poems than the birth of this reader. She must be indefatigable and resilient: further discoveries surely await in the labyrinth.

11
Interview with Medbh McGuckian
(Athol Hotel, Aberdeen, 6 May 2007)

SHANE ALCOBIA-MURPHY AND RICHARD KIRKLAND

Q. You've published six collections of poetry in the last six years, almost dou-
bling your number of publications. Why has that period been so productive for you?

A. My husband isn't working, so he's taking on all of the household responsibilities, the cooking and the shopping. Also, the children have
grown up – the youngest [her daughter, Emer] is eighteen – so that gives
me a bit more leeway. Although I now have my mother to look after instead of them, I do feel I have more time for writing. I also have a regular job, with a regular income, whereas before that I was travelling and
always looking for a writer's-in-residence job and feeling insecure about
money. Now I'm actually paid to write. Also, the RAE [Research Assessment Exercise] provides a certain amount of pressure: the more books
you bring out the better.

Q. It is unusual for a publisher to agree to bring out a collection every year
by a single author. How has that agreement come about?

A. My relationship with Peter [Fallon; editor of Gallery Press] is very good.
We came to this crisis when he was doing a book every four years or so,
and in the meantime I had stockpiled work – a nuclear armament that I
thought was going to explode! When he'd say, 'Maybe we should do a new
book?' I would have two hundred poems and we'd have to consider how
we'd bring them out. Meanwhile, Michael Schmidt from Carcanet Press
tried to seduce me away from Gallery by saying, 'We have John Ashberry
and the reason we have him is that we do a book for him every year.' And
he was soft-soaping me by saying, 'You're just as good as John Ashberry and
we'll do you a book every year if you leave Peter and come to us.' I liked
Michael Schmidt, but I just wasn't sure. I suppose I might have got on better having a British publisher but Peter has always been good for me and

I just didn't want to leave him. So I went back to Peter and told him about the agreement with Michael. I said, 'Look, you bring out a book every four years, and Michael can do the other three years – he can soak up the inferior poems and I'll give you my best poems.' He was aghast and mortally offended. He agreed to do a book whenever necessary. He's been very good and *would* do one every year if I insisted. I don't think he makes much money on the books or that he sells many of them. He probably only does a small run of about five hundred. He probably only gets rid of a couple of hundred of them. But it's nice for me.

Q. You were first published by Oxford University Press. What were the circumstances of your move from them?

A. The first three books were with Oxford and they were reasonably successful. I was still considered as a British poet – I had won the Cheltenham award. I was not emphasising my Irishness too much because I didn't really think of myself that way. But I wasn't an English goody-two-shoes! Anyway, the controversy arose when I was getting my poems ready for the *Marconi's Cottage* collection and I was becoming something else. I felt I had changed. I had been to America and had a difficult time there, and the *Marconi* poems were a coming home. I had decided I wouldn't emigrate – I wouldn't do what Paul Muldoon or Seamus Heaney had done. I would stick to my guns, as it were, and not leave. So what happened was, I was getting together these poems which were so different – I felt the *Marconi* poems were more complicated and I was beginning to get more political. So I think the voices were twofold. The Oxford people didn't like the new style. They couldn't understand some of the poems – they were set in other voices, particularly the one about Gwen John ['Road 32, Roof 13-23, Grass 23'] – and they weren't sure whether it was poetry or just madness. And so that was a difficult time. I didn't realise this was the way they were thinking until afterwards. The crux of it was that they had the manuscript and they were shilly-shallying and were saying that they wanted me to explain them. They said they couldn't publish them. They were being hard to live with and being very negative about the new stuff. At this point, Peter came in. Ciaran [Carson] would insist that it was *he* who persuaded Peter that I was good. I don't buy that, but I'm sure he *had* something to do with it. Peter had to work a fast one somehow. Peter was blackmailing both of us somehow! The Oxford people were afraid of losing me, so I think they conceded at some point – and I suppose I would have liked to have stayed with them as it was a British centre. In the end, I went to Peter. Letters were exchanged between all parties which weren't very nice. I wanted a quotation from [Roger] Casement on the front of *On Ballycastle Beach* and someone in the Oxford office was a relative of Casement and didn't approve of this – I later heard that. So that had something to do with the move as well. I eventually got the Roger Casement quotation put in.

Q. As you say, your style has been changing – but do you have a writing method which has remained constant?

A. Yes. Those very early poems weren't based on texts, they were memory poems. But I was imbibing influences from the male and female poets. When I started borrowing texts to begin with it was very awkward as the seams were always showing. I wasn't always expert at fusing what I wanted to say with what someone else had said. But gradually I became more and more at ease at going into a book and finding these flowers of poetry and making, as you know, my first notebook, then my second notebook and then writing my poems, usually pretty quickly. [McGuckian first makes a long list of selected quotations in one notebook, then a second, shorter selection. And then she works with this list to create her poems.] But the building up of it, for the nuggets of wisdom, can be quite slow. Also, in re-lation to your first question, I meant to say that, since I'm now working, for good or ill, at Queen's University, I now have access to a pretty good library where I can get twenty-five books out for six months, whereas be-fore that I was getting six books out for three weeks, and out of not very good libraries (though I used to go to the Linen Hall Library). Before I was starved, and now I'm kind of sated.

Q. So to do my kind of criticism on your work, I should go to Belfast and stalk you when you visit the library?!

A. Do you know, I'll give you fair warning: there's this theological library in Queen's where they give you the old books – they actually give you them. There are all these sermons! I would say I'll be trying that library.

Q. Given that your poems are usually based on sources, I wonder if you could resolve a contradiction which seems to have arisen between accounts you've given in two different interviews. In one, you've talked about how you 'don't talk about [yourself]' in your work, that you 'erase [your] expe-rience', yet in another you've said that your work is 'almost totally auto-biographical'.

A. I don't write exactly about what I did. So, I wouldn't write 'I went to Ab-erdeen and had coffee with Shane [Alcobia-Murphy] and Richard [Kirk-land].' I'm not saying that'd be boring, but it's on the level of prose. I write about my emotional life. So, if I was writing about this experience I might talk about how I felt during the meal last night with you and Patrick [Crotty]. I write about things which are deeper than the surface experience. I erase my daily experience for the paranormal or for experiences which happen to me on another plane, the one where poetry exists. Poetry exists to tap into that life, the life of the mind, the spirit, the inner life. There's a distinction here between the body and the soul. It's more important to tap into the deeper levels of your consciousness, of dreams.

Q. Because of that, many critics have gone on to complain that you write in a 'private language' and that this renders your work overly obscure. Indeed, Patrick Williams infamously said that your 'lines were so arbitrary', that they 'mean more or less anything'. Does such criticism put pressure on you as a writer?

A. I would need a lot of theory about what 'meaning' actually means. The kind of meaning that I'm after is beginning in the private, but belongs in the privacy of the ultimate or ideal reader. Sometimes I think only women could understand certain poems, that only a woman who had had a child could understand some of them, or only a man whose child had died might understand a certain poem. It doesn't worry me. I think Patrick Williams is typical of that time, a time when maybe women poets weren't as thick on the ground as they are in the North now. It's easier to be more accommodating now.

Q. Dillon Johnston, your former editor from Wake Forest University Press, once wrote to you to say, 'In my own readings I found some poems immediately beautiful and others apparently forbidding. On re-readings I bounced my head against these poems, until I decided I was not offering them the appropriate organ.' What *is* the appropriate organ with which to read your work?

A. I think he *didn't* mean the sexual organ! I think he meant his heart and not his head. I think he was being too rational when reading them, looking at them in a much too logical way. He refused to publish the first three collections on that ground. He just couldn't get his head around them. But I think with the new language that I was evolving in *Marconi's Cottage* he came around. And by that time he had gone through quite a few changes in his life and of course Guinn Batten [his partner] was very much in favour of them and steered him towards taking me on. So what he meant in the letter is that he had to allow the emotions to dominate rather than a word-to-word mathematical reasoning. And so he was then able to appreciate them. Readers just need to relax and swim in the stuff. To attack it with the 'what does it all mean'? – it doesn't always work. But you *can* go through it all with a fine instrument and I can do this with my work.

Q. Perhaps we could try this with 'Constable's *Haywain*' from *Captain Lavender*?

A. The poem isn't about Constable or his painting, *The Haywain*. My father
    was an educated man and he had a teacher's diploma and if things had
    been otherwise in the North he would have been a university lecturer.
    There was no way Catholics in the North could integrate so he had to
    leave to go to England to get educated and his family had to pay for that.
    Ironically, my father was the eldest of twelve children and he would have
    inherited the family farm, which would have suited me and suited my
    sense of connection to that place, but because he got this education he
    forfeited the farm which then went to the dissolute younger sons. So
    my father was a Constable type of person. He loved the countryside. To
    please his family and fulfil his own nature he became a teacher – but he
    was really a farmer. He was happier in the field. So *The Haywain* is like
    the meadow which he bought back from the family. So I felt that the
    price that he paid for his growth as a person . . . it was a bit like Seamus
    Heaney's poem 'Digging' – he didn't have the pen, he only had the spade.
    My father also enjoyed carpentry. While he didn't buy paintings, he liked
    getting prints and making frames for them and we had at least four or five
    different Constable prints. There were two that I got when he died. The
    poem was written before he died. The painting for me summed up a lot
    about my father's tragedy, his desire for art and his desire for heaven and
    stability and his love of the country and his masculinity and tenderness.
    I was preparing in poetry for my father's death, like I'm now preparing
    for my mother's death. He started having heart attacks when he was
    sixty-three and he died when he was seventy-three. So the first verse is
    about the time before he died. A week before he died, I was sent a form
    to fill in. It asked me to fill in the parent's birth-date and, if applicable,
    the date of his death and it was very strange. I felt this was a warning. It
    was very clinical. The other thing about his birth-date was that he was
    always wrong about it, he never seemed to know the exact date. When
    asked about it, he'd say maybe it was the 28th or the 29th. The 28th was
    the feast of St Peter and 'Paul and we always preferred that date since it
    was the more holy day. The 'incised triangle' in the poem was very phys-
    ical. It's like what they were doing to him. They were constantly open-
    ing him and cutting him. He had one of those very brutal deaths. All of
    those are about my emotions about this. And of course the 'piano' refer-
    ence is important too. My father was one of those mad people who was
    never happier than when he was sitting up on the roof pointing the
    chimney. He climbed the roof and was fearless in that way. He had this
    old piano and carried it into the house. So the piano was like his coffin,
    it was a symbol for me. He didn't play the piano and I failed to play it
    properly – I always wanted to. There's a mixture of truth in the poem and

a mixture of quotation in it. To me, the sources are a crutch and help.

Q. Did the reading of source texts at this period help when you were trying to write about the death of your father?

A. There's so much energy in books. They are arenas where you are likely to find true words. I don't feel I appropriate as such. The person who has published the book wants it to be read, and doesn't mind it being read and going straight into someone's head. If it's enshrined in the work of art, even in a truncated or bowdlerised form, still I think when I meet the people who wrote all the books I think they will forgive me. I think that they would think that their work was being given further life. Everybody you read has alluded to works. It's really satisfying. You can't think up all the words. It's a shorthand. It's like getting a blood transfusion into your system and to feed off other writers who don't need the words any more. I would rarely go into poetry itself for poetry. That has been the only way that I have existed. English isn't my native language or my mother tongue. English is this huge empire of signs, that because I'm not able to write or speak in Irish, I have the texts as a resource for my pleasure or my taking. It's my only way of asserting my rights; it's a way of getting back my freedom in the language.

Q. It seems like such an authoritative strategy to appropriate the words of others and put them into your own texts. It's a curious strategy, since some might argue that this is a sign of a *lack* of authority. Perhaps it's akin to how you used to describe the persona of the writer as necessarily male (and *not* female), as the one who was sanctioned by tradition to write. Do you still think in those terms?

A. Well, I suppose I'm an older woman now. My femininity is less of a barrier. Although I'm still a woman, I'm through all the cycles and not having babies, and I'm not tied to the menstrual cycle any more. I think now those demarcations are less important to me. I wouldn't talk about 'male' and 'female' as rigid boundaries. I still feel that the writing of poetry is such an unusual thing for a woman to do. It's still a challenge. It's quite competitive. And the people that I want to impress with my poetry, or have to keep up the standard with, are people like [Seamus] Heaney and [Michael] Longley. There is a network of women who wouldn't dream of being heard by them at all.

Q. Have your reading and writing about female writers of the past helped to change your thoughts about gender and authority?

A. There's been a lot more work done about women writers and I'm finding more about them, like Sappho. There is a thread of energy that is open to me that I didn't know was there. The experience of doing the Irish women's anthology [for Cork University Press], which I still haven't got published, and finding about Irish women poets, even though they weren't from my class, that has helped me. I could see that they had suffered greatly for what they were trying to do. I still have a long way to go to work it all out.

Q. You once said that Emily Brontë's 'No Coward Soul is Mine' was your favourite poem. Has she been an influence? As a female writer, with, some might argue, an Irish background, did Brontë's experience help you or make you angry, given that the Irish connection is rarely adverted to?

A. My father lost two sisters; one of them had tuberculosis. They lived in this very isolated place. So the connection with Emily is a haunting presence. I have a couple of poems about Brontë. The main problem I have with her is the religious influence. I've been to Haworth and was very intimidated by the emphasis on death. All the gravestones are horizontal. And Sylvia Plath is buried near there as well. I'm a bit frightened by the intensity of these women. I don't have that absolute devotion to my art, over all else. That one has to die for it. For me, I don't think I have that amount of dedication. But it is important to me; it's my way of surviving.

Q. When did you first conceive of yourself as a writer?

A. When I was sixteen or seventeen, I began to write poetry. But for me the studying of English and the writing of poetry seem to cancel each other out. You could spend two hours on your poem or two hours writing an essay about Keats, and usually I ended up writing the essay on Keats. When I went to Queen's there was no encouragement to write. It was always 'write about the people who wrote'. But there was a very repressed desire to write. I suppose I kept my diaries at that time because they were very easy to write. After that, I did an MA on Gothic literature, and that was again putting off the day of writing. I just got so dried up by that. At the end of that time I was twenty-two/twenty-three, and I was doing a teaching course when I met Ciaran [Carson] and he was extremely active. He was writing his first book, and I was deeply involved with that, helping him and seeing how he wrote. And it was he who taught me to go to texts. In order to build his collection he would get books. That was the first time I realised that you don't just sit down with your head, your pen and your paper and sit there in a vacuum. That you can draw on a resource. I owe him for that. I never realised that that was possible or that it was right even. He'd sit in the room and then a few hours later he'd have this miracle, this text he'd concocted from what he was reading. Yet it was his, it surely was his. This was a revelation to me, and I would like to thank him for that.

Q. Could you say a little more about this process of 'going to texts' – what do you look for when reading them?

A. What you look for in the texts are images, striking conjunctions of maybe two or three unusual words, esoteric vocabulary; in other words, the poetry which is there, embedded in what people write and say, and what they themselves quote from. My methods would be a sort of speed reading through unpromising books and a very slow reading even again of highly poetic texts, of which there are very few. So, one has to read maybe ten to twenty books, sometimes for just a few nuggets of wisdom. Then these separate phrases from different places are fused together in a paradoxical, contradictory way to give or get at the truth of something in my life. For instance, my last poem is called 'Sung Death', a phrase I found put together somewhere, but not from a title. I used it to write about my aunt's recent death, to express both the reality of the loss, and the excitement of the event, for her – the rejoicing, as I see it, of her family, including my father, who liked to sing, in Heaven, or wherever they all may be. I do have a firm belief in these however outmoded ideas from my modish experience of them. I am not sure that I enact a transformation. I suppose I yoke together disparates. Nietzsche says, 'beauty in Art is power over opposites'. I suppose I select the most incongruous, the ones you would least expect to make the poem. I edit the first lot of phrases by almost ninety per cent since they are mostly useless, and only appealed to what I was thinking at the time I was reading – so very dull. Silly stuff. I think, 'Why in hell did I write that down?' But then, as you go through them, there are some gold bits that seep up, and eventually I have on a clean lined page enough words on their own, or together, from all over the place to begin [the poem]. I usually read them aloud at this stage to see if any rhyme or fit each other. The more ludicrous, often the more poetic sense. Then I will see that it is falling into a pattern concerning what is my most unconscious anxiety, fear, love or anger at the time I am working on it, not the time I was reading. So I may have picked up things about my life that are later discarded. The poem will end up itself being about what is most on my heart, although when I begin it I rarely know exactly what this deepest thing is. I may begin thinking, 'Oh, this looks as if I am writing about my sister,' which was that 'Sung Death' one, but really it was for the aunt, although my sister is also there. A poem may be, in fact, mostly about two people. I forget the texts totally because I have to – like a diving board – otherwise I would be left up there. They provide the means, but my dive is each time my own skin into the world. Ciaran still does use books, but I do not, as he has done in his latest collection, quote and twist from poems themselves (as he does with some of mine). I feel that is wrong. If I were to turn people's lines and poems on their head, I think that would be decadent and insulting. I have a poem called 'District Behind the Lines' which is intended as a reaction to Seamus [Heaney's 'District and Circle'], but that, I think, is fair enough – no disrespect and nothing personal.

Q. Do you mind when critics unearth your sources?

A. I am actually pleased to have critics unearth the sources as they are usually good books that people might enjoy. Also, it is payment to that author for my use of him or her, and it's only right. However, if I were to detail it all myself it would be too scholarly and a pain, as if I were saying, as some do, 'look at all the work I have done.' And also, I do change and adapt [the material], so the crossover is not simple. But I feel critics should go further sometimes and explain what the poem means again in the light of their findings.

Q. Many of your more recent sources have focused on religious topics. To what extent has religion, or religious belief, shaped your work?

A. The religion question is enormous. I can only allude to it. Northern Ireland is and was a place where 'religion' meant to be on a losing side, for me. It meant to be less, to be excluded, not to qualify, not to fit or belong. To be Irish and a woman and, therefore, tainted. To be afraid to say what I was. To hide and twist and cower behind words, hoping no one will know what they mean. I guess your distinction between religion and belief is accurate. Until I was in my twenties, we learned to survive really like Jews in a ghetto by disguise and subterfuge. We practised our faith secretly, covertly, as we tidied away our womanhood and sexuality as we spoke English and repressed what remained of our Irishness. We stared at the British news and read their weather. All of this affected my poems to begin with, and it is only very recently, and painfully, that I am even approaching considering openly what joy there might be in confessing publicly a Christianity which is labelled or tattooed 'Roman Catholicism'. It is fundamental to my work: it inhabits every poem. The births and deaths, the loves and relationships, all are viewed sacramentally, if I can. The idea of sin is never absent, nor the concern with salvation, nor the awareness of Christ's voice as poetry. So water and blue have this duality. The body fluids, the amniotic, the sea, its colour range, Ballycastle, my family: so wide and changeable. They are at once romantic and chaste, to do with washing and sky benevolence, rain and fertility. I love their vastness for different modes and their elasticity. In ever onward contexts they continue to work and illuminate with their eternal simplicity. Of English words, they seem the most Latin. But every appearance of them is a special meditation in itself.

Q. In your diaries, it's very clear that you were aware about what was going on in the political world. Critics, looking at your early collections, often go to them to work out your 'position' regarding the Troubles. Do you think of those works as 'political'?

A. I lived in cloud cuckoo land. We had left school promising the nuns (a) that we'd keep our virginity forever, or until we got married, and (b) that we'd not get involved with any political struggles. We had to swear that before we left the school, that we'd keep ourselves immune, that we'd keep ourselves closeted away from men and politics. I was an ostrich. I knew that the Troubles were building, but I just hoped it would all go away. I didn't get involved for religious reasons. But then of course all of these defences broke: I went through a total period of rejection of religion from the time I met Ciaran. That was the cost of being with Ciaran, as he was a Marxist–Leninist. He had this card-carrying communist persona at the time. I had a closed ear to the Troubles that were happening around me. I wouldn't look at stuff on the television or in the newspapers, but I did have a sense of it all. I had a sense of where I fitted in, and whose side I had to be on. But I'd an equal sense of the fluidity of it all and how I didn't want to be tarred and feathered in an absolute way. Not like Bernadette McAliskey. I feared her, just as much as Emily Brontë, her direction. She had been the one I had sympathised with, but I didn't really understand her.

Q. With the publication of *Captain Lavender*, your work seemed to suddenly become more overtly political. How did that change come about?

A. My father died in 1992 and that ended that time when I was preparing for the worst possible experience that I could imagine, that of losing my father. Having experienced that, I could feel him in his afterlife. That afterlife sustained me. So to vindicate him, I could deal with the things that had made his life so difficult and which gave him his heart condition, all his suffering, his tensions, his trying to please the church. He spent his whole time trying to please the clergy and fit in. At the same time, there was nothing in that world which met his desires. So I got very angry and his resentment came out in me. Also, going into the Maze prison [to teach poetry classes to the prisoners] was crucial to that.

Q. Did the teaching that you did in the Maze affect what you were writing?

A. These were people I would normally never have access to, on either side (either the loyalist or republican paramilitaries). I suddenly realised this was the absolute truth of Bobby Sands and all of that battle. I could see very clearly the very entrenched positions of everybody there. Basically, what illuminated it was that I was going through this very cosy world of being a British poet and being spoiled with all this English stuff, and these people wanted to be Irish. They desperately wanted to speak Irish. They wanted the pride of having a nation. So it was hard not to respect them and they led me to look at the history of the country. The poems for *Shelmalier*, and the poems for Robert Emmet and the poems for Thomas Ashe would never have been written unless I had met these people.

Q. Were they receptive to your work? One of the prisoners, Tarlach O'Conghalaigh, with whom you developed a correspondence, once wrote to you saying how even mentioning Wormwood Scrubs in conjunction to the prisoners was an insult to them, how it made them criminals. So how did they react to your writing?

A. I had used the word 'criminals' but in an ironic way, that they had this ambiguous status in prison. They had a huge amount of autonomy. It was like a picnic the way that, within the prison, they had an immense amount of freedom of thought and freedom of soul. He [Tarlach] was in the *Gaeltacht* wing. They weren't all the same. The relationship with Tarlach was different to the relationship with, say, Danny Morrison. They wouldn't have all been on the same wavelength. There were divisions within there. There were some who were very violent. There were some who were more political, and some who were more verbal. Actually, I only discovered this recently, but the guy whom Heaney meets on the train [in 'The Flight Path'] is Danny Morrison. And Danny Morrison was a very outspoken sophisticated manipulator of the media, like [Gerry] Adams. Recently I went to a poetry reading by Martin McGuinness. Right enough, they were very political poems, but they were so awful. The vanity of it! This is what it's come down to, the whole struggle – it's enough for him to read these poems. It's so sad. The different people I met in the Maze had different effects on me. This man in particular [Tarlach] affected me because he was doing the longest time. Danny Morrison was doing ten years, and he was doing twenty-three for four murders. He wouldn't even tell me what he had done. He convinced me that he had been victimised and that he was definitely innocent. So then I became interested in the legal system and realised how unjust the system is. In my last book [*The Currach Requires No Harbours*], the experience of my daughter brought it all home to me. The police knew who had done that [violence] to her and they would not go ahead and prosecute.

Q. What actually happened?

A. In the book, the first sixteen poems are about Emer. We have four children, nd the eldest boy went to my husband's school, which was a Catholic school in a Protestant area. That was difficult, but since it was the school that my husband was in we thought it would be safe. A lot of the people started sending their children to the local state school, and so we sent our other three children there, which seemed to be the safer option. The two boys were fine. They went through the system, which was like the English public-school system, and they ended up playing rugby and reading the bible, rather than serving mass and playing Gaelic games. Anyway, we sent the girl [Emer] to this school rather than the Convent which I had ended up swearing allegiance to. She was there about six weeks and was on the school bus. This bus would take all the children to begin with, but would then drop off the Protestant children in the Protestant area, and then ferry the Catholics up to the more Catholic districts. It's very clear where this border is. The bus was attacked there. All the Protestants got off and at- tacked the bus because they knew there were only Catholics left. Emer got a brick thrown at her head. She took an epileptic fit. It had hit her eye. In the book there are so many 'eyes' because she could have lost her eye. Anyway, my son Fergus was on the bus and he chased the people who had thrown the brick. They were Rangers supporters, and they were definitely identifiable. Obviously, I felt very guilty at having sent her. It was one of the many dilemmas of living in the North. When it happened, the police came around and were very helpful, but as we got further into the legal sys- tem we realised there was no point in trying to do anything. And I didn't really want to prosecute the guy.

Q. Has it been easier for you to talk about the Troubles since the ceasefires?

A. It's been easier to live day by day. But I don't find it easier to refer directly to violence. I still find it enormously difficult. All of the poems about Emer never actually say what happened to her. They skirt around it. It's too painful, it's too immediate and it's too shocking. I was saying to Richard [Kirkland] yesterday that 'The Flitting', my poem which won the National Poetry Competition [in 1979], was the most crucial thing. It was about the experience of my husband's sister's husband being murdered. They had hotels which were all destroyed in one night. There was no possible com- pensation for his family, and yet I got my poem out of that. I owe the vi- olence my work, but I've never really stated it as such.

Q. Clearly there's a sense of social injustice which you work through in your poems. But about that particular poem, 'The Flitting', isn't there another kind of injustice about the way you were treated when you won the National Poetry Competition?

A. Yes. You had to give yourself a pseudonym, so I called myself 'Jean Fisher'. And I thought this was quite innocuous, a fairly bland name, almost Scottish. So they rang me up and said I had won, but because Frank Ormsby, who was the editor of The *Honest Ulsterman* and who had been rejecting my poems religiously for years (for good reason), because he had got second place, and because he was an authority figure at the time, what they did was they bumped him up. So instead of me getting a thousand pounds, which were my legitimate winnings, they said that they were only going to give me five hundred. They bumped up Frank's winnings. People in the *TLS* wrote about this. The British sense of injustice was outraged by this. They asked why it was that this unknown woman didn't get the thousand pounds. And there was a whole flurry of letters asking was she discriminated [against] because (a) it turns out she was Catholic, (b) because she's from the North of Ireland. They justified this by saying that because I had sent in three poems – 'The Flitting', 'Tulips' and 'Mr McGregor's Garden' (not my original title) – the poems taken together had a force, but that when you isolated the poems there wasn't a single one that deserved the thousand pounds, so there was a whole other controversy.

Q. Clearly those judges will never become your muses. Could you talk about a more enabling muse: Gregory Peck? How did his influence come about?

A. Well, as you mentioned before my reading [the previous night at Aberdeen University], I had picked up various awards and prizes along the way. I have never won the major awards. I'm not unhappy about that, but I know that I don't fit in with the culture's notion of what poetry is and will never probably make that world, being popular. But I'm never going to be totally excluded from it, I'll be on the edge of it. Anyway, there was one prize that I did covet – the Irish-American one [The American Ireland Fund Literary Award] – which everyone had got. So in 1998 I won it and they always get prestigious Americans to come over to present it, and Gregory was the one giving the prize that year. I met him through that prize-giving. It was love at first sight. Absolute love. He had incredible charisma. I know this sounds schoolgirlish. But he was so very normal and down to earth. He was near to death at that time. He knew that he had extended his life. But he was still travelling and working. We became friends and we corresponded and I met him in New York and in Chicago, I went to his house in Los Angeles. I would phone him once or twice a month for maybe three years. He was a lovely person. He sent presents to the family.

His connection to Thomas Ashe reinforced my respect for him. Thomas Ashe was, in some way, filtered through him. In some of his films, he thought he was playing Thomas Ashe.

Q. To conclude this interview, could you sum up how your work has progressed in the years since *The Flower Master*?

A. I have stylistically moved from slim to fat as befits a lady! My poems were small and slender – I suppose virginal. Several babies later, I became rotund and exuding: longer poems, more moralising. Then came my death sequence, so drawn out, for my father. Then came my political poems – a rather pedantic historical questioning [regarding the] tragic awareness of the rebellion [and] the Famine, very elegiac. Lately [there is] a sort of serenity, accepting things, suspicious of the peace process, my loss of the last main muse, Gregory [Peck], a sort of full stop. My last book looks at women in my family, my next at poets and poetry.

Afterword

CLAIR WILLS

I first encountered Medbh McGuckian's work soon after the publication of *Venus and the Rain*, in 1984. There was a stand devoted to the Oxford Poets series in the middle of the ground floor of Blackwells in Oxford, where I was then living, and, amongst Penelope Shuttle and Peter Porter and D.J. Enright, I found Medbh's work. *Venus and the Rain* led me back to *The Flower Master*, which had been published in 1982, but which I had missed. Then in 1988 came *On Ballycastle Beach*. By that time it was clear that here was a poet with an unmistakable voice, intellectually challenging and richly sensuous at the same time, a poet who sounded like nobody else. The terms used to describe her work tended towards the sensual. She was 'beguiling', 'bewitching', and sometimes 'frustrating'. Later the word was 'gorgeous'.

With the benefit of hindsight these early volumes seem almost dazzling in their clarity. This is especially true of *The Flower Master*, even in the Oxford Poets rather than the revised Gallery Press version. This has partly to do with the formal, syntactical structure of these early works. Many of the poems are built around a loose question and answer format. In 'Lychees', for example, past and present versions of relationships set one another in balance. Then there's that direct and confiding voice. Even where the metaphors stretch at the seams, there's a conversational tone to the *Flower Master* poems, and a relatively stable central figure who leads us through the narratives of suppressed desire, sexuality, fertility and growth.

The clarity also derives from the underlying lucidity of the pool of metaphors from which she drew in her early work – the precision of the images relating to areas of personal and intimate experience: clothing, interiors, gardens, seeds. We were good, as readers, at noticing the ramifying meanings of images of growth and fertility, of ownership, and of the relationship to the past, and to a defining tradition. We noted the power of the grandmother's history as a containing narrative in 'The Seed Picture', for example, or the story of moving in and taking one's place which is tracked through many of the poems and which is both familial and 'national' at the same time.

We were perhaps less good at understanding McGuckian's intense concern with her place in a poetic tradition, which was not only national and gendered, but international. Yes, we saw the allusions to women poets and artists – Dickinson, Plath, Beatrix Potter. (Later Tsvetaeva, Kahlo, Modersohn-Becker and many others.) But the very tough intellectual stand she was taking on the relationship between art and sexuality sometimes did get lost in vague commentaries on writing the body, and particularly writing parturition. It is perhaps easier to see through the lens of her more recent concerns with female folk remedies, and the relationship between image and writing in the private space of the home, just how radical McGuckian's vision was. For all the references to grandmothers in *The Flower Master*, the last thing McGuckian offers us is a celebration of woman's tradition. Plath is as much raided as revered. Just like those women pushed aside in 'The Soil Map' – she drinks to them as she takes their place.

As Richard Kirkland notes in his essay here, McGuckian's unfolding drama of unconscious desire, containment and control was compressed into the very early poem 'Smoke', which stands as the opening lyric in the revised version of *The Flower Master and Other Poems*. The idea that containment is beyond the poet ('I am unable even / To contain myself') is of course belied by the structure of the lyric, with its emphasis on control through half-rhyme and line-break. A better term for control might be deliberation, or indeed, to use a metaphor from Robert Frost which haunts much of McGuckian's work as it does those of several of her Northern Irish contemporaries, design. For all McGuckian's statements about vatic inspiration (discussed here by Leontia Flynn) it is the deliberateness with which she creates ambiguity and even opacity which is most striking, using stretched and unhooked metaphors, yes, but also more traditional poetic techniques such as the pun, the line-break, enjambment, and grammatical and syntactical shifts. Think of those endlessly migrating pronouns.

It is deliberation and control, as much as co-dependence (of the mother and child, or woman and lover) which lie at the heart of McGuckian's exploration of attraction, repulsion and interdependence in *Venus and the Rain* and *On Ballycastle Beach*. The metaphors of weather and interplanetary influence do give rise to a pattern of images focused on traditional feminine symbols such as the moon, but McGuckian also figures attraction as a means of derailing or undermining authority. References to silent appropriation abound: in 'To the Nightingale' 'our neighbour's Mirabelle' is 'unacknowledged as our own'; in 'Slips' a series of flirtatious tricks and sleights of hand lead to 'my own key slotted in your door'. Her way of finding a place in a tradition is by 'studied' moves rather than a straightforward assault on authority.

Despite the emphasis on 'natural' force and inspiration characteristic of her interviews, as many of the essays here show, that tradition is securely literary and European; her engagement is with English romanticism and its legacies, with European modernism – the work of Mallarmé, Mandelstam, Rilke and Céline – with the visual arts, and, to an extent which has probably still not been fully realised, with the poetry of W.B. Yeats.

Unacknowledged borrowing is by now a well-known aspect of McGuckian's aesthetic, though we should note she was drawing attention to it long before any of her readers fully took the measure of it. And as critics have begun to understand, this borrowing has had as much to do with historical as literary tradition. McGuckian's poetry throughout the 1990s articulated a growing concern with her place in Northern Ireland, with the legacy of a history of violence. As she says in the interview printed here, this concern partly grew from her work as writer-in-residence at the Maze prison, and a parallel period of intense reading in the history of Irish republicanism. Yet a striking feature of what McGuckian herself designates the 'political' period of her writing is her continuing exploration of the polarities of tradition and liberation. In *Captain Lavender*, for example, the poems circle around images of caging and flight, repeatedly suggesting limitation and control (such as the constraints provided by organised religion) as the necessary basis for redemption. The analogy with the formal constraints of poetry is explicit, as McGuckian plays with the idea of the poem as a formal 'cage' or prison of meaning (with more than a nod towards Louis Mac-Neice's 'The Sunlight on the Garden') as a vehicle for transcendence and even healing.

As readers we can acknowledge the different 'phases' of her work, as McGuckian herself delineates them in the interview published here: the 'virginal', the moralising, the death sequence, the political and the period of serenity, 'suspicious of the peace process'. But at the same time we can notice the common concerns that bind these phases into a whole. Her abiding preoccupation with her relation to literary and political tradition is explored through textual borrowings, and through metaphors of growth and constraint. The sense of the past as both a constraining and productive legacy is a constant in McGuckian's work, occurring in volume after volume, from *Captain Lavender*'s understanding that 'We are half-taught our real names, from other lives' to the more troubled recognition in *Shelmalier* that 'your eighteenth century fingers spice the soil, with blood and bone'.

But it is also important to recognise that the lineaments of tradition are explored through the formal dynamics of the lyrics themselves. Set in the context of the work of her fellow Northern Irish poets, McGuckian's poems may appear to reject traditional forms as means of organising poetic thinking – we might compare her style to the baroque formal experiments of Paul

Muldoon and Ciaran Carson, or the loose stanzaic patterns of an older generation of poets (Heaney, Longley, Mahon) which are characteristic of much
post-war Anglo-American poetry. Unlike her contemporaries, McGuckian
never uses formal rhyme schemes and indeed rarely uses rhyme at all. When
she does so, as in *Shelmalier's* 'Script for an Unchanging Voice', it tends to
bear an 'ironic' meaning, signifying closure and lack of creativity. Yet she
retains a strong commitment to the stanza as an organising principle of her
poetry – the stanza acts as a room or cage allowing the fragments of bricolage to be juxtaposed to one another, forming patterns of repeated images
which are productive of new meanings.

We can approach the formal dynamics of McGuckian's poetry another
way, by considering the critical lag which has characterised responses to her
work. Arguably, a rather narrow British poetic critical tradition has been slow
to respond to the challenges posed by her poetry. As Shane Alcobia–Murphy
recalls in his introduction to this volume, McGuckian's style has given rise to
extreme forms of critical anxiety – one might argue that the more negative
the appraisal in those early reviews the more acute the anxiety, for why write
a review at all if the poetry has so little to recommend it? Several of the
essays here note reviewers' inability to 'read' the symbolist and avant-garde
aspects of her work, their habit of putting her style down to confused or
sloppy thinking. Undoubtedly the difficulty experienced by her early readers
was in part a consequence of her radically unfamiliar style, but we might add
that the post-Movement consensus which characterised the British poetry
establishment didn't help. The failure to appreciate her engagement with the
poetic avant-garde, or to understand bricolage and cut-up as 'legitimate'
poetic techniques, revealed the insularity of that poetic tradition, unschooled
in the broader traditions of European modernism and experimental poetry
in Britain and the United States.

One of the many strengths of this collection is the essayists' willingness to
consider McGuckian's poetry in the context of broader developments in
contemporary philosophy, art and linguistic theory, drawing on the theoretical perspectives of thinkers such as Kristeva, Wittgenstein, Deleuze, Levinas
and Heidegger to illuminate her avant-garde practice. Yet the general reluctance to read McGuckian's work as engaged with experimental poetic
techniques cannot simply be put down to the blindnesses of the critical
establishment. It is also a consequence of McGuckian's uneasy relationship to
linguistically innovative poetry as it has developed in Britain. Despite
McGuckian's lack of interest in the qualities of balance, coherence and integration there is a deeply traditionalist element to her work, and a belief in
the vatic and even redemptive possibilities of lyric poetry, which sets her
apart from many of the experimental poets associated with the small presses
in Britain.

Let us turn to a recent volume such as *The Book of the Angel* to examine
how her central drama of desire and containment has developed in her
current mode of poetic thinking. The volume is steeped in images and
metaphors derived from the visual arts, from the iconography of medieval
and Renaissance religious painting and stained glass. Many of the poems
draw attention to their reliance on fragments of analysis and descriptions of
particular paintings for their composition:

> It is impossible to tell
> from the brocade and feathers
> of the robes, wings and hair of Gabriel,
> from the tartan cloth of the angel,
>
> whether he has already spoken.

The preoccupation throughout the volume is with annunciation as a figure
for inspiration and fertility. As in this quotation from 'A Chrisom Child', it is
the eccentric details in the paintings and stained-glass compositions which
draw the attention; they stand in for the moment of transition, about which
it is 'impossible to tell'. The moment of annunciation is a moment between
motion and stasis – caught in paint annunciations represent ever-unresolved
confrontations, or mediations, between the secular and the divine. In a barely
disguised allusion to Yeats's 'Leda and the Swan' (with the 'push' of the terri-
fied fingers, and the broken line, 'Being so caught up, / [. . .] Did she put on
his knowledge with his power') McGuckian reminds us in 'Studies for a
Running Angel' that this concern with the moment of incarnation, the
passage between inner and outer worlds, is fundamental to post-romantic
poetry:

> Did she build up
> any depth of shadow, pushing away
> the darkness of the universe [. . .]?

We should note, however, that McGuckian's interest in these moments of
transition between orders of knowledge and understanding goes far beyond
theme and subject matter. Like the composition of religious representations
in stained glass from tiny abstract fragments of colour, the poems themselves
work by means of juxtaposition and bricolage. She places 'note against note',
building up a narrative through fragments: 'your story, in pieces, as it is'. The
poems draw attention to this method of 'overlapping' fragments (the word
'overlapping' itself appears several times in the collection, surely a knowing
reference to critical discussion of her works as composed of 'overlapping'
fragments of text), and an almost clumsy use of repetition. Terms such as
'leaves', 'cloak', 'separation', 'dream', 'blue', 'possess' are repeated not only

across poems but between the lines of single poems and single stanzas, so that the use of repetition as a principle of composition is impossible to ignore. The reader is forced to notice the process of building up the picture through careful piecing together of fragments which echo and spark off one another. As so often in McGuckian's work, it is in the relationship between the containment provided by the form of the poem and the possibilities provided by that containment for liberation that understanding occurs.

For a long time now, McGuckian's readers have been 'caught up' by her lyrical experiments, the dream logic of her poetry which occupies a space somewhere between an act of divination and an act of devotion, and which continually asks us to consider the relationship between pre-conscious inspiration and artfulness or design. As this timely collection of essays shows, her critics are now finding the appropriate languages with which to discuss and commend her strange and wonderful work.

Notes and references

INTRODUCTION

1. Rui Carvalho Homem, 'Looking for Clues: McGuckian, Poems and Portraits', in Maria de Fátima Lambert (ed.), *Writing and Seeing: Essays on Word and Image* (Amsterdam: Rodopi, 2006), p. 187.
2. Dennis O'Driscoll, 'Picturesque Debut', *Sunday Tribune*, 8 June 1982. McGuckian Papers, MS 770, Special Collections, Emory University, box 35, folder 2.
3. Eamon Grennan, 'Trades People', *The Irish Times*, 31 July 1982. McGuckian Papers, MS 770, box 35, folder 2. See also Kevin T. McEneaney, 'Flower Masters and Winter Works', *Irish Literary Supplement*, and Douglas Sealey, review of *The Flower Master*, *Poetry Ireland Review*, 5–6, pp. 57–8. Both reviewers express their concern about *The Flower Master*'s obliquity.
4. Avril Forrest, 'Flowers and War', *The Connaught Tribune*, 2 July 1982, p. 1.
5. Medbh McGuckian, 'Mr McGregor's Garden', *The Flower Master* (Oxford University Press, 1982), p. 14. McGuckian's poem is cited on the right and the intertext from which she composes the poem is cited on the left (Margaret Lane, *The Magic Years of Beatrix Potter* [London: Frederick Warne, 1978]).
6. Robin Lane Fox, 'Poetry Now', *Financial Times*, 8 January 1983. McGuckian Papers, MS 770, box 35, folder 2.
7. Deryn Rees-Jones, *Carol Ann Duffy* (Plymouth: Northcote House, 1999), p. 17.
8. Lane, *Magic Years*, p. 9.
9. Ibid., p. 61.
10. See Clair Wills, *Improprieties: Politics and Sexuality in Northern Irish Poetry* (Oxford: Clarendon Press, 1993).
11. McGuckian, 'The Rising Out', *Venus and the Rain* (Oxford University Press, 1984), p. 35.
12. Aidan C. Mathews, 'Mandrin Muse', *The Irish Times*, 13 October 1984. McGuckian Papers, MS 770, box 35, folder 3.
13. Peter Porter, 'Pleasures of Obscurity', *The Observer*, 19 August 1984, p. 19.
14. Jon Cook, 'New Found Land', *New Statesman*, 31 August 1984, p. 26.
15. James Simmons, 'A Literary Leg-pull', *Belfast Review*, 8 (Autumn 1984), p. 27.
16. Robert Nye, 'An Irish Parnassian at Work', *The Times*, 24 January 1985. McGuckian Papers, MS 770, box 35, folder 3.

17. Karen Petersen and J.J. Wilson, *Women Artists: Recognition and Reappraisal from the Early Middle Ages to the Twentieth Century* (London: The Women's Press, 1978).
18. Ibid., p. 3.
19. Ibid., p. 3, emphases added.
20. Ibid., p. 4.
21. Lebrun cited in ibid., p. 52.
22. Ibid., p. 135, emphasis added.
23. Rilke cited in ibid., p. 110, emphasis added.
24. Joanna Griffin cited in ibid., p. 62.
25. Alan Jenkins, 'Hearts on the Right Place', *The Observer*, 10 July 1988. McGuckian Papers, MS 770, box 35, folder 4.
26. David Herd, 'Other Rooms', *New Statesman and Society*, 28 August 1992, p. 36.
27. Sean O'Brien, 'Athletic Aesthetics', *The Sunday Times*, 12 July 1992, Books, p. 12.
28. Allison Rolls, review of *Marconi's Cottage*, *Krino*, 15 (Spring 1994), p. 99.
29. See Guinn Batten, '"The More with Which We Are Connected": The Muse of the Minus in the Poetry of McGuckian and Kinsella', in Anthony Bradley and Maryann Gialanella Valiulis (eds.), *Gender and Sexuality in Modern Ireland* (University of Massachusetts Press, 1997), pp. 212–44; Moynagh Sullivan, 'The Informal Poetics of Medbh McGuckian', *Nordic Irish Studies*, 3.1 (2004), pp. 75–92; Erin C. Mitchell, 'Slippage at the Threshold: Postmodern Hospitality in Medbh McGuckian's Poetry', *Literature Interpretation Theory*, 17.2 (2006), pp. 137–55.
30. Julia Kristeva, *Powers of Horror: An Essay on Abjection*, trans. Leon S. Roudiez (New York: Columbia University Press, 1982).
31. McGuckian, 'To Such a Hermes', *The Soldiers of Year II* (North Carolina: Wake Forest University Press, 2002), p. 40. McGuckian's text is on the right, the quotations from Kristeva on the left.
32. Ibid., p. 1.
33. Ibid., p. 207.
34. Ibid., p. 198, emphasis added.
35. Ibid., p. 188, emphasis added.
36. McGuckian, '*Comhrá*: A Conversation between Medbh McGuckian and Nuala Ní Dhomhnaill', interview by Laura O'Connor, *The Southern Review*, 31.3 (Summer 1995), pp. 605–6.
37. McGuckian, '"My Words Are Traps": An Interview with Medbh McGuckian', interview by John Hobbs, *New Hibernia Review*, 2.1 (Spring 1998), p. 114.
38. Kristeva, *Powers of Horror*, p. 191.
39. Ibid., p. 155, emphasis added.
40. Floyd Skloot, 'Tracking the Muse', *Notre Dame Review*, 17 (Winter 2004), p. 150.
41. Ray McDaniel, review of *The Book of the Angel*, *The Constant Critic* http://www.constantcritic.com/ray_mcdaniel/the_book_of_the_angel/ (accessed 20 July 2009).
42. Dillon Johnston and Guinn Batten, 'Contemporary Poetry in English: 1940–2000', in Margaret Kelleher and Philip O'Leary (eds.), *The Cambridge History of Irish Literature*, vol. 2 (Cambridge University Press, 2006), p. 398.
43. Robert Brazeau, 'Troubling Language: Avant-garde Strategies in the Poetry of Medbh McGuckian', *Mosaic*, 37.2 (2004), pp. 127–44.
44. McGuckian, 'Pulsus Paradoxus', *Shelmalier* (Oldcastle: Gallery Press, 1998), p. 40.
45. Ray Monk, *Ludwig Wittgenstein: The Duty of Genius* (London: Jonathan Cape, 1990).

46. St Augustine cited ibid., p. 364.

47. Wittgenstein cited ibid., p. 365, emphasis added.

48. Ibid., p. 578.

49. Ibid., p. 533.

50. McGuckian, 'Sky in Narrow Streets', *Marconi's Cottage* (Oldcastle: Gallery Press, 1991), p. 100.

51. C.S. Lewis, *Studies in Words* (Cambridge University Press, 1960) – referred to above as 'CL'; George D. Painter, *Marcel Proust: A Biography*, 2 vols. (London: Chatto and Windus, 1959 and 1965) – referred to above as 'MP1' for volume 1 and 'MP2' for volume 2; Henri de Lubac, *The Faith of Teilhard de Chardin* (London: Burns and Oates, 1965) – referred to above as 'TC'.

52. Seán Hand, 'Introduction', *The Levinas Reader* (Oxford: Blackwell, 1989), p. 6.

53. Ibid., pp. 5, 6.

54. McGuckian, 'A Book of Rains', *The Currach Requires No Harbours* (Oldcastle: Gallery Press, 2006), p. 24.

55. Emmanuel Levinas, *The Levinas Reader*, ed. Seán Hand. McGuckian's poem is cited on the right, quotations from Levinas are on the left.

56. McGuckian, 'Sky-Writing', *Marconi's Cottage*, p. 79.

57. Rainer Maria Rilke, *Selected Letters of Rainer Maria Rilke, 1902–1926*, trans. R.F.C. Hull (London: Macmillan, 1946). Quotations from this text cited on the left.

58. Susan Stanford Friedman, 'Creativity and the Childbirth Metaphor: Gender Difference in Literary Discourse', *Feminist Studies*, 13.1 (Spring 1987), pp. 65–6.

59. McGuckian, 'The Over Mother', *Captain Lavender* (Oldcastle: Gallery Press, 1994), p. 64.

60. David Mason, *The Poetry of Life and the Life of Poetry* (Ashland, Oregon: Story Line Press, 2000), p. 112.

61. McGuckian's text is cited on the right. The quotations on the left are from the poem's main intertext, Diane Wood Middlebrook's *Anne Sexton: A Biography* (Boston: Houghton Mifflin Company, 1991) – referred to in the text as 'M'.

62. Interview with McGuckian, Marine Hotel, Ballycastle, Co. Antrim, 19 August 1996.

63. McGuckian cited in Catherine Byron, 'A House of One's Own: Three Contemporary Irish Women Poets', *Women's Review*, 19 (May 1987), p. 33.

64. McGuckian 'A Religion of Writing', *Had I a Thousand Lives* (Oldcastle: Gallery Press, 2003), pp. 22–3.

65. Armando Petrucci, *Writing the Dead: Death and Writing Strategies in the Western Tradition*, trans. Michael Sullivan (Stanford University Press, 1998) – referred to as 'W'. Theodor Adorno, *Beethoven: The Philosophy of Music*, trans. Edmund Jephcott (Cambridge: Polity Press, 1998) – referred to as 'B'.

66. See the 'Afterword' by Clair Wills in this collection of essays.

67. McGuckian, 'Sealed Composition', *My Love Has Fared Inland* (Oldcastle: Gallery Press, 2008), p. 17. The quotations from the poem's intertext, Glauco Cambon's *Dante's Craft* (Minneapolis: University of Minnesota Press, 1966), are cited on the left and are referred to as 'GC'. The other intertext is Mary Carruthers and Jan M. Ziolkowski (eds.), *The Medieval Craft of Memory* (Philadelphia: University of Pennsylvania Press, 2004) – referred to as 'MC'.

68. Interview with McGuckian, Marine Hotel, Ballycastle, Co. Antrim, 19 August 1996.

69. John Ahern, 'Between the Love of Clizia and Mosca', *New York Times*, 23 February 1986, http://www.nytimes.com/1986/02/23/books/between-the-love-of-clizia-and-mosca.html.

CHAPTER ONE

1. Christopher Benfey, 'A Venusian Sends a Postcard Home', review of 'Venus and the Rain', *Parnassus: Poetry in Review*, 12 (1985), p. 507.
2. Michael Allen, 'The Poetry of Medbh McGuckian', in Elmer Andrews (ed.), *Contemporary Irish Poetry: A Collection of Critical Essays* (Basingstoke: Macmillan, 1992), pp. 286–309.
3. Jonathan Hufstader, *Tongue of Water, Teeth of Stones: Northern Irish Poetry and Social Violence* (University of Kentucky Press, 1999), pp. 262, 265–6.
4. William Butler Yeats, 'Cathleen Ní Houlihan', in John P. Harrington (ed.), *Modern Irish Drama* (New York: Norton, 1991), p. 11.
5. For a detailed analysis of the female allegory of Ireland, cf. my chapter '"A Very Real Dragon": The Myth of Ireland as a Woman', in Michaela Schrage-Früh, *Emerging Identities: Myth, Nation and Gender in the Poetry of Eavan Boland, Nuala Ní Dhomhnaill and Medbh McGuckian* (Wissenschaftlicker Verlag Trier, 2004), pp. 3–11.
6. Seamus Heaney, 'Act of Union', *Opened Ground: Selected Poems, 1966–96* (New York: Farrar, Straus and Giroux, 1998), p. 120.
7. Clair Wills, *Improprieties: Politics and Sexuality in Northern Irish Poetry* (Oxford University Press, 1993), p. 57.
8. Rebecca E. Wilson, 'Medbh McGuckian', in Gillean Somerville-Arjat and Rebecca E. Wilson (eds.), *Sleeping with Monsters: Conversations with Scottish and Irish Women Poets* (Dublin: Wolfhound Press, 1990), p. 3.
9. Medbh McGuckian, *The Flower Master* (Oldcastle: Gallery Press, 1993 – originally published by Oxford University Press in 1982); *On Ballycastle Beach* (Oxford University Press, 1988); *Venus and The Rain* (Oxford University Press, 1984); *Marconi's Cottage* (Oldcastle: Gallery Press, 1991); *Captain Lavender* (Oldcastle: Gallery Press, 1994). References to these collections are cited in the text as *FM, VR, OBB, MC* and *CL* respectively.
10. The last line of the original version of the poem reads: 'The grass is no bed after dark.'
11. Alexander G. Gonzalez, 'Celebrating the Richness of Medbh McGuckian's Poetry', in Alexander G. Gonzalez (ed.), *Contemporary Irish Women Poets: Some Male Perspectives* (Westport, Connecticut: Greenwood, 1999), pp. 47–49.
12. See Thomas Docherty, 'Postmodern McGuckian', in Neil Corcoran (ed.), *The Chosen Ground: Essays on the Contemporary Poetry of Northern Ireland* (Bridgend: Seren Books, 1992), p. 195.
13. Medbh McGuckian, 'Drawing Ballerinas: How Being Irish Has Influenced Me as a Writer', in Lizz Murphy (ed.), *Wee Girls: Women Writing from an Irish Perspective* (North Melbourne: Spinifex Press, 1996), p. 196.
14. Michaela Schrage-Früh, 'An Interview with Medbh McGuckian', *Contemporary Literature*, 46.1 (2005), p. 6.
15. Yeats, 'Cathleen Ní Houlihan', p. 7.
16. *The Táin*, trans. Thomas Kinsella (London: Oxford University Press, 1970), p. 53. See also Wills, *Improprieties*, pp. 72–3.
17. Michaela Schrage-Früh, '"Uncharted Territory": An Interview with Medbh McGuckian', in Renate von Bardeleben und Patricia Plummer (eds.), *Gender und Globalisierung* (Tübingen: Stauffenburg, forthcoming).

18. Schrage-Früh, 'An Interview with Medbh McGuckian', p. 10.

19. W.B. Yeats, *Collected Poems* (London: Macmillan, 1982), p. 204 (my emphasis).

20. Ibid., p. 204.

21. See Wills, *Improprieties*, p. 163.

22. Schrage-Früh, 'An Interview with Medbh McGuckian', pp. 11–12.

23. See Lewis Carroll, *Alice's Adventures in Wonderland, Through the Looking-Glass and Other Writings* (London: Collins, 1954). The tale of Alice seems an appropriate literary allusion, since Alice, too, moves between different worlds, and is 'very fond of pretending to be two people' (Carroll, p. 31).

24. Sarah Broom, 'McGuckian's Conversations with Rilke in *Marconi's Cottage*', *Irish University Review*, 28.1 (1998), p. 140. Broom discusses Rilke's aesthetics, his relationship with Paula and 'Requiem für eine Freundin' in the context of *Marconi's Cottage*. She does not mention, however, the evident impact of Rilke's work on *Venus and the Rain* and 'The Rising Out' in particular.

25. Rainer Maria Rilke, *The Selected Poetry of Rainer Maria Rilke*, ed. and trans. Stephen Mitchell (New York: Vintage, 1982), pp. 76–7.

26. Broom, 'McGuckian's Conversations', p. 140.

27. Schrage-Früh, 'An Interview with Medbh McGuckian'.

28. Michael Ferber, *A Dictionary of Literary Symbols* (Cambridge University Press, 1999), p. 48.

29. Ad de Vries, *Dictionary of Symbols and Imagery* (Amsterdam: North-Holland Publishing Company, 1974), p. 125.

30. Ferber, *Dictionary*, p. 49.

31. McGuckian, 'Drawing Ballerinas', p. 199.

32. Wills, *Improprieties*, p. 63.

33. Schrage-Früh, 'An Interview with Medbh McGuckian', p. 12.

34. John Brown, 'Interview with Medbh McGuckian', *In the Chair: Interviews with Poets from the North of Ireland* (Knockeven: Salmon Poetry, 2002), p. 180.

35. For a detailed interpretation of this poem in terms of spirituality see Patrick Grant, *Breaking Enmities: Religion, Literature and Culture in Northern Ireland, 1967–97* (Basingstoke: Macmillan, 1999), pp. 140–4.

36. Schrage-Früh, personal conversation with Medbh McGuckian, autumn 2001.

37. J.E. Cirlot, *A Dictionary of Symbols* (London: Routledge and Kegan Paul, 1971), p. 275.

38. See, for instance, 'The Unplayed Rosalind' where the speaker provides an imaginative though scarcely veiled description of the womb as 'a rose-red room, a roseate chamber' (*MC* 59); 'The Delivery of Charlotte', where she addresses her newborn daughter: 'Your morning sounds are a womb of roses, / Sinking into life and whoness' (*MC* 83); and 'The Rosary Dress' in which a woman, about to give birth in a sterile, clinically white delivery room, defensively tries to turn herself into a rose (*MC* 55).

39. See, for instance, Patricia Boyle Haberstroh, *Women Creating Women: Contemporary Irish Women Poets* (Dublin: Attic Press, 1996); Wills, *Improprieties*; Eileen Cahill, '"Because I Never Garden": Medbh McGuckian's Solitary Way', *Irish University Review*, 24.2 (1994), pp. 264–71.

40. Medbh McGuckian cited in Shane Murphy, '"You Took Away My Biography": The Poetry of Medbh McGuckian', *Irish University Review*, 28.1 (1998), p. 120.

41. For this intertextual vein in Medbh McGuckian and its manifold functions, see, for instance, Wills, *Improprieties*; Murphy, '"You Took Away My Biography"' and '"The Eye That Scanned It": The Picture Poems of Heaney, Muldoon, and McGuckian',

New Hibernia Review, 4.4 (2000), pp. 85–114; Broom, 'McGuckian's Conversations'.

42 Breda Gray, *Women and the Irish Diaspora* (London: Routledge, 2004), p. 223.

43. Hufstader, *Tongue of Water*, p. 267.

CHAPTER TWO

1. Cecile Grey, 'Medbh McGuckian: Imagery Wrought to its Uttermost', in Deborah Fleming (ed.), *Learning the Trade: Essays on W.B. Yeats and Contemporary Poetry* (West Cornwall, Connecticut: Locust Hill Press, 1993), p. 168 (Inset Interview dated 1991).

2. Susan Shaw Sailer, 'An Interview with Medbh McGuckian', *The Michigan Quarterly Review*, 32.1 (1993), p. 113.

3. Thomas Docherty, 'Initiations, Tempers, Seductions: Postmodern McGuckian', in Neil Corcoran (ed.), *The Chosen Ground: Essays on the Contemporary Poetry of Northern Ireland* (Bridgend: Seren Books, 1992), pp. 191–210.

4. Clair Wills, *Improprieties: Politics and Sexuality in Northern Irish Poetry* (Oxford University Press, 1993).

5. See Michael Allen, 'The Poetry of Medbh McGuckian', in Elmer Andrews (ed.), *Contemporary Irish Poetry: A Collection of Critical Essays* (Basingstoke: Macmillan 1992), pp. 286, 299, 302, 308; James McElroy, 'The Contemporary Fe/Male Poet: A Preliminary Reading', in James Brophy and Eamonn Grennan (eds.), *New Irish Writing: Essays in Memory of Raymond J. Porter* (Boston: Twayne, 1989), p. 189; Alan Robinson, *Instabilities in Contemporary British Poetry* (Basingstoke: Macmillan, 1988), p. 208.

6. Robinson, *Instabilities*, p. 208.

7. Ibid., p. 202.

8. Neil Corcoran, *English Poetry since 1940* (Harlow, Essex: Longman, 1993), pp. 222–4.

9. Richard Kearney, in conversation with Ciaran Carty, 'Why Ireland Needs a Fifth Province', *Sunday Independent*, 22 January 1984, pp. 14–15.

10. Seamus Deane, in conversation with Ciaran Carty, ibid.

11. Kearney, ibid.

12. Corcoran, *English Poetry*, p. 222.

13. Peter Sirr, '"How Things Begin to Happen": Notes on Eiléan Ní Chuilleanáin and Medbh McGuckian', *The Southern Review*, 31.3 (Summer 1995), pp. 461, 450.

14. Ibid., p. 451.

15. Moynagh Sullivan, 'The In-formal Poetics of Medbh McGuckian', *Nordic Irish Studies*, 3.1 (2004), pp. 75–92.

16. Ibid., p. 77.

17. Sirr, '"How Things Begin to Happen"', p. 460.

18. Wills, *Improprieties*, p. 50.

19. Medbh McGuckian, 'Emotion Recollected in Tranquillity . . .', in Susan Sellars (ed.), *Delighting the Heart: A Notebook by Women Writers* (London: The Women's Press, 1989), p. 59.

20. Laura O'Connor, '*Comhrá*: A conversation between Medbh McGuckian and Nuala Ní Dhomhnaill', *The Southern Review*, 31.3 (Summer 1995), p. 606.

21. Kimberly Bohman, 'Surfacing: An Interview with Medbh McGuckian', *The Irish Review*, 16 (Autumn-Winter 1994), p. 99.

22. McGuckian, 'There is no Feminine in Eternity . . .', in Sellars, *Delighting the Heart*, p. 179.

23. McGuckian, in Gillean Somerville-Arjat and Rebecca Wilson (eds.), *Sleeping with Monsters: Conversations with Scottish and Irish Women Poets* (Dublin: Wolfhound Press, 1990), p. 2.
24. Docherty, 'Initiations', p. 209.
25. Ibid.
26. Ibid., pp. 200, 201.
27. Ibid., p. 192.
28. For examples, see ibid., pp. 195, 196, 197, 198, 199.
29. Ibid., p. 205.
30. Wills, *Improprieties*, p. 191.
31. We will not know the details of her life – McGuckian has asserted they are irrelevant. See Sailer, 'An Interview with Medbh McGuckian', pp. 112, 113.
32. Wills, *Improprieties*, p. 159.
33. Ibid., p. 75.
34. Ibid., pp. 166, 167.
35. Ibid., pp. 168, 169.
36. Ibid., p. 76.
37. Ibid., p. 49.
38. Ibid., p. 76.
39. Ibid., p. 49.
40. Ibid., pp. 173–82.
41. Ibid., p. 182.
42. Ibid., p. 76.
43. McGuckian, *Venus and the Rain*, revised edition (Oldcastle: Gallery Press, 1994), p. 11. Subsequent references to this text will be incorporated parenthetically using the abbreviation *VR*.
44. Kathleen McCracken, 'An Attitude of Compassions: Q & A with Medbh McGuckian', *Irish Literary Supplement*, 9.2 (Fall 1990), p. 20.
45. Sailer, 'An Interview with Medbh Mc Guckian', p. 113.
46. McCracken, 'An Attitude of Compassions', p. 20.
47. Ibid.
48. McGuckian, 'Balakhana', *On Ballycastle Beach* (1988), revised edition (Oldcastle: Gallery Press, 1995), p. 36. Subsequent references to this text will be incorporated parenthetically using the abbreviation *OBB*.
49. McCracken, 'An Attitude of Compassions', p. 20.
50. Ibid.
51. Wills, *Improprieties*, pp.172–82; Shane Murphy, '"You Took Away My Biography": The Poetry of Medbh McGuckian', *Irish University Review* 28.1 (Spring-Summer 1998), pp. 110–32.
52. Sullivan, 'In-formal Poetics', pp. 75–92.
53. Ibid., pp. 75–82.
54. I am indebted for the honing of this argument to the insights of Moynagh Sullivan's work on how McGuckian brings the mother object of traditional poetics into visibility as an autonomous entity. See Sullivan, 'In-formal Poetics', pp. 82–92.
55. Docherty, 'Initiations', p. 208.
56. McGuckian, *Marconi's Cottage* (Oldcastle: Gallery Press, 1991). Subsequent references to this text will be incorporated parenthetically using the abbreviation *MC*.
57. Bohman, 'Surfacing', p. 97.

58. McGuckian, *The Flower Master* (1982), revised edition (Oldcastle: Gallery Press, 1993), p. 13. Subsequent references to this text will be incorporated parenthetically using the abbreviation *FM*.

59. Sullivan, 'In-formal Poetics', pp. 84–90.

60. Bohman, 'Surfacing', p. 103.

61. O'Connor, *Comhrá*, p. 606.

62. McGuckian, 'There is no Feminine in Eternity . . .', p. 179.

63. McGuckian, in Somerville-Arjat and Wilson, *Sleeping with Monsters*, p. 5.

64. Clair Wills notes the phallic projection of the aeroplane model. Wills, *Improprieties*, pp. 170–1.

65. McGuckian, 'Sky-Writing', *Marconi's Cottage*, p. 79, and McGuckian, 'Open Rose', *Marconi's Cottage*, p. 80.

66. See Sullivan, 'In-formal Poetics'.

67. See McGuckian in Sailer, 'An Interview with Medbh McGuckian', p. 125: 'And a pendulum: you have a measure for time through the poems, a measure of time.'

68. See McGuckian's remark: 'And therefore, snow that has dissipated and spread out, is pressed into the earth, sort of like water, to bring something new up [. . .] but [. . .] something of the waters will come back to you somehow.' Ibid.

69. McGuckian's 'The Dream-language of Fergus' finds a direct heir in the exploration of 'trans-sense language' in her poem 'Elegy for an Irish Speaker' (*Captain Lavender*, p. 42), collected six years later. Here the association of self and language ('your speaking flesh') is far more directly developed, McGuckian associating the essence of her poetry, the invisible active anti-self of text, with the unspoken Irish language – both functioning as the 'Roaming root of multiple meanings'. The voice of the poem mourns the death of the Irish speaker as the bearer of a dead language that, *through* being lost or invisible, paradoxically propels itself forward into the world.

70. McCracken, 'An Attitude of Compassions', p. 20.

71. Angela Bourke, 'The Virtual Reality of Irish Fairy Legend', *Éire-Ireland*, 36 (1991), pp. 7–25. Quotations here are taken from the republished version of this essay in Claire Connolly (ed.), *Theorizing Ireland* (Basingstoke: Palgrave Macmillan, 2003), pp. 27–40.

72. Bourke, 'Virtual Reality', p. 31.

73. Ibid.

74. Ibid., pp. 30, 31.

75. Ibid., p. 29.

76. Luke Gibbons, 'Narratives of the Nation: Fact, Fiction and Irish Cinema', in Luke Dodd (ed.), *Nationalisms: Visions and Revisions* (Dublin: Film Institute of Ireland 1999), pp. 66–73. Quotations here are taken from the republished version of this essay in Claire Connolly (ed.), *Theorizing Ireland* (Basingstoke: Palgrave Macmillan, 2003), pp. 69–75.

77. Ibid., p. 72.

78. For a more sustained exploration of the concept of good faith in relation to Irish poetry, see Catriona Clutterbuck, 'Good Faith in Religion and Art: The Later Poetry of Eiléan Ní Chuilleanáin', *Irish University Review*, 37.1 (2007), pp. 131–56.

CHAPTER THREE

1. Kathleen McCracken, 'An Attitude of Compassions: Q & A with Medbh McGuckian', *Irish Literary Supplement*, 9.2 (Fall 1990), p. 20.

2. Helen Blakeman, 'I am Listening in Black and White to What Speaks to Me in Blue': Interview with Medbh McGuckian, *Irish Studies Review*, 11.1 (April 2003), p. 68.

3. Arthur Symons quoted in Karl Beckson and Arthur Ganz, *Literary Terms: A Dictionary*, third edition (London: André Deutsch, 1990), p. 275.

4. Michael Groden and Martin Kreiswirth (eds.), *The Johns Hopkins Guide to Literary Theory and Criticism* (Baltimore: Johns Hopkins University Press, 1994), p. 484.

5. Clive Scott's essay 'The Poetry of Symbolism and Decadence', in Patrick McGuinness (ed.), *Symbolism, Decadence and the Fin de Siècle: French and European Perspectives* (University of Exeter Press, 2000), explores the interconnections of Symbolism and decadence or, as he states, 'the Symbolist and Decadent aspects of the same poet', and the differences between them. The term *fin de siècle* is related to the term 'decadence' and the writings of the 1880s and 1890s that embodied a sense of decline and despair as the end of the century approached. Often employed to signify a historical period, *fin de siècle* has also, however, been used to describe specific works *inspired* by decadence. That titles such as *Symbolism, Decadence and the Fin de Siècle* include all three terms, therefore, illustrates both their interrelation and their singularity.

6. Chris Baldick, *The Concise Oxford Dictionary of Literary Terms* (Oxford University Press, 1990), p. 220.

7. Walter Benjamin, 'On Some Motifs in Baudelaire', *Illuminations*, trans. Harry Zohn (London: Fontana Press, 1992), p. 170.

8. Wallice Fowlie, *Poem and Symbol: A Brief History of French Symbolism* (Pennsylvania State University Press, 1990), p. 32.

9. Scott, 'Poetry', p. 60.

10. J.A. Cuddon, *A Dictionary of Literary Terms and Literary Theory*, fourth edition (Oxford: Blackwell, 1998), p. 885.

11. Michael Temple, 'M'introduire dans ton histoire', in Michael Temple (ed.), *Meetings with Mallarmé in Contemporary French Culture* (University of Exeter Press), p. 13. Temple footnotes 'theory of our times', inviting the reader to '[c]ompare the coinage of this term in the special issue entitled 'Mallarmé: Theorist of our Times', *Dalhousie French Review*, 25 (1993), p. 229, fn. 14.

12. Edmund Wilson, *Axel's Castle: A Study in the Imaginative Literature of 1870–1930* (Glasgow: Fontana Library, 1976), p. 23.

13. Julia Kristeva, 'The Revolt of Mallarmé', in Robert Greer Cohn (ed.), *Mallarmé in the Twentieth Century* (Madison: Associated University Press, 1998), p. 36.

14. George Craig, 'Reading Mallarmé', *Modern Language Review*, 78.3 (1983), p. 564.

15. Mary Jacobus, *Reading Woman: Essays in Feminist Criticism* (London: The Athlone Press, 1994), p. 148.

16. Anne-Marie Smith, *Julia Kristeva: Speaking the Unspeakable* (London: Pluto Press, 1998), p. 23.

17. Judith Butler, *Gender Trouble: Feminism and the Subversion of Identity* (New York: Routledge, 1990), p. 82. Interestingly, in *Revolution in Poetic Language* (New York: Columbia University Press, 1984), Kristeva states 'We understand the term "semiotic" in its Greek sense [to mean] distinctive mark, trace, index, precursory sign, proof, engraved or written sign, imprint, trace figuration', a description which displays many similarities with the Greek definition for 'symbol' discussed above.

18. Butler, *Gender Trouble*, p. 81.

19. Kristeva, 'Sémanalyse', cited in Roland Barthes, 'Theory of the Text', in Robert

Young (ed.), *Untying the Text: A Post-Structuralist Reader* (Boston: Routledge and Kegan Paul, 1981), p. 38.

20.   Kristeva, *Revolution in Poetic Language*, p. 88.

21.   Ibid., p. 86.

22.   The translation of '*Ses purs ongles*' is taken from Robert Greer Cohn, *Toward the Poems of Mallarmé*, expanded edition (Berkeley: University of California Press, 1980). I have placed the English translation alongside the original poem in French as the sound of the poem is as integral a part of its 'meaning' as any semantic interpretation. As there are inherent difficulties in discussing any poem in translation, my consideration of '*Ses purs ongles*' will focus primarily on graphemic and phonetic characteristics.

23.   Cohn, *Toward the Poems of Mallarmé*, p. 138.

24.   Groden and Kreiswirth, *Johns Hopkins Guide*, p. 485.

25.   Butler, *Gender Trouble*, p. 82.

26.   *Johns Hopkins Guide*, p. 485.

27.   Ibid., p. 484.

28.   Beckson and Ganz, *Literary Terms*, p. 285.

29.   Ibid.

30.   Fowlie, *Poem and Symbol*, p. 13.

31.   Victor Shklovsky, 'Art as Technique', in David Lodge (ed.), *Modern Criticism and Theory* (London: Longman, 1988), p. 20.

32.   Cohn, *Toward the Poems of Mallarmé*, p. 140.

33.   See also *Stephane Mallarmé: Selected Poems*, trans. C.F. MacIntyre (Berkeley: University of California Press, 1957) and Octavio Paz, 'Commentary on the "Sonnet in IX" of Mallarmé', in Robert Greer Cohn (ed.), *Mallarmé in the Twentieth Century* (Madison: Associated University Press, 1998).

34.   For example, Charles Chadwick in his introduction to *The Meaning of Mallarmé: A Bilingual Edition of his Poésies and Un Coup De Dés* (Aberdeen: Scottish Cultural Press, 1996) states that 'in the following pages, the original text, has, on occasions, been expanded in the translation and obscure images have been interpreted in order to achieve the goal of giving meaning to the poems'. Chadwick offers a radically revised version of Mallarmé's poems that ironically attempts to 'smooth out' the radical indeterminacy that Mallarmé desired.

35.   Craig, 'Reading Mallarmé', p. 568.

36.   Ibid.

37.   Paul de Man, 'Lyric and Modernity', in Harold Bloom (ed.), *Modern Critical Views: Stéphane Mallarmé* (New York: Chelsea House Publishers, 1987), p. 71.

38.   Cohn, *Toward the Poems of Mallarmé*, p. 141.

39.   Ibid., p. 144.

40.   Ann-Marie Smith, *Julia Kristeva*, p. 21.

41.   Octavio Paz notes in his essay 'Commentary on the "Sonnet in IX"' that 'In a letter of 3 May 1869, addressed to Eugène Lefébure, the poet confided to his friend: "I have written a sonnet and I only have three rhymes in *ix*. Try to ascertain the real meaning of the word *ptyx*. I assure you that no language has it, which does not stop pleasing me, as I would love to have created it through the magic of rhyme"' (p. 120). As Cohn notes, however, Hugo had already used the word in his 'Satyre'.

42.   Paz defines Ptyx as a marine conch and yet, recalling Cohn's comment, Paz maintains that this 'structure that coils in on itself' is simultaneously 'carnal: The sex organ of

the woman refolds in on itself and hides beneath a dark fleece' (pp. 123–4).

43. E.S. Burt, 'Mallarmé's "Sonnet en yx": The Ambiguities of Speculation', in Bloom, *Modern Critical Views*, p. 111. Burt provides both a thorough and insightful discussion of the word 'ptyx'.

44. Ibid., p. 111.

45. Ibid., p. 115.

46. Hans-Jost Frey, *Studies in Poetic Discourse: Mallarmé, Baudelaire, Rimbaud, Hölderlin*, trans. William Whobrey (California: Stanford University Press, 1996), p. 20. Interestingly, in discussing '*A la nue accablante tu*' Frey adopts the word '*baver*', signifying the 'foam of the sea' in Mallarmé's poem, as representative of his use of language. Frey notes how negative connotations of this word include the 'babbling of children' and 'to speak nonsense'. He states, 'Comprehension begins when *baver* is no longer understood as a negative thing' but rather 'revaluation requires the renunciation of instrumentality and the recognition of a discourse that does not communicate or that does so in another way' (p. 25). This recalls for me Bowie's description of the work of Mallarmé and Lacan as 'pre-semantic babble' and reinforces my reading of Mallarmé as fracturing instrumental discourse.

47. Sigmund Freud, *The Interpretation of Dreams* (London: Penguin, 1991), p. 383.

48. See Frey's discussion of the *simultaneity* of multiple readings and the irreducible ambiguity of the text.

49. Frey, *Studies*, p. 31.

50. Patrick Ffrench, 'Revolution in Poetic Language? Kristeva and Mallarmé', in Temple, *Meetings with Mallarmé*, p. 194.

51. Ibid., p. 194.

52. Edgar Allan Poe, *Selected Writings* (Middlesex: Penguin, 1984), p. 485.

53. See Derrida's discussion of '*sonor*' in his essay entitled 'Mallarmé', in Derek Attridge (ed.), *Acts of Literature* (New York: Routledge, 1992), pp. 110–26.

54. See Roger Pearson, *Unfolding Mallarmé: The Development of a Poetic Act* (Oxford: Clarendon Press, 1996).

55. Charles R. Lyons, 'Mallarmé and Representation in the Theatre', in Cohn, *Mallarmé in the Twentieth Century*, p. 100. The collaboration between Mallarmé and Manet to translate and illustrate 'The Raven' was completed in 1875. Mallarmé's first version of '*Ses purs ongles*', entitled '*Sonnet allegorique du lui-meme*', was written in 1868 and the final version appeared in 1887. Both versions contain the 'or' and 'yx' rhyme and it is conceivable that Poe's poem and his critical writing influenced Mallarmé's own choice of rhyme scheme. Roger Pearson notes how in a letter to Cazalis dated January 1864 Mallarmé explicitly mentions Poe's essay on 'The Raven' in relation to his poem '*L'Azur*'. Pearson also states that 'the twin operations of transcription and translation (of Poe) were Mallarmé's way of assimilating and transcending the poetic language of his mentors' *Unfolding Mallarmé* (p. 22).

56. Kristeva, '*Poésie et négativité*', translated and cited by Patrick Ffrench in 'Revolution in Poetic Language? Kristeva and Mallarmé', in Temple, *Meetings with Mallarmé*, p. 189.

57. Ffrench, 'Revolution in Poetic Language', p. 189.

58. Kristeva, '*Poésie et négativité*', pp. 189–90.

59. Cohn, *Toward the Poems of Mallarmé*, p. 143.

60. Derrida, 'Mallarmé', p. 120.

61. Kristeva, *Revolution in Poetic Language*, p. 86.

62. Cohn, *Toward the Poems of Mallarmé*, pp. 3–4.

63. Malcolm Bowie, 'Lacan and Mallarmé: Theory as Word-Play', in Temple, *Meetings with Mallarmé*, p. 73.

64. Ibid. Bowie provides the following translation of this stanza, taken from *Mallarmé: The Poems* trans. Keith Bosley (Harmondsworth: Penguin, 1977):

So that they all, enormous,	Telles, immenses, que chacune
Were adorned with clear outlines	Ordinairement se para
Commonly, a hiatus	D'un lucide conour, lacune
Between them and the garden.	Qui des jardins la separa.

65. Ibid.

66. Ibid., p. 72.

67. Derrida, 'Mallarmé', p. 114.

68. Ibid.

69. Craig, 'Reading Mallarmé', p. 563.

70. Burt, 'Mallarmé's "Sonnet en yx"', p. 108.

71. Ffrench, 'Revolution in Poetic Language?', p. 185.

72. Ibid., p. 193.

73. Craig, 'Reading Mallarmé', p. 561.

74. Peter Sirr, '"How Things Begin to Happen": Notes on Eiléan Ní Chuilleanáin and Medbh McGuckian', *The Southern Review* 31.3 (1995), p. 451.

75. Kimberly S. Bohman, 'Surfacing: An Interview with Medbh McGuckian', *The Irish Review*, 16 (1994), p. 98.

76. Sue Vice, *Introducing Bakhtin* (Manchester University Press, 1997), p. 21.

77. Blakeman, 'I am Listening', p. 68.

78. All quotations taken from Shklovsky, 'Art as Technique', pp. 19–20. Shklovsky promotes 'defamiliarization' as one means of avoiding the 'automatism of perception', which I have discussed above in relation to Mallarmé.

79. Blakeman, 'I am Listening', p. 63.

80. McCracken, 'An Attitude of Compassion', p. 20.

81. Andrea Nye, 'Woman Clothed with the Sun: Julia Kristeva and the Escape from/to Language', *Signs: Journal of Women in Culture and Society*, 12.4 (1987), p. 673.

82. Medbh McGuckian, 'Time-Words', *Marconi's Cottage* (Newcastle upon Tyne: Bloodaxe Books, 1992), p. 106.

83. Frey, *Studies in Poetic Discourse*, p. 5.

84. For further discussion on the rift between the signifier and signified in McGuckian's poetry, see 'Metaphor and Metonymy in Medbh McGuckian's Poetry', *Critical Survey*, 14.2 (2002), pp. 61–74.

85. Patricia Boyle Haberstroh, *Women Creating Women: Contemporary Irish Women Poets* (Dublin: Attic Press, 1996), p. 125.

86. Maggie Humm, *A Reader's Guide to Contemporary Feminist Literary Criticism* (Hertfordshire: Harvester Wheatsheaf, 1994), p. 105.

87. Frey, *Studies in Poetic Discourse*, p. 11.

88. Smith, *Kristeva*, p. 23.

89. Ibid.

90. Chris Baldick, *The Concise Oxford Dictionary of Literary Terms* (Oxford University Press, 1990), p. 220.

91. Kristeva, *Kristeva Reader*, p. 93. I am aware that Kristeva's use of the pronoun 'he' in this comment relates to her assertion that due to women's 'incomplete' separation from the mother, men are more capable of representing the semiotic.

92. Bowie, 'Lacan and Mallarmé', p. 79.
93. Paul Ricoeur, 'Myth as the Bearer of Possible Words: Interview with Richard Kearney', in Mario J. Valdes (ed.), *A Ricoeur Reader: Reflection and Imagination* (Hertfordshire: Harvester Wheatsheaf, 1991), p. 465.
94. Fowlie, *Poem and Symbol*, p. 52.
95. Blakeman, unpublished interview notes.
96. Burt, 'Mallarmé's "Sonnet en yx"', p. 99.
97. Philippe Sollers, 'Literature and Totality', in Bloom, Modern Critical Views, p. 43.
98. Scott, 'Poetry', p. 64.
99. Derrida, 'Signature, Event, Context', in Peggy Kamuf (ed.), *A Derrida Reader* (Hertfordshire: Harvester Wheatsheaf, 1991), p. 94.
100. Ibid., p. 83.
101. Ibid., p. 91.
102. Blakeman, 'I am Listening', p. 63.
103. Sirr, 'How Things Begin to Happen', p. 464.
104. Blakeman, 'I am Listening', p. 64.
105. McGuckian, '*Comhrá*: A Conversation between Medbh McGuckian and Nuala Ní Dhomhnaill', interview by Laura O'Connor, *The Southern Review*, 31.3 (1995), p. 606.
106. Blakeman, 'I am Listening', p.67.
107. Barthes, 'Theory of the Text', p. 43.
108. Ricoeur, 'Myth', p. 452.

CHAPTER FOUR

1. Eileen Cahill, '"Because I Never Garden": Medbh McGuckian's Solitary Way', *Irish University Review*, 24.2 (Autumn-Winter 1994), p. 267. Cahill refers to an interview from 1990, where McGuckian says that 'poetry must almost dismantle the letters'. See Kathleen McCracken, 'An Attitude of Compassions: Q & A with Medbh McGuckian,' *Irish Literary Supplement*, 9.2 (Fall 1990), p. 20.
2. Susan Porter, 'The "Imaginative Space" of Medbh McGuckian', *Canadian Journal of Irish Studies*, 15.2 (December 1989), p. 95.
3. Thomas Docherty, 'Initiations, Tempers, Seductions: Postmodern McGuckian', in Neil Corcoran (ed.), *The Chosen Ground: Essays on the Contemporary Poetry of Northern Ireland* (Bridgend: Seren Books, 1992), p. 205.
4. Cahill, '"Because I Never Garden"', pp. 265–6.
5. Ibid., p. 268.
6. Mary O'Connor, '"Rising Out": Medbh McGuckian's Destabilizing Poetics', *Éire-Ireland*, 30.4 (Winter 1996), p. 156.
7. Medbh McGuckian cited in McCracken, 'An Attitude of Compassions' p. 20.
8. McGuckian, *Venus and the Rain* (Oxford University Press, 1984), p. 36. Further references to this edition will henceforth be cited parenthetically as *VR*.
9. O'Connor, '"Rising Out"', p. 157.
10. Hélène Cixous, for instance, argues that feminine writing is "working (in) the in-between". Cixous, 'The Laugh of the Medusa', in Elaine Marks and Isabelle de Courtivron (eds.), *New French Feminisms: An Anthology* (Brighton: Harvester, 1981), p. 254. Similarly, Tilman Küchler describes postmodern thinking as follows: 'the "new" and "properly" speaking postmodern site for thinking is always an (improper) site inbetween.' Tilman Küchler, *Postmodern Gaming: Heidegger, Duchamp, Derrida* (New York: Lang, 1994), p. 5.

11. Jacques Derrida, *Margins of Philosophy* (University of Chicago Press, 1982), p. 6.
12. McGuckian, 'The Sailor', *The Flower Master and Other Poems* (Oldcastle: Gallery Press, 1993), p. 46. Further references to this edition will henceforth be cited parenthetically as *FM*.
13. McGuckian, 'Circle with Full Stop', *Shelmalier* (Oldcastle: Gallery Press, 1998), p. 31. Further references to this edition will henceforth be cited parenthetically as *S*.
14. McGuckian, 'A Different Same', *Marconi's Cottage* (Oldcastle: Gallery Press, 1991), p. 49. Further references to this edition will henceforth be cited parenthetically as *MC*.
15. 'Hotel' thus offers an alternative to the idea sometimes voiced by post-structuralist and French feminist critics that all speaking inevitably gets caught in oppressive, logocentric concepts. Luce Irigaray, for instance, states that "to speak *of* or *about* woman may always boil down to, or be understood as, a recuperation of the feminine within a logic that maintains it in repression, censorship, nonrecognition". See Luce Irigaray, *This Sex Which Is Not One*, trans. Catherine Porter and Carolyn Burke (New York: Cornell University Press, 1985), p. 78.
16. Paul Ricoeur, *Oneself as Another*, trans. Kathleen Blamey (University of Chicago Press, 1992), p. 27.
17. McGuckian, *On Ballycastle Beach* (Oxford University Press, 1988), p. 25. Further references to this edition will henceforth be cited parenthetically as *OBB*.
18. For an analysis of negativity and the surplus of meaning in McGuckian's poetry, see Guinn Batten, '"The More with Which We Are Connected": The Muse of the Minus in the Poetry of McGuckian and Kinsella', in Anthony Bradley and Maryann Gialanella Valiulis (eds.), *Gender and Sexuality in Modern Ireland* (Amherst: University of Massachusetts Press, 1997), pp. 212–44.
19. McGuckian, *Captain Lavender* (Oldcastle: Gallery Press, 1994) p. 16. Further references to this edition will be cited parenthetically as *CL*.
20. Derrida, *Writing and Difference* (University of Chicago Press, 1978), p. 177.
21. Maurice Merleau-Ponty quoted ibid., p. 11.
22. Martin Heidegger, *Poetry, Language, Thought*, trans. Albert Hofstadter (New York: Harper & Row, 1975), p. 215.
23. Derrida, *Writing and Difference*, p. 70.
24. What is remarkable about Odysseus is, first, his heroic overcoming of hardships and vanquishing of strange creatures, and, second, his complete lack of development. As Erich Auerbach notes in his famous essay 'Odysseus's Scar': the Homeric heroes 'have no development, and their life-histories are clearly set forth once and for all. So little are the Homeric heroes presented as developing or having developed, that most of them – Nestor, Agamemnon, Achilles – appear to be of an age fixed from the very first. Even Odysseus, in whose case the long lapse of time and the many events which occurred offer so much opportunity for biographical development, shows almost nothing of it. Odysseus on his return is exactly the same as when he left Ithaca two decades earlier.' Erich Auerbach, *Mimesis: The Representation of Reality in Western Literature* (Princeton University Press, 1953), p. 17.
25. Emmanuel Levinas, 'The Trace of the Other', in Mark C. Taylor (ed.), *Deconstruction in Context: Literature and Philosophy* (University of Chicago Press, 1986), p. 346.
26. Ibid., p. 354.
27. William Shakespeare, *Hamlet* (London: Routledge, 1982), 3.1.79–80.
28. In an interview, McGuckian states that Yeats's Fergus is one of the inspirational sources for 'The Dream-Language of Fergus'. See Susan Shaw Sailer, 'An Interview

with Medbh McGuckian', *Michigan Quarterly Review*, 32.1 (1993), p. 123.

29. W.B. Yeats, *The Collected Poems of W.B. Yeats*, ed. Richard J. Finneran, revised second edition (New York: Scribner, 1996), p. 32.

30. Derrida, *Writing and Difference*, p. 73.

31. Roland Barthes, *Writing Degree Zero* (New York: Hill and Wang, 1968), p. 48.

32. See Jacques Derrida's chapter 'Différance' in Derrida, *Margins of Philosophy*, trans. Alan Bass (University of Chicago Press, 1982), pp. 1–27.

33. Michael Roth, *The Poetics of Resistance: Heidegger's Line* (Evanston: Northwestern University Press, 1996), p. 148.

34. Derrida, *Of Grammatology*, corrected edition (Baltimore: Johns Hopkins University Press, 1998), p. 158.

35. Docherty, 'Initiations', p. 209.

36. Richard Rorty, *Contingency, Irony, and Solidarity* (Cambridge University Press, 1989), p. 7.

37. Docherty, 'Initiations', p. 192.

38. Ibid., p. 193. For a critique of Docherty's reading of the self in McGuckian's poetry, see Shane Murphy, '"You Took Away My Biography"', *Irish University Review*, 28.1 (Spring-Summer 1998), pp. 110–32.

39. Derrida, *Writing and Difference*, p. 11.

40. Neil Corcoran, *English Poetry since 1940* (London: Longman, 1993), p. 222.

41. Molly Bendall, 'Flower Logic: The Poems of Medbh McGuckian', *Antioch Review*, 48.3 (Summer 1990), p. 369.

42. Paul Celan, *Collected Prose*, trans. Rosmarie Waldrop (Manchester: Carcanet, 1986), p. 46.

CHAPTER FIVE

1. Shane Alcobia-Murphy, 'Safe Houses: Authenticity, Nostalgia and the Irish House', in Gerry Smyth and Joanna Croft (eds.), *Our House: the Representation of Domestic Space in Modern Culture* (Amsterdam and New York: Editions Rodopi, 2006), p. 117.

2. See, for example, Scott Brewster, 'Building, Dwelling, Moving: Seamus Heaney, Tom Paulin and the Reverse Aesthetic', ibid., pp. 141–60.

3. Lucy Collins, 'Architectural Metaphors: Representations of the House in the Poetry of Eiléan Ní Chuilleanáin and Vona Groarke', in Scott Brewster and Michael Parker (eds.), *Irish Literature Since 1990: Diverse Voices* (Manchester University Press, 2009), p. 144.

4. Gerry Smyth, *Space and the Irish Cultural Imagination* (London: Palgrave, 2001), p. 56.

5. Philippa Tristram, *Living Space in Fact and Fiction* (London: Routledge, 1989), p. 2.

6. Kathy Mezei and Chiara Briganti, 'Reading the House: A Literary Perspective', *Signs: Journal of Women in Culture and Society*, 27.3 (2002), p. 839.

7. Heather Zwicker, 'Gendered Troubles: Refiguring "Woman" in Northern Ireland', in A. Kibbey, K. Short and A. Farmanfarmaian (eds.), *Sexual Artifice: Persons, Images, Politics* (New York and London: New York University Press, 1994), p. 251.

8. Collins, 'Architectural Metaphors', p. 143.

9. Gaston Bachelard, *The Poetics of Space*, trans. Maria Jolas (Boston: Beacon, 1994), p. xxxvi.

10. Ibid., p. 5.

11. Ibid., p. 6.

12. Ibid.

13. Collins, 'Architectural Metaphors', p. 157.
14. Patricia Boyle Haberstroh, *Women Creating Women: Contemporary Irish Women Poets* (Syracuse University Press, 1996), p. 147.
15. Bachelard, *Poetics of Space*, p. xxxvii.
16. Thomas Docherty, 'Initiations, Tempers, Seductions: Postmodern McGuckian', in Neil Corcoran (ed.), *The Chosen Ground: Essays on the Contemporary Poetry of Northern Ireland* (Bridgend: Seren Books, 1992), p. 201.
17. Medbh McGuckian, *Selected Poems* (Oldcastle: Gallery Press, 1997), p. 33.
18. Haberstroh, *Women Creating Women*, pp. 21–2.
19. Smyth, *Space and the Irish Cultural Imagination*, p. 72.
20. McGuckian, *Selected Poems*, pp. 21–2.
21. Clair Wills, *Improprieties: Politics and Sexuality in Northern Irish Poetry* (Oxford: Clarendon Press, 1993), p. 73.
22. Luce Irigaray, *An Ethics of Sexual Difference*, trans. C. Burke and Gillian C. Gill (London: The Athlone Press, 1993), p. 15.
23. Irigaray, *Speculum of the Other Woman*, trans. Gillian C. Gill (Ithaca: Cornell University Press, 1984), p. 365.
24. McGuckian, cited in Wendy J. Eberle, 'Painting a Pictographic Language, Beyond Sound Boundaries: Medbh McGuckian's Poetic Making', *Canadian Journal of Irish Studies*, 22.1 (July 1996), p. 67.
25. Ann Beer, 'Medbh McGuckian's Poetry: Maternal Thinking and a Politics of Peace', *Canadian Journal of Irish Studies*, 18.1 (July 1992), p. 195.
26. Mary O'Connor, '"Rising Out": Medbh McGuckian's Destabilizing Poetics', *Éire-Ireland*, 30.4 (Winter 1995–1996), p. 159.
27. McGuckian, *Captain Lavender* (Oldcastle: Gallery Press, 1994), p. 64.
28. McGuckian, *Marconi's Cottage* (Oldcastle: Gallery Press, 1992), p. 79.
29. Wills, *Improprieties*, p. 63.
30. Guinn Batten, '"The More with Which We Are Connected": The Muse of the Minus in the Poetry of McGuckian and Kinsella', in Anthony Bradley and Maryann Gialanella Valiulis (eds.), *Gender and Sexuality in Modern Ireland* (Amherst: University of Massachusetts Press, 1997), p. 217.
31. Susan Porter, 'The "Imaginative Space" of Medbh McGuckian', *Canadian Journal of Irish Studies*, 15.2 (December 1989), p. 103.
32. Wills, *Improprieties*, p. 68.
33. Hélène Cixous, 'Utopias', trans. Keith Cohen and Paula Cohen, in Elaine Marks and Isabelle de Courtivron (eds.), *New French Feminisms: An Anthology* (New York: Schocken Books, 1981), p. 258.
34. Erin C. Mitchell, 'Slippage at the Threshold: Postmodern Hospitality in Medbh McGuckian's Poetry', *Lit: Literature Interpretation Theory*, 17 (2006), p. 143.
35. McGuckian, *On Ballycastle Beach* (Oxford University Press, 1988), p. 11.
36. Wills, *Improprieties*, p. 191.
37. Elin Holmsten, 'Double Doors: An Interview with Medbh McGuckian', *Nordic Irish Studies*, 3.1 (2004), p. 93.
38. Bachelard, *The Poetics of Space*, p. 222.
39. Emmanuel Levinas, *Totality and Infinity*, trans. Alphonso Lingis (Pittsburgh: Duquesne University Press, 1969), p. 14.
40. Levinas, *Ethics and Infinity: Conversations with Philippe Nemo*, trans. Richard A. Cohen (Pittsburgh: Duquesne University Press, 1985), p. 86.

41. See Jacques Derrida, *Adieu à Emmanuel Levinas* (Paris: Galilee, 1997).
42. Christina Howells, *Derrida: Deconstruction from Phenomenology to Ethics* (Cambridge: Polity, 1998), p. 146.
43. In this regard, see Levinas's 'Substitution', in Séan Hand (ed.), *The Levinas Reader* (Cambridge: Basil Blackwell, 1989), pp. 88–126.
44. Mitchell, 'Slippage at the Threshold', p. 138.
45. Forbes Morlock, 'Home Economics/Household Words: Disciplining Rhetoric and Political Economy', *Angelaki*, 2.1 (1997), p. 165 n. 35.
46. Jacques Derrida, *The Politics of Friendship*, trans. George Collins (London: Verso, 1994), p. 201.
47. Derrida, *Of Hospitality: Anne Defourmantelle Invites Jacques Derrida to Respond*, trans. Rachel Bowlby (Stanford University Press, 2000), p. 29.
48. Mitchell, 'Slippage at the Threshold', p. 140.
49. Ibid., p. 142.
50. McGuckian, *Selected Poems*, p. 73.
51. McGuckian, *Shemalier* (Oldcastle: Gallery Press, 1998), pp. 24–5.
52. Ibid., p. 90.
53. Ibid., p. 53.
54. Eluned Summers-Bremner, 'History's Impasse: Journey, Haunt and Trace in the Poetry of Medbh McGuckian', in Irene Gilsenan Nordin (ed.), *The Body and Desire in Contemporary Irish Poetry* (Dublin: Irish Academic Press, 2006), p. 46.
55. McGuckian, *The Currach Requires No Harbours* (Oldcastle: Gallery Press, 2006), p. 53.
56. Janet Carsten and Stephen Hugh-Jones (eds.), *About the House – Lévi-Strauss and Beyond* (Cambridge University Press, 1995), p. 2.
57. Bachelard, *Poetics of Space*, p. 45.
58. Ibid., p. xxxvii.

CHAPTER SIX

1. Medbh McGuckian, *Had I a Thousand Lives* (Oldcastle: Gallery Press, 2003).
2. W.B. Yeats, 'Easter 1916', *The Poems* (London: J.M. Dent, 1994), pp. 229–30.
3. Ibid., p. 230.
4. McGuckian, 'A Religion of Writing', *Had I a Thousand Lives*, pp. 22–3.
5. McGuckian, 'The Finisher', *Had I a Thousand Lives*, p. 53.
6. McGuckian, *Shelmalier* (Oldcastle: Gallery Press, 1998).
7. McGuckian, 'The Walking of the Land', *Had I a Thousand Lives*, p. 61.
8. McGuckian, 'Low Low Sunday', *Had I a Thousand Lives*, p. 51.
9. McGuckian, 'Forcing the Music to Speak', *Had I a Thousand Lives*, pp. 103–4.
10. Ibid., p. 104.
11. Ibid.
12. I take this version of Emmet's speech from the fifty-first edition of T.D., A.M. and D.B. Sullivan's *Speeches from the Dock, or Protests of Irish Patriotism* (Dublin: Gill and Macmillan, 1905), p. 54.
13. McGuckian, 'Ring Worn Outside a Glove', *Had I a Thousand Lives*, p. 63.
14. Ibid.
15. Ibid., p. 91.
16. S.T. Coleridge cited in Marianne Elliot, *Robert Emmet: The Making of a Legend* (London: Profile, 2004), p. 123.

17. Yeats, 'Emmet as the Apostle of Liberty', *Uncollected Prose of W.B. Yeats*, vol. 2, ed. John P. Frayne and Colton Johnson (New York: Columbia University Press, 1976), pp. 310–17.
18. McGuckian, 'The Flower of Tullahogue', *Had I a Thousand Lives*, p. 45.
19. Terry Eagleton, *Heathcliff and the Great Hunger: Studies in Irish Culture* (London: Verso, 1995), p. 15.
20. Fredric Jameson, *The Political Unconscious: Narrative as a Socially Symbolic Act* (London: Routledge, 1981).
21. See Luke Gibbons, 'Identity Without a Centre: Allegory, History and Irish Nationalism', *Transformations in Irish Culture* (Cork University Press, 1996), pp. 134–48.
22. McGuckian, 'Slieve Gallion', *Had I a Thousand Lives*, p. 15.
23. Ibid.
24. Ibid.
25. McGuckian, 'The Mirror Game' and 'Asking for the Alphabet Back', *Had I a Thousand Lives*, pp. 35 and 31 respectively.
26. McGuckian, 'Cathal's Voice', *Had I a Thousand Lives*, p. 34.
27. McGuckian, 'Reading in a Library', *Had I a Thousand Lives*, p. 33.
28. Ibid.
29. Ibid.
30. See Patrick M. Geoghegan, *Robert Emmet: A Life* (Dublin: Gill and Macmillan, 2004), pp. 268–9.

CHAPTER SEVEN

1. Andreas Huyssen, *Twilight Memories: Marking Time in a Culture of Amnesia* (New York: Routledge, 1995), p. 249.
2. Barbara Misztal, *Theories of Social Remembering* (Maidenhead: Open University Press, 2003), p. 13.
3. Colin Graham, '"Every Passer-by a Culprit": Archive Fever, Photography and the Peace in Belfast', *Third Text*, 19.5 (September 2005), p. 568.
4. Michael Longley, '"Walking Forwards into the Past": An Interview with Michael Longley', Interview by Fran Brearton, *Irish Studies Review*, 18 (Spring 1997), pp. 35–6.
5. Jack Pakenham, *A Broken Sky* (Derry: Orchard Gallery, 1995), n.p.
6. Willie Doherty, *Ghost Story*, in *Willie Doherty*, ed. Yilmaz Dziewior and Matthias Mühling (Osfildern: Hatje Cantz Verlag, 2007), p. 160.
7. Ibid., p. 162.
8. See David Park, *The Truth Commissioner* (London: Bloomsbury, 2008).
9. Bill Rolston, 'Visions or Nightmares? Murals and Imagining the Future in Northern Ireland', in Brian Cliff and Éibhear Walshe (eds.), *Representing the Troubles: Texts and Images, 1970–2000* (Dublin: Four Courts Press, 2004), p. 118.
10. Aaron Kelly, 'Walled Communities', *All Over Again* (Belfast: Belfast Exposed, 2004), n.p.
11. Longley, 'Blackthorn and Bonsai: Or, a Little Brief Authority', *Tuppeny Stung: Autobiographical Chapters* (Belfast: Lagan Press, 1994), pp. 75–6.
12. Medbh McGuckian, email correspondence, 11 September 2008.
13. McGuckian, 'Corduroy Road', *Had I a Thousand Lives* (Oldcastle: Gallery Press, 2003), pp. 80–1.

14. David W. Blight, *When This Cruel War Is Over: The Civil War Letters of Charles Harvey Brewster* (University of Massachusetts Press, 1992), p. 4. Hereafter cited as 'DB'. Blight's text is on the left, McGuckian's poem is on the right.

15. Ibid., p. 68.

16. McGuckian's text is on the right; quotations from Blight are on the left.

17. Martin Gilbert, *The Boys: Triumph over Adversity* (London: Phoenix, 1997), referred to as 'MG'; Samuel Clark and James S. Donnelly, Jr. (eds.), *Irish Peasants: Violence and Political Unrest, 1780–1914* (Manchester University Press, 1983), referred to as 'IP'. An analysis of the manuscript and word sheets for this poem held in the Special Collections at Emory University confirms the presence of these intertexts.

18. Hélène Cixous's *Three Steps on the Ladder of Writing* (New York: Columbia University Press, 1994). Hereafter cited as 'HC'.

19. Kevin Whelan, 'Between Filiation and Affiliation: The Politics of Postcolonial Memory', in Clare Carroll and Patricia King (eds.), *Ireland and Postcolonial Theory* (Cork University Press, 2003), p. 93.

20. Paul Ricoeur, 'Memory and Forgetting', in Richard Kearney and Mark Dooley (eds.), *Questioning Ethics: Contemporary Debates in Philosophy* (London: Routledge, 1999), p. 10.

21. Dominick LaCapra, *History and Memory after Auschwitz* (Ithaca: Cornell University Press, 1998), p. 9.

22. Ronit Lentin, *Israel and the Daughters of the Shoah: Reoccupying the Territories of Silence* (New York: Berghahn Books, 2000), p. 2.

23. Primo Levi, *The Drowned and the Saved* (New York: Vintage, 1989), p. 31.

24. McGuckian, 'She Thinks She Sees Clarissa', *The Currach Requires No Harbours* (Oldcastle: Gallery Press, 2006), pp. 53–4.

25. Michel de Certeau, *The Practice of Everyday Life* (Berkeley: University of California Press, 1984), p. 36.

26. Cathy Caruth, *Unclaimed Experience: Trauma, Narrative, and History* (Baltimore: The Johns Hopkins University Press, 1996), p. 2.

27. McGuckian, email correspondence, 11 September 2008.

28. Glenn Phillips and Thomas Crow, *Seeing Rothko* (London: Tate Publishing, 2005). The quotations from this text are cited above as 'R'.

29. Seamus Deane, 'Reading Deane', interview with Carol Rumens, *Fortnight* (July-August 1997), p. 30.

30. See Marianne Hirsch and Susan Rubin Suleiman, 'Material Memory: Holocaust Testimony in Post-Holocaust Art', in Shelley Hornstein and Florence Jacobowitz (eds.), *Image and Remembrance: Representation and the Holocaust* (Bloomington: Indiana University Press, 2003), pp. 79–80.

31. McGuckian, interview by Rebecca E. Wilson, in Gillian Somerville-Arjat and Rebecca E. Wilson (eds.), *Sleeping with Monsters: Conversations with Scottish and Irish Women Poets* (Edinburgh: Polygon, 1990), p. 5.

32. Robin Silbergleid, '"Treblinka, a Rather Musical Word": Carole Maso's Post-Holocaust Narrative', *MFS: Modern Fiction Studies*, 53.1 (Spring 2007), p. 2.

33. Berel Lang, *Act and Idea in the Nazi Genocide* (University of Chicago Press, 1990), p. xi.

34. Sidra DeKoven Ezrahi, *By Words Alone: The Holocaust in Literature* (University of Chicago Press, 1980), p. 1.

35. Claude Levi-Strauss cited in Ruth Linn, *Escaping Auschwitz: A Culture of Forgetting*

(Ithaca: Cornell University Press, 2004), p. 83.

36. Adorno, *Notes to Literature*, cited in Irving Howe, 'Writing and the Holocaust,' *Selected Writings, 1950–1990* (New York: Harcourt, Brace, Jovanovich, 1991), p. 429.

37. Ezrahi, *By Words Alone*, p. 4.

38. McGuckian, 'The Stone-word', *Eureka Street*, 7, 24 April 2006, http://www.eurekastreet.com.au/article.aspx?aeid=344.

39. Ash Amin and Nigel Thrift (eds.), *Cities: Reimagining the Urban* (Cambridge: Polity Press, 2002), referred to as 'C'; Gary D. Mole, *Beyond the Limit-Experience: French Poetry of the Deportation, 1940–1945* (New York: Peter Lang, 2002), referred to as 'M'.

40. McGuckian, 'Notice', *Poetry* 189.4 (January 2007), p. 276.

41. Ken Worpole and Lorraine Worpole, *Last Landscapes* (London: Reaktion Books, 2003), p. 180. The list which McGuckian cites in full is translated from a text by the architect R. Auzelle.

42. James Bacque, *Crimes and Mercies: The Fate of German Civilians under Allied Occupation, 1944–1950* (London: Time Warner, 2002). Stanza two is taken from p. 99 and stanza four is cited from p. 43.

Chapter Eight

1. Gilles Deleuze, 'Control and Becoming', *Negotiations: 1972–90* (New York: Columbia University Press, 1995), p. 173.

2. Medbh McGuckian, 'In the Country of Comparative Peace', radio interview with Margaret Coffey, broadcast 12 December 2004, ABC (Australia), http://www.abc.net.au/rn/relig/enc/stories/s1259334.htm.

3. Peggy O'Brien, 'Reading Medbh McGuckian: Admiring What We Cannot Understand', *Colby Quarterly*, 28.4 (December 1992), p. 241.

4. Gilles Deleuze and Félix Guattari, *A Thousand Plateaus: Capitalism and Schizophrenia* (London: Continuum, 2004), p. 276.

5. Ibid., p. 117.

6. Ibid.

7. Ibid., p. 118.

8. Ibid., p. 117.

9. Deleuze, 'Control and Becoming', p. 174.

10. Ibid., p. 175.

11. McGuckian, 'Emotion Recollected in Tranquility. . .', in Susan Sellers (ed.), *Delighting the Heart: A Notebook by Women Writers* (London: The Women's Press, 1989), p. 59.

12. Peter Sirr, '"How Things Begin to Happen": Notes on Eiléan Ní Chuilleanáin and Medbh McGuckian', *The Southern Review*, 31.3 (Summer 1995), p. 464.

13. McGuckian, *Selected Poems* (Oldcastle: Gallery Press, 1997), p. 34.

14. McGuckian, 'Charcoal Angel', *The Book of the Angel* (Oldcastle: Gallery Press, 2004), p. 82.

15. Deleuze, 'Control and Becoming', p. 176.

16. McGuckian, 'Smoke', *Single Ladies: Sixteen Poems* (Budleigh Salterton, Devon: Interim Press, 1980), p. 8.

17. McGuckian, *Selected Poems*, p. 13.

18. McGuckian, 'The Seed-Picture', *The Flower Master* (Oxford University Press, 1982), p. 23.

19. See, for instance, Catriona Clutterbuck's PhD thesis 'Self-Representation and the Politics of Authority in Contemporary Irish Poetry: Eavan Boland and Medbh McGuckian' (Oxford University, 1996).

20. McGuckian, *Captain Lavender* (Oldcastle: Gallery Press, 1994).

21. Shane Murphy, 'Sympathetic Ink: Intertextual Relations in the Poetry of Paul Muldoon and Medbh McGuckian', DPhil thesis (Cambridge University, 1998), p. 123.

22. This wariness persisted despite the example set by Clair Wills's productive reading of McGuckian's 1984 poem 'Dovecote' in the context of the Hunger Strikes of 1981. See *Improprieties: Politics and Sexuality in Northern Irish Poetry* (Oxford University Press, 1993), pp. 167–9.

23. Leontia Flynn, 'Reading Medbh McGuckian', PhD thesis (Queen's University of Belfast, 2004).

24. Wills, *Improprieties*, p. 193.

25. Ibid., p. 63.

26. Shane Murphy, '"You Took Away My Biography": The Poetry of Medbh McGuckian', *Irish University Review*, 28.1 (Spring–Summer 1998), p. 122.

27. Wills, *Improprieties*, p. 173.

28. Murphy, 'Sympathetic Ink', p. 230.

29. Murphy writes: 'despite the absence of footnotes and clear acknowledgement of her source material, one should not describe her work as in any way "plagiaristic". Like Mandelstam, she is a "builder", one who transforms the given material with all the imaginative skill, poise and genius of a poet' ('"You Took Away My Biography"', p. 132). It is ironic that the next essay in the journal, also on McGuckian, begins: 'After five collections of poetry Medbh McGuckian continues to write with steadfast originality and independence of mind' (Sarah Broom, 'McGuckian's Conversations with Rilke in *Marconi's Cottage*', *Irish University Review*, 28.1 (Spring–Summer 1998), p. 133).

30. Murphy, '"You Took Away My Biography"', p. 124.

31. Ibid., p. 110.

32. Murphy, 'Sonnets, Centos and Long Lines: Muldoon, Paulin, McGuckian and Carson', in Matthew Campbell (ed.), *The Cambridge Companion to Contemporary Irish Poetry* (Cambridge University Press, 2003), p. 201.

33. Tim Pat Coogan, *Michael Collins: A Biography* (London: Arrow, 1991).

34. McGuckian, *Delighting the Heart: A Notebook by Women Writers*, p. 59.

35. McGuckian, interview with Heidi Lynn Staples, *The Argotist Online*, http://www.argotistonline.co.uk/McGuckian%20interview.htm (accessed 31 October 2006).

36. Edward J. Mallot's thoughtful comments on this issue in a recent essay are valuable: 'Murphy seems fine with this creative borrowing, and perhaps rightfully so: McGuckian uses other sources for intensely, insistently personal reasons, and the results are so radically different from their sources that one can hardly consider her products literary travesties. Still, Murphy's discoveries certainly do little to protect a highly contested poet from further controversy surrounding both the nature and the worth of her work.' ('Medbh McGuckian's Poetic Tectonics', *Éire-Ireland*, 40.3–4 (Fall–Winter 2005), p. 255).

37. Flynn, 'Reading Medbh McGuckian', p. 15.

38. McGuckian, 'Rescuers and White Cloaks: Diary, 1968–9', in Patricia Boyle Haberstroh

(ed.), *My Self, My Muse: Irish Women Poets Reflect on Life and Art* (New York: Syracuse University Press, 2001), pp. 137–54.

39. McGuckian, 'Women are Trousers', in Kathryn Kirkpatrick (ed.), *Border Crossings: Irish Women Writers and National Identities* (University of Alabama Press, 2000), pp. 157–89. The peculiarity of this title is worth reflecting upon. McGuckian's own reference to it in the diary ('I laughed at the wind's struggles – men are the wind, women are trousers, they are measured against us', p. 160) suggests a number of alternative readings, although none is particularly satisfactory. More engaging is Flynn's perception of it, which notes in the 'absurdity of this metaphor, a refusal of any such definitions – including, perhaps, those suggested by the anthology in which the diary appears. That is, that in light of the many claims about what women poets *are* (that they "wear the trousers", that they are "border crossing"), "trousers" might be as representative as an epithet as any' ('Reading Medbh McGuckian', p. 43).

40. Kirkpatrick, *Border Crossings*, p. 10.

41. McGuckian, 'Rescuers and White Cloaks', p. 151.

42. Kirkpatrick, *Border Crossings*, p. 10.

43. John Brown, *In the Chair: Interviews with Poets from the North of Ireland* (Knockeven: Salmon Poetry, 2002), p. 172.

44. Flynn, 'Reading Medbh McGuckian', p. 106.

45. Examples of this are numerous. See, for instance, McGuckian's comments on the English language: 'Because it's an imposed language, you see, and although it's my mother tongue and my only way of communicating, I'm fighting with it all the time. I mean even the words "Shakespeare" and "Wordsworth" – at some level, I'm rejecting them, at some level I'm saying get out of my country, or [. . .] get out of me.' See '*Comhrá*: A Conversation between Medbh McGuckian and Nuala Ní Dhomhnaill', interview by Laura O'Connor, *The Southern Review*, 31.3 (Summer 1995), pp. 605–6.

46. McGuckian, *Horsepower Pass By!: A Study of the Car in the Poetry of Seamus Heaney* (Coleraine: Cranagh Press, 1999), pp. 6–7.

47. McGuckian, 'Curtains', *Portrait of Joanna* (Belfast: Ulsterman Publications, 1980), p. 15.

48. Ashley Tellis, 'The Poetics and Politics of Contemporary Irish Women's Poetry: A Study of the Poetry of Eavan Boland, Medbh McGuckian and Eiléan Ní Chuilleanáin', DPhil thesis (Cambridge University, 1998), p. 67.

49. Tom Paulin, *The Strange Museum* (London: Faber & Faber, 1980).

50. Seamus Heaney, *Death of a Naturalist* (London: Faber & Faber, 1966).

51. McGuckian, 'Rescuers and White Cloaks, p. 139.

52. Ibid., p. 142.

53. Danielle Sered, interview with Medbh McGuckian, Emory University, Atlanta (April 1998), cited at http://www.english.emory.edu/Bahri/McGuckian.html (accessed 31 October 2006).

54. Seamus Deane, 'Irish Poetry and Irish Nationalism: A Survey', in Douglas Dunn (ed.), *Two Decades of Irish Writing: A Critical Survey* (Manchester: Carcanet, 1975), p. 18.

55. Seamus Heaney, *Preoccupations: Selected Prose 1968–78* (London: Faber & Faber, 1980), p. 30.

56. McGuckian in Brown, *In the Chair*, p. 171.

57. McGuckian, 'Drawing Ballerinas: How Being Irish Has Influenced Me as a Writer', in Lizz Murphy (ed.), *Wee Girls: Irish Women's Writing* (Melbourne: Spinifex Press, 1996), p. 194.
58. McGuckian and Dhomhnaill, '*Comhrá*', pp. 591–2.
59. Edna Longley, review of *Single Ladies*, *New Statesman* 24 April 1981, p. 20.
60. Flynn, 'Reading Medbh McGuckian', p. 106.
61. McGuckian, 'Rescuers and White Cloaks', p. 146.
62. McGuckian, 'Women are Trousers', p. 159.
63. Ibid., p. 171.
64. McGuckian, 'Rescuers and White Cloaks', p. 149.
65. Ibid., p. 138.
66. Bernadette Devlin, *The Price of My Soul* (London: Pan Books, 1969). I discuss this work at greater length in *Identity Parades: Northern Irish Culture and Dissident Subjects* (Liverpool University Press, 2002).
67. Devlin, *The Price of My Soul*, p. 9.
68. McGuckian, 'Women are Trousers', p. 165. Devlin had been sentenced to six months' imprisonment after admitting to organising the throwing of petrol bombs during the 'Battle of the Bogside' in Derry in August 1969.
69. McGuckian, 'Rescuers and White Cloaks', p. 137.
70. Ibid., p. 143.
71. 'White on white, I can never be viewed / Against a heavy sky', Medbh McGuckian, 'Venus and the Rain', *Venus and the Rain* (Oxford University Press, 1984), p. 31.
72. *Irish News*, 22 July 2005, p. 9.
73. McGuckian, 'Women are Trousers', p. 168.
74. Ibid., p. 169.
75. Ibid., p. 189.
76. Helen Blakeman, 'Metaphor and Metonymy in Medbh McGuckian's Poetry', *Critical Survey*, 14.2 (2002), pp. 69–70.

CHAPTER NINE

1. Elin Holmsten, 'Double Doors: An Interview with Medbh McGuckian', *Nordic Irish Studies*, 3.1 (2004), p. 96.
2. Medbh McGuckian, 'The Seed Picture', *The Flower Master* (Oldcastle: Gallery Press, 1993), pp. 28–9. The collection was first published by Oxford University Press in 1982.
3. McGuckian, 'The Seed Picture', p. 28.
4. Ibid.
5. Ibid.
6. Ibid.
7. McGuckian, 'Ode to a Poetess', *Venus and the Rain* (Oldcastle: Gallery Press, 1994), p. 13.
8. Ibid.
9. Robert Brazeau, 'Troubling Language: Avant-Garde Strategies in the Poetry of Medbh McGuckian', *Mosaic*, 37.2 (June 2004), p. 135.
10. See Susan Stanford Friedman's notion of the 'childbirth metaphor'. Friedman argues that, when used by women writers, this metaphor originates in conflict with themselves as other. Quoted ibid.

11. Ibid.
12. Ibid.
13. Ibid.
14. Ibid.
15. Medbh McGuckian, 'Open Rose', *Marconi's Cottage* (Oldcastle: Gallery Press, 1991), p. 80.
16. Ibid.
17. Ibid.
18. Toril Moi, *What is a Woman?* (Oxford University Press, 1999), p. 290.
19. See Bourdieu's argument, that the process of symbolic consecration is essential to the reproduction of 'mythico-ritual' systems. Quoted ibid., n. 30.
20. See a discussion of Bourdieuian 'capital', ibid., pp. 288-95.
21. McGuckian, 'Open Rose', p. 80.
22. McGuckian, 'Venus and the Rain', *Venus and the Rain*, p. 40.
23. McGuckian, 'The Potter', *Shelmalier* (Oldcastle: Gallery Press, 1998), p. 32.
24. Ibid.
25. Ibid.
26. Ibid.
27. Ibid.
28. Ibid.
29. In an Irish context the most famous poet to refute the stereotype of the lyrical muse is probably Eavan Boland, particularly in her poems 'Tirade for the Mimic Muse' and 'Tirade for the Lyric Muse'. Eavan Boland, *Collected Poems* (Manchester: Carcanet Press, 1995), pp. 55, 130.
30. McGuckian, 'Dear Rain', *Marconi's Cottage*, p. 22.
31. McGuckian, 'The Brownstone Bride', *Shelmalier*, p. 93.
32. McGuckian, 'The Tamarind Tree', *Shelmalier*, p. 107.
33. McGuckian, 'The Flora of Mercury', *Drawing Ballerinas* (Oldcastle: Gallery Press, 2001), p. 57.
34. McGuckian, 'The Marital We', *Drawing Ballerinas*, p. 65.
35. Medbh McGuckian, 'The Face of the Earth', *The Face of the Earth* (Oldcastle: Gallery Press, 2002), p. 12.
36. McGuckian, 'Reading the Earthquake', *The Face of the Earth*, p. 26.
37. McGuckian, 'A River Pebble', *The Face of the Earth*, p. 61.
38. McGuckian, 'The Change Worshipper', *The Face of the Earth*, pp. 50–1.
39. McGuckian, 'Interview with Medbh McGuckian', in John Brown (ed.), *In the Chair: Interviews with Poets from the North of Ireland* (Knockeven: Salmon Poetry, 2002), p. 174.
40. For a detailed discussion of this topic see David Fuller, 'Poetry, Music, and the Sacred', in David Fuller and Patricia Waugh (eds.), *The Arts and Sciences of Criticism* (Oxford University Press, 1999), pp. 180–99.
41. McGuckian, *The Book of the Angel* (Oldcastle: Gallery Press, 2004).
42. McGuckian said: 'The next book the only thread I've got through it is the word "angel". It's going to be for Gregory [Peck] and it's going to be called *The Book of the Angel*. [. . .] But this is just corroborating, because I have this thing about angels.' Leontia Mary Flynn, 'Interview with Medbh McGuckian', in 'Reading Medbh McGuckian', PhD thesis (Queen's University, Belfast, 2004), p. 253.
43. McGuckian, 'The Chrisom Child', *The Book of the Angel*, p. 30.

44. Ibid.
45. Ibid.
46. James Joyce also makes this connection when Stephen ponders on inspiration in *A Portrait of the Artist as a Young Man*. He says: 'In the virgin womb of the imagination the word was made flesh. Gabriel the seraph had come to the virgin's chamber.' James Joyce, *The Portrait of the Artist as a Young Man*, ed. Richard Ellmann (London: Jonathan Cape, 1956), p. 221.
47. McGuckian, 'Saint Faith', *The Book of the Angel*, p. 38.
48. Ibid.
49. Ibid.
50. McGuckian, 'Poem Rhyming in "J"', *The Book of the Angel*, p. 85.
51. Medbh McGuckian, 'Kaddish', *The Currach Requires No Harbours* (Oldcastle: Gallery Press, 2006), p. 26.
52. Ibid.
53. Simon Critchley, *Very Little . . . Almost Nothing: Death, Philosophy, Literature* (London: Routledge, 1997), p. 26.
54. McGuckian, 'Kaddish', p. 26.
55. Ibid.
56. Ibid.
57. Maurice Blanchot, *The Space of Literature*, trans. Ann Smock (Lincoln, London: University of Nebraska Press, 1982), p. 193.
58. 'Inventiveness' is a term used by Derek Attridge to denote a creation, 'the effect of which goes beyond the created entity' and which 'may bring about permanent alterations in cultural norms'. It is intended as a reinterpretation of earlier terms such as 'originality', or 'inspired', arguing that 'inventiveness' implies the process of making simultaneously with the achieved result. See Derek Attridge, *The Singularity of Literature* (London: Routledge, 2004), pp. 41–54.
59. Ibid., p. 79.
60. Ibid., p. 80.
61. Ibid.
62. Ibid., p. 81.
63. Ibid., p. 83.
64. McGuckian, 'The Over Mother', *Captain Lavender* (Oldcastle: Gallery Press, 1994), p. 64.
65. Ibid., p. 64.
66. Ibid.
67. McGuckian, 'Breaking the Blue', *Marconi's Cottage*, p. 84.
68. Ibid.
69. Ibid.
70. Ibid.
71. Since it is desire which keeps them together, this forms another unlikely link to the attributes of the pre-Platonic muses. The poem says that for the 'inaccessible, mineral world' of the authorial subject the reader 'seems a town garden', again creating a simultaneous link and a severance.
72. It is possible to read in the act of writing (a writer can read what s/he writes), but a writer cannot read and write the 'other' simultaneously, unless, like McGuckian, s/he *writes* the reading subject. That is why reading McGuckian is also, necessarily, a writing of McGuckian.

73. McGuckian, 'Breaking the Blue', p. 84.

CHAPTER TEN

1. Medbh McGuckian, *On Ballycastle Beach* (Oldcastle: Gallery Press, 1995), p. 61.
2. Patrick Williams, 'Spare that Tree: Review of *On Ballycastle Beach*', *The Honest Ulsterman*, 86 (Spring-Summer 1989), pp. 50, 52.
3. Michael Allen, 'The Poetry of Medbh McGuckian', in Elmer Andrews (ed.), *Contemporary Irish Poetry: A Collection of Critical Essays* (Basingstoke: Macmillan, 1992), p. 287.
4. Shane Murphy, '"Roaming Root of Multiple Meanings": Intertextual Relations in Medbh McGuckian's Poetry', *Metre*, 5 (1998), p. 105. Murphy's findings also appeared in the essays '"You Took Away My Biography": The Poetry of Medbh McGuckian', *Irish University Review*, 28.1 (Spring-Summer 1998), pp. 110–132; 'Obliquity in the Poetry of Paul Muldoon and Medbh McGuckian', *Éire-Ireland*, 3.4 (1996), pp. 76–99; '"A Dove Involving a Whole Nation": Politics in the Poetry of Medbh McGuckian', *Études Irlandaises*, 24.1 (1999), pp. 91–108; 'Writing in the Shit: The Northern Irish Poet and Authority', *Canadian Journal of Irish Studies*, 24.1 (1998), pp. 1–22, '"The Eye that Scanned it": The Picture Poems of Heaney, Muldoon, and McGuckian', *New Hibernia Review*, 4.4 (2000), pp. 85–114; '"A Code of Images": Northern Irish Centos', *Irish Studies Review*, 10.2 (2002), pp. 193–204. Alcobia-Murphy's findings then appeared in book form in *Sympathetic Ink* (Liverpool University Press, 2006) and *Governing the Tongue* (Newcastle-upon-Tyne: Cambridge Scholars Press, 2005).
5. McGuckian, 'Little House, Big House', *On Ballycastle Beach*, p. 32.
6. Meva Maron, 'The Stamps Had Squirrels on Them', *The Honest Ulsterman*, 88 (1989–90), pp. 33, 34.
7. Olga Ivinskaya, *A Captive of Time: My Years with Pasternak*, trans. Max Hayward (London: Collins and Harvill Press, 1978), p. 191. First noted by Murphy in '"Roaming Root of Multiple Meanings"', pp. 100–1.
8. Murphy calls it 'a meditation upon Tsvetaeva's suicide' ('"Roaming Root"', p. 101). To a certain extent I have caricatured Alcobia-Murphy's position to make a point about McGuckian's indeterminacy. Frequently he comments shrewdly on McGuckian's sources, as when he notes that she allows 'her voices to become a medium for precursor poets and prior texts' ('"You Took Away My Biography"', p. 110), as well as her preoccupation with literary paternity. In general, though, in *Sympathetic Ink*, his intertexts are presented as previously missing interpretative keys and readers who are unaware of them as guilty of misreadings.
9. Murphy '"You Took away My Biography"', p. 121.
10. Osip Mandelstam, 'Conversation about Dante', *The Complete Critical Prose and Letters*, ed. Jane Gary Harris, trans Jane Gary Harris and Constance Link (Ann Arbor, Michigan: Ardis, 1979), p. 397.
11. Marina Tsvetaeva, *Marina Tsvetaeva: Selected Prose*, ed. J. Martin King (Ann Arbor, Michigan: Ardis, 1980); Elaine Feinstein, *A Captive Lion: The Life of Marina Tsvetaeva* (London: Hutchinson, 1987); Simon Karlinsky, *Marina Tsvetaeva: The Woman, Her World and Her Poetry* (Cambridge University Press, 1985), and Marina Tsvetaeva, *Art in the Light of Conscience: Eight Essays on Poetry*, trans. Angela Livingstone (London: Bristol Classical Press, 1982). See Murphy '"You Took Away My Biography"', pp. 114–19.

12. Karlinsky, *Marina Tsvetaeva*, pp. 97, 98. First noted by Murphy in '"You Took Away My Biography"', p. 115.
13. Thomas Docherty, 'Initiations, Tempers, Seductions: Postmodern McGuckian', in Neil Corcoran (ed.), *The Chosen Ground: Essays on the Contemporary Poetry of Northern Ireland* (Bridgend: Seren Books, 1992), p. 191.
14. Murphy, '"You Took Away My Biography"', p. 114.
15. McGuckian, 'Harem Trousers', *On Ballycastle Beach*, p. 40.
16. McGuckian, 'The Dream Language of Fergus', *On Ballycastle Beach*, p. 57.
17. McGuckian, 'The Time Before You', 'A Dream in Three Colours', *On Ballycastle Beach*, pp. 43, 42.
18. McGuckian, 'The Dream Language of Fergus', *On Ballycastle Beach*, p. 57.
19. Mandelstam, 'Conversation about Dante'.
20. Clair Wills, *Improprieties: Politics and Sexuality in Northern Irish Poetry* (Oxford University Press, 1993), pp. 174–5.
21. Mandelstam, 'Conversation about Dante', p. 402.
22. Clarence Brown, *Mandelstam* (Cambridge University Press, 1973), p. 67.
23. Seamus Heaney, 'The Government of the Tongue', *The Government of the Tongue: The 1986 T.S. Eliot Memorial Lectures and Other Critical Writings* (London: Faber and Faber, 1988), pp. 91, 92.
24. Ibid., p. 71.
25. 'The police agents failed to find the poems I had sewn into cushions or stuck inside saucepans and shoes.' Nadezhda Mandelstam, *Hope Against Hope: A Memoir*, trans. Max Hayward (London: Collins and Harvill Press, 1971), p. 271. Alcobia-Murphy notes this in *Sympathetic Ink*, pp. 127–8. Alcobia-Murphy has found that the first line of the second stanza of 'Balakhana', 'Compare the most metallic of sounds, the sound of elevators at night', is also drawn from this memoir.
26. Seamus Heaney, 'The Indefatigable Hoof-taps: Sylvia Plath', *The Government of the Tongue*, p. 148. In concluding his analysis of Elizabeth Bishop's 'At the Fish-houses' in 'The Government of the Tongue' itself, Heaney also writes that the 'lines are inhabited by certain profoundly true tones, which, as Robert Frost put it, were before words were living in the *cave of the mouth*' (p. 106). This may be the same 'cave' as the mouth of the infant in McGuckian's 'The Dream-Language of Fergus'.
27. McGuckian, 'Frost in Beaconsfield', *On Ballycastle Beach*, p. 35.
28. See Shane Murphy, 'Sonnets, Centos and Long Lines: Muldoon, Paulin, McGuckian and Carson', in Matthew Campbell (ed.), *The Cambridge Companion to Irish Contemporary Poetry* (Cambridge University Press, 2003) p. 199.
29. Alan Jenkins, 'Private and Public Languages', *Encounter*, 59.5 (November 1982), pp. 56–63. For Jenkins, McGuckian possessed 'erotic fluency', which 'if it is anything at all, is a quality of rhythm and, especially, of syntax; it may partake of "the abstract vitality of speech", "the sound of sense" (as Frost defined it)', p. 59.
30. McGuckian, 'My Brown Guest', *On Ballycastle Beach*, p. 12.
31. McGuckian, 'Death of a Ceiling', *On Ballycastle Beach*, p. 24.
32. The notion of things lurking behind doors recurs in the poems of *On Ballycastle Beach*: 'None of my doors has slammed / Like that' ('What does "Early" Mean?', p. 9); 'The door I found / So difficult to close let in my first / European feeling' ('Balakhana', p. 36).

33. See Murphy, 'Sonnets, Centos and Long Lines', p. 200.

34. Brown, *Mandelstam*, p. 175. Nadezhda Mandelstam also learned Mandelstam's poems by heart, and the labial quality of Dante's work is commented on in Mandelstam's 'Conversation about Dante'.

35. Karlinsky, cited in Murphy, '"You Took Away My Biography"', p. 115.

36. Mandelstam, 'Conversation about Dante', p. 401.

37. Ibid., pp. 297, p. 442.

38. Tsvetaeva, *Art in the Light of Conscience*, p. 136.

39. Roland Barthes, 'From Work to Text', *Image, Music, Text: Essays Selected and Translated by Stephen Heath* (London: Fontana Press, 1977), p. 160.

40. 'It is like the seduction of a letter unread, a letter which remains tantalisingly visible beneath or within its envelope; but the tearing open of the envelope reveals that the letter is not there after all: what we thought was a meaningful missive turns out to be a pattern on the envelope.' Docherty, 'Initiations', p. 201.

41. McGuckian, 'Mazurka', 'Balakhana' and 'Querencia' are the titles of poems. The 'French-born sea' is found in the title poem of *On Ballycastle Beach*, p. 61.

42. As Patricia Boyle Haberstroh points out, McGuckian's father came from Bally-castle Beach, and McGuckian had recently bought 'Marconi's cottage' at the end of Ballycastle beach. This was the house in which Guglielmo Marconi, the inventor of wireless telegraphy, sent the first wireless messages to and from Rathlin Island. Haberstroh, *Women Creating Women: Contemporary Irish Women Poets* (Syracuse University Press, 1995; Dublin: Attic Press, 1996), p. 149.

43. McGuckian, in Gillian Somerville-Arjat and Rebecca Wilson (eds.), *Sleeping with Monsters: Conversations with Scottish and Irish Women Poets* (Dublin: Wolfhound Press, 1990), p. 2, and Kimberly S. Bohman, interview with Medbh McGuckian, 'Primordial Voices: Culture and Consciousness in the Poetry of Medbh McGuckian', dissertation (Queen's University, Belfast, 1994), p. 51.

44. Tsvetaeva, *Art in the Light of Conscience*, p. 172, in Murphy '"You Took Away My Biography"', p. 117.

45. Tsvetaeva cited in Murphy, '"You Took Away My Biography"', p. 117.

46. Barthes, 'The Death of the Author', *Image, Music, Text*, p. 147.

47. Murphy, '"You Took Away My Biography"', p. 120.

48. Karlinsky, *Marina Tsvetaeva*, p. 180.

49. The Russian poet was also considered a '*mythomaniac*' and 'fantasist', wrote intensely, hugely prolifically, her poetic sensibility inclined not simply towards inspiration, but to mysticism, and her work, like McGuckian's, was considered 'unique and unprecedentedly original'. See ibid., p. 191.

50. Frankie Sewell, 'Interview with Medbh McGuckian', *Brangle*, 1 (1993), p. 54.

51. McGuckian in conversation with Murphy, *Sympathetic Ink*, p. 65.

52. Boris Pasternak, Marina Tsvetaeva and Rainer Maria Rilke, *Letters: Summer 1926*, ed. Yevgeny Pasternak, Yelena Pasternak and Konstantin M. Azadovsky, trans. Margaret Wettlin and Walter Arndt (London: Jonathan Cape, 1986). See Wills, *Improprieties*, p. 173. In the letters, Tsvetaeva continues to write to Rilke after his death, rather in the way that, in *The Book of the Angel*, McGuckian continues to write to Gregory Peck.

53. For the individual words and phrases borrowed in 'Visiting Rainer Maria' see

pp. 48, 82, 89, 94, 21, 22, 242, 86, 88, 95, 79 in Brown's *Mandelstam*.

54. Indeed, Tsvetaeva actually planned to publish the poetry she wrote between 1922 and 1925 under the title 'Secret Intentions'. Another work, 'Side Streets', is, as Karlinsky notes, completely baffling without reference to the Russian fairy tale which it 're-tells'. He notes further that her book *Craft*, which is addressed to Karolina Pavalova, deleted the epigraph to her, 'not wishing to facilitate anything for the reader out of respect for the reader'. She also wrote long poems ('From the Seacoast', 'Essay of a Room', 'New Year's Greetings') which 'readers, unaware of Tsvetaeva's relationships with Pasternak and Rilke reflected in these poems, found incomprehensible' (Marina Tsvetaeva, p. 188). Until now readers were similarly unaware of McGuckian's relationships with Tsvetaeva, Pasternak and Rilke.
55. Ibid., p. 181. See also Michael Makin, *Marina Tsvetaeva: Poetics of Appropriation* (Oxford: Clarendon Press, 1993).
56. Brown, *Mandelstam*, p. 173.
57. Ibid., p. 207.
58. Ibid., p. 213.
59. Mandelstam, *Complete Prose and Letters*, p. 436.
60. McGuckian, '*Comhrá*: A Conversation bdtween Medbh McGuckian and Nuala Ní Dhomhnaill', interview by Laura O'Connor, *The Southern Review*, 31.3 (Summer 1995), p. 608.
61. Pasternak et al., *Letters: Summer 1926*, p. 26.
62. Murphy, 'Obliquity', p. 95. Tatyana Tolstoy's *Tolstoy Remembered*, trans. Derek Coltman (London: Michael Joseph, 1977) is used in the poem 'Choorka' and 'Garbot at the Gaumont'. See 'Obliquity', pp. 91–7.
63. 'Word, dialogue and novel', *The Kristeva Reader*, ed. Toril Moi (Oxford: Basil Blackwell, 1986), p. 37.
64. Barthes, 'From Work to Text', *Image, Music, Text*, p. 160.
65. Mandelstam, 'Conversation about Dante', p. 398.
66. McGuckian, 'Visiting Rainer Maria Rilke', *Marconi's Cottage*, p. 10.
67. Brown, *Mandelstam*, pp. 77, 78. The 'quotations' of Mandelstam's translation of his wife were first noted by Sarah Broom, who uses a slightly different translation of Mandelstam's letter as the 'source' of McGuckian's poem (contained in the *Collected Prose*, p. 484), one in which Nadezhda's smock is dark blue. See Sarah Broom, 'McGuckian's Conversations with Rilke in *Marconi's Cottage*', *Irish University Review*, 28.1 (1998) pp. 133–50.
68. Brown, *Mandlestam*, p. 166.
69. Ibid., p. 165. If poetry, for Mandelstam, is *there in the silence*, ironically, it is the absence of this clear link between the word and the thing described which creates the very difficulties of accurate translation experienced by Brown himself. Mandelstam says the word 'is, after all, not a thing. Its signification is not in the slightest degree a translation of the word itself. As a matter of fact, it never happened that someone baptised the thing and gave it some name that had been dreamed up' (Brown, *Mandelstam*, p. 236).
70. Ibid., p. 236.
71. McGuckian uses Susan Chitty's *Gwen John 1876–1939* (New York: Franklin Watts, 1987) in 'Road 32, Roof 13-23, Grass 23', *Marconi's Cottage*, p. 42. See Alcobia-Murphy, *Sympathetic Ink*, pp. 201–3.

72. Murphy, 'Obliquity', p. 97.
73. See Murphy, 'Obliquity', pp. 86–91, and 'Picture Poems', pp. 106–8. As Murphy notes, the texts that McGuckian uses are Winifred Gérin, *Emily Bronte: A Biography* (Oxford: Clarendon Press, 1971) and Susan Chitty, *Gwen John 1876–1939* (New York: Franklin Watts, 1987). The issue of plagiarism is raised in relation to Emily Brontë by Winifred Gérin, as it is in Clarence Brown's book about Mandelstam. Gérin describes Brontë as 'a visionary' (p. 182), while Gwen John was, according to Susan Chitty, also a religious mystic and an enigma: 'something of a shadow Gwen John still remains' (p. 7).
74. McGuckian, 'To Call Paula Paul', *Marconi's Cottage*, p. 16. A footnote at the back tells us: 'The title is adapted from a statement of Rilke's about the artist Paula Modersohn-Becker.' 'During 1906 and 1907 Gwen John wrote three letters a day to Rodin, unable to resist the temptation to talk to him [. . .]. In two years he (Rodin) received close to two thousand letters from Gwen John' (Chitty, pp. 82, 83).
75. *I Love: The Story of Vladimir Mayakovsky and Lili Brik* (London: André Deutsch, 1979). See Alcobia-Murphy, *Sympathetic Ink*, p. 63.
76. McGuckian, 'Journal Intime', *Marconi's Cottage*, p. 26. The lines are borrowed from *The Madwoman in the Attic: The Woman Writer and the Nineteenth-Century Literary Imagination* (New Haven and London: Yale University Press, 1979), and in turn refer to other women writers: Mary Shelley's *Frankenstein*, where the characters' histories 'echo and re-echo each other' (p. 229), is 'like the solipsistic relationships among artfully placed mirrors' (p. 228) – 'Victor Frankenstein is slated to marry his "more than sister" just as 'Caroline Beaufort was clearly a "more than" wife [. . .] to her father's friend' (p. 228); in George Eliot's *Middlemarch* Casaubon is 'weak-eyed' (p. 215), and Dorothea here is compared to 'Milton's wailing six-fold Emanation, his three wives and three daughters gathered into a single grieving shape'. See Alcobia-Murphy, *Sympathetic Ink*, pp. 68–72.
77. McGuckian, 'A Deserted Landing Stage on the Rhine', *Had I a Thousand Lives*, p. 99. See Alcobia-Murphy, *Governing the Tongue*, pp. 56–8. David Irving, *The Destruction of Dresden* (London: William Kimber, 1963), Stephen Spender, *The Thirties and After: Poetry, Politics, People, 1933–75* (Glasgow: Fontana/Collins, 1978).
78. Tim Pat Coogan, *Michael Collins: A Biography* (London: Arrow, 1991). See Alcobia-Murphy, *Governing the Tongue*, pp. 49–51. Angela Bourke's *The Burning of Bridget Cleary* (New York: Penguin Putnam, 2000) is used in 'Manteo', *Drawing Ballerinas* (Oldcastle: Gallery Press, 2001), p. 67 (see Murphy, 'Sonnets, Centos and Long Lines', p. 201).
79. John Elderfield's *The Drawings of Henry Matisse* (London: Thames and Hudson, 1984) is used in the title poem of *Drawing Ballerinas*, p. 14. See Alcobia-Murphy, *Sympathetic Ink*, pp. 203–7. Elias Canetti, *The Torch in My Ear*, trans. Joachim Neugroschel (London: Granta, 1982) is used in 'The Dead are More Alive', *Drawing Ballerinas*, p. 14, and 'Reading in a Library', *Had I a Thousand Lives* (Oldcastle: Gallery Press, 2003). See Alcobia-Murphy, *Sympathetic Ink*, pp. 207–11 and 51–2.
80. See Murphy, *Governing the Tongue*, pp. 59–60.
81. Barthes, 'From Work to Text', *Image, Music, Text*, p. 157.

82. McGuckian, 'Mazurka', *On Ballycastle Beach*, p. 20.
83. McGuckian, 'The Time Before You', *On Ballycastle Beach*, p. 43.
84. Barthes, 'From Work to Text', *Image, Music, Text*, p. 158.
85. McGuckian, 'Balakhana', *On Ballycastle Beach*, p. 37.
86. McGuckian, 'The Most Emily of All', *On Ballycastle Beach*, p. 38.
87. Barthes, 'Death of the Author', *Image, Music, Text*, p. 146.
88. Barthes, 'From Work to Text', *Image, Music, Text*, pp. 162, 163.

Bibliography

I Primary Sources

Poetry Collections

Selected Poems by Medbh McGuckian (Oldcastle: Gallery Press, 1997).
Portrait of Joanna (Belfast: Ulsterman Publications, 1980).
Single Ladies (Budleigh Salterton, Devon: Interim Press, 1980).
The Flower Master (Oxford University Press, 1982).
Venus and The Rain (Oxford University Press, 1984).
On Ballycastle Beach (Oxford University Press, 1988).
Marconi's Cottage (Oldcastle: Gallery Press, 1991).
The Flower Master and Other Poems (Oldcastle: Gallery Press, 1993).
Captain Lavender (Oldcastle: Gallery Press, 1994).
Shelmalier (Oldcastle: Gallery Press, 1998).
Drawing Ballerinas (Oldcastle: Gallery Press, 2001).
The Face of the Earth (Oldcastle: Gallery Press, 2002).
The Soldiers of Year II (North Carolina: Wake Forest University Press, 2003).
Had I a Thousand Lives (Oldcastle: Gallery Press, 2003).
The Book of the Angel (Oldcastle: Gallery Press, 2004).
The Currach Requires No Harbours (Oldcastle: Gallery Press, 2006).
My Love Has Fared Inland (Oldcastle: Gallery Press, 2008).

Articles, Reviews, Diary Entries

'Mystical Island in a Dusky Bay', review of *Real Ireland: People and Landscape*, by Liam Blake, *Fortnight*, 211 (December 1984–January 1985), p. 23.
'Room of Calm, Room of Thunder ...', in Susan Sellers (ed.), *Delighting the Heart: A Notebook by Women Writers* (London: The Women's Press, 1989), pp. 25–26.
'Emotion Recollected in Tranquility', in Susan Sellers (ed.), *Delighting the Heart: A Notebook by Women Writers* (London: The Women's Press, 1989), pp. 59–60.
'If Poetry Come Not as Naturally as the Leaves to a Tree', in Susan Sellers (ed.), *Delighting the Heart: A Notebook by Women Writers* (London: The Women's Press, 1989), pp. 142–7.

'There is No Feminine in Eternity ...', in Susan Sellers (ed.), *Delighting the Heart: A Notebook by Women Writers* (London: The Women's Press, 1989), pp. 177–9.

'Visiting Poet', *Irish Review*, 11 (Winter 1991–2), pp. 47–9.

'Don't Talk to Me about Dance', review of *Philomena's Revenge*, by Rita Ann Higgins, *Poetry Ireland Review*, 35 (Summer 1992), pp. 98–100.

'The Timely Clapper', *Krino*, 14 (1993), pp. 45–6.

'How Precious Are Thy Thoughts Unto Me', review of *Art in the Light of Conscience: Eight Essays on Poetry*, by Marina Tsvetaeva, *Common Knowledge*, 2.1 (Spring 1993), pp. 132–41.

'Death Withstood', review of *The Redress of Poetry: Oxford Lectures*, by Seamus Heaney, *Fortnight*, 344 (November 1995), p. 36.

'Drawing Ballerinas: How Being Irish Has Influenced Me as a Writer', in Lizz Murphy (ed.), *Wee Girls: Women Writing from an Irish Perspective* (North Melbourne: Spinifex Press, 1996), pp. 185–203.

'Horsepower, Pass By!: A Study of the Car in the Poetry of Seamus Heaney', *Metre*, 3 (Autumn 1997), pp. 70–83.

'Women Are Trousers', in Kathryn Kirkpatrick (ed.), *Border Crossings: Irish Women Writers and National Identities* (University of Alabama Press, 2000), pp. 157–89.

'Rescuers and White Cloaks: Diary, 1968–1969', in Patricia Boyle Haberstroh (ed.), *My Self, My Muse: Irish Women Poets Reflect on Life and Art* (Syracuse University Press, 2001), pp. 137–54.

'Michael Longley as a Metaphysical', *Colby Quarterly*, 39.3 (2003), pp. 215–20.

Interviews

'Interview by Rebecca E. Wilson', in Gillean Somerville-Arjat and Rebecca E. Wilson (eds.), *Sleeping with Monsters: Conversations with Scottish and Irish Women Poets* (Dublin: Wolfhound Press, 1990), pp. 1–7.

'An Attitude of Compassions: Q & A with Medbh McGuckian', interview by Kathleen McCracken, *Irish Literary Supplement*, 9.2 (Fall 1990), pp. 20–1.

'An Interview with Medbh McGuckian', interview by Susan Shaw Sailer, *Michigan Quarterly Review*, 32.1 (1993), pp. 111–27.

'Surfacing: An Interview with Medbh McGuckian', interview by Kimberly S. Bohman, *Irish Review*, 16 (Autumn-Winter 1994), pp. 95–108.

'A Hinge into Something Larger: Meetings with Medbh McGuckian', interview by Helen Kidd, *Oxford Poetry*, 8.2 (Winter 1994–5), pp. 53–7.

'*Comhrá*: A Conversation between Medbh McGuckian and Nuala Ní Dhomhnaill', interview by Laura O'Connor, *Southern Review*, 31.3 (Summer 1995), pp. 581–614.

Interview by Rand Brandes, *Chattahoochee Review*, 16.3 (Spring 1996), pp. 56–65.

'The Resolution of Opposites: Part Two', interview by Sarah Broom, *Poetry and Audience*, 37.2 (Summer 1996), pp. 10–17.

'A Dialogue with Medbh McGuckian', interview by Rand Brandes, *Studies in the Literary Imagination*, 30.2 (Fall 1997), pp. 37–47.

'"My Words Are Traps": An Interview with Medbh McGuckian', interview by John Hobbs, *New Hibernia Review*, 2.1 (Spring 1998), pp. 111–20.

'An Interview with Medbh McGuckian', interview by Danielle Sered, *Nua*, 2.1–2 (1998–9), pp. 151–62.

'Under the North Window: An Interview with Medbh McGuckian', interview by Sawnie Morris, *Kenyon Review*, 23.3–4 (Summer-Fall 2001), pp. 64–74.

'Medbh McGuckian', interview by John Brown, *In the Chair: Interviews with Poets from Northern Ireland* (Cliffs of Moher: Salmon Publishing, 2002), pp. 169–84.

'I Am Listening in Black and White to What Speaks to Me in Blue', interview by Helen Blakeman, *Irish Studies Review*, 11.1 (April 2003), pp. 61–9.

'Double Doors: An Interview with Medbh McGuckian', interview by Elin Holmsten, *Nordic Irish Studies*, 3.1 (2004), pp. 93–100.

'An Interview with Medbh McGuckian', interview by Michaela Schrage-Früh, *Contemporary Literature*, 46.1 (Spring 2005), pp. 1–17.

Interview by Gerald Dawe, *The Poetry Programme*, RTE Radio 1, 6 December 2008.

II Secondary Sources

Alcobia-Murphy, Shane, '"Re-reading Five, Ten Times, the Simplest Letters": Detecting Voices in the Poetry of Medbh McGuckian', *Nordic Irish Studies*, 5.1 (April 2006), pp. 123–47.

Alcobia-Murphy, Shane, '"The Name Flows from the Naming": The Key to Understanding Medbh McGuckian's Poetry', *Estudios Irlandeses*, 3 (2008), pp. 1–10.

Alcobia-Murphy, Shane, '"If I Prolonged the Look to Rediscover Your Face": Medbh McGuckian's Ekphrastic Elegies', in Shane Alcobia-Murphy and Margaret Maxwell (eds.), *The Enclave of My Nation: Crosscurrents in Irish and Scottish Culture* (Aberdeen University Press, 2008), pp. 1–17.

Alcobia-Murphy, Shane, '"The Same Seed that Carried Me till It Saw Itself as Fruit": Medbh McGuckian's Exemplars', in Shane Alcobia-Murphy (ed.), *What Rough Beasts?* (Newcastle-upon-Tyne: Cambridge Scholars Publishing, 2008), pp. 12–24.

Allen, Michael, 'The Poetry of Medbh McGuckian', in Elmer Andrews (ed.), *Contemporary Irish Poetry* (Basingstoke: Macmillan, 1992), pp. 286–309.

Andrews, Elmer, '"Some Sweet Disorder" – The Poetry of Subversion: Paul Muldoon, Tom Paulin and Medbh McGuckian', in Gary Day and Brian Docherty (eds.), *British Poetry from the 1950s to the 1990s* (London: Macmillan, 1997), pp. 118–42.

Batten, Guinn, '"The More with Which We Are Connected": The Muse of the Minus in the Poetry of McGuckian and Kinsella', in Anthony Bradley and Maryann Gialanella Valiulis (eds.), *Gender and Sexuality in Modern Ireland* (Amherst: University of Massachusetts Press, 1997), pp. 212–44.

Beer, Ann, 'Medbh McGuckian's Poetry: Maternal Thinking and a Politics of Peace', *Canadian Journal of Irish Studies*, 18.1 (July 1992), pp. 192–203.

Bendall, Molly, 'Flower Logic: The Poems of Medbh McGuckian', *Antioch Review*, 48.3 (Summer 1990), pp. 367–71.

Blakeman, Helen, 'Metaphor and Metonymy in Medbh McGuckian's Poetry', *Critical Survey*, 14.2 (2002), pp. 61–74.

Blakeman, Helen, 'Medbh McGuckian and the Poetics of Mourning', in Irene Gilsenan Nordin (ed.), *The Body and Desire in Contemporary Irish Poetry* (Dublin: Irish Academic Press, 2006), pp. 197–212.

Bohman, Kimberly S., 'Borders or Frontiers?: Gender Roles and Gender Politics in McGuckian's Unconscious', *Irish Journal of Feminist Studies*, 1.1 (1996), pp. 119–32.

Brazeau, Robert, 'Troubling Language: Avant–garde Strategies in the Poetry of Medbh McGuckian', *Mosaic*, 37.2 (June 2004), pp. 127–44.

Broom, Sarah, 'McGuckian's Conversations with Rilke in *Marconi's Cottage*', *Irish University Review*, 28.1 (Spring-Summer 1998), pp. 133–50.

Byron, Catherine, 'A House of One's Own: Three Contemporary Irish Women Poets', *Women's Review*, 19 (May 1987), pp. 32–3.

Byron, Catherine, 'The Room is a Kind of Travel Also: An Appreciation of the Poetry of Medbh McGuckian', *Linen Hall Review*, 5.1 (Spring 1988), pp. 16–17.

Cahill, Eileen, '"Because I Never Garden": Medbh McGuckian's Solitary Way', *Irish University Review*, 24.2 (Autumn-Winter 1994), pp. 264–71.

Daniels, Kate, 'Poet to Poet: A Look at Medbh McGuckian's Language', *Shenandoah*, 51.2–3 (Summer-Fall 2001), pp. 46–54.

Docherty, Thomas, 'Initiations, Tempers, Seductions: Postmodern McGuckian' in Neil Corcoran (ed.), *The Chosen Ground: Essays on the Contemporary Poetry of Northern Ireland* (Bridgend: Seren Books, 1992), pp. 191–210.

Eberle, Wendy J., 'Painting a Pictographic Language, Beyond Sound Boundaries: Medbh McGuckian's Poetic Making', *Canadian Journal of Irish Studies*, 22.1 (July 1996), pp. 61–70.

Emmitt, Helen V., 'Rhyming Hope and History: Medbh McGuckian's Recent Poetry', *Shenandoah*, 51.2–3 (Summer-Fall 2001), pp. 55–67.

Faragó, Borbála, '"Self–Portrait in the Act of Painting a Self-Portrait": Tropes of Inspiration in Medbh McGuckian's *Shelmalier*', *Études Britanniques Contemporaines*, 25 (2003), pp. 31–44.

Faragó, Borbála, '"The Meeting of Two Tidal Roads": Tradition and Identity in Medbh McGuckian's *The Face of the Earth* and Eiléan Ní Chuilleanáin's *The Girl Who Married the Reindeer*', *Hungarian Journal of English and American Studies*, 10.1–2 (Spring-Fall 2004), pp. 331–40.

Fogarty, Anne, '"A Noise of Myth": Speaking (as) Woman in the Poetry of Eavan Boland and Medbh McGuckian', *Paragraph*, 17.1 (March 1994), pp. 92–103.

Fulford, Sarah, 'Medbh McGuckian's Disidentification', *Gendered Spaces in Contemporary Irish Poetry* (Oxford: Peter Lang, 2002), pp. 171–97.

Gonzalez, Alexander G., 'Celebrating the Richness of Medbh McGuckian's Poetry: Close Analysis of Six Poems from *The Flower Master*', in Alexander G. Gonzalez (ed.), *Contemporary Irish Women Poets: Some Male Perspectives* (Westport, Connecticut: Greenwood, 1999), pp. 43–63.

Gray, Cecile, 'Medbh McGuckian: Imagery Wrought to Its Uttermost', in Deborah Fleming (ed.), *Learning the Trade: Essays on W.B. Yeats and Contemporary Poetry* (West Cornwall, Connecticut: Locust Hill, 1993), pp. 165–77.

Haberstroh, Patricia Boyle, 'Medbh McGuckian', *Women Creating Women: Contemporary Irish Women Poets* (Syracuse University Press, 1996), pp. 123–58.

Holmsten, Elin, '"Those Deeply Carnal Moments": The Hermeneutics of Flesh in Medbh McGuckian's Poetry', *Nordic Irish Studies*, 2.1 (2003), pp. 29–45.

Holmsten, Elin, '"Like a Wished-for Body": Dialogues of Desire in the Poetry of

Medbh McGuckian', in Irene Gilsenan Nordin (ed.), *The Body and Desire in Contemporary Irish Poetry* (Dublin: Irish Academic Press, 2006), pp. 163–81.

Homem, Rui Carvalho, 'Looking for Clues: McGuckian, Poems and Portraits', in Maria de Fátima Lambert (ed.), *Writing and Seeing: Essays on Word and Image* (Amsterdam: Rodopi, 2006), pp. 187–98.

Hufstader, Jonathan, 'Medbh McGuckian', *Tongue of Water, Teeth of Stones: Northern Irish Poetry and Social Violence*' (University of Kentucky Press, 1999), pp. 261–86.

Kennedy-Andrews, Elmer, 'Medbh McGuckian: The Lyric of Gendered Space', *Writing Home: Poetry and Place in Northern Ireland, 1968–2008* (Cambridge: D.S. Brewer, 2008), pp. 225–48.

Mallot, J. Edward, 'Medbh McGuckian's Poetic Tectonics', *Éire-Ireland*, 40.3–4 (Fall–Winter 2005), pp. 240–55.

Maron, Meva, 'The Stamps Had Squirrels on Them', *The Honest Ulsterman*, 88 (1989), pp. 33–4.

Melander, Ingrid, 'The Use of Traditional Symbols in Three Poems by Medbh McGuckian', *Moderna Sprak*, 83.4 (1989), pp. 298–303.

Mitchell, Erin C., 'Slippage at the Threshold: Postmodern Hospitality in Medbh McGuckian's Poetry', *Lit: Literature Interpretation Theory*, 17.2 (2006), pp. 137–55.

Murphy, Shane, 'Obliquity in the Poetry of Paul Muldoon and Medbh McGuckian', *Éire-Ireland*, 31.3–4 (Fall–Winter 1996), pp. 76–101.

Murphy, Shane, '"You Took Away My Biography": The Poetry of Medbh McGuckian', *Irish University Review*, 28.1 (Spring–Summer 1998), pp. 110–32.

Murphy, Shane, 'Writing in the Shit: The Northern Irish Poet and Authority', *Canadian Journal of Irish Studies*, 24.1 (July 1998), pp. 1–21.

Murphy, Shane, '"Roaming Root of Multiple Meanings": Intertextual Relations in Medbh McGuckian's Poetry', *Metre* 4 (Winter 1998), pp. 99–109.

Murphy, Shane, '"A Dove Involving A Whole Nation": Politics in the Poetry of Medbh McGuckian', *Études Irlandaises*, 24.1 (Spring 1999), pp. 91–108.

Murphy, Shane, '"The Eye That Scanned It": The Picture Poems of Heaney, Muldoon and McGuckian', *New Hibernia Review*, 4.4 (Winter 2000), pp. 85–115.

Murphy, Shane, 'A Code of Images: Northern Irish Centos', *Irish Studies Review*, 10.2 (2002), pp. 193–203.

Murphy, Shane, 'Sonnets, Centos, and Long Lines: Muldoon, Paulin, McGuckian and Carson', in Matthew Campbell (ed.), *The Cambridge Companion to Irish Contemporary Poetry* (Cambridge University Press, 2003), pp. 189–209.

Murphy, Shane, 'Intertertextual Relations in the Poetry of Medbh McGuckian', in Patricia A. Lynch et al. (eds.), *Back to the Present: Forward to the Past: Irish Writing and History since 1798*, vol. 2. (Amsterdam: Rodopi, 2006), pp. 271–86.

O'Brien, Peggy, 'Reading Medbh McGuckian: Admiring What We Cannot Understand', *Colby Quarterly*, 28.4 (December 1992), pp. 239–50.

O'Connor, Mary, '"Rising Out": Medbh McGuckian's Destabilizing Poetics', *Éire-Ireland*, 30.4 (Winter 1996), pp. 154–72.

O'Neill, Charles L., 'Medbh McGuckian's Poetry: Inhabiting the Image', in Alexander G. Gonzalez (ed.), *Contemporary Irish Women Poets: Some Male Perspectives* (Westport, Connecticut: Greenwood, 1999), pp. 65–78.

Porter, Susan, 'The "Imaginative Space" of Medbh McGuckian', in Anne E. Brown and Marjanne E. Goozé (eds.), *International Women's Writing: New Landscapes of Identity* (Westport, Connecticut: Greenwood, 1995), pp. 86–101.

Rees-Jones, Deryn, 'Motherlands and Mothertongues: Writing the Poetry of Nation', *Consorting with Angels: Essays on Modern Women Poets* (Newcastle: Bloodaxe Books, 2005), pp. 174–215.

Robinson, Alan, 'Declarations of Independence: Some Responses to Feminism', *Instabilities in Contemporary British Poetry* (Basingstoke: Macmillan, 1988), pp. 202–8.

Sered, Danielle, '"By Escaping and [Leaving] a Mark": Authority and the Writing Subject of the Poetry of Medbh McGuckian', *Irish University Review*, 32.2 (Autumn–Winter 2002), pp. 273–85.

Sirr, Peter, '"How Things Begin to Happen": Notes on Eiléan Ní Chuilleanáin and Medbh McGuckian', *The Southern Review*, 31.3 (1995), 450–67.

Sullivan, Moynagh, 'The In-formal Poetics of Medbh McGuckian', *Nordic Irish Studies*, 3.1 (2004), pp. 75–92.

Summers–Bremner, Eluned, 'History's Impasse: Journey, Haunt and Trace in the Poetry of Medbh McGuckian', in Irene Gilsenan Nordin (ed.), *The Body and Desire in Contemporary Irish Poetry* (Dublin: Irish Academic Press, 2006), pp. 40–54.

Volsik, Paul, 'Engendering the Feminine: Two Irish Poets – Eavan Boland and Medbh McGuckian', *Études Anglaises*, 56.2 (2003), pp. 148–61.

Wheeler, Lesley, 'Both Flower and Flower Gatherer: Medbh McGuckian's *The Flower Master* and H.D.'s *Sea Garden*', *Twentieth Century Literature*, 49.4 (Winter 2003), pp. 494–519.

Wills, Clair, 'The Perfect Mother: Authority in the Poetry of Medbh McGuckian', *Text and Context*, 3 (Autumn 1988), pp. 91–111.

Wills, Clair, *Improprieties: Politics and Sexuality in Northern Irish Poetry* (Oxford: Clarendon Press, 1993).

Wills, Clair, 'Voices from the Nursery: Medbh McGuckian's Plantation', in Michael Kenneally (ed.), *Poetry in Contemporary Irish Literature* (Gerrards Cross: Colin Smythe, 1995), pp. 373–99.

Index